TRANSLATIONS FROM THE CLASSICS
INTO ENGLISH
FROM CAXTON TO CHAPMAN
1477-1620

By

HENRY BURROWES LATHROP

1967

OCTAGON BOOKS, INC.

New York

Originally published by the University of Wisconsin

Reprinted 1967

by special arrangement with The University of Wisconsin Press

OCTAGON BOOKS, INC.
175 FIFTH AVENUE
NEW YORK, N. Y. 10010

LIBRARY OF CONGRESS CATALOG CARD NUMBER: 67-18773

Printed in U.S.A. by
NOBLE OFFSET PRINTERS, INC.
NEW YORK 3, N. Y.

PREFACE

This book, begun twenty-five years ago, has taken much longer to complete than I anticipated. It has had to be done in intervals of time snatched from a busy life. This must be my excuse if I have failed to note some of the publications bearing on the subject which have appeared while the book has been under my hand.

Begun before the appearance of Miss Palmer's bibliography (Palmer, Henrietta R., *List of English Editions and Translations of the Classics printed before 1641,* Bibliographical Society Publications, London, 1911), the work was greatly facilitated by the appearance of that useful book. Here and there I have been able to supplement or correct her titles, but only with gleanings. I have been indebted to the authorities of the Congressional Library, the Libraries of Columbia University, Corpus Christi College, Cambridge, and the University of Chicago, the Bodleian Library, the British Museum, Dr. Williams's Library, and the Library of Cambridge University for their hospitable policy and for kindly assistance going far beyond the mere opening of their resources to me. I cannot forbear mentioning especially the generosity with which Mr. Falconer Madan, Bodley's Librarian, Mr. Strickland Gibson, of the Bodleian Library, and Mr. A. W. Pollard, Keeper of the Printed Books in the British Museum, took from their precious time to guide and help me. Professor Ruth C. Wallerstein has given me invaluable assistance in reading proof. The University of Wisconsin has been freely helpful in granting me the money for photostats and in obtaining special facilities for me. And so many of my colleagues, specialists in various fields, have assisted me in points of difficulty that I cannot mention, or even remember, all their names.

It will be noted that in most cases when the sources of translations are given, no evidence is cited. To have added the evidence, namely a minute comparison of texts, would have overladen a book already burdened with detail. In many cases, es-

5

pecially of translations at second-hand from the Greek, the translators announce their sources, and they tell the truth. When the English version does not give its source, it generally becomes obvious upon what books then extant the translator might have drawn, such as translations from Greek into a foreign language, or editions of classic authors. In general it is important to consider contemporary editions, because the text then current often differs widely from that accessible at the present time, and the English version is often guided by an editor's notes. When the present work contains a statement that a translation is direct from the Greek, all the old versions known to bibliographers, especially those into Latin, French, and Italian, have been examined. When for any reason it has not been practicable to make such an examination, nothing is said about sources.

H. B. LATHROP

The University of Wisconsin
    June 1, 1932.

TABLE OF CONTENTS

INTRODUCTION

We ordinarily read and speak about "a knowledge of *the classics.*" "—an old fashioned *classical* education," as if the classics and the education based on the classics had meant substantially the same thing for every generation, at least since the Revival of Learning. So far is this from the truth, that a student of classical influences and of the interest felt in Greek and Latin authors in successive periods cannot but feel surprised and sometimes even startled at the different points of view to which he must adjust himself in order to follow the thought of past generations about the classics. The authors read in schools are not the same, the values set on those read are not the same, the whole aim of classical training is not the same, so that *The Classics* of Shakespeare's youth in the reign of Elizabeth, and Byron's in the Regency, or even of Gibbon's in the mid-eighteenth century, and Jebb's in the mid-nineteenth differ essentially in spirit or content; and the *classical education* of the younger Pitt is far from that of Lord Burghley

All the histories of Elizabethan literature speak with emphasis of the influence of the Greek and Latin classics in that era. Certainly sixteenth-century books are full of references to Greeks and Romans. The learned allusion is a trimming as necessary as the fur of the learned gown. All serious argument is supported by classical authority and illustration, and nearly all the literature of delectation is enriched from the store of classical legend. The theory of conduct is drawn from Cicero and Plutarch, of policy from Isocrates and Tacitus; the physician and the farmer, the wit and the dramatist, quote Latin. The pertness of *Euphues* is as learned as the weight of the *Schoolmaster* or the *Advancement of Learning;* and when Shakespeare is most full of romance he is most full of Ovid.

Yet the sixteenth-century references to Greek or Roman matters do not convey that special quality which we of this day perceive in classic letters, and especially in Greek thought. Authors and works which were familiar then are obscure now, and on the other hand much that would now be foremost in

9

the mind of anyone thinking of Greek and Roman things is hardly present or is not present at all in the works of that age, a rich and various age, and one full of the classics, but certainly not a classic age. What then did the classic past mean to that great era of English life and thought, which looked toward it so reverently, and which was colored by it so constantly? What ancient authors were actually at that day generally known to English readers? How were they regarded? Was the feeling for them one of dim and distant reverence? or of defined practical respect for efficiency, or of uncritical enthusiasm, or of imaginative sympathy? Were they oracles, or guides, or good story-tellers, or helps to those that would live in the spirit? How wide-spread was the knowledge of Greek? What formative influence on style can be traced to the classics?

It is as a contribution to the answering of these and the like questions that the present study has been undertaken. To be sure, the real significance of the classics for the era is to be found in what was absorbed, in what entered freely into English general culture, and especially into English literature— in the ideas which spread into general consciousness and came to be accepted without question as fundamental (such as Isocrates's ideal of education), in formative and imponderable literary influences (such as the elevation of tragic conception and style in the University Wits), in familiar allusions to classic story (such as Shakespeare's unforced references). But these things are vast and often impalpable, the study of them is likely to run into a mere hunting of the letter or else to become merely impressionistic and inconclusive. The translations offer definitely secure and verifiable data. The substance and spirit of the originals are manifest; and translators often make known why they have chosen particular works, and how they regard their own function. Even the extent to which individual translations became current can be measured in some cases. Thus from the study of the translations assured certainties about the classics, their place in the thought of the time, their influence, and their meaning may be ascertained, and upon this basis some ideas about the more general and less definitely determinable aspects of the matter may be securely founded.

The study concerns itself primarily with *printed* English translations. It begins with the first printed English translations; for one reason, because they slightly antedate the coming of the New Learning into England, and partly by contrast, partly by agreement, define the nature of that learning. The study ends with 1620, the date of the completion of Chapman's *Homer,* the culminating Elizabethan version.

The investigation traces the full flood of sixteenth-century translation from its beginning to its end. At first sight it is difficult to separate the translations into periods; the same works are frequently reprinted, the same purposes once conceived continue to be aimed at by the later translators, and successive movements or streams seem to flow into each other and into the main current, blending and mingling inextricably. But upon longer scrutiny four quite clearly marked divisions can be made out, on the basis of the new work done in each of them. The first is the period from the introduction of printing to the advent of the New Learning—say the forty years from 1477 to 1517; an essentially medieval period when Boethius, "Cato," and "Aesop" were translated, Ovid and Vergil represented by summaries and *rifacimenti,* and Cicero alone of recognized classic authors was directly known, and he only as a graceful moralist. Caxton himself, Chaucer, Benedict Burgh, and John Tiptoft, Earl of Worcester, are among the most important of the translators, who lean heavily on the French. The second period covers the era from the introduction of the New Learning to the appearance of Tottel's *Miscellany,* say the forty years from 1517 to 1557. The period is marked by the many translations from Greek moralists, especially Lucian and Plutarch, under the influence of Erasmus and his group, and by a number of translations of historians. Latin moral works of Cicero and Seneca fill a less important place. The works translated are in general short,—from a brief pamphlet to a small book. The most important name among translators is perhaps that of Sir Thomas Elyot, but the diligent labors of Robert Whitinton deserve mention, and Alexander Barclay, Nicholas Udall, Richard Taverner, and John Brende have each done work possessing some individual character. Among the poets Wyatt, Surrey, and Grimald are the most important, and Surrey's is the most significant name. The third period covers the thirty-five years after the appearance of Tottel's *Miscellany*. In the first fifteen years of the period appeared the bulk of the versions which meant the most to the age of Elizabeth, in popularizing works which really entered the English mind of the time. There were large undertakings of permanently important books; among imaginative works Phaer's Vergil, Golding's Ovid, Adlington's *The Golden Ass*, Underdowne's *Theagenes and Chariclea*, and the plays of Seneca by various hands. Among works of information there were likewise large and important books; Billingsley's Euclid, Golding's Caesar, Stocker's Dionysius Periegetes and Diodorus Siculus, besides a large number of useful but less notable books of the same kind, such as Golding's other translations of historical, geographical, and ethical works. During the latter part of this era, some twenty years, say from 1572 to 1592, there were important additions to the histories,—Aelian, Appian, two books of Herodotus, Tacitus. Above all, there was North's Plutarch. But in poetry less ambitious things were undertaken, and they were done in a petty spirit. Abraham Fleming published a *Panoplie of Epistles*, including the *Praise of Baldness*, Abraham Kendall *Flowers of Epigrams*, an anthology of trifles, Abraham Fraunce *The Countess of Pembroke's Ivychurch*, an assembly of fragments and miscellanies. The secondary works and pseudepigrapha of Ovid and Vergil were translated: the *Tristia*, the *Ibis*, the *Bucolics*, the *Alexis*, the *Culex*. Gascoigne and Kinwelmersh adapted from the Italian the one Greek play of the age, *Jocasta* (the *Phenissae* of Euripides). In the last period, that from 1592 on, large works were courageously undertaken, and although the period includes Chapman's Homer, most of the important translations were of serious prose, historical and ethical, Lodge's Josephus and Seneca, Healey's Epictetus, Cebes, and Theophrastus, Philemon Holland's manifold spirited versions of Pliny, Plutarch's *Morals*, Livy, Suetonius, Ammianus Marcellinus, and Xenophon's *Cyropedia*, besides versions of Boethius, of Caesar, of Justin, of Julius Florus, and of Aristotle's *Politics*.

It is obvious that the classics meant something different to readers in the century and a half covered by this study from what they mean to readers now. The authors read, with a few great exceptions, are not those who would be thought of today as the greatest or the most representative.   The aspect under which the classic past was seen was widely different from that in which it is seen today.   The sixteenth century was one of autocracy and of large territorial states, and the minds of students turned naturally to the imperial period first of Rome, secondarily of Greece.   The lesson the translators of history never weary of insisting upon is the evil of rebellion against the Prince.   The Greek city-state and the conflicts of democracy and oligarchy were shocking and even unintelligible to them.   Here is one reason for their attention to late authors, and to those whom most classical students would now call inferior authors.   Chapman at last got back to Homer.   He could boast at the end of a quarter of a century,

> The work that I was born to do is done.

But it proved impossible to finish Herodotus or Thucydides. They are typical cases.   There is no early Greek lyric, no central drama or philosophy or oratory; nothing that is greatest and most significant in the Greece that still lives in thought. The great wall of the Roman Empire rose before the eyes of the sixteenth century.   They could not see beyond it, still less break through it and struggle to the heights of the Attic citadel above the mists.   The Greece they knew was one that somewhat weariedly handed on a great tradition, not the Greece that formed it.   There is not in these Greek works the free play of mind on life distinguishing the Greek literature of the classic era, and there is still less of the conflict of intense political experiment which abounded in the great period of Athens.   To the sixteenth-century reader the great classic past was the imperial age in which the order of human life had been best understood and organized by the intelligence of man.   It gave a fixed norm.   One went there for the best ideas on gardening, medicine, and the art of war, for the soundest detail of practical ethics, for the most vital history, for the most vivid personal character, for the best anecdotes, for the highest poetry and the richest imaginative view of the world.   But in our day this is no longer true.   Columella and Galen and Vegetius have become merely objects of curious inquiry.   The history of Rome has become merely a part of the history of the world, one of the most important parts, but no higher in *quality* than the history of Paris or Mexico. In the Middle Age and in the Modern Age we see a gallery of portraits no less brilliant than those of the men of old. Barbarossa and the first Duke of Marlborough, Thomas Aquinas, Gambetta, Benjamin Franklin, Lenin, and Mussolini are not pale beside Alcibiades and Vespasian. In every practical art, including politics and the art of living together in civilized life, the modern world has met and has to meet problems more difficult than antiquity ever knew. In the fields of imaginative creation and of metaphysical speculation alone does the classic past hold a place of unsurpassed excellence, and in these it does not now stand alone, but sees worthy companions, the work of later days, installed rightfully in a place of honor beside its own productions of creative genius. The classic past, however it may be loved and admired, cannot thrill us as it did the readers of a bygone day with the awe and excitement inspired by a new, sacred, beautiful, and perfect world of thought.

The learned in the sixteenth century believed themselves to be reaching back across an abyss of darkness to the enlightenment of an earlier age, to be re-enkindling the long extinguished lamp of knowledge. In fact they could take from the classic past only that which their own experience and the experience of immediately preceding generations had prepared them to take, a fruitful but a definitely limited influence.

CHAPTER I: THE AGE OF CAXTON
1477-1517

Caxton's public was composed of ecclesiastics, noblemen, gentlemen, and wealthy tradesmen, all belonging to the ruling class.[1] The ecclesiastics needed service books and devotional works, including the sermons of some celebrated preachers; as teachers of youth they required some textbooks, especially of elementary Latin;[2] thoughtful men among the upper classes read the national history with serious attention, and all the nobility and gentry delighted in romances. The only art systematically treated in a book was the art of war. Everybody respected a few great poetic names;—Chaucer, and after him Gower and Lydgate.[3] In brief, the age was far from being intellectually dead, but it was practically untouched by the Renaissance. The circle in which Caxton moved, and the members of which shared his tastes, was, then, a group of aristocrats and prosperous merchants, whose point of view was medieval.[4] The approach of humanism to England was gradual and not rapid; and at the time of the invention of printing it would have been impossible that more than a very few of the gentlemen and churchmen who were his most liberal patrons should have had any tincture of the new learning. The translations of this period inevitably present in one field the same aspects which are to be found in other English books of the time. Speaking broadly, they are translations of standard works popular during the later Middle Ages; and they are from the hands of an earlier generation of French or English writers

[1]Aurner, Nellie S., *Caxton, Mirrour of Fifteenth Century Letters*, Boston, 1926, pp. 200 *et seq.*

[2]Gasquet, Rt. Rev. F. A. *The Bibliography of some Devotional Books Printed by the Earliest English Printers*, in *Transactions of the Bibliographical Society*, London, 1904, vii, 163.

[3]v. sub Gower and Lydgate in D. N. B.

[4]For the view that Caxton followed rather than guided the taste of his patrons, see Lathrop, H. B., *The First English Printers and their Patrons*, in *The Library*, 4th ser. iii (1922), 19; for a vigorous statement of the opposite view, Plomer, H. R., *William Caxton*, 1925.

15

whose names carried some weight of authority. Indeed, they do not at all represent, in scope or quality, even the larger culture possible in medieval times, but the conventional taste and narrow outlook of ordinary people who accepted the ordinary books. There is but one man who presents an exception to what has been said, and who brings Caxton and early English printing into some relation with the contemporary Italian revival of learning, namely, John Tiptoft, the Earl of Worcester, who translated Cicero's *De Amicitia,* a man of many-sided activity, of whom it will be necessary to speak later.

The list of actual translations from classic authors published in England between the introduction of printing and the time when the spirit of the new learning began to be felt in England is indeed a short one. In strictness it includes only Cicero's two graceful moral essays on *Friendship* and *Old Age* printed in one volume in 1481, and translated at some time before 1460. Boethius may be reckoned as coming at least from the ancient world, if he is not to be called a classic. Caxton printed Chaucer's version of *De Consolatione,* made before 1400, in or before 1479. Caxton himself made versions from the French of several medieval books which had some basis in classic antiquity. He translated and prepared for the press in 1480, and perhaps printed the allegorization of Ovid's *Metamorphoses,* and printed about 1483 a version of Premierfait's paraphrase of the *Disticha* of Dionysius Cato, in 1484 a translation of Machault's French version, made from Steinhöwel's German translation, of the late Latin form of Aesop's *Fables,* and in 1490 a translation of the prose romance based on the *Aeneid.* He had earlier (1477-78) printed Benedict Burgh's paraphrase of Cato's *Disticha* in verse, and later (in 1495) printed a translation of Christine de Pisan's *Book of Fayttes of Armes,* which contains passages drawn directly from Vegetius and Frontinus. Two other printers printed schoolbooks: *Vulgaria Terentii,* a phrase-book of commonplaces based on Terence (Oxford, about 1483), and *The Flores of Ouide,* another school phrase-book, drawn from *De Arte Amandi* (Wynkyn de Worde, 1513.)

The medieval tradition with regard to each of the works translated is, of course, plain and familiar. "Cato" was *par excellence* the first of schoolbooks, and the fundamental elementary moral treatise of the Middle Ages. Boys learned from Cato the application of rules of syntax, profiting at the same time by his wise moral maxims. So popular was it that it was expanded by the addition of many maxims, and then the expanded form was made the subject of selection, then arranged and divided into books, and provided with an outline. In time the work, thus edited and transformed, was translated into nearly every "vulgar tongue" in Europe, first as a means to assist in the understanding of the original, and then in prose, amplifying and elaborating the original, or in verse,[5] emulating the Latin in a modern language. Its marvelous popularity is attested by the existence of such versions or *rifacimenti* in a dozen vernaculars.

Of the author of the English version printed by Caxton, Benedict Burgh, "late archdeacon of Colchestre, and high canon of St. Stephens at Westmestre," Max Förster[6] gives a careful account based on a searching study of the documents. Burgh was a clergyman who owed his preferments to the favor of the Bourchiers. The book, Caxton tells us, was made "for the erudicion of My lord Bousher, son and heir at that time to my lord the erle of Estsex." Of the relation between Burgh and young Lord Bourchier there is no evidence beyond the information given by Caxton and the tone of the translation itself. Burgh was in his day a person of recognized standing, a writer next to Occleve and Lydgate in general esteem.[7] The

---

[5]Schanz, M., *Geschichte der römischen Literatur*, Munich, 1896, pt. iii. p. 32 *et seq.*, contains an extended account by Max Förster of the translations and *rifacimenti* of Cato, with bibliography.

[6]Repr. Camb. 1906, in *A series of photogravure facsimiles of rare fifteenth century books in the University Library*, F. J. H. Jenkinson, ed.; Förster prints a critical text, with an account of the manuscripts and printed texts and a lexical appendix of the words worthy of note, many of which are older than examples given in the Oxford Dictionary, in *Archiv*, vol. 115, p. 258; vol. 116, p. 25; his account of Burgh's life is in *Archiv*. 101, 29. Caxton's preface is reprinted in Blades, W., *Life and Typography of William Caxton*, London 1861-1863, 1, 169; in Crotch, W. J. B., *The Prologues and Epilogues of William Caxton* (EETS, Orig. Ser. 176, Oxf. 1928); and in Aurner, Nellie S. *op. cit.* See also the valuable introduction to Chase, W. J., *Catonis Disticha*, in *University of Wisconsin Studies in the Social Sciences and History*, 1922.

[7]The eldest son of Henry Bourchier, created Earl of Essex in 1461, was William, Lord Bourchier by courtesy. Of him Polydore Virgil speaks in terms that indicate that even at the accession of Edward IV he at least began to assume serious public responsibilities, and he was married in February, 1466 (to Anna Woodville, the sister of Edward IV's queen). The form of Burgh's address ("my child") and the whole tone of the Cato show that it must have been written when Lord Bourchier was of tender

work of Burgh itself is a diffuse and stodgy paraphrase, each distich being expanded into the seven lines of "rime royale." For example:

Incipiens esto cum tempus postulat aut res
Stulticiam similare loco prudencia summa est

It is no wisedom a man alwey to be sage
But sumtyme to be nyce and feyne folye
Who that hath this fet shal fynde auantage
Whan tyme and thing desireth that espye
And than dissimile that is gret pollecye
For sumtyme to be vnwyse by apparence
Among the wyse is cleped hye prudence.[8]

It may be permitted to wonder whether the young Lord Bourchier received with much enthusiasm these admonitions of prudence, in which all the force of the original, which depended wholly on the pithy brevity of the axioms, is washed away in the shallow and vapid flood of Burgh's verbosity. The translation certainly commanded respect, having been reprinted twice by Caxton, and again by Copland, from a different manuscript, as late as 1557.

Burgh's translation did not exhaust the interest of Cato for Caxton, inasmuch as he printed a few years later (in 1483) a paraphrase with a prolix commentary from the French, perhaps of Premierfait. There is nothing to show that this second version was ever reprinted.

The fables of "Aesop" stood forth like Cato, as a work of moral doctrine, suitable for the discipline of youth. The fables, or some of them, had been used as material for elementary exercises in composition in the Greek schools of rhetoric,[9]

---

years. If at his marriage he may have been from fifteen to twenty-five, the translation must date between 1447 and 1461. Bourchier died before his father, leaving a son; hence Caxton speaks of him as "at that time son and heir." The version, then, came to Caxton from a generation antecedent to his. He printed no contemporary work, except his own and Lord Rivers's translations. (Rolls Series—Calendar of Patent Rolls, Edw. IV; Virgil, Polydore, ed. Sir Henry Ellis, Camden Socy. 1844, p. 113; Worcester, W. Annales, ed. Hearne, in Liber Niger Scaccarii, etc. London, 1774, II, 505-506.)

[8] Sig. A viii, verso.

[9] Aphthonius begins his Progymnasmata with stories from Aesop.

and had continued without interruption to be employed in the same way in Roman schools and then in the Christian schools of all Europe during the whole period of time intervening right down to Caxton's day. The book of fables, like Cato's distichs, had been so much modified, now added to from popular sources, now excerpted, now rearranged, that the "Aesop" of the late middle ages, like the Cato, is indeed no classical work, but a creation of the medieval period itself, though resting upon a solid ancient basis.[10] Caxton's English is from a French version of a German version of a Latin recension.

Closely related to these elementary works of morality were two actual school-books—collections of phrases, drawn, one from Terence, one from Ovid, to assist in the learning of Latin. The *Vulgaria Terentii* first printed at Oxford by T. Rood and T. Hunt in 1483 was evidently an acceptable school-book, going through four editions by 1486, and at least two more by 1529.[11] The phrases are not in the main quotations from Terence, but commonplaces of conversation, for example, greetings and expressions of compliment, based on Terence's idiom.

God spede you, save you or rest mery.
Saluete, Salue. Saluus sis chrito. Iubeo te saluere . . .

I thanke you for the grete chere ye made me at London.
Gracias vobis habeo de ingenti humanitate londoniis facta.

---

[10]Jacobs, J., *The Fables of Aesop, as first printed by William Caxton in 1484* (Bibliothèque de Carabas, voll. 4, 5, London, 1887 etc.) is a reprint of Caxton's translation, with a good introduction. Jacobs's remark on the quality of the translation: "At times he stumbles in his rendering, at times he calmly reproduces a French word for which he had no translation handy; most of the words in our glossary are Gallicisms of this sort,"— is not justified. "Most of the words" are: (1) obsolete spellings, *abhominable, threst* (thrust); (2) related forms not now in use: *retcheth* (recks), *thiefly* (like a thief); (3) obsolete words once in good use: *dommage* (danger); *procurator* (the long form for proctor) etc. On Steinhöwel *v.* Keller, A. von, in his edition of Steinhöwel's translation of the Decameron (Bibliothek des litterarischen Vereins in Stuttgart, no. 51); Steinhöwel's Aesop, ed. Oesterley, H., (Tübingen, 1873, Bibliothek des litt. Vereins in Stuttgart, No. 117).

[11]The filiation of the various editions would be worth investigation. The Oxford edition (1483) was followed in the same year by a close copy (W. de Machlynia); Machlynia printed another edition that year or the next, with the misprint *Salvus sis clerico* for *Salvus sis chrito*. The Antwerp edition (1486) reads *Salvus sis christo*. It will be seen that Mr. Foster Watson is not quite accurate in saying: "This latter part consisted of sentences from Terence with English translations," and, "This consists of sentences from Terence translated into English, without any apparent connection," (*The English Grammar Schools*, Camb. 1908, p. 402).

Variants are suggested:

It is soon acquytte
Cito vel facile fertur vel rependitur.

Ware thy hede thy handys or fete.
Caue capiti manibus pedibus.

Sometimes the passage of Terence which justifies the idiom is cited. "The modyr makyth most of hyr yongist sonne. Mater filium natum minimum maximi semper facit. Terencius. Siue hec to semper fecit maximi."—"I wott not what thou manyste. Quid tibi vis (sic) nescio. Quis animus tibi sit ignoro. Terencius Quid igitur sibi vult pater."—"It is harde to disceyue him. Difficile est ei verba dare Teren. Cui verba dare difficile est."

Much, indeed, is taken from Terence, especially many slightly figurative phrases, or specific phrases translated in literal or general terms.

I am hyer unhappily. Haud auspicato huc me appuli. [When I slung myself here I was out of luck].—All the matere is safe now Omnis res iam est in vado. [The whole business is by now out of deep water].

There are many gnomic speeches:

The condicyon or disposicyon of wymen is whan a man will thei will not And whan a man will not than thei desyre moste. Mulierum ingenium est Nolunt ubi velis ubi nolis cupiunt vltro.— For thof I am worthy this rebuke Yitt it was nott thy parte to do itt. Nam si ego digna hac contumelia sum maxime. At tu maxime indignus qui faceres tamen.

The Middle Ages agree in regarding the purpose of Terence as primarily a moral one. The maxims scattered through his plays and the typical nature of his characters give some ground for this view; and hence he passed into the schools as the author of moral apophthegms and quotable dicta, which thus became part of the stock of accepted moral doctrine. He was a sage, quoted freely at second-hand, from the collections of moral sayings to which the age inclined. Terence, therefore, takes a place with "Cato" and "Aesop," while the colloquial nature of his style made him important as a source of Latin idiom, at a time when Latin was a means of general communi-

cation.[12]   In the same spirit he passes into the Renaissance
text-books.   Valla, for instance, in his *Elegantiae* quotes Terence more than any other author.[13]

Another school-book is *Ars Amatoria.   The flores of Ouide
de arte amandi,* printed by De Worde in 1513.   The book consists of eighty-five distichs from *De arte amandi.*   It is odd to
see on the title-page of Ovid the familiar woodcut of a teacher
on a high seat, with a bundle of switches in his hand, addressing pupils hunched on a low form.   But there is no "dishonest"
meaning in the verses, which are soberly gnomic.   In one or
two a moralizing turn is given which evades the sense of the
original:

> Neyther the violetis be freshe continualy ner the lilyis floreshe
> alway stil in there feyre whyte coloure. and lykewyse the stalke
> left be hynde waxid styf / dry / & harde: when his rose is goon.

> > Nec semper viole: nec semper lilia florent
> > Et riget amissa spina relicta rosa.

> And so lyke wyse feyre childe white heers wol com to the withyn
> a whil whan the floris of thy vthe been goon: ther wol also
> shortly come eyuyls the whiche wole ere thy body with pletis lyke
> sorows.

> > Et tibi iam venient cani formose capilli
> > Iam venient ruge; que tibi corpus arent.

There is no "carpe diem" in the translation.

The English, considerably expanded, precedes the Latin.   As
the translator says: "We haue added moche anglysh more than
in laten fore [i.e., in what precedes; the explanation is given at
the end of the selections] in the versis to make the sentens
playn . . ."   An "Englyshe alphabet" [i.e., an English-Latin

---

[12]Buccioni, U., *Terenzio nel rinascimento* (Rocca San Casciano, 1911)
pp. 12, 13, 15; Graf, Arturo, *Roma nella memoria e nelle imaginazioni del
medio evo* (Turin, 1882).

[13]The word *Vulgaria* seems to have been used in two senses.   Brinsley,
John, *Ludus Literarius,* 1612, p. 148, says: "I have given them *vulgars,*
or Englishes, such as I haue deuised, to be made in Latine: and at the
first entrance I haue taught and heard them, how to make euery word in
Latine, word by word, according to their rules.   After a while I haue
only given them such vulgars, and appointed them a time, against which
they should bring them made in Latine . . . . and so haue giuen them
new Englishes . . ."   But such vulgars are not vulgaria *Terentii.*   In spite
of the fact that I have not yet found illustrative citations verifying the
meaning, the word must mean *expressions about everyday affairs; practical commonplaces.*

vocabulary] and a *"Latinum alphabeticum"* follow. " . . . we haue also addid laten for chyldren [i.e., many synonyms in the vocabulary] : that they shuld lacke not laten worde by worde as nygh: as the dyuersite of the langage wol soffer."—"Si cui anglica ortographia non placeat: non det impressorem vicio. Ut lingua mutatur: ita & noster calamus." I have not been able to observe that the English spelling is more arbitrary than was usual at the time, though *vthe* [youth], and *eyuyl* are extreme. But the comment proves how uneasy the irregularity of English spelling made even the men before Dr. Johnson.

Mnemonic devices are employed to help in remembering the distichs, which were evidently meant to be learned by heart. Ovid, it may be remarked, like Terence, was a source of worldly wisdom, and the author of grave proverbs. The enthusiasm of the Middle Ages for collections of *sententiae* is a commonplace of literary history. Ovid took his place with the other favorite authors; and it is no wonder that a school-book should be made from his neat and easily remembered elegiacs.[14]

The only handbook of practical arts at all dependent upon the Latin is Christine de Pisan's *Book of the Feats of Arms,* in which much use is made of the treatises of Vegetius and Frontinus on the art of war. Although Christine's work is not a mere translation or even a compilation, but an intelligent and original reworking of Vegetius, Frontinus, and still more of Bonnor, it still contains fairly long passages of direct though free translation from Vegetius. Frontinus appears in unsystematic extracts, in general pretty accurate, rather than in extended passages.[15]

With Cicero and Boethius we pass into a higher intellectual region. Cicero and Boethius, if they were not ethical philos-

---

[14]T. C[ooper] in his dictionary of proper names following the Latin-English Vocabulary *Thesaurus linguae Romanae et Britannicae,* (1565); *"Ovid*—excellent in facilitie and abundance of sentences [i.e. pithily expressed generalizations]."

[15]Jähns, M., *Geschichte der Kriegswissenschaften,* in *Geschichte der Kunstwissenschaften,* published by the Royal Academy of Munich (1889) vol. i, pp. 186, 187, 350: Vegetius had considerable influence throughout the Middle Ages, which increased in the thirteenth century; the warfare of the last days of antiquity corresponded in many details with that of developed feudal conditions. Jähns draws out the resemblance with some fullness. William of Worcester's son speaks of a book compiled by his father from the same materials as Christine de Pisan's work; preface to the collections of William of Worcester. Rolls Series, No. 22, vol. ii, pt. 2, p. 522, (1864).

ophers in any strict sense, yet in some measure uplift and set free the soul, which is something that the beggarly rudiments of Cato or of Aesop or the tatters of Terence and Ovid in meagre school-books do not essay at all. Of the place of Boethius in medieval life and thought there is no need to speak here.[16] He linked the classics to the Christian Era. The best and finest spirits of the Middle Ages followed his wistful gaze, turned toward the other world for solace. It is an instructive and rather painful study to see how even in the hands of a genius like Chaucer prose remained so refractory when verse had developed into so flexible a means of expression. Chaucer's version is a bald and literal translation into clumsy and helpless prose, direct from the Latin with the help of Jean de Meung's French.[17] Chaucer often merely gives to a Latin word an English form, and often reproduces Latinisms or Gallicisms not to be found or seldom to be found in his poems. Chaucer draws from the manuscript of Boethius which lay before him many glosses and interpretations,—footnotes, as it were,—and sometimes extends interpretations of allusions or figures of speech. The translation is full of inaccuracies and errors, showing that Chaucer's Latin, however fluent, was not scholarly.

Cicero was not read in all parts of Europe and in every period of the Middle Ages with the same unbroken regard as the other writers who have been named. He was of course reputed to be the supreme master of rhetoric for schools of which rhetoric was the central study until logic ousted it, but his rhetorical works did not receive the same attention in northern as in southern Europe.[18] The nature of his speeches made them unadaptable as direct models to the needs of the Middle Ages. His letters had been forgotten. The vogue of his philosophical dialogues waxed and waned from age to age;

---

[16]Stewart, Hugh Fraser, *Boethius, an Essay*, (1891); Fehlauer, H., *Die englischen Uebersetzungen von Boethius*, in *Normannia* No. II, Berl. 1909.

[17]Chaucer's Boethius is reprinted from the mss., ed. R. Morris, in E E T S, 1st ser. 5; extra ser. 5, (1868); v. Liddell, in *Academy*, (Lond. No. 1220, Sept. 21, 1895, p. 227); Skeat, Walter W., *The True Source of Chaucer's Boethius*, in *Ath.*, July-Dec. 1891, p. 549.

[18]Deschamps, P., *Essai bibliographique sur Cicéron*, (Paris, 1863), brings together details as to libraries and their contents in the Middle Ages and the early Renaissance, and of the proportion and distribution of manuscripts. The greater interest in Cicero in the south of Europe is an inference from his data.

about their soundness and innocence there had been serious differences between church fathers, and even tragic conflicts in the hearts of great and devout churchmen who were drawn to them by their charm and their nobility.[19]   The two graceful dialogues *De Senectute* and *De Amicitia* were so true and so attractive that it was hard not to love them; and they were less liable to theological question than the longer and more fundamental philosophical disquisitions.   Yet in the printing of them there is some slight touch of contact with the Renaissance.· The *Laelius* and the oration of Accursius on Honor, as Caxton tells us, were translated by John Tiptoft, Earl of Worcester.   Tiptoft is the only one among the earliest translators who links England to Italy and the New Learning.   Unlike the body of English noblemen of the time, who came into relations with continental Europe chiefly through Flanders, commercial though romantic and chivalrous,[20] Tiptoft both in the elegancies and the business of life was governed by Italian ideals.   Like Duke Humphrey he was a noble book-buyer, sufficiently magnificent to win a place and a panegyric in the record which Vespasiano da Bisticci, the Florentine bookseller, kept of the notables who bought books of him,[21] while his English eulogy is written by another bookseller, namely Caxton himself.[22]   But unlike Duke Humphrey he was not satisfied to be a mere patron, but strove to practise the rediscovered art of Latin rhetoric, as he did with brilliant success before the accomplished audience that gathered about the Pope.   In the spirit of Italy, he made his vigorous personality and his studies subservient to despotism, utilizing the Civil Law which he had studied in Padua to support the cruel reprisals of Edward IV.[23] And finally—the thing that gives him a place here—he had the courage to enrich and develop the capabilities of his native tongue by using it to express the ideas of Cicero.   His prose

---

[19]Graf, *Roma etc.*, ii. 260.

[20]Kirk, J. F., *History of Charles the Bold* (Phila. 1863-68), pp. 75 *et seq.*, 464-470, 524-533.

[21]Bisticci, Vespasiano da, *Vite di uomini illustri dèl secolo XV*, (Florence, 1859) p. 402.

[22]Caxton's memorial of the earl follows the translation from Accursius.

[23]The populace rejoiced at his death, "perchè egli aveva fatta una legge ch'era contro al popolo la quale l'aveva portata da Italia, che si chiamava la legge di Padova"; Bisticci, *loc. cit.;* "juged by lawe padowe," Warkworth's *Chronicle*, Camd. Soc. 1st ser. vol. x, p. 5.

is certainly stammering and unsure, but the mere effort is significant.

The *Laelius* is translated direct from the Latin, with timid literalness;[24] the *De Honestate* is in a more free and flowing style. These are the only two translations from the hand of Tiptoft. The *Cato Major* is by another writer,[25] and is from de Premierfait's French, an expanded and interpreted version, with three synonyms for every important word, in order to be sure to get the right one in, and with the explanation of the allusions and of the figures of speech incorporated in the text, as in Chaucer's Boethius.

The two authors whom the Middle Ages enjoyed above all others for sheer delightsomeness were of course Vergil and Ovid. They were the best of Latin story-tellers, the richest and the most ample in variety of material and information, the sweetest in diction, the most beautiful in style. Of these two, then, Caxton prepared versions for his press.

Ovid was never forgotten and never ceased to be loved; shocking to some, suspect to many more, he was yet in secret or avowedly a favorite with nearly all.[26] Hence, as was done with all the important familiar classical writers, attempts were made in the Middle Ages to "moralize" his writings, that is, to interpret them allegorically, so as to enjoy the charm without suffering from the contamination of the apparent immorality. The systematic allegorization of Ovid was made by the French bishop, Pierre Berçoir, in the fourteenth century, though later attributed to Thomas Whaley or Walleys, an English Dominican.[27] A French translation of Berçoir's Latin prose was printed by Colard Mansion, Caxton's sometime partner in May, 1484; Caxton, using the French of Mansion either in manuscript or from an earlier edition as his main though not his sole reliance, made an English version, omitting most of the rationalization of the material. The manuscript of the

---

[24]Lathrop, H. B. *The Translations of John Tiptoft*, in MLN xli, (1926) 8.

[25]The version of *De Senectute*, often attributed to the Earl of Worcester, cannot be by him; it it very probably by W. Botoner, *alias* Worcester. v. Hazlitt's Warton, III, 110, n. 6.

[26]Bartsch, K., *Albrecht v. Halberstadt und Ovid im Mittelalter* (1861); Taylor, A. O., *The Classical Heritage of the Middle Ages* (N. Y., 1901); Schrötter, W. *Ovid und die Troubadours*, (Halle, 1908).

[27]On the authorship of the moralization, see Hauriau, *Mémoires de l'Acad. des Inscriptions et des Belles Lettres*, tom. xxx, pt. 2 a (1881).

last six books of the Metamorphoses is in existence, with this
note or colophon at the end:

> Thus endyth Ouyde hys booke of Methamorphose, translated
> & fynysshed by me Willm Caxton, at Westmestre the xxii day of
> appryll the yere of our lord m^i iiii^c iiii^xx. and the xx yere of the
> regne of Kynge Edward the fourth.[28]

It is possible, but not probable, that Caxton printed the Ovid.
On the whole, the version has Caxton's usual charm. Here
and there are quaint Gallicisms, and there are some errors.
Lui ardit ses blons cheveux becomes *brent his blonke herris;
fardoit sa crueuse face* [daubed her wrinkled face] is turned
into *clensyd his cruel face*. The trees that gather about Orpheus
are *alyes, lauriers, mespliers, cyphos* [cypres], *fresnes, corny-
liers;* he speaks of an *vmbrous valuye, tenebres of helle, dey-
tees infernals, charmes* and *deuynailles,* the birdes that *jar-
gonned* on the riuer, the *groundeling* of the riuer,—*"They bar-
bette with gronyng voys."*

The Ovid is not a romance, but a summary of the narrative
of the *Metamorphoses* itself. The Vergil is from the French
version of the prose romance founded on the *Aeneid,* published
at Lyons in 1483. Caxton supposed he was making a direct
translation of Vergil. The vocabulary is even more unintelli-
gently French than that of the Ovid: "thexcersite and hoost"
(*exercitus*) ; "it was made of so," (*ouuraige de si*) ; "trymory-
site insolute," (*tremeurs insolits*). The version has less charm
than most of Caxton's work, except in the preface. The truth
is that Caxton had an overmodest reverence for aureate rhetoric. He is quite sincere in characterizing his own style as
simple, and in calling himself uncunning; he at one time speaks
of Skelton as the author rightfully qualified for the high effort of translation. Now Skelton's conscious style in serious
work is of the most stuffed and swelling bombast. An example
may be found in his translation of Diodorus Siculus. The introduction to Book v. is in part as follows:

> To vs not vnknowen how historyens in recountyng former actes
> and fayttes of antyquyte / as it fortuneth many seasons they
> faylle ofte of thyr sure fotyng by encheson that the Wilde wayes

---

[28] The date of the colophon, of course, proves that Caxton completed his
version before the extant edition of Mansion's version; Caxton's Ovid
printed Oxf. 1924.

and pathis discontynued of our auncyente gestis be moche slypper / and somwhat enderkyd wyth the busshy shadowes of ambiguite. So that wrytars be moche endoubted to arette theyr pennys in reportyng ony assuraunce of trouthe / where as they be destitute of the relucent lanterne that shold be theyr directorye vnto theffecte of theyr processe as it was in dede / . . . . . .
We in our inwarde aduertisement ponderyng the comodyous allectyues that may ensiewe of an hystoryous mater / yf it be orygynally contynued / suspensyfly protensyd & duly enlengthed processe fro his prymordiall & fyrst bygynnyng / take vpon vs the weyghty engroced burden of alle former auctoritees ensummed to gydre of a membrancer afforcyng thoffyce / whos charge is as ferforth as he may by mannes reson no thyng to passe ouer vntouched by remyssyue neclygance / of whiche consyderacion moeued we be determyned as euydently as we can alle former auncyent specyaltees of olde recorded compactly to gyder to engroce in this treatys compyled of our translacion / The noble actes of our former predecessors of olde such as longe tyme were byfore vs . . . . / Whos famous names inscrybed be / wyth laureate lettres Inviolably euermore to endure / emong the celestial senatours entrouanysed & crowned with the contynuel enverdured laureate leues of victoryous tryumphe in the gloryous cyte of fame.[29]

This was what Caxton admired, but what his better instinct kept him from doing; and this he quite crudely attempts in the Vergil.

We can now look back over the works of this era just before the dawn of a new classic culture in England. There are only eleven printed books which by the most inclusive definition can be regarded as coming within the scope of this study. All are of Latin origin, and of these six are from the French; two are elementary phrase-books for schools; only two are serious efforts to translate Latin authors from the Latin tongue. A moralistic bias is evident in all the group; nearly all are moral essays or works of directly didactic purpose, or moralizations. There is some interest of story, especially of romantic story. There is no history, no lyric, no satire, no oratory, no drama. Livy, Tacitus, Catullus, Plautus, Seneca, Horace, Juvenal, even Lucan and Statius, are not represented.

---

[29]Skelton's translation of Diodorus is no. ccclvii in Archbishop Parker's Mss. in the Library of Corpus Christi, Cambridge; Nasmyth Cat. p. 362; Rotograph No. 29, Library of Congress, Modern Language deposit; his source is Poggio's Latin version.

Terence is a mere source of phrases. Vergil and Ovid are hidden under a thick cloak, and they with Cicero the essayist are the only genuinely classic writers who are touched. Boethius, "Cato," "Aesop" are the really important authors. As for the style of the translations, it is naïvely helpless. The writers cannot put sentences together with any regularity of syntax, or definiteness of emphasis, or clearness of connection. Translators who worked direct from the Latin generally felt bound by multiplying synonyms to cover the meaning of the original words somehow, and "resolved," that is explained and made literal, the metaphors of the original. Those who depended upon a French intermediary are less constrained and more natural. Caxton, at least, wrote a graceful, rhythmic English, which though not at all highly organized is very attractive. Even his writings are immature, and most of the work of his contemporaries is simply crude.

CHAPTER II: THE INFLUENCE OF ERASMUS
1517-1557

The publication of Chaucer's *Boethius* in 1477 marks the beginning of the first period with which we have to deal; there is no similar landmark for the conclusion of that period, but it may fairly be reckoned as lasting for about forty years. The second period, after another forty years, comes to a fairly definite end with the appearance of Tottel's *Miscellany* in 1557. Perhaps the first work signalizing the new spirit characteristic of the second period is a version of Lucian's *Necromantia,* published about 1520,—the first English version of a Greek author; the end of the period is marked, as has been indicated, by Tottel's *Miscellany*, in which was gathered a body of representative verse, consisting in great part of translations, and written within some twenty-five or thirty years preceding the date of publication.

The new era—that of Henry VIII, Edward VI, and Mary —compared with the preceding is modern; it reflects a larger knowledge and a more critical understanding than the age of Edward IV, Richard III, and Henry VII. At the same time, it carried on some of the tendencies of the earlier period. It is true that of the earlier translations almost none were reprinted; the *Vulgaria* of Terence disappeared completely as soon as Udall's more vigorous *Flowers* were published.[1]   Tiptoft's

---

[1] The sixth and last known edition of *Vulgaria Terentii* (Wynkyn de Worde) appeared in 1529; the first edition of Udall's *Flowers* in 1532 or 1533. Udall's *Flowers* contains translations of phrases from Terence, not for their own sake, but for the purpose of aiding pupils to obtain a knowledge of Latin colloquial idiom; it is not meant to contribute to the edification or delight of the mere English reader, but is a school-boy's Latin book. As such it is a very important work. The title, *Flowers for Latin speaking selected and gathered out of Terence*, etc. indicates its purpose. The word *flowers* has no rhetorical intent; it means nothing more than *selections*, and the selections illustrate merely Latin idiom, not decorations or elegancies. In a Latin preface dated "pridie Calendas Martias, Anno post natum Christum M. D. XLIII," addressed to his pupils, Udall says: "Although I came into this business of teaching not by my own will,

Laelius (reprinted by William Rastell about 1530) and the *Cato Major* printed with it could not hold the respect of readers accustomed to more finished work; Caxton's Aesop alone held a place by its own interest, as it does still. But if the actual work of the earlier period was too crude to maintain its ground, some of the objects to which it was directed continued to prevail. There was the same desire for text-books of colloquial Latin, met by phrase-books; Cato, Boethius, Cicero's *De Amicitia* and *De Senectute* were translated as practical guides to life, as in effect the work of Christian doctors, by Whitinton, Rychard, and Burrant, in the same spirit as by Burgh, Chaucer, and Worcester; and Frontinus epitomized the art of war for Morison (Morysine, 1539) as for Christine. Similar works by the same classic authors, or by others known to the Middle Ages were added to Caxton's list; Cicero's *De Officiis* and *Paradoxa* were added to *De Senectute* and *De Amicitia,* Publilius Syrus to Cato, and Seneca to the other Latin moralists. In truth, scholars in both eras depended upon the classics mainly for specific direction in conduct; they looked for practical doctrine, for guidance to health of body and mind. The new era had somewhat different standards of health, and was acquainted with new authors. But there is comparatively

---

but partly because of the urgency of friends, partly by fortune, yet I see such promise in you that I am proud of my occupation, and am determined to do something professionally creditable. To improve the command of Latin no author is better than Terence; he is the fittest of all to form and develope a boy's Latin style, and without controversy is accepted as *facile princeps* in this field, inasmuch as he provides formulas suited for ordinary intercourse. He was the model of Cicero himself. I have added needful notes on syntax, idiom, and figurative language, and such other helps as seemed useful." The extracts are taken from *Andria, Eunuchus,* and *Heautontimoroumenos.* There is an index to Latinity and to points of syntax illustrated.

The book held an important place as a text-book for fifty years, and was revised and enlarged in 1575 by John Higgins, who added extracts from *Adelphi, Hecyra,* and *Phormio.* The edition of 1581 is a reprint of the edition of 1575, except that a set of hendecasyllabics by "Thomas Newtonus, Cestreshyrius" is prefixed.

The English translations have a value, as giving examples of English idiom, and sometimes of current colloqualisms, for example:

Habet patrem quendam auidum, miserum atque aridum. He hath to his father a certain felowe, greedie of money, a wretched feloe in his house, and a very pinchepenie, as drie as a kixe. (Ed. 1560, Fo. 144)

Haud stulto sapis. You are no small foole,

Istaec intro auferte. Haue in this geare,

Quid obstat? What let is there? (Fo. 136)

Mulier lacrimis opplet os totum sibi. The woman all to washes her face with blubbreyng and weepyng. (Fo. 134)

little of literary intent to be discovered in the translations of either period. The writers aim to improve the art of life as followed in their day, and they believed the ancients to have understood the art of life. Thus the horizon widened, the scope of knowledge was extended, more authors were read, and those who were read were better known; but the standpoint was the same, and the outlook was in the same direction. The Ovid and the Vergil of the first period were primarily books of morals and information. In this second period, except for a few trifling epigrams, the only complete poetical or imaginative work translated was the *Andria* of Terence, apparently prepared for acting by schoolboys. Although this somewhat Philistine practicality directed the minds of many students of antiquity throughout the hundred and fifty years which are comprehended within the scope of the present treatise, it was more exclusively dominant in the first and second periods than later.

The second era, of course, is in many particulars unlike the first. It has a direct and fresh contact with antiquity, and with really representative authors. The "Cato" and "Aesop," the Ovid and Vergil, of the earlier period were either not truly classic names at all, or were known to the earlier translators in a garbled form. Terence is a mere source of copybook maxims. Authors were still *auctores*—not individual men but mere sources. But such translators as Sir Thomas Elyot, or Alexander Barclay, or Richard Taverner had a personal contact with the authors whom they translated. Cicero and Plutarch were to them men, individuals with a history and a character, a personal method and a style. The new era also went for its most important moral and critical ideas not to Latin but to Greek sources, though usually through the medium of Latin translations. They went to the wise men of Greece for their pregnant sayings and anecdotic wisdom; to Lucian and Plutarch for the critical analysis of life, to Cebes and Isocrates for formative moral doctrine, to Xenophon for practical worldly wisdom, to Plutarch, Galen, and Hippocrates for hygiene. Ancient history now also appeared with ethics as a guide of life—no very large works were undertaken, but central parts of the narrative of Livy, Thucydides, and Caesar were given to the English public, together with such shorter works as the histories of Sallust, Herodian, and Quintus

Curtius. Finally, the art of rhetoric was adapted to the English language, and an oration of Cicero's was translated and presented as an example in a text-book.

The second period of this study was crucial in English life and thought; it was the age of Henry VIII, when the New Learning was endenizened in England and the beginning was made of a developing culture which culminated at the end of the century. The translations of this time grew out of a set of conditions and represented a school of thought quite definite though complicated, and having a real organic unity and fundamental principles. They were the principles conceived by Linacre and Grocyn, accepted by Colet, promulgated by Erasmus, accepted and enforced by a band of his associates and followers, including such eminent personages as Sir Thomas More and Reginald Pole, and brought into English literature by less distinguished men of letters, the translators of the age, among them such men as Sir Thomas Elyot, Gentian Hervet, at this time a tutor in the Pole family, John Rastell, More's brother-in-law, an adventurous man of many affairs, Alexander Barclay, and Richard Taverner. What were the ideas of these men in their view of the classics?

The New Learning in England was of a character that may be called Erasmian, for though it was clearly apprehended by Colet and Linacre, it was typically embodied and most energetically set forth by Erasmus. His object, his conscious object, pursued with all his strength, was a reform of European intellectual and moral life on the basis of ideas drawn from Greek sources. The Greeks had conceived of a civilized life, a life directed toward the achievement of proportion and beauty, and had developed what may be called a technique of the art of life applicable in the day of Erasmus as a basis of practical reform. This is the meaning of Erasmus's proverbs, his anecdotes, his letters, his editions. Nobody, not St. Bernard or Voltaire or Herbert Spencer, ever had a clearer programme or a more definite platform. The programme was to attack the rooted irrationality of the age and especially its superstitions, by every intellectual weapon—learning, invective eloquence, wit and direct exhortation—and the platform was enlightenment, knowledge, critical soundness of mind, sanity, especially as conceived by the later Greek philosophers and the large-minded early fathers of the Church.

Erasmus in no way thought of himself as anything but a true son of the Church. He believed himself to be modestly illuminating the Christian doctrine, and working not to change it but to deepen and clarify its essential spirit. And this he did by the method of criticism, by "a disinterested effort to learn and propagate" the nature and meaning of the fundamental documents which contained its truest and deepest thought. With absolute candor and sacrificial labor he edited, translated, interpreted, and made accessible first the New Testament and then, one after the other, the works of the great early Christian doctors, doing his best that, apart from anything personal to him, Christianity might be truly known in its inmost meaning.

The double purpose of Erasmus was to inculcate intelligently and afresh, the double ideal of modern Europe as defined by Arnold, *Hebraism and Hellenism,* and to make "reason and the will of God prevail."[2]

How his associates and followers regarded him in the early years of the sixteenth century is shown in the dedication of Gentian Hervet's translation of Erasmus's sermon on the Mercy of God, addressed to the Countess of Stafford:

> I have translated out of Latin in to englyshe a sermon of Erasmus of the mercy of god: the which translated for you, and dedicate for your ladyshyp I thought it shuld be a good dede, if for your ladisshypps pleasure it were printed and sprede abrode: and where as afore lerned men only it got out bothe pleasure and great fruite in readyng of this boke, now every man, as well rude as lerned, may have this sermon of the mercy of god as common unto him as the mercy of god it selfe is. And as touching the commendacion either of the author or of the werke, I knowe the tendrenes of my wit much more slendre, than that I can be able to beare the weyght of suche an enterprise, and I reken to be much better to hold my tonge utterly from the praisyng than of theym to speake to littell, and for faulte of wyt to minishe theyr excellence. Yet nethelesse it semeth expedient unto me, that by this your ladyshyp meane briefely other folke maye knowe how noble is the autor of this worke and how much we be bounde to him for it. The autor of the boke is Erasmus Roterodemus; whom my praises can no more ennoble, than the sun with a candle maie be made clearer. He is the man, to whom in learnyng no lyvyng man maie hymselfe compare; and not

---

[2] Glöckner, G., *Das Ideal der Bildung und Erziehung bei Erasmus von Rotterdam.* In *Jahrb. des Vereins fur wissenschaftliche Pedagogik* xxii, 1.

onely passeth theim that be alyve but also from the moste parte
of olde authours hath beraft the prize, and not onely painems
and gentils, but also Christen doctors. He is the man, that when
in his fyrst daies trouthe was far hyd in the depe veines of the
grounde and more over it was prohibited as a thyng beyng worthy
deth, that no man shulde for hir enquere, he dyd not suffre the
world to be confounded with such a meruelous darkness and
either he hath dygged up many lymmes of trouth, or at the leste
he hath restored us free libertee to serche her. He is the man,
that to Isaac maie be compared, the whiche dygged up the goodly
springyng welles, that the Philistens destroyed, and with dyrte
and donge overfilled. The clere springes of the holy scripture,
that the Philistines had so troubled, so marred, and so defiled,
that no man coude drynk or have the true tast of the water,
thei be nowe by his labour and diligence to their olde purenesse
and cleannesse so restored, that no spotte nor erthly filth in theim
remaineth. And though the Philistins dyd all that thei coude to
disturbe him from his holy purpose, and that among the people
by the reason of theym, he was greatly hated and envied, yet at
last, as it chanceth always unto them, that with a bolde stomacke
in their good dedes do continue excellent vertu hath overcome
enuy, whan both it is excedyng profitable and on every syde all
perfecte, me thinketh that this lyttell treatise, beyng in every
poynte as perfecte as any other be in profite, not onely geueth no
place but also greatly passeth: for where afore the workes that
he made were profitable but specially to one kinde of men his
Proverbes, his New Testament and many other treatises onely
to lerned men, of the boke of the Instruction of princes the most
profit redoundeth to princes. This boke onelye with the boke
called the knife or wepon of a Christen souldiour hath so far
sprede abrode his fruitefull branches, that there is no man, but
great fruite gether he maie out of it except he that thynketh that
it maketh no mater whether he be dampned or saved. And as
for the knife of a Christen souldiour, whiche he nameth Enchiridion, it bryngeth a man out of the waie of vices, and leadeth him
in the waie of vertu and the path of saluacion.

A few years later a second edition of the sermon appeared.[3]
All references to the Countess were suppressed, her whole family now being under suspicion. Gentian Hervet was an exile,
having fled from the ferocity of Henry VIII. Only a generation passed, and Hervet was acting first as one of the most useful secretaries, and then as one of the most vigorous propa-
gandists of the Council of Trent, with which the work of Erasmus was suspect.

---

[3]The first edition of Hervet's translation of the sermon on the Mercy of
God appeared in 1533, the second in 1547.

The conception that ancient philosophy and Christian doctrine are in no essential conflict was of course not new; in point
of fact when the Christian church was called upon to be the
efficient agent in organizing the life of civilization, it had to resort to Greek philosophy for a refined analysis of the relations
of life, such as neither the Old Testament nor the New provided. And alike in the East and the West the formative men
of the church were the product of the ancient schools of rhetoric, in which the theory of conduct was a part.[4] And alike
in the East and the West, the fathers claim heathen philosophy
as of right belonging to the church.

The Protestant scholar De Mornay expressed the current
idea forcibly—it was universal, indeed self-understood, among
all the learned of the age. De Mornay in *Six Excellent Treatises on Life and Death,* brings together the *Axiochus* believed
to be by Plato, Cicero *De Senectute,* a number of the letters of
Seneca, a sermon of St. Cyprian, and one of St. Ambrose. In
his advertisement to the reader he says:

> Whereas *Plato, Cicero* and *Seneca,* who were called Philoso-
> phers, are brought in, speaking by way of Dialogue, after the
> first Discourse [i.e., De Mornay's own] let not this be understood,
> of any want we had of more authentike aultors, that is to say,
> amongst the ancient Christians, vpon this argument (seeing we
> have in like manner produced two in this second edition, which
> are Saint *Cyprian* and S. *Ambrose*): but this was onely thought
> a better meanes to awake vs thorowly, by the crie of these
> strange witnesses, who tasting only, but out of their naturall
> iudgement, and some knowledge and experience which they had
> of the vanities of man; it seems, they would fain hail vs along to
> some better Port, and Retrait than themselves have attained for
> them, or witnessed vnto others by their example.[5]

Erasmus and his associates addressed themselves to an élite
—to an aristocracy in a double sense, the learned and the prosperous classes. The public of Erasmus was the international
body of educated people, who read Latin and who were accustomed to reflection and deliberate thought. To address the

---

. [4]*e.g.* Basil, Gregory Nazianzen, Chrysostom, Ambrose, Augustine, *v.*
Hatch, E., *The Influence of Greek Ideas and Usages upon the Christian
Church.* Hibbert Lectures, 1888, (Lond. 1891), p. 109.

[5]Cited from the English translation (1607); DeMornay's version dates
from 1576; see also Budé on "history and sapience," Delaruelle, Louis,
Études sur l'humaniste français Guillaume Budé (1917) p. 206-207.

great public, the emotional, instinctive, undeliberating public, would have been abhorrent to him. Like Plato, he recognized the great gulf between the philosopher and the common man. And again, like the other teachers of the Renaissance, he has in mind the well-to-do, the leaders, as an important part of his public, and the main subject of his educational programme. For this view, he had Greek and Roman precedent, education in classical times being essentially aristocratic.[6]

From these considerations it follows that the vernacular works, including the translations into the vernacular, are secondary and slight in comparison with the writings of the scholars in Latin and their commentaries upon the classics. The translations are indeed typical, they are imbued with the spirit of the Erasmian group, but they are not adequately representative; they include but a small part of the classics known, and they are not written with the same care for style as the works addressed to the international public. In England the translations were the casual labors of less distinguished men; the greater personalities were too busy with their own work to engage in the business of adapting the classics to the English public. The ideal of a French style and a French fame preceded by a generation the analogous ideal in England.

Two Greek writers were particularly valuable in serving the ends of Erasmus as sources and as models; Plutarch for his abundance of cheery and significant anecdote, and Lucian for his lively criticism of contemporary superficiality and obscurantism. Erasmus and More put out a collection of Latin translations of a number of small works of Lucian's which approved themselves to them by their spirit.[7] More's preface is addressed to Thomas Ruthall, private secretary to Henry VII. In it More declares that highly as he prizes all of Lucian's works, he delights most of all in those dialogues which he has himself translated;—*Cynicus, Necromantia,* and *Philopseudes.* Though other men may have different preferences, he thinks he can give a reason for his taste. He cites Chrysostom's use of the *Cynicus,* which depicts a life truly Christian in its austerity. He praises the *Necromantia* for its satire on the tricks of the magicians, the figments of poets, and the inconclusive

[6]Rostovtzeff, M. *The Social and Economiic History of the Roman Empire.* Oxf. (1926) p. 178-9.

[7]Luciani *Opuscula,* Aldus, Ven. 1516; Frobenius, Basle, 1521.

conflicts of philosophers; and he is not afraid to value the *Philopseudes* for its irony against superstition, not deterred by the fact that Lucian was of the sect of Democritus, Lucretius, and Pliny. Even Saint Augustine, a hater of falsehood, would have been protected from one deceit [perhaps his youthful Manichaeism], if he had known Lucian. And much more the coarse vulgar who have contaminated the religion of truth with falsehood, and done much harm thereby, for as Augustine says, the mixture of falsehood weakens truth . . . "Accept then these first fruits of my Greek studies."

It is impossible to read these words without finding in them the same spirit as in Erasmus's friend, Colet, girding at the relic-hunters and quizzing the guides at the great pilgrim shrines of Walsingham and Canterbury.[8] The English translator indicates no such purpose in his version; the *Necromantia* was to him amusing and instructive, so he printed More's Latin and his own English on opposite pages, "for the erudicion of them, which be disposyd to lerne the tongis." The English version is in crude verse, one page containing the earliest instance which I have found of the imitation of classic verse in English. It is curious that the very beginning of the attempt to popularize the substance of Greek literature in English included an effort to adapt classical metre to the English language.

Menippus.	*Menippus.*
Nay syr I was not dede But the hell alyue me receyued	Non: sed me ad huc viuum recepit tartarus
Philonides.	*Philonides.*
What causyd the to take the way Of this incredeble and new Iourney	Quenam causa tibi fuit nouae huius atque incredibilis viae?
Menippus.	*Menippus.*
Exam. Youth thereto dyd me Prouoke and also the boldnes Pent. Which for the youth alway Stronger it is in effect.	Iuuenta me incitauit, atque audacia Que pro iuuenta haud paululum impotentior

---

[8]*Peregrinatio Religionis Erga* in *Colloquia; Modus Orandi,* Erasmi *Opera,* Lugd. Bat. (1704), v. 1119, 1120.

Philonides.	*Philonides.*
O thou tragidian I pray the hartely	Siste o beate Tragica :
Stand styll and leaue thy versyfyeng	et ab iambis descendens [climbing down from your iambs]
Speke and shew me open and playnly	sic potius simpliciter loquere :
What was the cause of thy strange clothyng	quaenam haec vestis :
And of thy Iourney to hell descendyng	quae causa tibi itineris inferni fuit :

More's Latin, like the original, is in prose, of course, and the English version, as has been said, is in rough verse—a verse rougher than doggerel. Menippus, clad in tragic costume, speaks iambic trimeters, the verse of tragic dialogue. The English version strives to mark out his response by adapting the elegiac distich to the English language. Like nearly every English experimenter since, he compromises between quantity and stress in his metre. The general effect is quantitative, but *Which for the* cannot stand as a quantitative dactyl, especially for the age when R was "the dog's letter." In modern southern English it might. *Is* in *Stronger it is in effect* is easily pronounced long, while the first syllable in *effect* is probably short in most pronunciations.

Youth there|to did|me pro|voke and|also the|boldness
Which for the|youth al|way stronger it|is in ef|fect

This is not so bad for a first attempt; it has only one plainly false quantity.

The translator indicates on the title-page that his object in putting forth the Latin with the English text is pedagogical: ". . . now lately translated out of Laten into Englissh for the erudicion of them, which be disposyd to lerne the tongis." It has been suggested that the English as well as the Latin version is by More; but though More's known verse is rough, it is not so crude as that of this translation.

The *Cynicus* is likewise from More's Latin, but is in prose, more vigorous and effective than the verse of the *Necromantia.* An English version of the *Philopseudes,* printed first in 1669, it has been suggested, may be by More, but this is impossible; the translation cannot even come from More's era.[9]

"Opuscula" of Plutarch, as of Lucian, were popularized, if the term may be used—that is, made accessible to the generally educated international public of the day—by being turned into Latin. The essays, dealing with miscellaneous problems of domestic and personal life, with the art of choosing a friend, with the method of deriving benefit from an enemy, with the education of children, and with the care of health, were translated by various hands.

The first of the little works of Plutarch to be given an English form was *De Tranquillitate Animi, "Quyete of Mynde,"* translated by Sir Thomas Wyat from the Latin of Budaeus, to be presented to Queen Catherine as a gift for the New Year of 1528. The queen (whose life is a better treatise on fortitude and self-mastery than any book) had made to Wyat the pathetic request that he should translate for her Petrarch's *De Remediis Utriusque Fortunae;* and Wyat finding Petrarch's inexhaustible rhetoric of variations on his single theme tedious substituted Plutarch's briefer treatment of the subject. The style of the version is not so good as that of Wyat's *Defense,* entirely English in spirit as well as in language.

His laudable attempt to hold close to his original puts him under constraint, and causes him to depart from the natural idiom of the English language. He is helpless before a complicated construction; often un-English in the translation of even a simple one. Latin participles especially tempt him by their neat brevity away from the normal syntax of his own language. His diction, like that of all the earlier English humanists is studiously simple; the whole impression produced by the translation that of an awkward first attempt. Wyat's

---

[9] An English version of the *Philopseudes,* printed with L. Wagstaffe's *The Question of Witchcraft Debated,* (1) 1669; (2) 1671, has been thought to be possibly by More (D.N.B.). This is the third of the Lucianic dialogues translated by More into Latin; and a note in Wagstaffe—". . . I only ordered the Bookseller to Reprint it . . ."—shows that the translation had been actually printed before 1669; but it cannot be by More. The vocabulary is later: *intimate* as an adjective, first instance in Murray 1632 (substantive 1609); *application* of a medicament, 1601; *gangrene,* transitive verb, 1607; *spectrum,* a spectre, first in any sense, 1611; *conveyance,* (conduit), 1577; *motion,* a self-moving mechanism, 1605; and many more. The sentences are precise and studiedly various in syntax in a style not conceivable in More's time. The version is evidently from the early part of the seventeenth century.

version, which long remained unnoticed, has been made accessible (1931) by the authorities of the Huntington Library in a heliotype fascimile preceded by a scholarly introduction from the pen of Professor Charles R. Baskervill.

The essay *On the Education of Children* was translated by Guarino (first printed in 1497); and on this Latin version Sir Thomas Elyot based an English one, *The education or bringing up of children, translated by T. Eliot Esquire.* In the dedicatory preface, addressed to "his only entierly beloued syster Margery Puttenham," Elyot says that he expanded Plutarch's brief allusions to classical story, and excised the passages dealing with classical vice.

> I haue not onely vsed therin the office of a translatour, but also haue declared at lengthe dyuers histories, onely touched by Plutarch: to thentent that difficultie of vnderstandynge shall not cause the matter to be to you fastidious, as it often tymes hath hapened to other. Also of pourpose I haue omitted to translate some part of this matter, conteyned as well in the Greke as in the Latin, partly for that it is strange from the experience or vsage of this present tyme, partly that some vices be in those tonges reproued, whiche ought rather to be unknowen, than in a vulgare tonge to be expressed.

Thus the stories of the victory of Cadmus, of the insult to Socrates, and of Polyphemus are additions of Elyot's.

As for his style he says:

> . . . I wolde not that any man shuld exacte of me the exquisite diligence of an interpretour, syns I wryte not to clerkes, ne desire not to haue my boke conferred with the delectable styles of Grekes or Latines: But as I haue sayde, I haue this done for my pastyme without moch studie or trauaile. And it shall only suffice me, if by this littel labour I may cause you myn entierly beloued syster to folowe the intent of Plutarche in brynginge & inducing my littell neuewes into the trayne and rule of vertue, whereby they shall fynally attayne to honour (god so disposinge) to the inestimable comforte of theyr naturall parentes, and most specially to the high pleasure of god, commoditye and profite of theyr contray.

For all this, Elyot is no contemptible writer. He is unaffectedly vigorous, his sentences are firmly constructed, and his syntax is not incorrect. There is neither sprawling helplessness nor fantastic adornment in his writing. The following passage is a fair example of his work and presents an idea central in the educational theory of both writers.

> What is that to the purpose, sayth some man to me? For where thou dyddest promyse to gyue aduertisementes concernynge the bryngynge vp of honest mens children, notwithstandynge thou passest ouer poure men and commune people, that thou goest aboute to instructe onely ryche menne and noble [*noble* is the English translator's characteristic addition] whereunto it is no great difficultie to replie: Certeynly myn entent is, that my exhortation shulde be commune and also profitable to euery man. But if any be of suche pouertie that he is not able to vse this my counsayle, he shal blame fortune and not me, that do the best I can to aduise hym. It is to be assayed with all that may be, that the beste ways of bryngynge vp of chyldren may be knowen also to poure men and at the leste to do that that is possible.

Another of the little Plutarch essays discusses the question how to derive profit from having enemies. This was translated into Latin by Erasmus, and Erasmus's Latin was Englished about 1535. Mr. Croft says in the introduction to his edition of the *Gouernour* (p. cxlvi): "No author's name appears on the copy in the British Museum Library but it has always been attributed to Elyot." The book is not mentioned by Elyot in his enumeration of his works in the preface to *The Image of Governance,* and I know of no evidence that he was the translator. This essay, also, it need hardly be said, is characterised by the aristocratic spirit common to Greek and Renaissance education.

> Me thinketh that it were meete for a man of auctoritee, and that medleth in the rule of the commonwealth that amonge other businesse he shoulde haue also consideracion of his enemies, and to take good heede, that this was not spoken for nought of [i.e. *by*] Xenophon: It is a substanciall wise man's part, to take profytte of his enemies.

A third Greek author who expressed the ideals of the group to which Sir Thomas Elyot belonged was Isocrates. He combined high-minded morality, practical sense, an aristocratic spirit, and the point of view of the educator. Elyot, therefore, regarded his letter to Nicocles (*The Doctrinal of Princes*) with great respect; and he translated it direct from the Greek—the first work, so far as I know, thus translated into English. The preface, also, for the first time speaks with appreciation of the literary capacity of the English tongue.

Sir Thomas Eliot knight to the reader

This little booke (whiche in mine opinion) is to be compared in counsaile and short sentence [i.e. brief pregnant sayings] with any booke, holy scripture excepted, I haue translated out of greeke, not presumyng to contende with theim, whiche haue doone the same in latine: but to thintent onely that I wolde assaie, if our Englishe tunge mought receiue the quicke and propre sentences pronounced by the greekes. And in this experience I haue founde (if I be not muche deceiued) that in the forme of speakyng, vsed of the Greekes, called in greeke, and also in latine, *Phrasis*, [*i.e.* style, here applied particularly to conscious art in the construction of sentences] muche nere [more closely] approcheth to that, whiche at this daie we vse: than the order of the latine tunge: I meane in the sentences, and not in the wordes: whiche I doubte not shall be affirmed by them, who sufficiently instructed in all the saide three tunges, shall with a good iudgement read this worke. And where I haue put at the beginnyng this word: vessell, plate, or for that which is in greeke, brasse or golde wrought, it is perceiued of euery wise man, for what intent I did it. Finally the chiefe cause of this my litle exercise was: to the intent that thei which do not vnderstande greeke nor latine, should not lacke the commoditee and pleasure, which miae be taken in readyng therof. wherfore if I shall perceiue you to take this myne enterprise thankefully, I shall that litle porcion of life, which remaineth (God sendyng me quietnesse of minde) bestowe in preparing for you such bookes, in the readynge wherof, ye shall finde bothe honest passe tyme and also profitable counsaile and lernyng.

Fare ye well

Isocrates is the great founder of that school of practical but not ungenerous prudential morality which was a part of the training for active life given by the rhetorical schools of Greece to those who were to be leaders of men. His tradition passed on into the Roman schools, and gained renewed life at the Renaissance, affecting the ideals of the "Prince," the "Magistrate," and the "Gentleman."

Nor is Isocrates alone the founder of the moral ideal and discipline which passed on through the Greek schools to the Roman and the Christian, to Cicero, Quintilian, Libanius, even to Augustine, Basil, and Chrysostom, to Guarino and Vittorino and to St. Paul's, Winchester, Eton, and Harrow; he is the fundamental creator of prosaic prose, of prose which was comely without borrowing the special beauties of poetry. His predecessors, Herodotus, Thucydides, and Plato, are more beautiful and interesting writers than he, but they gain their charm from imagination, and normally adopt at the high points of writing the spirit and even the diction of the poets. Isocrates set about making a practical prose style suited for affairs and business. He avoided the extravagances of his master Gorgias, but adopted his fundamental principle of giving to prose an agreeable pattern by a system of balancing and measurement dealing with large groups instead of single syllables, and thus avoiding the form of verse. He added or carried farther the method of giving to prose style its own charm by striving for a smooth flow of syllables and an unobtrusive continuity of structure in the period, and in all his work was governed by the purpose of producing gracious ease without excess or shock. From his school of style filiated the ideals of Cicero, especially as exhibited in his philosophical writings. Cicero has at command a greater body of resource in the methods of obtaining effect, and above all possesses a bolder and warmer temperament, not afraid of a surprise in metaphor or paronomasia or jest, yet in general he creates an ample period of easy flow, unobtrusively connected, and kept always within the bounds of moderating taste and judgment.

This fairly long exposition has been necessary, since Isocrates is little read nowadays. For Elyot he was the guide and foundation not only of practical morals, but of style; and English prose, which had been rough and incondite or naïvely unformed, is by Elyot regularized,—not only made accurate in syntax, but made so far as he could make it flowing in movement, and given a pattern after the ideas of Isocrates. Roger Ascham is generally given the credit for inaugurating the influence here attributed to Elyot; but Elyot is half a generation earlier; and though the classical studies and the temper of Ascham might easily have led him to Elyot's point of view and to a style not unlike his, he had before him the encouraging example of the elder writer.

Sir Sidney Lee comments unfavorably on these cool-tempered humanists governed by classical principles of restraint.

The tuition of Latin (and in this case he might add Greek) influence on English prose "while it gave a more businesslike regularity to syntactical structure, was touched by no warmth of feeling, by no artistic expansiveness, by small originality or exuberance of thought."[10] He comments on the coldness of the three most notable humanist works that contributed to the formation of prose style: Elyot's *Gouernour,* Wilson's *Art of Rhetorique,* and Ascham's *Schoolmaster.* This coldness and reserve were intentional. They were the expression of a reaction against the fantastic excesses of popular writing, with its neologisms, especially its ink-horn terms, its jerky over-emphasis, its puerile ingenuity, its chiming plays on sound and its trifling plays on words. And if they were fairly dry and dull, had they not a good example, for is not Isocrates the most respectable bore in classic literature?[11]

The union of Christian and pagan morals, of the elder medieval tradition and the Newer Learning, are curiously illustrated by the way in which works from each realm of thought are brought together into one volume. Thus Erasmus made a book [T. Martinus, printer, Louvain, 1517] of Cato's *Distichs,* the *Mimes* of Publilius Syrus, his own *Institutio Christiani Hominis,* the *Epistola de philosophia Christiana* of Eucherius, Bishop of Lyons, his own translation of the *Sayings of the Wise,* and Isocrates's *Letter to Demonicus.* The letter to Demonicus teaches a high and generous morality, though I find it hard to reconcile its fundamental principles with Christian humility; and it was by many of the earnest and thoughtful men of that time accepted with reverence and enthusiasm as a systematic outline of practical duty. It was a work of Isocrates, probably this letter, it will be remembered, that Tyndall chose as a trial piece, by translating which he showed his skill in Greek to the bishop of London.[12] No translation seems to have been printed, however, until 1558. In that year John Bury's version, executed in 1557, appeared with the following dedicatory preface.

---

[10]*The French Renaissance in England,* 1900, pp. 136-7.

[11]On the influence of Isocrates on prose style, *see* Whipple, T. K., *Isocrates and Euphuism,* in M L R xi (1906), pp. 15 and 129.

[12]Preface to Genesis in Tyndall's version of the Pentateuch *apud* Baikie, Jas., *The English Bible and its Story* (Lond., 1928), p. 164.

To the ryght worshypfull Syr Wylliam Chester knyght, my syngular good Uncle.

Wherfore when it fortuned me to find cast in a corner, the booke whiche is cleped commenly Cato, Englyshed of an vncerten olde autor [Benedict Burgh] : me thought vnmete for so auncient a monument, to lye in suche case hyden from common vse. For the doctrines therin conteined, are most necessary for guiding this life, ne yeat the stile or phrase so vnacustomed or olde, but that the vulgar people may lyghtly vnderstande the same. If either we couet to araie and decke our mindes with morall lessons, or study to ben somwhat speciall in our mother tongue: this booke to bothe, wyll further vs right well. In consideracion wherof, I caused this Caton to be imprinted. And for that *Isocrates parenesis,* was of like argument and matter, and not hetherto published in our vulgar language: I also translated the same, and linked together do dedicate them bothe to your worship: that passing vnder your name & patronship, they might be of more authorite and credit to the readers: and also therby gratifie and auayle a multitude. My trauayle in traducing the same, although percase it shall not satisfie all mens expectations: neuertheles I trust it shal notbe vnprofitable. For in this *parenesis* we may learne howe to behaue our selues to all degrees, and howe in all tymes and tempestes also to dispose vs. How to god, howe to our prince, how to our parentes & kyndred: how to our frendes, howe to our enemies, how in prosperite & howe in aduersite, howe in peace and how in warre: nothing perdie wanteth in this oration which may lerne vs to liue either wysely or vertuously; nothyng almoste conteyned in the huige and ample volumes of morall philosophie, whiche here is not brefely touched. The stile is principall, the beauty singular, the lessons so vniuersall, so pithie, so sententious, and so ful of matter: that not any one of *Isocrates* orations in my opinion, is vnto it any whit comparable. May it please you therefore (ryght worshipfull) so well in worth to accept the same, as I with good intent do offer it: regardyng rather the greatnes of my good will, then the quantitie of the thyng: you shall both cause me to thinke my labour in this wel bestowed, & also encourage me to publishe shortly a woorke of greter trauaile.

Your louing cosin
Iohn Bury.

It is the epistle to Demonicus, so seriously and so widely accepted, that is the ultimate source of Polonius's advice to Laertes:

Be gentell and plesaunt to all men: be familiar but only with ye good.

Become sloly a frende, but after you haue professed amite endeuour so to continue . . . Trie your friendes by such aduersities as happeneth in this present lyfe . . . be to your familiars compayghniable, and not haughty . . . Be neate and clenly in your apparell: but not braue and sumptuous . . . Do your vter endeauor to lyue in safetie. But if it fortune you to come in perill, so defende yourselfe by batayle and force of armes, that it may redounde to your renoume. [Aviii *verso* to Bii *verso.*]

Isocrates suggests also some principles of courtly wisdom and manners, which Polonius applied:

Neyther proue your frendes with your annoyance: nor yet be ignorant of their condicions. And this you may do, if you fayne to haue nede of them when you haue no nede at all: and committe vnto them for great secretes, matters which may without danger be discouered. For albeit contrary to your expectacion they bewraye you, yet shall you not be endamaged thereby: and if they satisfie the truste and confidense you hadde in theim, then haue you a better tryall of their maners . . . Imitate the manners of kynges, and followe their wayes and trade of liuinge, (so shal you both seme to approue their doinges, and also to loue and folowe them) . . . .

Bury's version, it may be remarked, is direct from the original Greek, very likely with occasional reference to the Latin of Rodolphus Agricola for a word. Bury is quite adequate to his original, and expresses himself if not with the accomplished smoothness of Isocrates, yet with far more secure command of a period than was possessed by More or Elyot.

The composition which goes under the name of the *Table of Cebes* appealed to the temper which blended Christian doctrine and Greek philosophy in one moral ideal. The teaching of the "Table"—a picture representing emblematically the higher and lower ways of life—was indeed all but Christian. Below the life of real blessedness, the life of virtue and truth, to which even the lowly and ignorant may attain, it set the life of worldly pleasure and its deceits, and likewise scientific culture, a handmaid to truth, but not able to divine and reveal truth of itself. The mystic, ascetic, allegorical tone of the work—and it may be added its obviousness and essential lack of imagination—commended it where a subtler and profounder or a more sceptical and naturalistic work would have been unacceptable. An English version of the *Table* was made, probably between 1523 and 1527, and certainly before 1527, by Sir Francis

Poyntz.[13]   The printer tells us that it was "translated out of
latine into english by sir Frances Poyngz, at the request of his
brother sir Anthony Poyngz, which translacion is woorthy of
high commendacion.   And if any faute be therein, I knowe
well, it is mistakyng for my copie was somewhat combrouse,
what for the enterlinyng and yll writyng."   Poyntz's original
was the Latin version of Lascaris.

The following passage illustrates well both the ideas and
the style of this work:

> Have not men learned in these sciences, preheminence to be
> better than other men?   How can they excell or haue prehemin-
> ence whan men maie see them deceiued in the opinion of good
> and euyll, as other folke bee: and also bounde and tangled with
> all vngraciousnesse?   For knowledge of letters, nor vnderstand-
> yng of other sciences, doe nothyng let but that a bodie may be
> also droncke, intemperate, couetouse, vniuste, a traytour, and
> fynallie a foole.   Forsoth a man maie see many such.   Than how
> (quoth he) haue thei preheminence, by reason of those sciences,
> to be made the better men?   it seemeth not by this reason.   But
> what (quoth I) is the cause?   Because (quoth he) they dwell
> stylle in the seconde Compasse, as it were men approachyng to-
> ward true Learnyng.   And what helpeth that (quoth I) when we
> maie see many times, they come out of the first compasse from
> Incontinence and other vngraciousnes, to the third compasse, to
> true Learnynge, the whiche dooe passe by these learned men.
> And howe can men learned onely in these lyberall sciences excell
> other, whan they be more obstinate, and more vnable to bee
> taught, than other folke be?   Howe is that (quoth I?)   For
> (quoth he) in the second compasse that thyng that they knowe
> not, they doe feigne theim selfe to knowe.   If there were none

---

[13]The date of the writing is proved by the consideration that Sir Anthony,
who had been much abroad on public service, was at home in 1523.   Sir
Francis went as ambassador to the Emperor in 1527, and died in 1528.
The date of the printing is perhaps not so clear.   Hazlitt, VII 60, cites an
edition printed by Berthelet with the king's printer's colophon.   Of this
edition, which must have appeared between 1530 and 1547, I do not find
any copy recorded in the catalogue of any library that I have examined.
The printer's preface, according to the custom of the time, must have been
taken verbatim from it, and plainly indicates that it is posthumous.   A
second edition, with Berthelet's colophon without the title of king's printer
must date between 1547 and 1555.   This is in the British Museum, in one
volume with Plutarch's *De capienda ex inimicis utilitate* and Erasmus
On the death of a friend.   A third edition contains the same works; it is
printed in the *House late Thomas Berthelettes*, and must come not long
after 1555.   It is in the Bodleian.   The entries in *Hand-lists of English
Printers*, pt. iii, Thomas Berthelet, p. 18, "Table of Celebs the philosopher,"
are unlucky misprints, taken over in Miss Palmer's bibliography.   The
dates given are not possible.   Such accidents in such authorities warn all
us workers to be humble.

other thyng but this, as long as they haue this opinion, they must needes be vnable to be steered to come to true Learnyng. More-ouer, seist thou not an other thyng, that the opinions out of the firste compasse, come also into them? Wherfore these be no whit better, than those of the first compasse: excepte they doe re-pent, and be perswaded that thei haue not the true knowlage, but the vntrue Lernyng, by whom they be deceyued. And thincke, that as long as they remayne in the contrarie opinion, that thei can neuer be made safe and whole. Nor you nother frendes, except you so doe, and that these saiynges remain stedfastly in your remembraunce, tyll suche tyme as ye have ingendred in you by practyse, an habite or custome. Wherfore ye must con-sydere these saiynges continually, and not by startes, and thinke all other thynges pertayne nothyng to your pourpose. If ye doe not so, of these thynges, that ye haue nowe harde, ye shall haue no profitte.

When after all these slight and superficial discussions the reader comes upon the Ethics of Aristotle, he cannot but think, "At last!" But he is disappointed. The translation, by John Wylkinson, is from Brunetto Latini's summary, itself written in French and made from a Latin version, and translated into Italian as early as the thirteenth century by Bono Giamboni. The text of Giamboni, then, is at third-hand from the original, and is a medieval work; and Wylkinson's copy of Giamboni's text was a tattered and incorrect one. Hence only the very general outlines of Aristotle's teaching are to be seen behind a vague mist of discussion. Wylkinson's knowledge of Ital-ian is fair, though he sometimes makes confusing mistakes; but the connection often cannot be made out because of a lacuna or perhaps because of an ill-punctuated text.[14]

To the philosophy of the Renaissance as to Hebrew and Greek philosophy the art of life was one; practical wisdom was a part of ethics. Hence came the request from one of the excellent family of the Poles that Xenophon's *Oeconomicus* should be put into the vernacular.

---

[14] I have not been able to determine just what text Wylkinson used (not that of 1474); but all the seriously confusing departures from the best text of Giamboni are to be found in some printed text, as appears from the text-ual notes of Luigi Gaiter's edition of Giamboni. (Reale commissione pe' testi della lingua nelle provincie dell' Emilia. *Collezione di opere in-editi* etc. Bologna, 1878-1883).

To the Reader

> This boke of householde, full of high wisedome, written by the
> noble philosopher Xenophon, the scholer of Socrates, the whiche
> for his swete eloquence, and incredible facilitie, was surnamed
> Musa Attica, that is to saie, the songe of Athenes: is right coun-
> nyngly translated out of the Greke tonge into Englisshe, by
> Gentian Heruet, at the desyre of Maister Geffery Pole, which
> boke for the welth of this realme, I deme very profitable to be
> red.[15]

The author of the translation, Gentian Hervet, was a French
scholar, a conscientious student with a talent for language. The
fullest account of him and his works is given in the *Nouvelle
Biographie Générale,* Paris 1858, vol. XXIV. It should be
corrected as to his relations with the Pole family. Hervet
came first into relations with their circle when he was associated with Thomas Lupset in supervising the printing of Linacre's translation of Galen into Latin, which appeared at Paris
in 1528. He afterward went to England, and later became the
tutor of little Arthur Pole, born 1531, grandson, not as the
article says son, of the countess of Salisbury, and nephew,
therefore, not brother of Reginald Pole, the cardinal. This
Arthur was the son of Geoffrey Pole; and when Geoffrey with
his mother and brothers was arrested in 1538, because of the
course of Reginald, then out of Henry VIII's reach, it seems
certain that Hervet left England—the more so as he fully
shared the convictions of the cardinal. He would have had to
flee for his life, and may well have gone earlier. His connection with England would then have lasted at most ten years,
but little Arthur could have been under his care only a short
time. He certainly knew Greek enough to translate the Xenophon direct, as the translation shows, for he was later employed systematically in translating Greek authors, especially
early Greek fathers, into Latin. His preface to his English
translation of Erasmus's sermon *On the Mercy of God* proves
that he could write vernacular English with perfect ease. He
translated the little dialogue of Xenophon so well as to convey
its homely charm even in a language foreign to himself. This
book, translated by a French scholar, is the only one of the little
Greek philosophical essays translated at this time which

---

[15]From Berthelet's preface to the first edition; text of 1537.

achieved a real success. Miss Palmer lists seven editions in the sixteenth century, and the dialogue was reprinted, though only as a curiosity, in 1767, among "Certain Ancient Tracts concerning the Management of Landed Property."

Xenophon vindicated the dignity and interest of husbandry, the honor of thrift, orderliness, system, and the honor of commanding the forces of a household in the arts of peace, and claimed the theory of such matters as a rightful part of philosophy. The Greek philosophers and the Renaissance scholars also believed that the care of the body as of the mind and soul came within the purview of the wise man, as one aspect of the art of life. Linacre urged this liberal view of the art of medicine, and did his part not only to elevate the standard of medical practice by giving to the world an accurate Galen in Latin, but addressed himself to the generally educated man in the same work. Thus the title-page of his translation of Galen *De Temperamentis,* Cambridge, 1521, bears the words: *Opus non medicis modo, sed et philosophis oppido q[uam] necessariu[m].* Plutarch's brief dialogue on the care of the health naturally received attention at the hands of the humanists. It was translated by Erasmus into Latin, and his version, dedicated to John Yonge, Master of the Rolls, was printed by Pynson in 1513. A complete translation of Erasmus's Latin was made later, and probably, almost certainly, printed. The complete English version is now lost, but there are extant several editions of an imperfect text printed by Robert Wyer. Half the book is gone, lost or cut bodily out, and the remnant is printed without a hint that it is not complete. The version is the crudest of all the translations printed in the entire period, and betrays the most complete ignorance of even very simple and straightforward Latin. Wyer's edition of the *De tuenda sanitate,* then, is one of the first examples of the work of the hack-writer, and of the dishonest abridgment of a book by a cheap printer. Somewhat later, Wyer issued an even more completely fraudulent book based on the little essay of Plutarch, *Practica Plutarche,* containing three pages clipped out of the translation of Erasmus's version of Plutarch's *De tuenda sanitate.* The first sentence is so framed as to look reasonable, but the rest repeats the errors and nonsense of the earlier book. Then besides, both parties to the dialogue which composed the earlier book are now reduced to one speaker, Plutarch. Since they were in a lively dispute, he is made to contradict himself in the absurdest manner. After these three pages, the book is filled up with receipts and prescriptions, not from Plutarch, which had been appended to the earlier work.[16]

These books have only the interest of contributing their mite to social history, in illustrating the wide-spread demand for books of medicine, and of confirming the extent of Erasmus's influence. A more respectable version was one by John Hales, printed in 1543. This is at least correct and complete. It is expanded and colloquial in style. Phryne and Lais become *Julian of Rumford;—Quod ni sphaera ludas, aut umbratilia pugna exerceas*: "Because ye play not at the sphere, whirlegyg, or table or dooe not exercise to fyght with your own shadow"; —*Ridiculum*: "He was a *very lobcocke* that after he passed the age of .lx. yeares dyd desyre a physician to fele his handes."

Plutarch was chosen wittily by Erasmus for his purpose, because Plutarch had claimed the right of the non-professional man to speak sense about the care of the health.[17]

The translation of the standard manuals of the art of medicine into the vulgar tongue was a bolder step. It had been taken in France. Robert Copland, the old printer, made use of his knowledge of French in imitation of his master Caxton, issuing several translations in his old age. He added to a version of Guido de Cauliaco's catechism of surgery (*The Questyonary of Cyrurgens*) and other similar handbooks a translation of Galen's *Methodus Medendi,* Book IV, *the fourth book of the Terapentyke* [sic: i.e., of course Therapeutic], *or method curatyfe of Claude Galyen prynce of Physyciens.* This is from the French of a certain Philiatros. Philiatros's reasons for making the translation are interesting.

> *Philiatros the translatour in to Frenche to the Reader grettynge.*
> [Philiatros urges that all parts of medicine are so bound together that for proper practise physicians trust too much to apothecaries.]
> . . . . And as touchyng the Cyrurgery—(which is but a manuall occupatyon) the physytions esteme it a thyng to vyle and vnworthy of their professyon. And not onely *the* sayd manuall

---

[16]Lathrop, H. B. *Some Rogueries of Robert Wyer,* in *The Library* (1914), Ser. 3, vol. v, p. 349.

[17]*De tuenda sanitate praecepta, ad init.*

occupation the which Hipocrates and Galyen have not shamed to treate of and to exercyse, but also the methode to cure the vlceres and tumoures against nature, hath ben lefte by them in suche manere that the Barbours and Cyrurgyens in these dayes are more studyous than many physytions. Whiche is the cause wherfore I haue traducte out of latyn in to frenche this fourth boke of the methode of Galien moued of the great and ardaunt desyre that I haue knowen among the sayd Cyrurgiens to haue knowlege of some thynges. Wherin I wolde desyre gladly the grekysshe tongue or the latyn, bycause of the great payne takynge in the translation, and also bycause that euery tongue hath his properte in such wyse that many thynges cannot be sowned in the frenche speche, so well as they be written in the Greke or Latyn . . .[18]

George Baker in 1579 revised the work of Copland and added the third book, basing his translation on Linacre's Latin.

The *Aphorisms* of Hippocrates were included in another compilati'on, *The Treasuri of Helthe,* translated from the Latin of Petrus Hispanus (probably Pope John XXI), by Humphrey Lloyd (1550?-2nd ed. 1585). Lloyd rearranged the *Aphorisms* in order, from the head to the feet. It will be noticed that the translations of ancient medieval writers include only small extracts from their works, and are ancillary to elementary general manuals.

Of genuine ancient science there is little enough. Masquerading under the name of Aristotle and Ptolemy are medieval works of superstition, astrology, and physiognomy: *De cursione lune* (1530, 1535), *Secreta secretorum* (1528), Ptolemy's *Compost* (a falsification, 1535), a compilation on physiognomy, translated by Thomas Hill (1550), who also translated Artemidorus on dreams. The one book truly representative of ancient science is Proclus, *De Sphaera.* The dedication by Wyllyam Salysbury to his "verye louynge Cosen Iohn Edwardes

---

[18]The process by which the vernacular tongue in all European countries came very gradually and with much conflict to be acceptable for scientific exposition is an interesting chapter in social history. Naturally enough, it began with the practical demands of the art of war and the art of surgery. Neither military experts nor barber surgeons could be obliged to know Latin. Physicians, however, could hold their place with pride in the ranks of the learned. In France an amusing compromise was reached in the seventeenth century. At lectures on surgery the operative barber-surgeon performed the demonstration, the medical lecturer not deigning to touch the dead body, and speaking in a pigeon-Latin, so framed that the French-speaking audience of prospective barber-surgeons could understand it. (*Dictionnaire Encyclopédique des Sciences Médicales*, vol. xxxii (1875), p. 368).

of Chyrke Esquyer" tells how Edwards had asked for a book
treating in English of the sphere of the world :—

> . . . . I walked my selfe, rounde about all Poules Churche
> yearde, from shop to shop, enquyryng of such a treatyse neyther
> coulde I heere of any that eyther wrote of this matier proposely,
> nor yet occasyonallye. But what trowe you dyd I than by my
> fayth syr, I returned backe euen the same way (but wondryng
> moche at the happe) and asked agayne for the same workes in
> laten, wherof there were, iii. or iiii. of sondrye Aucthoures
> brought, and shewed vnto me, amonge all whiche (for the breuyte
> and playnes) I chose Proclus his doynge. And this a Goddes
> name entended I than (for the accomplysshement of your wyll)
> to traducte into the Englysshe tonge. But wolde God that he
> [marginal note: That man M. Thomas lynacre], whiche trans-
> lated it into the Laten, had taken so moche paine, as for his
> countre sake, as to englysshe the same also English was his
> natyue tonge. Greke and Laten, ar well knowen, where as En-
> glysshe to me of late yeares, was wholy to lerne, the Laten not
> tasted of, the Greke not once hurde of, whom although euen at
> this present I might rather and truelye with lesse reproche,
> denye to haue any knowledge in it at all, than to professe the
> perfect phrase of any of theym three. Why than shall I attempt,
> for any mannes pleasure, to go aboute to translate a Scyence
> vnknowen, out of a tonge vnknowne, in to a tonge no better
> knowen vnto me . . . .

For all this protesting the translation is clear enough, and not
more crude than most of the English prose in the time of
Henry VIII.

If the versions of Greek writers who deal with the conduct
of life of the best moral and practical ends be considered in
retrospect, it will be seen that though they are not many or
profound or rich, they do contribute a new element to culture,
however slightly they contain and express the humanist spirit.
The similar works from the Latin do not mark so distinct a
separation from medieval tradition. They include only a few
essays of Cicero, and some pseudo-Seneca, and interestingly
enough begin and end with Boethius.

In 1410 a certain John Walton, depending largely upon
Chaucer's prose version, turned the *De Consolatione* into English verse. His work cannot be praised. Though he compared
Chaucer with the Latin, he falls into a greater number of down-
right errors than his predecessor. His style is heavy, and as
ten Brink says, he flattens out his original with its varying form

and spirit in his monotonous prolix verse. Not alone is the
book a real voice speaking from the fifteenth century to the
sixteenth, but the initiative attributed to the patron sounds already old-fashioned.

> Here endeth the boke of comfort called in latyn Boecius de
> consolatione Phil. Emprented in the exempt monastery of Taue-
> stok in Denshyre. By me Dan Thomas Rychard monke of the
> sayd Monastery/ To the instant desyre of the ryght worshypfull
> esquyer Mayster Robert Langdon. Anno d' MDxxv
> Deo Gracias

In the days of the fall of the monasteries, Dan Thomas
Rychard might well be seeking the consolations of philosophy;
and let us hope that Mayster Robert Langdon was a generous
patron. The book is one of the last works the printer of which
is thus patronized and refers to his obligation in the colophon.

The never-ceasing interest in Boethius is shown by the appearance in 1556 of another version by "George Colvile, *alias*
Coldewel," as the title-page names him, dedicated by the author
to Queen Mary after her marriage, and therefore probably
made not long before it was printed. Colvile knew his Latin
grammatically, and was able to follow unhesitatingly the
scholastic subtleties of Boethius's reasoning. He can also express himself in English clearly and vigorously without apparent effort. He is free from affectation and pedantry of style,
and makes no attempt to give a spurious interest to his writing
by colloquialism or ingenuity. His version, therefore, gives a
just and adequate view of Boethius's thought. Unfortunately,
like his predecessors, he does not attempt to distinguish the
meters from the proses by their form, writing wholly in prose.
But as L. J. de Mirandol says at the end of the introduction to
his edition of the *Consolations* in Latin and French (1861), to
translate the meters in prose is to do an injustice to the thought
of Boethius, for the verses spring from the train of thought
presented by the prose, but by no means always carry it on;
they are skilfully managed pauses for refreshment, which rest
the mind of the reader without distracting it. Moreover the
mingling of the metaphysical dissertation with the poetical
visions in a continuous sequence confuses and baffles the
reader.

Colvile cannot escape giving a certain lyric tone to his

meters, but feels it his duty to "open" the numerous metaphors, thus producing an incongruous mingling of the imaginative and the flatly prosaic, and destroying the emotional effect which simple accuracy would have communicated.

For example, the first meter of the third book (the explanatory words are italicized):

> He that wyll sowe a goodly felde wyth corne, fyrst he must ryd the same felde of shrubs and thorns and cutte awaye the bushes and ferne with his *hoke or* syth, *that* the newe corne may grow and encrease with ful eres. [lit. that Ceres may go heavy with the new corn].
>
> The laboure of the bees, *that is to sai*: *the honye,* is swete to the mouth, that hath tastyd some euyl tast *or bytternes* before. And after that *the south wynde called* Nothus, cesseth to geue his sheury blasts, then do the sters shyne more plesaunt *and bryght.* And after that *the day sterre called* Lucifer hath chased awaye the darkenes *of the nyght.* Then the bryght daye ledyth fourth the shinyng horse[s] of the sonne, *that is to sai; after the darke nyght the clere day shineth more plesaunt.* So lykewyse thou fyrst beholdyng false goods, *that is to saye: false felycytie of worldely things* begynne thou to wythdrawe thy neck from the yoke *of the sayd false felicitie or worldely thynges.* And after that, trewe goodes, *that is to saye: vertue, or trewe felicite* wyll enter *the better* into thy mynde.

The prose disquisitions, which to be sure impose an easier task upon a translator, are meritorious because of the manly directness and clear intelligence of Colvile. Take the end of the fourth prose of the fourth book:

> Phi. Then it semeth the, that he that doth wrong is more wretche than he that taketh wronge. Boe. I saye it foloweth well. Phi. Therefore for thys cause and for other lyke causes of the same sorte, it appeareth that syns of it self, by nature maketh men wretches. And it semeth to euerye man that the wronge that is done, is not the wretchednes of hym that taketh the wrong but of hym that doeth the wrong. Boe. Certes the orators do contrarye for they do labour to moue the iudge, to haue pitie vpon *th*em, that haue done some haynous and greuous offence, where as more pytie ought to be shewed vnto them that haue suffred wrong and it behoueth that they *th*at haue done such offences should be broughte (not with angre, but rather with merciful accusers) vnto iudgemente, as sycke folke be broughte vnto the phisicion, that the iudge myght put awaye the syckenes, of the offence, with ponyshment, by whych meanes the dyligence of the orators should either holye cesse, or els if they would profyte offenders,

their diligence shoulde be turned into the habyte of accusation, that is to say they shoulde rather accuse offenders, then excuse them or intreate for them. And so the offenders (if it were lawefull for them to se by any chyn [chine] or clifte the vertue and goodnes that they haue loste, and that they shoulde expulse the vylenes of theyr synnes, by tormentes of paynes, to optayne some recompence of theyr goodness) woulde not esteme thys for ponyshments, but wold forsake the diligence of suche orators and defenders, and commyt them selfe holy to the accusars and to the iudges. Whereby it happeth that hatred hath no place emongeste wise men. For who hateth good folk but he be a very fole? And he hath no wyt that hateth wicked folke. For lyke as syckenes is the dyssease of the bodye, euen so vyce and synne is as the syckenes of the mynde, or soule. And when we doe iudge that men that be sycke in their bodyes, be not worthy to be hated but rather worthy to be pytied, euen so much the more are they not to be hated, but to be pitied whose myndes wickednes greaueth, that is more fierse and cruell, than any syckenes of the body.

Most conscientious, most diligent, and most stupid of translators was Robert Whytinton, "laureat poete."[19] This laborious schoolmasterly person had enormous loquacity and the best will in the world, enough Latin to write grammatical verses that scan to the finger, good confidence, and a grave Dogberry mind. Between 1534 and 1540 he published translations of Cicero's *De Officiis, Paradoxa,* and *De Senectute,* and in 1546 and 1547 Seneca's *The Dialogue between Sense and Reason* (*De remediis fortuitorum*) besides two works attribut-

---

[19]Wood, Anthony à, *Historia et antiquitates Universitatis Oxoniensis* (1674) Lib. II, p. 4. "Notandum his obiter duco; quod Gradus in Arte etiam Poeticâ & Rhetoricâ capessi solebant . . . Inter novissimos Gradus Rhetorici candidatos *Robertum Whittingtonum* Sacerdotem secularem, offendo, qui cum ad illam artem annis quatuordecim contendisset, pueros vero in eàdem annis duodecim informasset, ut ista sufficerent ad Gradum capessendum supplicavit, anno Dom. MDXII. qui postquam carmina centena condiderat, laurea in proximis Comitiis insignitus est. Hic celebris ille *Whittingtonus* est qui ob artis Grammaticae peritiam sub *Henrico VIII.* inclaruit, quique *Johannis Stanbridgii* discipulus erat, deque re Grammaticâ tractatus varios edidit, in quorum altero Laureatum sese diserte appellat.

"*Roberti Whittintoni Lichfeldiensis Grammatices Magistri, protovatis angliae in flòrentissima Oxoniensi Academia Laureati, de Octo partibus orationis.*

"De librorum vero ejus, eleganti stylo conscriptorum, numero erat, quem *de difficultate Justitiae servanda in Reipublicae administratione, in laudem* Thomas Wolsei *Cardinalis,* inscripsit, hoc initio, *Quae res in terris,* & Hunc autem tractatum inter *Whittintonianos* minime recensuerunt qui viri eruditi vitam exararunt."

Wood's *Athenae Oxonienses* is, unfortunately, not accessible to me at the moment.

ed to Seneca, an essay, *The Forme and Rule of Honest Living* (*De formula honestae vitae*) and a collection of *sententiae, The Mirrour or Glasse of Manners.*

Whytinton gives as his ground for translating the *De Officiis* the desire to meet the eager curiosity of the day with worthy substance.

> The fynall cause wherfore I toke in hande this noble monumente to be translate in to my natyue and Englysshe tonge is this: I se many yonge persones/ and rather all for the most parte that be any thyng lettred/ of whome some scantly can skyll of lettres/ very studyous of knowlege of thynges/ and be vehemently bente to rede newe workes/ and in especyall that be translated in to the vulgare tonge. All be it some of theym where as they iudge them selfe very fruytfully exercysed/ not withstandyng they seme vaynly occupyed/ and they perceyue very lytell fruyte to issue out of their studye.

Saint Cicero is the Latin author whom Erasmus in the *Colloquia* places beside the Greek Holy Socrates.[20] Cicero had been the inspiration of the early Renaissance. He massed together the diverse elements of the moral ideal of the best of antiquity with eloquence, taste, fervor, and the indefinable reality that comes from the experience of the world sincerely met. His was the most complete code of the better life. He maintained the cause, also, of that freedom of judgment without which there is no true activity of the reason, and of the freedom of the will which is so strong a support of the sense of personal dignity and responsibility. In brief, his doctrine, like that of Plutarch, was that of individualism and of rationalism, and of the ordered civilized life directed by reason.

The important service of communicating this central author of the Renaissance to the English reader was very ill done by Whytinton. The translations of the *De Officiis* and *De Senectute* simply mangle the original, mainly because of sheer stupidity. Whytinton has to put into English Latin which means:

---

[20]V. *Colloquia, Convivium Religiosum* (Opera Lugd. Bat., 1706. i, 682, A.), Fateor affectum meum apud amicos: non possum legere librum Ciceronis de Senectute, de Amicitia, de Officiis, de Tusculanis quaestionibus, quin aliquoties exosculer codicem, ac venerer sanctum illud pectus, afflatum coelesti numine . . . Proinde quum hujusmodi quaedam lego de talibus viris, vix mihi tempero, quin dicam, Sancte Socrates, ora pro nobis. Ch[rysoglottus]. At ipse mihi saepenumero non tempero, quin bene ominer sanctae animae maronis & Flacci.

"There is a difference between the precision attained when truth itself is brought to a fine edge (*limata*) in a discussion, and that which results when everything said is accommodated to the common way of thinking." He says: "The substylyte and quiddyte is a nother maner of thynge/ when truth it self is fyled or subtylly handled in disputacyon/ and an other maner of thynge when all altercacyon is applyed to the vulgare and commen opinyon."

Perhaps his measure is best given by his version of the famous and beautiful passage in *De Senectute* about the household of Appius:

> Quatuor robustos filios, et quinque filias, tantam domum, tantas clientelas, Appius regebat et senex et caecus. Intentum enim animum habebat, nec languescens succumbebat senectuti. Tenebat non modo auctoritatem, sed etiam imperium in suos: metuebant eum serui, verebantur liberi, carum omnes habebant: vigebat in eo domo patrius mos et disciplina.

> Appius gouerned foure sonnes bygge men/ and fyue doughters/ so greate an housholde/ so many seruauntes/ beynge bothe an old man and blynde: For he had his mynde bente therto as a bowe. Nor he waxynge weyke stouped therby in his olde dayes. For he kepte not onely his authorite/ but also his rule vpon his housholde meyny. His seruauntes stode in drede of hym/ his chyldren feared hym/ and all they loued hym. The maner of the father and discypline flouryshed in that housholde.[21]

Pontifices, as in every medieval translation, are always *bishops.* "What shall I speke of the study of Publius Scipio now of late in our days/ which was made archebyssop [*pontifex maximus*] within these few days?"

The *Paradoxa* is better. In it Whytinton was helped by an excellent commentary, expounding the whole and explaining allusions. But even in the *Paradoxa* there are some dreadful passages:

> Knowest not thou that exile is punishment of mischyefe? and that my iourney was taken to do very noble actes here before time [*because of very noble acts by me beforetime done*] al mischeuous & vngracious persones of whom thou professeth that thou arte captayne, whom the lawe wylle to be punysshed with exyle. Be they banysshed men, though they change nother soyle nor countrey? [*All mischievous and ungracious persons, of whom thou professest that thou art*

---

[21]Sig. Ciii *r.*

*captain, whom the law willeth to be punished with exile, are ban-
ished men, though they change neither soil nor country.*] Than
whether or no? whan/ all lawes iudge the to be a banysshed man,
wyll thou not be a banysshed man? He is not called an ennemye/
whiche hathe ben before the Senate with his weapon/ thy skeine
wher with thou slewest a man/ was taken all blodye. [*Then when
all laws judge thee to be a banished man, shall not an enemy so call
thee?—a man who was with his weapon in his hand? Thy skeine was
wrested from thee before the Senate.*][22]

Seneca (the "morall Senec" of Chaucer) filled an even larger
place in the medieval mind than Cicero. His pithy and ingenious style makes him eminently quotable, while the warm emo-
tionalism and spirit of renunciation of his moral essays caused
them to be very acceptable to Christian moralists. His vogue
continued so long as the classics were resorted to as sources of
moralizing. Seneca, to Whytinton, was the medieval Seneca,
about whose genuine works there had grown up an accretion
of supposititious moral writings, all accredited by his name. In
his "prologue vpon the workes of Lucius Anneus Seneca Dedicate to Syr Fraunces Bryan knyght," prefixed to the *Myrrour,*
Whytinton says:

> I haue taken payne in studye to translate thre bokes of the sayde
> Seneca. The first of maners [*The Myrrour or Glasses of Maners;*
> a supposititious work]. Seconde of the fourme of honest lyfe [*De
> formula honestae vitae;* also supposititious]. Thyrde of remedyes of
> all casuall chaunces [*De remediis fortuitorum;* probably genuine].
> And haue adioined the texte of the latin, with the translacion in Eng-
> lysshe, to *the* entent that nat onely scole maysters, teachers, & reders
> folowynge *the* olde tradicion of expart & excellent lerned men, maye
> instruct theyr scolers in good and honest maners in bothe tongues
> Englysshe and latin, but also all other *that* be lettred (whiche in thys
> oure tyme be verye studyous of knowledge) by of[t] redynge of these
> vertuous workes: may folowe the trade of morall wysedome. whiche
> is the nexte meane to amplyfye & encrease the commen welthe to the
> whiche not only nature and morall phylosophy: but also the holy
> deuine scripture, both exhorteth vs, & also byndeth vs vnto.

Whytinton's translation of *The forme and rule of honest liuinge* was printed in 1546; the other treatises in 1547. The
translations are not better than the translations from Cicero,
and Whytinton must in his own day have received criticism

---

[22]Sig. Bviii *v.*

that he resented, as is evident from the prologue to the *Myrrour*.

> I am bolde to dedicate this my poore lucubrations of the transla-
> cion of these thre morall workes traducte out of the monumentes of
> *th*e noble philosopher *Seneca,* to thende that these workes goynge
> forth/ vnder the recognysaunce of your name, maye the better be
> accepte to al gentyll reders that hathe delyte in morall wysdome, & nat
> onlly that, but also all other pers*o*ns that be of cankerde & enuyous
> stomake, whose maner is to depraue *th*e studyous workes of other
> menne, without cause, but onely of theyr malencoly mynde repleted
> with venym of intoxicate malyce, lyke vnto a curre dogge that barkes
> at euery waggynge of a strawe, shall *th*e rather refrayne theyr bark-
> ynge by deprauacion agaynst these morall monumentes, put forth
> vnder the tuicion of your name . . . .

The Myrrour or Glasse of Maners is a collection of stock sayings, many from classical sources, but not all by Seneca. They are mostly easy and are in the main correctly translated by Whytinton, though even here he takes fine advantage of opportunities to go wrong.

A very different book is Harington's *De Amicitia*. The author, who may be called John Harington the Elder, to distinguish him from the better known John Harington of Queen Elizabeth's court, was a gentleman of the county of Rutland, employed as treasurer of the forces under Hertford, afterwards Duke of Somerset.[23]   He was first vice-treasurer of the vanguard, at the siege of Montreuil in 1544, and afterwards treasurer of the forces in the campaign of 1546.[24]   He was for some reason now unknown in prison, probably a military prison, for a fairly long time, and used his leisure to make this translation.

The Epistle Dedicatory is addressed to Katharine, born Willoughby, the dowager Duchess of Suffolk.

> As my prisonment and aduersitee, most honorable lady, was
> of their owne nature ioigned with great and sundrie miseries, so
> was the sufferance of the same eased, by the chaunce of diuerse
> and many commodities. For thereby founde I great soule profite,
> a little minde knowlege, some holow hertes, and few feithfull
> frendes. Wherby I tried prisonment of the body, to be the lib-
> ertie of spirite: aduersitee of fortune: the touche stone of freend-

---

[23]Cal. State Pa., Henry VIII, vol. ix, pt. 1, 1544 (Lond. 1905) i, 632 ff.
[24]Rolls Series: *Letters and Papers Foreign and Domestic Henry VIII,* vol. xxi, pt. 1, 1546, (Lond. 1908) document 353.

ship, exempcion from the world to be a contempt of vanitees:
and in the ende quietnes of mind, the occasion of study. And
thus somwhat altered, to auoide my olde idelnesse, to recompense
my lost time, and to take profite of my calamities, I gaue myselfe
among other thynges to study and learne the Frenche tonge,
hauyng both skilful prisoners to enstruct me, and therto plenty
of bookes to lerne the language. Among whiche as there were
dyuerse notable, and for their sondry mattier woorthy readyng,
so none liked me aboue this Tullius booke of freendship, nor for
the argument any with it to be compared. The whole whereof
whan I had perused, and saw the goodly rules, the naturall order,
and ciuile vse of freendship. where before I but liked, than was
I rauished, and in a certain wonder with 'the heathen lernyng,
which chiefly for its sake I phantasied, and for my state I deemed
good to be embraced, as a glasse to discerne my freends in, and
a ciuile rule to leade my life by.

These causes moued me to thinke it mete for moe. Wherupon
I (as I coulde) translated it, and though not so liuely, nor so
aptly, as some coold loke for, and many culd doe, yet I trust thei
will rather beare with my good will, than rebuke my boldnes, for
that it proceded more of a good mind than of any presumpcion
of knowlage and so my enterprise is to be enterpieted rathei by
freendes, as a treatise of frendship, then by lerned clerks in an
argument of translacion. Well, how so euer it shalbe liked of the
learned, I hope it shalbe allowed of the vnlatined. Whose capa-
citees by my owne I consider, and for lacke of a fine and flowyng
stile, I haue vsed the plaine and common speache, and to thende
the sense might not be chaunged, nor the goodnes of the matter
by shift of tounges much minished, I caused it to be conferred
with the latine auctor, and so by the knowen wel lerned to be
corrected: after whose handelyng me thought a new spirit and
life was geuen it, and many partes semed as it were with a new
cote araied, as well for the orderly placyng and eloquently
changeyng of some woordes, as also for the plainly openyng and
learnedly amending of the sence, whiche in the Frenche translacion was somewhat darkened, and by me for lacke of knowlage
in many places missed.

Harington, in translating from the French, had a far easier
task than those of his contemporaries who essayed the Latin
originals directly. Shorter analytic sentences had already
been deftly substituted for the ample periods of Cicero, so that
he did not have to re-fashion the whole structure of his language in order to make the work English. Moreover, by the
time of Edward VI and Mary, English literary prose had begun to outgrow the stumbling weakness of the first generation

of the age of Henry VIII. If he is not eloquent, he is clear,
natural, and not ungraceful.

> Neyther do I so search the matter to the quicke, as they which
> reason this geare more subtillie although perchaunce truely, and
> yet little to any common profite. And be it so hardily. Yet such
> a thyng call they that wysedome as neuer earthely man atteigned
> hytherto. But we muste hope for such thynges as bee in vre,
> and in our daiely life, and not for those thynges, whiche be
> feigned or wished after. I wil neuer saie, that Caius Fabritius,
> Man. Curius, and Titus Cornucanus, whom our elders deemed
> wyse, were after these mennes rule accompted wyse. Wherfore
> let them keepe to them selues their name of wisedome, both
> enuied and vnknowen, so they confesse these afore were good
> men: but yet that wyll not they graunt, for they will deme that
> that can bee saied but by them that be wyse. Let vs goe then
> euen plainlie to woorke lyke a packe staffe, as the prouerbe is.
> They whiche behaue themselues, and doe so liue, that their faieth,
> their honestee, their vprightnesse and liberalitie is allowed, and
> in them neither couetousnesse, neither trecherie, neither rash-
> nesse is seene to be: and besyde this, be of great constancie, as
> they wer, whom before we named: All these lyke as they bee
> taken for good men, so we thinke them worthie to be called,
> who folow nature, the best guide of welliuyng, so far as mans
> power can leade them.

Nicholas Grimald, in comparison with most of his predecessors, might almost be called famous. He was a good scholar
and a clever and energetic man, the ablest of the early translators. However weak and shifty his character, his contributions
to the development of English prose and verse deserve recognition.[25]

Grimald's translation of Cicero *De Officiis,* first printed in
1553, is dedicated to Thomas Thirlby, Bishop of Ely under
Philip and Mary. In it Grimald says that returning to his
old studies, he has devoted himself to such learning as "wold
serue best bothe to the order of my studie, & also to the gou-
erraunce of my life; so that comparing my experience, and
reading togither, I might make my priuate diligence in studi-
eng do seruice to the open vse of liuing." He finds that by the
natural maturing of his judgment, and extended experience
he begins now to see into authors, and finds more in Cicero
De Officiis than he had ever before found. This book, then,

---

[25]Merrill, LeRoy, *The Life and Poems of Nicholas Grimald,* New Haven,
Conn., (1925) (Yale Studies in English, no. 69).

for private or public life is the "mirrour of wisdom, *the* fortres of iustice, the master of manlinesse, the schoole of temperaunce, the iewell of comlinesse." So he wished many more to be partakers of such sweetness as he had partly felt himself. Hence he set about translation, to do as much for his countrymen as "Italia*n*s, Fre*n*chmen, Spaniardes, Dutchme*n*, & other foreins haue liberally done for theyrs . . . . so that our me*n* . . . . beeing by nature most of all other nations giue*n* to ciuilitie, & humanitie: whe*n* thei shall be aided, & directed by these perfite preceptes: may, in all pointes of good demeanour, become people perelesse."

Grimald well understands Cicero's value as the epitomator of the good way of life elaborated by the Greeks: "the first, and the chief, that euer cladde ladie Philosophie in Romane attire." Philosophy, as he says in his address to the reader, has as its chief purpose to show the end of man and the means to attain it. "Nadoute, as welco*m* it was to *the* lerned Athenians: as *the* Greeks doings to the Romanes: or as now adayes, the French & Italians welframed writings to those Englishme*n*, that vnderstand the*m* . . . ." Erasmus, "the Roterodame," is cited at length as to the value of this "heathen"; and Grimald shows by his very emphasis on the word his sympathy with the anti-dogmatic tendency of Erasmus which found Cicero more Christian than many a Christian.

What Cicero did with the treasure of Greek wit and wisdom for Rome, Grimald aspired to do for England. "None other translation, in our tong haue I seen, but one [i.e. Whytinton's] : which is of all men of any lernyng so well liked: *that* thei repute it, & count it as none: yet if ye list to compare this somewhat *with that* nothing perauenture this somwhat will seeme somwhat *the* more."

Grimald is the first of the translators in whom I have discovered a clear statement of his ideals.

> Howbeit looke, what rule the Rhetorician giues in precept, to bee obserued of an Oratour, in telling of his tale: that it bee short, & withoute ydle wordes: that it be playn, and wi*th* oute derk sense: that it bee prouable, and withoute anye swaruing from *the* trouth: the same rule should be vsed in examining, & iudging of tra*n*slation. For if it be not as brief, as the verie authors text requireth: whatso is added to his perfite stile, shall appere superfluous, & to serue rather to the making of some paraphrase, or

commentarie. [The point of this remark is made plain by considering such expansions as the translations of Premierfait, reproduced in English by Caxton, in which all allusions are explained in additions to the text, and metaphors are "resolved" into flat and thin literality.]   Therto, if it be vttered *with* ynkhorne termes, & not with vsuall wordes: or if it be phrased *with* wrasted or farrefetched fourmes of speech: not fine, but harshe, not easie, but hard, not natural, but violent it shall seme to be. [Skelton's aureate rhetoric in the translation of Diodorus Siculus is an example.]   Then also, in case it yelds not the meaning of the author: but eyther following fansie, or misledde by errour, forsakes the true patern [like Whytinton]: it cannot be approued for a faithfull, & sure enterpretacion: which ought to be taken for the greatest praise of all. These pointes as I haue studied to parfourme: so where I haue not always attained vnto them: I shal desire you gentle reader, gently to consider bothe the excelence of the author, who is a perfit oratour & also *the* gretnesse of the matter, which is profound philosophie.

Grimald, indeed, believes that Cicero, the "perfit oratour," may do much to elevate English prose style, as his "philosophie" may do much to refine the standard of English conduct. He recognizes the existence of an English literary prose, idiomatic though not colloquial, and he contributed to the formation of such a prose. His ideal is the "plain style," excelling by the virtues of order, clearness, and directness, rather than by intensity of imagination or external qualities of beauty.

Neuerthelesse, such as be exquisite in both the languages already: may (& that with some profit, & pleasure) trye what I haue done, & what they can do, all vnder one: if, layeng my translation apart, they will set the latine before the*m*, & so assaye their owne veine. Eyther they shall like themselues the better: when they conferre it with my poore workma*n*ship: or els perchau*n*ce conne me the more thank for attempting folowing, & accomplishing of this enterprise. Be it so, one hath neither the latine, nor the english eloque*n*ce: yet, by the benefite of nature, syth a ma*n* may do much: namely if he therto adioyne vse, & exercise: here is for him occasion bothe to whet his wit, & also to file his toung. For although an English man hath his mother toung: & can talke apace, as he lerned of his dame: yet is it one thing to tittle tattle, I wot not how, or to chatter like a iay: and an other, to bestowe his woordes wisely, orderly pleasauntly, & pithiely. Such as haue english meatly well, & but a smattering, or small tast in *the* lattine, which noumber is great, among the scholars of this realme: may hereby fall into suche acquayntaunce,

and familiaritie with this excellent latine man: that neither shall
his deuise seme hard, nor his arte obscure, nor his style straunge.
I dare well say, if this worke happe into a good students hand:
he will not think it ynough to runne ouer it once; as we fare with
trifles, and toyes: but aduisedly, and with good leasure, three, or
foure, or fiue tymes, he will reade it, and reade it, and reade it
agayne: first, by the principall pointes, by the definitions, and
the diuisions: to see, what is treated, howe farre forth, in what
order, and with what varietie: then, to mark the preceptes, reasons, conclusions, & common places: after vnto the sayde places
to referre the stories, with the verses poeticall: finally, as well in
the englysh, as the latine, to weygh well properties of wordes,
fashions of phrases, and the ornamentes of both. Moreouer, many
clerks haue I knowne, eare thys: which could conceiue, & vnderstande full well: whose toung neuerthelesse in vtteraunce, and
vse of speache, was in a maner maymed: yes and some, that
could also speake latine reddily, and wel fauoredly: who to haue
done as much in our language, & to haue handled the same matter, wold haue bin half blank, what nede mo words? I desire, my
trauaill none otherwise to be taken in worthe, than the diligent
peruser shall in effect find frute thereof.

Carrying out Grimald's suggestion that it would be worth
while to compare his work with the Latin, as a benefit in
mastering both tongues, the translation was printed with the
Latin text from 1558 on. The translation is intelligent, neat,
and distinct, but is frequently too literal, becoming sometimes
awkward, sometimes obscure. The following passage is a favorable specimen of the style of this important work.

*How to get
a credit*

*Prudence with
iustice*

But, that a trust may be had in vs, by two thinges
it may be brought to passe: if we shall be thought to
haue attained prudence ioined with iustice. For bothe
to them we haue a trust, whom we suppose to vnderstand more, than ourselves: and also to them, who we
beleeue, be able bothe to foresee thinges to comme: &
also to dispatche the bysinesse, and forthwith to take
counsail: when the mater is in hand, and standes in
hasard. For all men do iudge this the profitable and
true prudence. But in such wise credit is giuen to
iust and trustie men (that is) to good men: that in
them there is no suspicion of deceite, and iniurie.
Therfor to these our life, to these our goodes, to
these our children we suppose verie well to be committed. Of these twoo then iustice is of more power
to win a credit: bicause it without prudence hathe

Prudence,
withoute
iustice, is
suspected.

sufficient authoritee, prudence without iustice is nothing worth to get credit. For, the sutteler, and the craftier that a man is: so much the more he is to be hated, and suspected, when the opinion of his honestie is pulled awaie. Wherfore iustice ioyned with vnderstanding, shall haue as much power, as it lest, to purchase credit: iustice withoute prudence shal be of much power, prudence without iustice shall be nothing worth. But leste some man haue maruail: seeing amongst all philosophers it is plaine, and by miself disputed often: him, that should haue one vertue, to haue all the vertues: why I do now sonder them so. as though ther may anie man be iust, which is not prudent: of one sorte is *the* suttleness, when verie trouth is leueled in disputation: & of an other sorte is *that* talk, when it is all applied to the common opinion. Wherfore we speake so in this place, as the common sorte doo/: that we call somme one sort manlie, somme other good men, somme other prudent. For with the peoples wordes, and vsuall termes we must treate, when we speake of the comon peoples opinion: & that did Panetius, after the same sorte. But the purpose let vs returne.

3.
That wee may be
reckened worthie
of honour

Great things

Of *the* three therfore, which should appertein to glorie, this was the third: that with admiration of men, we might by them be thought worthy of honour. Generallie then they haue in admiration doutelesse all things: which they haue noted to be greater and beyonde their wening: and seucrallie in euerie sere [individual] man, if they perfitlie see good thinges vnlooked for. Therfore they honour those men, and with highest praises set them alofte: in whom they think themselues to beholde certein passing, & singuler vertues. But those they despise, & set at nought: in whom no vertue, no corage, no strength they iudge. For all men do not despise them, of whom they think euill. Wherfore (as I said afore) they be despised: who neither to themselues, nor to other do good, as they saie: in whom ther is no painefulness, no diligence, no caring: but they be reuerenced with a certein admiration: who ar thought to go before others in vertue: & to be without bothe all vnseemlinesse, and also those vices, which other can not easilie withstand. For both pleasures, full flattering dames, do oftentimes wrest the greater part of the mind from vertue, and also when the brondes of paines be laid vnto them. most men beyond measure be alltofrayed.

Admiration for
stayednesse

Pleasures
flatering dames

Brondes of
paines

[Fo. 75 *verso-77 recto,* ed. 1556]

The vocabulary is often interesting:

barbarum, a kerne [Fo. 82 *recto.*]
et barbarum et stigmaticum, a kerne and an yronbronded slaue [Fo. 82 *rec.*]
hasta posita, when the salestaffe was pight [Fo. 83 *rec.*]
in singulis, in euery seere man [Fo. 86 *rec.*]
ostentatione, outshowe [Fo. 89 *rec.*]
ad multitudinem deleniendam, to clawe the multitude [Fo. 96 *rec.*]
theatra, porticus, sightcourtes, gallery-walkes [Fo. 98 *rec. Theatre* in its modern sense first as the proper name of Burbage's Theatre, 1576.]
secula, worldes [Fo. 106 *rec.*]
inhumane, vnkindly [Fo. 124 *rec.*]
inhumanum, vnciuill [Fo. 133 *rec.*]
sociorum, leagfriendes [Fo. 127 *ver.*]

Grimald's vigorous and solid translation of the *De Officiis* was so satisfactory and adequate that it was reprinted twice a decade for about sixty years.

That Cicero continued to be regarded as primarily a philosopher and moralist is illustrated by the fact that the single one of his speeches which was translated was intended merely as an illustration of the principles of rhetoric in a text-book, R. Sherry's *Treatise of the Figures of Grammar and Rhetoric.* The work is in Latin, by Sherry, adapted and often quoted from Cicero and Quintilian, each section being followed by its English equivalent. The speech chosen as an illustration, strangely enough, is the address to Caesar on the pardoning of Marcellus, and the translation, though correct, sounds perfunctory. The book is in itself of little value, but the fact that such a book should be printed in English is important, as a proof of the growing respect in which the English language was held.[26]

Properly to be reckoned among the dissertations on morals are a number of collections of aphorisms which were printed between 1525 and 1550. Whether wholly ancient, as are Publilius Syrus's so-called *"Mimi,"* or modified by tradition, but based on antiquity, as are the *Distichs* of Dionysius Cato, and the sayings of the Seven Wise Men of Greece, or newly gathered together, as are Sir Thomas Elyot's *Banquet of Sapience,* Baldwin's *Moral Philosophy,* and above all Erasmus's *Adagia*

---

[26]Haz. War. IV, 248.

and *Apophthegmata,* all these works were intended to give to the world the best teaching of the Greeks and Romans about conduct, and were in the main composed of sayings from classic sources. Hence they deserve a place here, among the books of ethics. Indeed they are among the most important of the translations of the period, since they were as regards their substance central in the intellectual movement of humanism, and since some of them achieved a popular success and familiarly entered the life of the English spirit. The collections of sayings were looked at as belonging entirely in the same class with the continuous treatises or dialogues. Erasmus's editions of Cato and Publilius Syrus and the Sayings of the Wise were printed in one volume with his revision of Rodolphus Agricola's Latin version of Isocrates to Demonicus. Elyot filled the empty pages following his version of *Ad Nicoclem* with *sententiae* on the principles of "rule," partly from Scripture, partly from classic writers; and the author of the translation of Plutarch *De Capienda ex Inimicis Utilitate* did likewise. "To fylle vp the padges that els wold haue ben void, I thoght it shuld nother hurt nor displese, to adde herevnto a fewe sayenges/ howe a man shulde chose and cherysshe a frend."

The first important work of Erasmus, and that which laid the foundation of his fame and influence was a collection of classical proverbs, edited and annotated with so much charm and learning that the book became not only widely popular, but fundamental to the culture of the age. This collection, the *Adagia,* had close connection with England. It was dedicated to Erasmus's young English friend and patron, Mountjoy, for whom Erasmus says in the dedication of the first edition he especially intended the work. Even in this undeveloped and relatively bare form, the book excited great enthusiasm among the English group of Erasmus's friends and followers. Mountjoy says everybody praised it, and Archbishop Warham delighted in it so much that Mountjoy could not manage to get the book away from him when he once had it in his hands. The *Adagia* constitute an introduction to the human and ethical side of Greek life, and incidentally to Greek and Latin linguistic usage. The book contains, first, the adage considered; secondly, its interpretation; thirdly, citations of the use of it, with explications when required, from classical authors. It gives then a store of information, as to the usage of language and as to ways of life, it interprets specific passages, it provides a mass of knowledge of mythology, biography, and history, and it digests a vast amount of wise and witty comment on human conduct. Ultimately, the collection of *Adagia* grew to include over four thousands—"Chiliads"—of proverbs. With the course of time, the *Adagia* as a source of information has been superseded by more orderly and complete if less genial manuals, while as a work to be read for its own interest, it has suffered the fate of all the Latin literature of the Renaissance: "Ciceronianism" and the disappearance of Latin as a language of practical use have caused it to be neglected. Moreover, its ethical method is out of fashion. Who, nowadays, could endure reading a collection of proverbs seriously, as a real basis of conduct and a guide of life?

The *Apophthegmata* are anecdotes of great men, embodying their pregnant and witty sayings. Though the book is mainly conversant with classic names, it is not wholly so. The earlier parts are based mainly on Plutarch; the later have a wider range, and include some anecdotes from history recent in Erasmus's day. The book is even more entertaining than the *Adagia,* and is as profitable in every way. The anecdotes of the *Apophthegmata* were so popular, as is shown by Mr. H. de Vocht, that they were even worked down into stories for the lower type of popular jest-books.[27] In *Jack of Dover* a narrative of Socrates from Diogenes Laertius is told of the Foole of Lincoln, and a tale of Demosthenes, from Valerius Maximus, of the Foole of Westchester, both coming through Erasmus. In *Merry Tales and Quicke Answers* nearly all the tales dealing with personages from history are borrowed from Erasmus. As de Vocht suggests, this is a saving of time: in place of reading through *Scriptores Historiae Romanae Minores,* or even Aulus Gellius or Plutarch, one had only to open the pages of the *Apophthegmata.* Moreover, it is to be noted that the compiler could check Erasmus with a Latin source, but not with a Greek source, and hence had to depend on him implicitly for much. Plutarch, through Erasmus, appears in *Pasquil's Jests,* and even in *Mother Bunch's Merriments.*

---

[27] De invloed van Erasmus op de Engelske tooneelliteratur der xvie en xviie eeuwen, deel 1 (Gent 1908).

The first Englishman to undertake in a serious way the translation of any substantial part of Erasmus's collections was Richard Taverner, whose *Garden of Wisdom* is a small collection of anecdotes, drawn from the *Apophthegmata.* Book I, which was probably first printed in 1538, perhaps in 1539, contains chiefly anecdotes from the earlier part of Erasmus's work; Book II, which was added in the next year, is drawn mainly from the later part, including some anecdotes of nonclassical worthies, such as Athanasius, Alfonso of Aragon, and the Emperor Sigismund. In the preface to the second book Taverner apologizes for his "incondite and grosse phrase," and his "confused order." In point of fact his expression is more neat and vigorous than was common in his day.

Taverner did not hesitate to add comments of his own to the explications of Erasmus. Lycurgus and Agesilaus serve to prepare a compliment to Henry VIII, and the Egyptians to celebrate the freedom of English courts from corruption.

> What tyme the valyaunte capytayne Memnon held warres agaynst the great Alexander on the behalfe of Darius kynge of Persia, it chaunced that a certayne hyred sowldyoure in the armie of Memnon made verye moche raylynge vpon kynge Alexander. Memnon hearynge hym, layde hym on the pate wyth hys speare and thus rebuketh hym. I gyue the wages, syr knaue, and meate and drynke to fyght wyth Alexander and not to rayle vpon hym. Let Crysten men at lest waye take example hereby, to leaue there fowle and detestable raylynges farre vnworthye for suche as professe Chrystes doctryne, that forbyddeth vs to calle our brother but fole. Some we cal Pharysees, we be knaue, we defye as naughtye papystes wyth other lyke opprobriouse wordes, vnmete for Chrysten mennes eares, but as for to fyghte agaynste theym, and to confounde them wyth pure doctryne and good lyuynge, that we woll not. Agayne other some, we beheretyke, we call Lutheranes, and all that *that* naught is, but to shewe them charitably where they erre, & ryghtly to instructe them, we wol not.[28]

Almost at the same time Taverner was at work on a version of selections from the *Adagia,* and in 1539 "Prouerbes or adagies with newe addicions gathered out of the Chiliades of Erasmus by Richard Tauerner" was printed, a second edition following in 1552. Taverner condenses Erasmus's comments, giving the explanation of the meaning of the proverb, but omit-

[28]Edition of 1550[?], ptr. W. Copland for Kele; Fo. xv *verso,* xvi *recto.*

ting references to the source and all scholarly apparatus, but sometimes adding a moral commentary of his own. For example, after the tale of the wolf whose calumny of the fox caused himself to be slain, he adds: "Let all counsayllors beare thys example wel in mynde, Yf they be nothing moued wyth fables: Let them at lest be admonyshed wyth the history of Aman in the boke of Hester, whych is in the Byble."[29]　He translated freely from Erasmus, as follows: "There be kynges, there be Cardinalles, there be Bishops, Prelates, and sondry other officers and magistrates in Christendome, whych do all by vycares and deputies, but them selues lyue in most ydelnes and in all kyndes of pleasure," and adds, "lyke popes. Wold god these wold take exemple of our most vigilant prince and soueraygne lord kinge Henry the eyght, who not only setteth vigilant deputies and ministers vnder hym, but also loketh hym selfe ryght busely vpon hys charge committed vnto him of god."[30]　So throughout the book, Taverner, in spite of his protests against the unkind abuse of erring fellow-Christians by applying offensive terms to them, introduces equally irritating slurs against papists and praises of Henry.

Erasmus, in 1514, had put forth a volume including the Sayings of the Wise (*Septem Sapientium dicta,* "e Graecis, ut habebantur, a nescio quo Graeculo utcumque collecta."), the *Mimi* of Publilius Syrus, with Cato's *Distichs,* the *Institution of a Christian Man,* and a translation of the letter to Demonicus. Taverner made up a little book mainly of the *Sayings* and the *Mimi,* and printed the Latin and English interlined, omitting Erasmus's commentary. He gave his work the title, *Flores aliquot sententiarum ex variis collecti scriptoribus. The flowers of sencies gathered out of sundry writers by Erasmus in Latine & Englished by Rychard Tauerner. Huic libello non male conueient Mimi illi Publiani nuper ab eodem Richardo versi. . . . .* The first edition appeared in 1540, the fifth, the latest which I have found, in 1574.

Taverner, then, in all these translations, is merely one more humble follower of Erasmus.

Almost contemporaneously with Taverner's first translation Sir Thomas Elyot published a small collection of aphorisms,

[29]Fo. xxi, *r.* and *v.*
[30]Fo. vii, viii.

The Bankette of Sapience. The dedicatory prologue addressed
to the King is an elaborate conceit on banqueting after labor.
"Considering the longe abstinance & fastyng of this presente
Lent, with also the continuall trauayle that your hyghnes, your
counsaylle, and dyuers your subiectes haue sustayned in con-
sultinge about the weale publyke of this your grace's most
noble realme . . . ." I have provided this banquet, with varied
dishes, seasoned by Sapience; I deserve no more praise than
"one of them that beareth a torche before euery course when
they come from the dresser." Yet I may be permitted to
scrape the dish. This banquet must be "wel masticate, and not
hastily deuoured." It is gathered "out of the workes of moste
excellent persons, as wel faythfull as gentyles." On the whole,
more than half is from Scripture and Christian authors: Solo-
mon is with Seneca and Periander, Lactantius with Plautus and
Euripides, and Paulus is cited as well as Plutarch. Of heathen
authors, Seneca is the most frequently quoted. Elyot's work
is not in the least like Erasmus's in tone. Elyot is literal and
sober, and draws from Scripture and grave authors, but Erasmus's *Adagia* have all some point of surprise, metaphor, or
allegory.

A trifle later (1544) Richard Morysine filled up the empty
pages at the end of his translation of Vives's *An Introduccion
to Wysedome,* itself a collection of devout aphorisms, with
"certain floures of most notable sentences of wise men, gathered together by Erasmus of Roterdam, and translated into
Englysh." These few pages are independent of Taverner.

In 1555 there was published a translation by Robert Burrant of some of the works in the collection edited by Erasmus
in 1514, namely the *Distichs,* the *Mimi,* and the *Sage Sayings.*
Burrant translated into roughly rhyming distichs, and added his
own amplification in imitation of Erasmus, the amplification
being in general a mere lot of redundancy, explaining the obvious. Burrant, however, makes a few comments that are related to his times. On the one hand, as Burrant displays none
of Taverner's intelligence in the expression of his ideas, so, on
the other he is without Taverner's generosity of heart. On
Cleobulus's fifth saying:

> Whosoeuer wyl good men fauour
> Of euyll persons, he wyll be a persecutour,

Burrant remarks:

> Loke whatsoeuer thing a man enterely loueth, he wyll the
> same safely kepe and defende from soche thinges as may destroy
> and hurte it. As yf a man loue gay apparel, he wyl prouyde a
> medecyne for moghthes. If he set by money, he wyll make it
> sure from theues, and do all that he can to hange theim. If he
> loue the trueth of Gods word, and the professoures of godly doc-
> tryne, he wyll be an earnest persecutour of Idolitors, Papistes,
> Heretikes, and scysmatikes. For he truely and vnfaynedly fau-
> oureth good men, who taketh away that which most offendeth
> them, that is euyl disposed persons.[31]

He shows especial delight and eagerness in expanding the commonplaces against women.

The most extensive and the best written translation of any of
Erasmus's collections was done by Nicholas Udall, the schoolmaster. He translated the third and fourth books of the *Apophthegmata,* omitting none except such as honesty persuaded
him to be better passed over than rehearsed or spoken of His
preface intelligently states the ideal of translation which he
followed,—"I haue laboured to discharge the duetie of a translatour, that is, kepyng and folowyng the sense of my booke, to
interprete and turne the Latine into Englyshe with as muche
grace of our vulgare toung, as in my slendre power and knowe-
lage hath lyen." (Ed. of 1542.) Here and there,—not often,
—he introduced for the benefit of young scholars Greek and
Latin verses and words, "Wherof *the* pith and grace of the saying depended." It is not "to be doubted but that such as are
towardes the disciplines of good litterature in diuerse tounges,
maye of such dooynges as this, picke out as muche vtilitie and
furtheraunce of their studies, as the vnlearned shall take
pleasure, and fruite of the Englyshe for their vse. Whoso
careth not for the Latine may passe it ouer and satisfie hymself
with the Englysshe. Who passeth not on the Greke, maie
semblably passe it ouer, and make as though he see none suche."
Udall has added a few annotations and comments of his own,
but mainly confines himself to his original. His translation is
pithy and vigorous but sometimes quaint.

Beeyng asked, whether philosophiers wer eaters of tartes or

---

[31]Fo. vi, *v.,* vii *r.*

sweet meates too? yea, of all thynges (saied Diogenes) euen
like other christian bodyes.[32]

When he had freely perdoned and leat goo at their libertee
the *Atheniens,* as many as euer had been taken priesoners in batail
at *Cheronea,* and thei, thynkyng that not to bee enough, required
also to haue restitucion of their apparell and all their bagguage, and
did for the same entre accions of detinue, and commense suite against
the *Macedonians, Philippus* laughed, saiyng: what? dooeth it not
appere the Atheniense to deme and iudge that thei haue been ouer-
comed by vs, at the hucclebones?[33]

Udall, though an accomplished writer of prose for his time,
cannot yet manage a *long* sentence with just emphasis.

It breided & areised greate enuie and grutchyng against *Caesar,*
that one of those persones, whom he had sent to Rome, standyng in
the senat hous, as soone as he knewe that the senate would not geue
ne graunte vnto *Caesar* prorogacion, that is to saie, a longer tyme in
his dictature, gaue a greate stroke with his hande vpon *the* hiltes
of his swerde, & saied: well yet this felo here shall geue it.[34]

It is worthy of remark that the book has seemed sufficiently
interesting to be handsomely reprinted, not for scholars as a
curiosity but for the thoughtful general reader, at Boston,
Lincs. in 1877.

The most popular collection of aphoristic wisdom was James
Baldwin's *Moral Philosophy.* The book consisted of selections
from the body of sayings of the wise ancients, not arranged
by authors or scattered at random, but distributed under topical
heads, with an appearance of system. The first edition appeared in 1547, and the author put forth a reprint in 1550.
One of the gentlemen of the Queen's Chapel—a chorister, that
is, and presumably a Roman Catholic by conviction—William
Paulfreyman by name, was a delighted reader of the book; and
as he read it, over and over, he began comparing part with part,
resorting the material, and putting the aphorisms on the same
subject together. Paulfreyman, in other words, found Baldwin's material valuable, but his arrangement illogical and in-
convenient. He might well do so. Baldwin arranged his work
according to a purely formal scheme, in three divisions; first of
counsels, laws, and precepts,—injunctions, that is, given liter-

[32]Ed. 1542, fo. 128 *r.*
[33]*Op. cit.* Fo. 163 *r.*
[34]Fo. 298 *v.*

ally; secondly, of proverbs and adages,—that is, of general truths, usually epigrammatic in expression; and thirdly of parables and semblables,—teachings delivered in metaphorical form. A book of the lives and notable sayings of famous men was prefixed; and the three books that composed the bulk of the work were divided into chapters according to subject-matter: God; the soul; virtue; vice; the accidents of life; and so on. Obviously this classification, based on three principles —authorship, form, and content, no one of them carried through consistently—was the product of a disorderly, illogical mind. To add to the confusion, Baldwin added theoretical problems to the topics treated, and prefixed chapters on the origins, divisions, and nature of philosophy. For this he had no gift; his mind was not really able to transcend the statement of rules and specific directions, and to see his subject as in any way a body of co-ordinated principles. Paulfreyman cast away all the prefatory matter, rearranged the confused body of precepts on a sounder basis, added sayings from his own reading, and printed his revision, at some time soon after 1550. No copy of this revision is known to be extant.

Baldwin was vexed—not unnaturally perhaps—most of all by the omission of his ambitious discussions. He accordingly re-issued his work, with slight additions (a chapter on *Marriage and Married Folk,* and some passages on *Freedom*) in 1555 (reprinted by Professor Arber in 1908).

Paulfreyman also issued a new edition, reprinting Baldwin's prefatory chapters this time, and adding again some new material of his own. This book, like his first revision, is lost.

Baldwin again revised his book, retaining Paulfreyman's additions and taking advantage of his improvements in arrangement except in some details. He added a table of contents, perhaps modified from Paulfreyman, but if so spoiled in the process. This was in 1564.

Paulfreyman again (in 1567) revised and enlarged the work, improving the table of contents, and rounding out the treatment of the subjects, to the great convenience of the reader. This edition was reproduced in 1575, and with slight additions in 1584. There were editions in 1587, 1591, 1596, 1600, 1610, 1620?, 1630?, 1651.

In the course of these alternating revisions both Baldwin

and Paulfreyman in their prefaces express disapproval of each
other's actions. Baldwin in his dedication of his edition of
1555 writes thus:

> The same treatyse of moral philosofie which eyght yeares
> passed I dedicate too your Lordship [the Earl of Hertford] I
> haue at the Printers request newly pervsed, picked, and augment-
> ed: which I was the willinger to doe, because that mayster Pal-
> freyman in his booke bearing the same title (wherein he hath
> couched most parte thereof though in an other order) hath lefte
> that oute, which many most desyer, as that which onelye answer-
> eth the name and title of the volum. For any thing is vnaptly
> called a treatise wherin *the* matter treated of is not formally de-
> fined, discussed, and sundred in to the partes: which caused me
> to searche out, and as wel as I could, to declare the beginnynge
> and originall with all the membres of Philosophie in my former
> treatise: which I woulde wysh had been with the rest of the
> booke alowed if it be alowable, or if it be not, to haue ben altered
> and made perfect, so should the booke haue ben rightly intituled.
> I saye not this (if it like youre Lordshyppe) to disalow mayster
> Palfreymans diligence, or anye others that would take payne in
> the like matter, for, as I said and say still in the fifth chapter of
> my first booke, the chefest cause why I did put of it furthe was
> to prouoke other, more learnedlye to handle my rude beginnyngs.
> Yet meaned I not neyther to haue my wourke aultered, but to
> haue had it remayne styll (as it was) a blunt whetstone. I hoped
> that sum learned therin woulde haue perused the Rabbines, sum
> other the sages of oure owne countrey, and haue seuerally gath-
> ered together theyr liues and sentences, and therout made suche
> lyke and better volumes, as I had stollen from among the Latined
> Grecians. I thought nothing lesse than to haue any other man
> plowe with my oxen, or to alter or augmente my doynges:
> whiche perchaunce (if I had thought mete) I could and would
> haue doen as wel as an other. It maye and will be thought I am
> sure, but vntruly, that I haue taken this labour in hande againe,
> rather to redeme my name and glory than for any other cause:
> which is not so. And yet is a good name such a losse to him that
> hath none other riches, as may prouoke a wyser than I and that
> by the wisest judgment, to endeuor with tooth and nayle, as well
> to preserue as to procure it. . . .

Paulfreyman responds with an unctuous and loquacious preface. "Gross, rude, and unlearned" as he is, he looks upon his
work as a "simple doings," and knows that it is "worthy but
of small commendation in comparison to the witty and learned
handling of thother: Unto thautoure wherof, (Maister
Bauldwin) I yet stil (as before) gladly, & most hartely referre

the whole commendacion and praise." If his little labors are worthy acceptation of God, he hopes men will not condemn them; man's work and glory are nothing, and there is nothing in which we should seek to be glorified; and he prays God to vouchsafe to give to us his unworthy servants a spirit of humbleness, so that we may have nothing to do with the "cursed spirit of envy and strife, scornfulness or disdain." Vain men flatter themselves with the "only taste of their own sugard phantasies," and scorn the patient labor of others, finding it "unpicked, emptie, barren of eloquence, void of profound learning, excellency, dainty or fine perfection (although in some godly matters, such exact diligence and nicety needeth not) . . . Such men cause others to despise good works. This I have noted, not that feeling myself pricked, I should swell or stomach against any man. I hope God will teach them better; I am not striving to enter into comparison with any man, etc."

Baldwin was uncritical, superstitious, and illogical. He begins his introduction by condemning Pericles for refusing to be frightened by an eclipse. "And so contemninge a good admonicion sent as then by God, he sayled forwarde, to the destruccion of hys souldiers, besides the greate detrimente of all the whole lande of Grecia . . . In lyke maner there be many nowe adayes, which as Pericles despysed Astronomie, dispise all other sciences." He accepts the fables of Trismegistus, and is ready to doubt with St. Augustine whether "he spake such things as he did by knowledge of Astronomy, or else by revelation of spirits"; or else with Lactantius to accept him as saint and sibyl. He tells with all reverence the tale of Epimetheus who slept fifty-seven years, and throughout displays a lamentable failure to catch any of that critical temper which was part of the ideal of his master Erasmus.

Baldwin sets forth the spirit in which he studies the ancients' philosophy, not as contradicting or even interpreting the Scriptures, but as supporting them.

> For although (good Reader) that Philosophie is not to be compared with the most holy Scriptures, yet is it not vtterly to be despised: whiche (yf men wil credyt the holy doctours) may be proued by the iudgment of S. Augustine, which in his booke *De doctrina Christiana,* cap. xl exhorteth vs to the reading therof, saying: Yf they whiche be called Philosophers, specially of Plato his secte, haue spoken ought that is true & appertinent to oure

faithe, we ought not onely not to feare it, but also to chalenge it as our own, from them whiche are ryght owners therof. For lyke as the Egipcians had not onely Idols and great burdens which the Israelites did hate and flye, but also vessels, ornamentes & goodly Iewels of golde & syluer, whiche the Israelites departing from Egypt, vnder the colour of borowing, stole priuely from them, not of their own mynd but by commaundement of god, to turne that to a better vse which the Egyptians abused; So in the doctrine of the Gentiles are not only contaiyned supersticious and fayned rites, with great burdens of vaine labour, all which we Christians following Christ out from among the vnbelieuyng Gentiles, should vtterly detest and auoyde: but also much good Learnyng, mete for to serue the trueth, with sum moste profitable preceptes of good maners, wherin are founde sum truth, how to worshyp the eternal and onely God. . . . These be the wordes, iudgment, and councell of that moste holy Doctour concernyng Philosophie.

Certainly Baldwin would never have kissed a codex, or exclaimed, "Blessed Saint Socrates!"

The design of the book being to make heathen philosophy contribute to the teaching of conduct, not a father of the church is cited in the didactic part of the work; all is "gentile philosophy." The most important source is the collections of Erasmus, though Baldwin was an independent gatherer of material from many sources, especially from the many translations into Latin of the Greek moralists. Professor Arber notes among the rhymes Ascham's version of a few lines of Euripides, and Surrey's of the Martial epigram incorrectly entitled *"Ad se ipsum."* The first edition bears date January 20, 1547. Surrey was executed January 21. The verses, in this edition anonymous, were printed with the name of the author in the edition of 1555.[35] Baldwin refers respectfully to Sir Thomas Elyot, praising him particularly for his translation of the *Education of Youth,* from Plutarch, and to Udall for his version of Erasmus's *Apophthegmata.*

Paulfreyman followed Baldwin at first in thus confining himself to classic heathen writers; but in the edition of 1567 he added chapters chiefly on virtue and vice, and conscience. These are drawn chiefly from the church fathers, and give the book a decidedly Christian, even an ascetic tendency, as in Chrysostom's rating of pure virginity as the first degree of

---

[35]*Cf.* Hudson, Hoyt H., *Surrey and Martial.* M L N (1923).

chastity, matrimony as second, and Jerome's commendation of fasting.

Paulfreyman's citations are longer and less epigrammatic than Baldwin's, but the style of both exhibits the great advance in the mastery of the English language which had been gradually acquired by the average cultivated man since the time of Barclay and Elyot, still more since the time of Caxton and Skelton. It would have been impossible for a writer in 1530 not to trip himself up in such sentences as the following:

> Whom peruerse fortune, long sicknesse, seruice, friendship, disloyaltie of them that were trusted, or that theeues and oppressours hâue brought vnto pouertie, to those let men extend foorth their compassion and Charitie.[36]
>
> There must bee vsed amongst men of a lowly and milde behauior, a decent reuerence one towards another (as becometh good and humble men) not onely vnto those of the higher sort; but also to all the rest of meaner degrees: for otherwise, it should not onely be a signe of great arrogancie and pride, but also a plaine cause of iudgment, that such a one sheweth himselfe to bee altogether not onely lawlesse, but also shamelesse and without honest re garde what euery man do thinke of him.[37]

The *Treatise of Moral Philosophy,* begun as a collection of a few of the most pregnant sayings of the ancients upon human conduct had grown to a much greater size and had been given an appearance of completeness and system. It had become a kind of compendium, drawn mainly but not altogether from antiquity, of moral and political virtue. The *Treatise* and Grimald's translation of "Tully's" *Offices* were the most popular and efficient of the works of this period in disseminating among "mere English" readers the moral wisdom of antiquity. Such works, without the attraction of surprise or the spice of originality, may seem dull and insignificant, but the commonplace has the advantage of the paradoxical that it is more often true. The claim of such works is no small one: they declare that their doctrines have been honestly tested in the only laboratory, the laboratory of human experience. Even cleverness has to take account of this traditional wisdom, and can correct it only by a finer test, and not by impatience.

Next to the works of ethical philosophers, and the sayings

---

[36]Ed. 1600, Fo. 129 *v.*
[37]Ed. 1600, Fo. 129 *v.*

of the wise culled from experience, the "Prince," the "Governor," or the "Gentleman" was to be formed by the study of history. It would be easy to fill a volume with the praise of history from the prefaces of scholars in the Renaissance. General as was the humanism of Nicholas V, it was in history that he was most interested. Even those who looked with hesitation on heathen poetry, or who carried their distrust of gentile ideas so far as to discredit profane philosophy, agreed on the importance of classical history. Indeed the more literary theorists sometimes admitted the superior necessity though not the superior importance of historical study for the training of the public man. In France, moreover, the princes themselves had received with favor translations of classic historians into the vernacular. These translations were amplified so as to resolve all difficulties of interpretation and to explain allusions, that they might be easily read by busy men little acquainted with classic story, but desirous of getting the facts quickly. English versions of the same kind do not begin to appear until a generation after the French. One of the earliest, perhaps the earliest, is William Rastell's version of Caesar's Gallic War, "as much as concernyth thys realm of England," which has erroneously been attributed to the Earl of Worcester. The brief tract, itself taken from the French version of Gaguin, intends to do for English readers what the printers in France had already begun to do for the French—namely, to make accessible at large the stores of information from classic sources hitherto shut up in the libraries of the great.[38]

Perhaps Alexander Barclay's version of Sallust's *Jugurtha* preceded the Caesar by a few years. The principle of the translation is like that of the French versions which had set Barclay his example. As Thomas Paynell says, in the dedicatory preface of his edition of Barclay's *Jugurtha* (1557),

> The translation dothe paraphrasticallie so open the hole matter, that no scruple remaineth to be douted vpon. For Saluste the noble historiographe, doth in the laten tonge so compendiouslie and briefly, but yet most eloquentlie and truely, knyt vp the whole historie of Iugurth, that the reader in diuers places (excepte he be very rype and perfecte in the eloquence and figures of the laten tonge, and phrases of the same) shal stumble and

---

[38]Reed, Arthur W., *The Editor of Sir Thomas More's English Works: William Rastell*, in *The Library*, 4th Ser., iv, 29-30, (1924).

stagger in the conueyance and vnderstandinge of the true mean-
yng and sence therof.

Barclay wrote an English dedication to the Duke of Norfolk, victor of Flodden, and a Latin one to John Veysey, Bishop
of Exeter, "Ex cellula Hatfeldensis regii, iii Idus Novembris."
Since Veysey was created bishop of Exeter very late in 1519,
the Latin preface cannot be earlier than November, 1520; and
since Norfolk died in May, 1524, the English preface cannot
be later than November, 1523.[39]
It is evident from the English preface that the method of
translation was consciously adopted by Barclay.

I haue considered what seruice I might do acceptable to your
magnificence: feeling unworthy to perform any. Neuertheles
after many consyderacions the gracious regarde of benynge grauite
which I beholde in your countenance: and the euident signes of
humilite which outwardly appereth radicate in your noble hert:
reconforteth myne insufficience & inboldeth my spirites/ some
thyng to write my custome which I may present into your gracious handes: as a perpetual memorial: an and [sic] euident testimony of my deuout seruice/ & amorous affection against your
magnificent hyghnes. In this consyderacion I haue reuolued
many & diuerse volumes/ studyeng of which/ one: the translacion: might correspond with your noble estat. But at last I haue
remembred that a mercyal matter is most congruent vnto a marcial
& victorious prince. Wherfore I haue attempted to translate
into our maternal language the auncient cronicle & famous hystorie of the warre: and dyuers batayls which the romayns dyd
agaynst the tyran Iugurth: vsurper of the kyngdome of Numidy.
Whiche hystorie is writen in latyn by the renowmed romayne
Salust: whose wordes in latyn I haue also added vnto the marge
of this my translacion to thintent that such as shal dysdayne to
rede my translation in englysshe: may rede this historie more
compendyously & more obscurely writen in laten. Which hystorie: parauenture shal apere more clere & playne vnto theym in
many placces by help of this my translation. Which shal nat be
tedyous to such as be lerned & vnderstande latyn: but vnto many
noble gentylmen which vnderstande nat latyn tong perfetly I dout
nat but that this my labour shalbe both pleasure & profet. For
by the same they shal haue some help toward the vnderstandyng
of latyn: whiche at this tyme is almost contemned of gentylmen.
And also they shal vnderstande a ryght fruytful hystorie: bothe
pleasaunt/ profitable/ & ryght necessary vnto euery degre: but
specially to gentylmen/ whiche coueyt to attayne to clere fame
and honour: by glorious dedes of chyualry.

[39]D. N. B. speaks of the work as "of unknown date."

The pompous style of this passage is not characteristic of the translation, but is maintained through the preface. Barclay defends himself for occupying his pen with matters of war in despite of his priestly character; and following the example of the scholars of the time in their editions of Latin histories he brings together a multitude of passages from authorities in favor of the value of historical study. As usual, the central passage is the eloquent sentence of Cicero: "An hystore is the recorder of tymes passed: the lyght of verite: the maistres of mannes lyueng: the presydent of memorie: the messanger of antiquite."[40]   Besides Livy and Diodorus (from Beroaldus's Latin), Quintilian is cited in favor of the histories of war, since by righteous wars vice and evils are corrected, and all things brought to order. Moreover the fortune of war should avail to the contempt of mundane pleasure and the misery of this uncertain life.

> For whan hystories represent before our syght the valyant and bolde herted knyghtes shyning in armour: & richely aparelled: on comely coursers barded and trapped with golde & syluor: the goodly order and ordynance of a great army of armed men shyning in harnesse: fyers/ & prepared redy to batayle: the trumpettes sounding: the golden stremers and standards blasyng & glisteryng agaynst the sonne: and brefely all the grounde ouercouered with men & riches. What els is all this: but a vayne ostentation of yertly [sic: i.e. earthly; inanis] opulence: and caduke glorie prepared besely/ assembled laboriously/ and exposed folysshly vnto distruction & perdicion. But agayn anon after: when we rede & se in the same hystories the valiaunt mennes bodyes prostrate, the carkases of kynges/ dukes/ erles/ knyghtes/ and pages mengled all togyder: all pride & contention abated. The bryght harnesse dyed with blode: the wounded coursers drawynge after them the deed bodyes of their lordes: the men cryeng. the tentes & townes brennyng. What is all this sight with otherlyke? Forsoth nought els but an euident spectacle of mannes brutall crudelite: and an example of mundayne vanite: declarynge the immoderat & insaciable desyr of dominion of yerthely princes: and prouing that vnto man welth is intolerable/ & confounded by his owne foly.

So much has been said about the expanded method of translation that it will be well to give an example of it. The matter added is italicized.

---

[40]*De. Or.* II, 36.

Vos autem, Adherbal et Hiempsal colite observate talem hunc virum,

But ye *my dere sonnes* Adherbal and Hiempsal se that ye worshyppe and loue this Iugurth *your* worthy *vncle. And bewarre that ye offende nor dysplease hym*: *but* folowe his *vertue & manly behauour.* And do your deuoir to the

imitamini virtutem et enitimini

best of your power *after his example behauynge yourselfe / so discretely and so wysely* that it be nat *hereafter* reported by [i.e. about][41] me /

ne ego meliores libros sumpsisse videar quam genuisse.

that I haue takenne vnto me by adoption / better chyldren thanne I haue begotten. *Thus concluded the kyng Micipsa his wordes.* Howbeit Iugurth well perceyued the kynges wordes :

ad ea Iugurtha, tametsi regem ficta locutum et ipse longe aliter animo agitabat, tamen pro tempore benigne respondit.

but fayned *and spoken agaynst his hert: if any other remedy might haue ben founde.* Neuertheles he answered benygnely for the tyme / all if he *thought and* reuolued in his mynde moche otherwyse / *and contrary to his humble and mylde answere.*

Micipsa paucis post diebus moritur

Not longe after the kynge Micipsa decessed *whose dethe was dolorous and sore bewayled of all his subgettes: but most of all to his naturall sonnes it was to be lamented; and not without great cause as the process of this hystorie shall afterwarde declare. But* after the kyngs

Postquam illi more regio justa magnifice fecerant, reguli in unum convenerunt, ut inter se de cunctis negotiis disceptarent. (Cap. x, 8; xi, 1 and 2.)

funerall exequies were magnificently ended as apertayned to his state royall. The *thre* princes *that is to say Adherball / Hiempsall / and Iugurth* anone assembled to the intent to *commen and* treat of busynesses of the royalme / *concernyng particion and separation of the same: and all other thynges conuenient.*

Barclay's *Jugurtha* was soon reprinted, and in 1557 was printed again, in one volume with the translation of Felicius Durantinus's *Catiline* by Thomas Paynell. Paynell, in the dedication, "To the ryghte honorable Lorde Antonye Vycounte Mountague, knyghte of the ryght honorable order of the garter, and one of the kynge and Queenes majesties pryuie counsayle," tells how a friend desiring to have the *Jugurtha* and the *Catiline* bound up together, had urged Paynell to peruse the work of Barclay, in order to correct mistakes of the press, which "had somewhat mangled and corrupted" the work. This, he

---

[41]By—about (in an unfavorable way): against. *v.* NED, *s.v. by;* and *cf.* Queen Elizabeth's distich:

"Much suspected by me;
Nothing prooued can be."

(Flügel, E., *Gedichte der Königin Elisabeth,* in *Anglia,* xvi (1892), p. 355).

says, he had done; but I have been unable to find any change
except a *with* for an *in;* the very colophon is reprinted, except
for the change in the printer's name.

Over twenty years passed before another translation of a
classical historian was attempted. The gentry and nobility of
the age of Henry VIII had their minds turned in other directions than towards the lessons of the past. In 1544, a year of
conflict with France and Scotland, on the verge of a still bit-
terer conflict with Rome, Sir Anthony Cope printed the story
of Hannibal and Scipio, drawn mainly from Livy. Of the
dedication to Henry VIII, two pages are devoted to exhibiting
by proofs drawn from nature, reason, learning, and experience, the fact that all things are governed by time, and that
there is a time for all things. For Henry it is now time for
war. "Wherefore well ponderyng the tyme of warre to be
nowe in hand, as a thyng so much needfull for many consider-
acions, I (for my poore part) thought, that I should dooe, not
onely to your hyghnesse acceptable service, but also to all noble
men, and ientilemen of the realme greate pleasure and com-
*m*oditie, if gatheryng to gyther out of Titus Liuius, and other
autours, the lyues, the policies, and the marciall actes of two
the most woorthie capitaynes, of the two moste renowmed em-
pires of the worlde, that is to saie, of Anniball of Carthage,
and Scipio of Rome, I woulde brynge the same into english
toung: whereby, besyde the pleasant bestowyng of tyme, in
the readyng therof, men also may learne bothe to dooe dis-
pleasure to theyr enemies, and to auoyde the crafty and daungerous baites, which shall be layde for theim." Hannibal and
Scipio, says Sir Anthony, are rightly renowned in history, and
made the subject of pictures. "For who is he that doeth not
muche reioyce, in beholdyng Hercules painted on a walle,
clothed in a lyons skynne, by his mighty hand spoyled, and
drawynge after hym Cerberus that hell hounde, with iii. hydeos
heades, whome he hath brought from the dominion of Pluto?
Who doeth not reioyce to heare the conquest of the golden
fliece, by Iason in the Isle of Colchos . . . . But sens of all other
that euer wer, Hercules in accoumpted moste woorthy the
crowne of honorable prayse, as the chief daunter of monsters:
I will nowe with his conquestes compare your moste famous
subduyng of the Romayne monster Hydra, . . . Those his

heddes . . . . be almost cleane cutte of, and mortified, the veno-
mous styng of ignorance plucked awaie, and his power suppressed: so that the walles of his denne of Rome tremble, beholdyng your cristall shielde of prudence. . ."

Cope's diction is fresh and vivid, but he cannot mass a sentence of any length as well as Barclay.

The number of the hooste was reckened to be. xl. M. fotemen,
and x. M. horsemen. Hasdruball gouerned the lefte wynge, Ma-
harball the ryght wyng, and Anniball with his brother Mago, kept
the myddell battayle. The Romans were tourned towarde the
southe, and the Carthaginenses toward the northe. The south-
east wynd was than vp, which blewe the dust, that with sterying
of the people, arose into the eies of the Romans, and that blynd-
ed them very soore. Anon with great rumor the forewardes
began the battels: And than the lefte wynge of the Frenchemen
and Spanyardes mette, and encountred the ryght wyng of the
Romanes, not after the maner of the batayle of men of armes on
horsbacke, bycause they lacked roume and space, they were soo
enclosed on bothe sydes, vpon the one syde with the ryuer, and
on the other the footemen letted them, so that they coulde none
otherwyse do, but runne streyght one vpon an other, and lyke
wrastlynge on horsebacke one tugge with an other, and with
force drawe one an other of theyr horsebackes, soo that in a
whyle it was more lyke a battayle of footemen than of horsemen.
This conflyct was vehement, but it endured not long: The Romans being put to the worse, incontinent left the batayle and
fledde. Whan the horsemen had done, the fotemen beganne the
batayle, which endured very long. The Frenchmen and Spanyardes were longe of lyke courage. The Romans toke great
peyne in breaking the myddell front of their ennemies, whiche
they apperceyued to be moste thynne and weake, which whan
they had brought to passe, and whan those that kept the fore-
warde with force, were put to vtteraunce, and were fledde to the
Affricans, than folowed the Romans without resistence for a
season, tyll at the last they were come betwene the two wynges
of the Affricans vnto the Frenche men and Spanyardes. Thus
the Romanes without order and vnwisely rushed into the prease.
Than the Affricans extended theyr wynges, compassyng and en-
closyng theyr ennemyes behynde theyr backes. Wherfore the
Romans leauing to fyght with the Frenchmen and Spaniardes,
began a freshe battayle aganst the Affricans, whyche was not
only vnlucky by reason they were enclosed on all partes, but
also they being weary, enterprised a new battaile against them
that were freshe and vnfoughten withall.[42]

[42]Fo. 33 *r.*

Six more years passed after the appearance of Cope's Scipio and Hannibal before the publication of another classical history. In 1550 there was printed Thomas Nichols's translation of Thucydides's Peloponnesian War, from the French of Claude de Seyssel, itself from the Latin of Laurentius Valla. The translation includes the prefatory matter of Valla and de Seyssel, besides a dedication, not only to a prince, Edward VI, but to a scholar, "Maister Iohn Cheke," who is desired to correct the work.

All the various prefaces have a considerable interest in exhibiting the spirit in which the translation had been performed.

The preface of "Iames Colyn," late secretary to Francis I, reprobates books of chivalry . . . . "Hence is it that in steede of Tristrams, Girons and Lancelotes and other, which do fylle bookes wyth dreames, and wherin many haue euill bestowed theyr good houres, ye haue, by the benefyt of the Kynge, no lesse frutefull than pleasante passetyme, for to knowe what people were Pericles, Nycias, Antigonus, Lysimachus, Eumenes, Hanibal, Scipion, and many other sage and valyant Capitaynes." Here the practical and almost ascetic realism of the classicists, such as Ascham and Cheke, is vigorously opposed to the romantic spirit of the time of Caxton.

Seyssel's preface, addressed to King Louis XII, illustrates that interest in history which caused so many translations of classic historians to be dedicated to French sovereigns from Charles VIII to Francis I. Valla's prologue, addressed to Nicholas V, declares that the original is so difficult that he would not have undertaken to translate it except by command, and could not have finished the translation except with the help of Lascaris. A translation at two removes from its original and transmitted through so cloudy a medium as Valla would have to be recommended by some literary power of its own if it were to be significant, and Nichols has no extraordinary gifts of imagination or language.

The best of the translations of classic historians before the time of Golding in the reign of Queen Elizabeth, was John Brende's version of Quintus Curtius's *History of the Acts of Alexander,* first printed in 1553. The work was dedicated to John, Duke of Northumberland, Earl Marshal. Northumberland became Earl Marshal September 2, 1551, and hence it would seem that the translation was made not long before it was put into print. So well was Brende's work esteemed that almost alone among these early translations it held its own even into the seventeenth century, being reprinted in 1561, 1570, 1584, 1592, 1602, and 1614.

Brende used the edition of Christopherus Bruno, Basle, 1545, who added as a supplement two books in place of the missing first two of Curtius, completed book v, and filled up missing parts of book x. Brende borrowed a great part of his dedication from Bruno's dedication to Albert Count Palatine, Duke of Bavaria—for example, the usual commonplaces on the importance of historical knowledge, especially to princes and others in authority, and the outlines of the life of Alexander. Brende's additions to the preface are not without interest. The insistence on the Scriptures as the sole rule of faith has a Protestant tone, characteristic of the reign of Edward VI. "There is required in all magistrates both a fayth and feare in God, and also an outwarde policye in worldlye thynges, wherof as the one is to be learned by *the* scryptures, so the other must chiefly be gathered by readyng of histories." The philosophy which history taught by example to Brende as to all humanists was the duty of humble obedience to rule, but perhaps it had special weight in England, whose bitter experience of civil faction had made the country so devoted to the autocracy which kept the country quiet, but under which such disturbing forces were moving. "In historyes it is apparant how daungerous it is to begyn alteracions in a commen wealth. How enuy & hatredes oft risyng vpon smal causes, haue ben the destruction of great kyngdomes. And that disobeyers of hygher powers, & suche as rebellyd agaynst magystrates, neuer escapyd punishment, nor came to good end." Brende expresses the usual sense of the superior importance of classical history, and hopes to do for England what had been done for other countries by translation. "Seing histories be then so good and necessary, it were muche requisite for mens instruccion, that they were translated into suche tounges as most men myght vnderstand them; and specially the histories of antiquitye, whych both for the greatnes of the actes done in those daies, and for the excellencie of the writers haue much maiestie and many ensamples of vertue. I therefore

hauyng alwaies desired that we, englishmen might be founde
as forwarde in that behalf as other nations which haue brought
all worthie histories into their naturall language, did a few
yeares paste attempte the translacion of Quintus Curtius, and
lately vpon an occasion performed & accomplished the same."

Brende expresses the ideas of the original after his own
manner, usually with a happy result in retaining the vivacity of
Curtius. (He says in his preface: "My trust is that your grace
will . . . . consider that in a translacion a man can not always
vse his own vaine, but shalbe compelled to tread in the aucthores
steppis: which is harder, and a more difficulte thynge to do,
then to walke his owne pace.") And although he departs from
his original in no vital matter, he also falls into error on almost every page, and frequently into grievous error. A good
example of his lively style is as follows:

> But they beyng slowe beastes, and not apte sodaynly to moue,
> were preuented by the swiftenes of the horses: and theyr bowes
> stoode not them in any great steade: for by reason their arrowes
> were so longe, and heauy, that they could not nocke them within
> theyr bowes except they staied first theyr bowes vpon the ground,
> and the grounde being so slipperie that they coulde haue no per-
> fite foting: whilest they were preparynge themselues to shoote,
> theyr enemyes were come emonges them. Then euery man fled
> from thordre that Porus had geuen, as it chaunceth oftentimes
> emongest troubled mindes, where feare beareth more rule, then
> the Capitaines appoinctment. For in so many partes as their
> armie was dyuyded, so many generalles became emonges theim.
> Some woulde ioigne all theyr battailes in one, other would haue
> them deuided. Some willed to stay, & other to go forwardes,
> and enclose theyr enemyes about: There was no general con-
> sultation emongest them. Porus notwithstanding accompanied with
> a few (with whome shame preuailed more than feare) assembled
> such together, as were disperkled abroade, and went forwardes
> against hys enemies, setting his Elephantes in the front of the
> battaile.
> They put the Macedons in feare, troubling with their vnwonted
> crie, not onely the horse, that naturallie do feare them [tam pauidum
> *ad omnia* animal], but also amased the men, and dysturbed theyr
> order; Insomuche that they whiche a litle before thought them-
> selues victours, looked aboute whyche waye to flie and saue them-
> selues: whyche thynge when Alexander perceiued, he sent against
> the Elephantes, the Agrians, and Thracians, that were men lighte
> armed, and apter to skirmishe a farre of, then to fighte hande to
> hande. They gaue the Elephantes, and their Gouernours muche
> a doe, and sore afflicted them withe *the* multitude of theyr dartes,

and arrowes that they bestowed emongest them: And the Phalanx
came constantly forwardes against theim that were in feare.
But suche as pressed ouer forwarde in fyghtinge with the Elephantes procured their manifest destruction [quidam auidius per-
secuti beluas, in semet irritauere uulneribus] : who being tramp-
led to deathe with their feete were an example to other, not to
bee ouer hastie in aduenturing theimselues. The most terrible
sight was, when the Elephantes with their long trunkes called
Proboscides, [orig. simply *manu*], tooke men in theyr armour from
the ground, and deliuered them vp to theyr gouernours. The battaile
was prolonged doubtfully, tyll the daye was farre spente: the souldiours sometime flienge from the Elephantes, and sometime pursuinge
after theim, vntill that wyth a certaine kind of crooked weapons called
copidae (prepared for *the* purpose) they cut *the* Elephantes vpon the
legges. [Donec securibus (id namque genus auxilii preparatum
erat) pedes amputare coeperunt. Copidas vocant gladios leuiter
curuatos, falcibus similes, queis appetebant beluarum manus.]
Those the Macedons had ryght aptly deuised [not in orig.] : for
not onely the feare of deathe, but also the feare of a new kinde
of torment in death, caused them to leaue nothing vnproued.
Finally Thelephantes weried wyth woundes, with theyr violente
struglyng did cast theyr gouernours to the earth, and tare theim
in pieces: for they were put in suche feare, that they were no
more hurtfull to theyr enemies, but driuen oute of *the* battaile
like shepe.[43]

The latest of the Greek historians to appear in an English
form during this period is Herodian, whose *History of the
Roman Emperors* was translated by Nicholas Smith from the
Latin of Angelo Poliziano. It seems strange that this late
Syrian writer, without distinction of substance or style should
have been chosen for translation when other earlier and better
writers were passed over. The era was one when the great
eagerness for abundant, easily acquired information caused
compendious works to be more highly appreciated than special-
ized ones, and Herodian gives a summary view of the history
of the early empire. His work also offers more information
about Britain than other ancient works. The translation, being
dedicated to "William [Herbert], Earl of Pembroke, Lord
President of the King and Queenes Maiestys Counsaile in the
marches of Wales, and one of their Matys Priuy Counsel,"
must date between 1554, the year of the marriage of Philip and
Mary, and 1558, the end of their reign. Smith's style is easier

---

[43]Fo. 179, edition of 1561, which differs slightly from that of 1553.

and smoother in movement than was common at the time,
except for an occasional period which is made cumbrous and
confused by too much grammatical suspense. The following
passage gives an account of the expedition of Severus against
the Britons.

As the olde man was thus in mynde molested, wyth the sensuall,
and vnhoneste lyfe, and delytes of hys Sonnes, he receyued letters
from hys lyuetenaunte of Englande, wherby he was enformed,
how the barbarouse people rebelled, and wasted thole Region
with invasions, and Commocions. Wherefore, he neaded a greater puyssaunce of men, to resiste, and suppresse them: there
wanted the Emperours presence also. Glad was Seuerus hereof:
for beynge a man of his owne nature, greadie of renowne, after
his vyctories, in thoriente, and Septententrion [sic] and his sur-
names by the fame obtained, he coueyted to make some Conquest,
ouer the Englyshemen. And to lede hys Sones, fourthe of the
Citie, that being farre from the pleasures thereof, thei might
accustome them selfes, to warlike, and sober dyet. Wherfore, he
proclaimed his expedicion into Britayne, beynge very olde, and
sore troubled with the goute, but yet of so valiaunte a stomake,
as neuer was any yonge man. In hys iorney, he roade moost
communely in a horse litter, neuer resting longe in any place.
When he had ended his voyage, and passed the Ocean Sea, with
as muche celeritee as can be thoughte, he entred into Brytaine,
mustered his Souldiours, hauing gathered a wonderfull power
togithers, and prepared hym selfe to batayle. The Britons,
beynge astonied, and agaste wyth thys so sodeine arriuall, of
themperour, And hearinge that so huge, an host was assembled
against them, sent Ambassadors unto him, to purge their mis-
demeanours, & entreate for peace. But Seuerus, makinge delaies
of purpose, lest he shuld retorne to Rome, without ani thing done,
& being very desyrous of the Conquest, & surname of Britaine,
dismissed the Ambassadors home againe, without any resolute
answere, geuen to their suite. Himselfe, with circumspecte in-
dustrie prepared all thinges expediente vnto the warre. And his
chiefest care, was to buylde bridges ouer, and in the marishes, to
thentente hys Souldiours myghte stande and fyghte in safetye.
For manye places in Britaine, are full of watery maryshes,
throughe the often flowynge ouer of the Ocean Sea. By those
maryshes dyd the Britons swymme and skyrmyshe therin wyth
theyr enemyes, beyng couered wyth water vp vnto the nauell,
and not muche caring, that men se the priuy partes of theyr naked
bodyes. Neyther dyd they knowe the use of apparaile, but accustomed to compasse their belyes and neckes onely wyth Iron,
whych they estemed an ornament, and token of richesse, as other
barbarous people supposed golde. They paynte theyr bodies,
wyth dyuerse pyctures, and fourmes of beastes, and therefore

weare no garments, lest the paynting shoulde be hydden, beynge a nacion verye valiaunte, and warlyke, gredye of slaughter, and contente onely wyth a small target, a speare, and a skeyne hangynge by theyr naked sydes, ignoraunte vtterlye of thuse of shyrtes of mayle, and helmettes for: they reckoned the same cumberous vnto them, when they should swim ouer the lakes, throughe whose vapours and heate, the ayre is there alwayes mystye and darke. Seuerus omytted nothyng vndone, that myghte auayle the Romaine Souldiours, and endomage the Britons.[44]

In review of the historical translations, it may justly be said of them, as of the philosophical ones, that in their character they are typical of the higher scholarship of their day, but that they are so few and so slight that they do not represent English learning. None of the greater English scholars engaged in making them; they turned their attention to the Scriptures. The genius of Tyndale, the amiable talent of Coverdale, the exact learning of Taverner and Cheke all found in the Scriptures the most worthy object of their attention. Contrast the production in France with that in England. In France whole works were translated, not mere scraps or fragments; and a body of translators each adding his contribution to what had been already done carried through the enterprise of providing French versions of all the important classic historians. A half century or more before the painful pen of Philemon Holland had given the country gentleman stately volumes of history, de Seyssel and his collaborators had done the same service for French gentlemen. The French had Livy, Caesar, Sallust, Tacitus, Suetonius, Quintus Curtius, Justin, Herodotus, Thucydides, Xenophon, Polybius, Arrian, Aelian, Appian, Herodian.[45] Amyot's Plutarch was the capstone of an already stately pile. England had not yet the public, the wealth, or the ideas for such large undertakings.

As has been said, the only complete work of the imagination translated during this period was Terence's *Andria*. It stands near the very beginning of the era, having been printed by Rastell, not far from 1520. The prologue and epilogue, and the stage directions make it obvious that the play was intended for acting, as Payne Collier suggests.[46] The prologue carries

[44]Fo. xliii, xliv.
[45]Tilley, Arthur, *The Literature of the French Renaissance* (1904) i, 36-39.
[46]Collier, J. Payne, *The History of English Dramatic Poetry to the time of Shakespeare: and Annals of the Stage to the Restoration.* (1879) vol. ii, p. 278, n. 2.

us far back, to the time when Gower and Lydgate were reckoned with Chaucer the greatest English authors.

The poet

The famous renown through the world is sprong
Of poetys ornate that vsyd to indyte
Of dyuers matters in theyr moder tong
Some toke vppon them translacions to wryte
Some to compile bokys for theyr delyte
But in our english tong for to speke playn
I rede but of few haue take any gret payn.

Except master Gowre which furst began
And of moralite wrote ryght craftely
Than master Chaucer that exellent man
Which wrote as compendious & elygantly
As in any other tong euer dyd any
Ludgate also which adournyd our tong
Whose noble famys through the world be sprong

By theis men our tong is amplyfyed so
That we therein now translate as well may
As in any other tongis other can do
Yet the greke tong & laten dyuers men say
Haue many wordys can not be englysshed this day
So lyke wyse in englysh many wordys do habound
That no greke nor laten for them can be found.

And the cause that our tong is so plenteouse now
For we kepe our englyssh contynually
And of other tongis many wordis we borow
Which now for englysh we vse & occupy
These thingis haue gyuen corage gretly
To dyuers & specyally now of late
To them that this comedy haue translate.

Which all discrete men now do besech
And specyally lernyd men to take no dysdayn
Though this be compylyd in our vulgare spech
Yet lernyng therby some men may attayn
For they that in this comedy haue take payn
Pray you to correct where faut shalbe found
And of our matter lo here is the ground.

The argument of the play follows at some length, and the prologue bows himself off to make room for the players. The translation itself is in a rough rhyming verse; perhaps a few examples of idioms and common proverbial expressions could be gleaned from it, but the only one of any interest upon which I have chanced is the following:

> Noua nunc religio in te ictec incessit
> Where dydyst all thys pope holynes fynd.[47]

Professor Bang has noted the unexplained phrase, "a tale of a rosted horse," the first examples of which in the Dictionary of the Philological Society are much later.

The verse translated in this period of confusion and disturbance, in which English poetry was beginning to stammer in the new accents of the Renaissance, was but little in comparison with the prose, but that little included Surrey's Vergil. The other translations in verse were of small importance except as they did their part toward creating a regular verse-form for the English language and as they indicated rather faintly the line which the later translators were to follow. Nearly all of the verse translations now extant, except of course the Vergil, were swept together into the *Miscellany* published by Tottel in 1557; and Wyat, Surrey, and—far behind them—Grimald are the most important translators, as well as the most important personalities in the general history of poetry during the two generations under consideration. The *Miscellany* gathered together and gave greater publicity to what was already not unknown. Unlike the prose translations, which were addressed to the large public direct, and which were too bulky to circulate widely in manuscript even if the authors desired it, the verse circulated pretty widely among a considerable group, the members of which passed manuscripts from hand to hand, and copied them freely. Thus, even after the publication of the *Miscellany,* we find evidence that the printed book was not known to all readers, even bookish readers, and that the poems were sometimes cited from manuscripts. Accordingly the date when the verses began to count in English life is rather the date of the manuscript circulation than of the printing.

Sir Thomas Wyat is of course best known as the introducer into English of the Italian conceptions of poetry which had been formed under the influence of Petrarch and maintained

---

[47]*Pope holynes,* Act iii, sc. 3; on *a tale of a rosted horse, v. Bausteine,* i (1906), p. 61.

by inferior imitators in France and Italy. He naturalized the sonnet and the ottava rima, and introduced other Italian metrical forms. With the form he naturalized the spirit; he made the conceit at home in England. He taught Surrey, and Surrey taught all the sonneteers, and especially Shakespeare, much that was good, something that was ill, but all effectively. And this vicarious glory is perhaps Wyat's best claim to remembrance—to have inspired the form and spirit of greater men who followed him. But as for the actual expression of Wyat's own genius, it is not in the sonnets but in his songs and his reflective poems, and especially in satires that it is to be found.

He was not made by nature to write of gallantry. He had not so warm a sense of womanly beauty as to bow before it with sincerity, even with imaginative sincerity; he had not the sense of the beauty of nature which could enable him to make it the gracious setting of his love; he is too serious to be an elegant trifler, and too kind to be cynical. He had not the imagination or the mastery of poetical rhetoric or rhythmic finish to give either energy or charm to the expression of passion. Hence he borrowed from his Italian masters only their faults, their tortured ingenuity of thought, their exaggeration, their thinness of ideas, and if possible made their ingenuity more ingenious, exaggerated exaggeration, and beat out the conceits which had been hammered thin into even thinner foil.[48]

There is grace and power in Wyat's songs. His psalms, though I cannot see in them the power which Miss Foxwell discovers, are dignified and sincere. But in the satires Wyat is most himself. They combine that energy, sagacity, easily carried scholarship, and gracious manner which we know from contemporary references distinguished him in real life, and correspond with the portrait of him, with countenance "stern and mild" which Surrey's pen and Holbein's pencil have left for us. The three satires are all in form (terza rima) of Italian descent, but are in substance of classic origin. The first satire "To John Poynz, *Of the mean and sure estate,*" is an adaptation of Horace's sixth satire of the second book— the story of the town mouse and the country mouse. Anno-

---

[48]Haz. War. iv, 41, 44, 45; Foxwell, A. K., *A Study of Sir Thomas Wyat's Poems* (Lond. 1911), pp. 80, 81, 87-88; Tillyard, E. N. W., *The Poetry of Sir Thomas Wyatt*, 1929.

tators have referred to a free paraphrase of this satire by Henryson as a possible source for Wyat. But a comparison shows that Wyat, to adapt the satire to his own circumstances, has represented the country mouse (a young man of good family) as going to her rich relatives (a favorite at court) to mend her own fortunes, instead of being invited by the town mouse. Neither Horace nor Henryson is copied; the poem takes its start, its spring and general idea, from Horace. The second half is Wyat's own outcry after the injustice which he had suffered. It followed his own disappointments after the downfall of the Boleyns. The end is an appropriate paraphrase of Persius.

> But to the great God, and to his high doom,
> None other pain pray I for them to be,
> But, when the rage doth lead them from the right
> That looking backward, Virtue they may see,
> Even as she is, so goodly, fair and bright;
> And whilst they clasp their lusts in arms across.
> Grant them, good Lord, as thou mayst of thy might,
> To freat inward, for losing such a loss.

The satire *To Sir Francis Bryan,* "A spending hand," is likewise a free imitation of Horace's fifth satire of the second book. These satires are favorable examples of the classic *imitatio*—the adaptation to new conditions of forms of art already developed. They are free from the servility of the herd of imitators, they are original in observation and in detail, but they gain weight from association and suggestion, and security of form from their models. In the satires Wyat, being in sympathy with his masters, and having a sincerely felt experience to communicate, is inspired by them to combine artistic form with reality of content. In the sonnets his imitation is purely superficial; there is no competition with his models, but mere subserviency to them.

In Wyat's works there are three or four reminiscences of Horace's *Odes* and of Vergil's *Aeneid.* Though not many, these reminiscences are so unforced as to make it plain that Wyat loved and remembered his boyhood studies. The "Song of Iopas" is not a translation from Vergil, but a set of verses on astronomy, developed from the song of Iopas in the *Aeneid,* the original of which has not been found. They cannot have

been composed by Wyat. The actual translations of Wyat
from sources that can be called in any way classical are con-
fined to three epigrams—poems expressing in condensed and
pregnant form serious reflections on life, akin in spirit to his
grave satires. "If thou wilt mighty be, flee from the rage"
is a combination of three "metres," the fifth, sixth, and third,
of the third book of Boethius. Miss Foxwell in her valuable
edition of Wyat, has spoken hastily of this poem as appearing
to be "*entirely* founded upon Chaucer." In Chaucer the
"metres" are in prose, with nothing distinctive about them,
while of course in the Latin they stand out on the page. Moreover, the Latin is clearer than Chaucer's version. It is impossible that Wyat should have picked out three metres from
Chaucer's third book, with nothing to direct his attention to
them, and there is nothing common to Chaucer and Wyat which
is not also in the original. The second epigram, "Stand who so
list," is from Seneca's *Thyestes*. Like the Boethius passage,
it is a dignified version of its original. In a letter to his son,
Wyat speaks of his studies in "Senec and Plato," and this epigram is a fruit of them. The third epigram is a version, somewhat expanded, of Ausonius's expansion (Bk. xix, Ep. 14) of
a Greek epigram (Anth. Pal. x, 30) appearing under the name
of Plato. It is a condensed anecdote of a man about to commit suicide with a halter, who chancing upon a treasure, left
in its place the halter, which served the need of the rightful
owner of the treasure, when he failed to find the treasure
where he had hidden it.

The little epigram has borne a much greater weight than
should have been put upon it. Inasmuch as Wyat's poem
contains the expansion of Ausonius and more, it cannot have
been translated from the Greek original, but must have been
based upon Ausonius's Latin, or upon a still later intermediary.
Moreover, the name Plato in the Anthology means little. This
trifle is certainly not very Platonic. Thus to suggest that the
great Plato had anything to do with this version, still more
that the version indicates any familiarity with Plato on the
part of Wyat, is quite unwarranted. The theme of the epigram recurs interestingly, of course, in many places; it is a
wide-spread folk tale.[49]

---

[49]*v. Heir of Linne* in *Percy's Reliques*, Ser. II, Bk. II, No. v; *cf.* Cinthio
Hecatommithi (Dec. ix, Nov. 8).

There is also an epigram, whether original with Wyat or not, based upon Josephus's story of the Jewish woman who slew and ate her child at the siege of Jerusalem.[50]   Now in commenting upon Wyat's verse, the remark is common that he was a man of learning.[51]   In point of fact, the actual contents of Wyat's poetry do not justify crediting him with any remarkable scholarship.   The reminiscences of Horace and Vergil certainly give evidence of familiarity with the originals; but the versions of isolated passages from Seneca, Boethius, and Ausonius, and the verses based upon Josephus are no proof of intimate acquaintance with the originals.   These all may have come to Wyat at second-hand.   In particular, there is nothing to show that he could read Greek.   His translation of an essay from Plutarch's *Morals,* for example, is from Latin.   It is much more important that he himself speaks of his devotion to "Senec and Plato," and that in a letter to his son he urges him to "gather an heap of good opinions [as the context proves, *sententiae*] and to get them perfectly, as it were on your finger's ends . . . . Of them of God [Scriptures] there is no question.   And it is no small help [support to the Scriptures] to them, the good opinion [wise sayings] of moral philosophers: among whom I would have Seneca your study; and Epictetus, because it is little, to be ever in your bosom."[52]   The works of Plato which would naturally accompany Seneca are *Crito,* the *Apology,* and *Phaedo,* and with them or even before them *Axiochus,* which was universally regarded as genuine; Wyat gives no evidence of being so far above English contemporaries as to enter on any wingy mysteries; but he did, like them, delight in sober moral teaching that accorded with Scripture.

The case is different with Surrey.   The very few reminiscences of classic writers which are to be found in his poems may be no more than commonplaces, which give no evidence one way or the other as to his classical reading.   *Cupid's golden and leaden arms,* out of Ovid, and the *unknown heir,* out of Horace, were part of every schoolboy's reading.   On the other hand, the translation of Vergil's *Aeneid,* Books II and

---

[50]Josephus, *Jewish War,* vi, 201-213.
[51]On Wyat's reputation for learning see Miss Foxwell's *Wyat,* vol. ii, p. xx.
[52]Wyat, Works, ed. Nott, (1816) p. 293, misprinted 275.

IV, is one of the monuments of English poetry, being fundamental as to verse-form and poetical rhetoric, including the evolution of the period, and the choice of words. The introduction of blank verse into English literature is an event of first-rate importance, justifying the most minute investigation into its details.

There has never been any serious question that Surrey in writing unrhymed ten-syllable verse was imitating Italian example; but what Italian example? Had Surrey simply caught the idea of the verse-form from one or more of the numerous Italian writers who had employed it in original works, or had some Italian translation of Vergil served him as a model? Warton and Sir Sidney Lee had supported the former view, the one suggesting Trissino, whose tragedy of *Sofonisba* was written in 1514-15 and printed in 1524, the other Alamanni, whose blank verse circulated in manuscript at Paris during Surrey's youth. Dr. Nott believed that a version of the second book ostensibly by Cardinal Hippolyto de Medici, printed first by itself in 1539, and afterwards in 1541 in a collection of versions of the first six books, had been the direct suggestion of Surrey's work. Who was right, and were there still other Italian translations to be taken into consideration? The problem was one requiring laborious attention in the minute collation of texts, and intelligence and sound judgment in estimating parallel passages, so as not to be deceived by accidental resemblances on the one hand or to miss real relationships on the other. Moreover, the second book has come down to us only in Tottel's edition of the two books, frequently reprinted; and as is well known all the early verse printed by Tottel was carefully edited to smooth out metrical irregularities, to correct syntax, to remove archaisms, and to improve expression according to the taste of the day. Hence Tottel's text has to be used with the greatest caution. For the fourth book, there are extant a separate edition printed by John Day (1554?), and a manuscript copy taken early in the reign of Elizabeth. These had to be compared in the endeavor to reach Surrey's original text as nearly as possible.

A succession of investigators took up the problem of the immediate sources of Surrey's versions from the *Aeneid*, and finally succeeded in solving it. Otto Fest, Hans Imelmann and Miss Gladys Willcock have each contributed to the study, and Professor Padelford has reviewed and summarized their results in his edition of Surrey's poems, reaching on the basis of the facts collected by Miss Willcock the same conclusions with her.[53]

The testimony of comparison shows a considerable number of close resemblances between Surrey's version of the second book and that attributed to Hippolyto. These resemblances involve deviations from the original in syntax or diction, usually slight, but sometimes quite definite; any one might be accidental, but the whole number are not likely to be so. It cannot be said that the dependence of Surrey on Hippolyto is absolutely proved, but it seems to me to be highly probable. Close scrutiny shows a number of resemblances between an Italian version of the fourth book by Nicolo Liburnio, published in 1534, and Surrey's English in the manuscript which gives the most authentic text. On the whole, then, investigation sustains the belief of Dr. Nott, that Surrey was influenced in the second book by the version which goes under the name of Hippolyto de Medici, and adds that for the fourth book he utilized Liburnio's version. There is no evidence that he read the translation of the fourth book by Bartolommeo Piccolomini which was printed in the collection of six books. There is no difficulty in point of date. The date when Surrey made his version is uncertain. It is a work evidently performed in the later part of his life, after he had acquired facility in poetical composition. There are two periods when he would seem likely to have had leisure for the work, the one within two or three years after his marriage in 1538, the other in 1544 between the two sieges of Calais and Boulogne; the latter date is supported by Fest, the former by Professor Padelford.

The Italian translator of the second book strove to hold close to his original, not expanding it, but rendering idiom for idiom, so as not servilely but accurately to give the sense of

---

[53]Fest, Otto, *Ueber Surrey's Virgilübersetzung*, etc. (Berl. 1903), in *Palaestra*, vol. 34; Imelmann, R. *Zu den Anfängen des Blankverses: Surreys Aeneis in ursprünglicher Gestalt*, in *Shakespeare-Jahrb.*, 41 (1905); Willcock, Gladys D., *A Hitherto Uncollated Version of Surrey's Translation of The Fourth Book of the Aeneid* in *Mod. Lang. Rev.* xiv (1919), p. 163; xv (1920), p. 113; xvii (1922), p. 131; Surrey, *Poems*, ed. Padelford, F. M., Univ. Washington Publications in Language and Literature, vol. v. revised edition (1928), p. 233 ff.

the Latin.   But he makes no effort to do justice to the rich and powerful diction of Vergil, commonly substituting tame literality for the imaginative single words of his original.   The following examples are fairly representative:

Infandum, regina, iubes renouare dolorem (1.3)
Tu voi ch'io rinouelli
Il *spietato* dolor, degna Reina
(Surrey: "the woe cannot be told.")

Fracti bello (1. 13) omitted
(Surrey: "all irked with the war.")

. . .   tot iam labentibus annis (1. 14)
. . .   molt' anno
(Surrey: "Wherein they wasted had so many yeres.")

Est in conspectu Tenedos (1. 21)
Giace Tenedo post *incontr'* à Troia
(Surrey: "There stands in sight an isle, hight Tenedon.")

. . .   timeo Danaos et dona ferentes (1. 49)
. . .   i *falsi* Greci io temo
Anchor ch'io veggia che n'apportin' doni
(Surrey: "I dred the Grekes; yea! when they offer gyftes!")

. . .   ficto pectore (1. 107)
. . .   con *parole* finte
(Surrey's "forged words" is close to the Italian.)

The Italian versions gave Surrey his verse-form, and the idea of modest obedience to his original. But he had another guiding help in the version of Gawain Douglas. The Scotch translator followed the usual custom of expansion in order to bolster out his rhyming couplets. His style, moreover, is homely and plain. His most interesting passages are marked by boisterous vigor, and he is most at home in fights, storms on sea or land, and the rush of streams in flood, in brief, in scenes of violent physical action. Surrey, as Dr. Nott proved,[54] was indebted to Douglas's version for a good many words scattered through his own translation, words often vigorous and appropriate; but he owes him nothing more: nothing fundamental or inspiring. Douglas is diffuse, Surrey terse; Douglas is fa-

---

[54]Nott, *op. cit.*, I, p. cciii.

miliar, Surrey dignified, Douglas is clumsy, Surrey aims at elegance, and sometimes attains it; when he fails he is stiff.

Surrey, then, owes a debt to both translations, adding something of Douglas's energy of conception to the formally more accurate Italian. He added something of his own. He strove to create a style appropriate to his lofty material in English. He had acquired a considerable facility in what may be called poetic rhetoric by his previous practice, but in the Vergil he attempts something higher. He consciously endeavored to create a heroic style and form; and so successful was he that his Vergil became a guide and support to Sackville and after him Spenser, and thus contributed to the formation of the great English style.

Nicholas Grimald is of interest to the historian of literature because in an age of transition he did first what many men came to do after him; he stands at the top of a literary watershed—not lofty but distinct. With Grimald English verse departed from the court to the schools, where it abode for a generation. The poets of his day and for ten years after him were either students or scholars, not courtiers. He replaced the Italian conventions of Wyat and Surrey by Latin conventions; he was the earliest of the English classical belles-lettrists—men to whom the classics were not primarily guides of life but models of form and sources of poetry. He first makes poems of which the entire poetical capital consists of classical allusions. Wyat has only an occasional Apollo, Venus, or Bacchus in his verse; once in a while he equips a Cupid. Surrey gives Cupid more of a place, arms him with a scourge, lets him inflict wounds, and introduces Boreas, Penelope, Iphigenia, Alexander, Caesar, Pompey, and Sardanapalus with quite individual attributes. On the whole the artificiality of these two poets, when it is present, is one of ideas; and they refer directly to the actual sensible world of experience. In Grimald's poems Daphne, Calisto, Dictynna, Adonis, and in general Ovid *quantum suff.* fill the page, and satisfy his needs of imaginative enrichment without any definite setting of actuality at all. His English poems in Tottel's *Miscellany* in the main are from the mould of the imitative neo-Latin poetry which he himself practised in the Latin language. Grimald's place, accordingly, as one of the three main contributors to

Tottel's *Miscellany,* is not accidental.   He was the most brilliant man of letters in England at the time of its publication
and led in the direction which English verse was to take in the
generation following him.

Professor H. H. Hudson of Swarthmore has shown that precisely those poems of Grimald's which have received the greatest praise for originality and imaginative vigor are translated
from the youthful Latin poems of Theodorus Beza (Théodore
de Bèze), who became in his later years the successor of Calvin as the leader of Genevan protestantism.[55]   These translations are eleven in number; all of course make use of classical
commonplaces both of allusion and of ideas, and they have the
classical merits of "terseness and distinctness" for which Professor Courthope gives Grimald credit.   Three seem to me to
filiate pretty directly from the Greek Anthology: *In praise of
measure-keeping,* (Arber's Tottel, p. 108; Beza, Elegia II.)
Description of virtue (Arber's Tottel, p. 108; Beza, Epigram
XXXI), and *Of M. T. Cicero* (Opp. Cit. p. 125; Icones).
Of the *Description of virtue* Professor Padelford says: "I
cannot discover a source for these particular symbols, though,
of course, the symbolical representation of the virtues and
vices was very common in the Middle Ages.   Cf. the descriptions in the Romant of the Rose."   The particular symbols
may have originated with Beza, but the idea of this form of
symbolism is classical.   The epigram may well have been imitated, as Professor Courthope suggests, from Ausonius's Epigram (bk. xix, ep. 33); but this is itself an imitation of a translation from the Anthology (Planudean Anth. 4, 275).

Four other poems of Grimald's also come ultimately from
the Anthology.   *Man's life after Posidonius* (*sic*: it should be
Posidippus) *or Crates* is *Anthologiae Palatinae* bk. ix, ep. 359.
This and the companion piece, *Metrodorus mind to the contrary* (Anth. Pal. IX, 360) had been translated by Erasmus.
The list of the Muses (Arber, p. 100) is slightly modified from
Anth. Pal. IX, 504.   *Cleobulus the Lydian's Riddle* (Arber
p. 102) is Anth. Pal. XIV, 101.

The late Professor G. C. Fiske called my attention to the
fact that *Musonius the Philosophers saiying* (Arber p. 101) is
from Aulus Gellius, *Noctes* XVI, 2, where a brief Greek form

---

[55]M L N, xxxix, 388 (1924).

is cited, followed by an expanded Latin version by Cato. *Marcus Catoes comparison of mans life with iron* is also from the *Noctes,* XI, 2.

Definite originals have been found for eighteen of the forty poems of Grimald in Tottel. Ten of the residue deal in a generalizing manner with classic material; and originals for them may turn up any day. The other twelve are poems of individual compliment or eulogy, most of them so essentially rhetorical, so imitative and reminiscent, that they would be little more original if assembled than if translated. An acrostic on Damascene Audley, a love-poem to the same lady, To L. I. S., the first elegy on Sir James Wilford, and—most of all—the elegy on Grimald's mother could not well have been translated. The last true and tender poem is sincerely and imaginatively grounded in life, after the artificial prologue by which Grimald strove to elevate it.

It was noted by Steevens, the Shakespearian editor, that the *Death of Zoroas,* a poem of some 115 lines in blank verse, is translated from the *Alexandreis,* written about 1200 by Philippus Gualterus de Castellione (Philip Walter of Chatillon), and Professor Merrill prints the passage followed by Grimald. The *Alexandreis* was frequently reprinted in the sixteenth century; but I cannot see anything in Grimald by which to identify the edition which he used. The other piece of blank verse is *Marcus Tullius Ciceroes Death.* Professor Berdan has recently suggested that these two pieces of Grimald's and not Surrey's translations of Vergil may be entitled to the honor of being the first blank verse in English.[56] Professor Berdan is arguing for a sceptical attitude with reference to the commonly accepted belief that blank verse was introduced by Surrey in imitation of Italian models.

"The further assumption, entirely without proof, must be made that he [Grimald] was an imitator of Surrey. In the first edition of Tottel, dated June 5, 1557, two poems by Grimald in blank verse, *The Death of Zoroas* and *Marcus Tullius Ciceroes Death* appear. Sixteen days later, Tottel published Surrey's translation of the second and fourth books of the Aeneid. Unless there be a prior issue of the Surrey [Day's edition of the fourth book almost certainly appeared in 1554],

---

[56]Merrill, *op. cit.* p. 443.

to Grimald belongs the honor of the first blank verse published
in England. But as Surrey was executed in 1547, his verse
must have been written before that date. On the other hand
Warton suggests—and the more the period is studied the
greater appears his scholarship and the little relative advance
made since his work—that Grimald's verses were prolusions or
illustrative practical specimens for our author's course of lectures in rhetoric. In that case they would have been written
between 1541 and 1547. I know no method of settling the
priority of either claimant. But until that be done, Surrey's
supposed indebtedness to the Italian merely explains half the
problem."

Now Surrey was executed in 1547 and the *Cicero* having
been taken from Beza's poems is doubtless posterior to 1548,
when they were printed. Though poems circulated freely in
manuscript, it seems unlikely that the work of the courtly
young Frenchman should have come so promptly into English
hands. Moreover the *Zoroas* must be posterior to the *Cicero*.
Nothing is more natural than that Grimald, finding in his
master Beza a striking poem on the self-sacrificing and dramatic death of a man of thought should have translated the
poem, and then finding in his reading another self-sacrificing
and dramatic death of a man of thought should have extracted
the brilliant incident from the *Alexandreis* as the material of a
second poem. On the other hand, it would have been a coinci-
dence approaching the miraculous for Grimald years before
seeing the *Cicero,* to have selected just this incident for treatment, and then to have found so pat a parallel in the author
to whom he looked for guidance in so many of his poems.
Here are the facts requisite to establish the priority of Surrey;
and the possibility that Grimald's work antedates Surrey's does
not arise to perplex the problem of the relation between English and Italian blank verse. Grimald's verse though less
beautiful than Surrey's is at all times more regular and more
skillfully patterned by means of variety of cesura and *enjambement*. It is such verse as a clever uninspired man might
well have been able to write upon the basis of Surrey's suggestions.

---

[57]Berdan, John M. *Early Tudor Poetry,* N. Y. 1920, p. 354-6.

CHAPTER III: FORMATIVE INFLUENCES
1558-1593

The third of our periods begins with the publication of the first part of Phaer's Vergil (1558); but its end is not so definite. The most important translations of the era were made by 1580, and from that time on a succession of trifles appeared, up to 1593, the year of the publication of the first of the translations of Marlowe. Perhaps the publication, in that year, of Barnabe Barnes's version of the first idyl of Moschus in *Parthenophil and Parthenope* may for the convenience of marking a definite point be taken as the end of the period. In this era the literature of delight takes precedence over the literature of instruction; and the center of interest turns from didactic essays on conduct to imaginative works dealing with adventurous and amatory subjects, whether in prose or verse. Not that the interest in ethical dissertation and history had disappeared—a fair number of moral essays were translated, and even larger and more important historical works than had appeared in the era which had just come to a close. But the emphasis, the general interest and outlook, were different.

This change in interest involves not merely the selection of new authors and books for translation, but expresses a different view about the classics from that held by the graver humanists of the earlier era. It turns to the classics for variety and excitement, for color, for the enrichment of life, and not for its guidance and restraint. The better translators wrote in that flush of joy at the revelation of the world of poetic delight which a long succession of youths, acolytes of verse, have felt first of all when Vergil's magic revealed it to their newly enlightened eyes. The imaginative ritual of Ovid's mythological story caught their minds and ordered their experience of life under forms of beauty, giving typical expression especially to the drama of love, so that there is something more than rhetoric in that full body of reminiscence which so enriches the English of the next generation,—

> . . . . In such a night . . . .
> Troilus, methinks, mounted the Trojan walls,
> And sigh'd his soul toward the Grecian tents,
> Where Cressid lay that night.
>
> In such a night,
> Did Thisbe fearfully o'ertrip the dew;
> And saw the lion's shadow ere himself,
> And ran dismay'd away.
>
> In such a night,
> Stood Dido with a willow in her hand
> Upon the wild sea banks, and waft her love
> To come again to Carthage.
>
> In such a night,
> Medea gather'd the enchanted herbs
> That did renew old Aeson.

This is not wholly serious, but neither is it wholly without seriousness. It is a playful memory of

> Such sights as youthful poets dream
> On summer eves by haunted stream.

The new translators were not in general men of affairs, like Sir Thomas Elyot, nor had they come to poetry through courtly life and the contact with foreign ideas, as had Wyat and Surrey, but they were from the schools. They were students, young professional men, enthusiastic for letters, or elder pedants, with the dry and warped interest in crochets which marks the tribe.

It was of course to Latin authors that the translators turned, and first of all to the poet-narrators consecrated by long tradition—to Vergil and Ovid, the beloved story-tellers of the schools, and to Seneca, whose name had been consecrated during the Middle Ages like the names of Vergil and Statius by his supposed contact with Christianity. From Ovid to the late Greek writers of amatory romances was a natural step; the French had set the example of taking it, and had given translations which the English writers could exploit. And finally there were versions of epigrams from the Anthology, from Martial, and from Ausonius, and of a few pastorals, also under the leading of the French. The interest in post-classical verse

was new in English literature. Some hint of the interest in
Vergil, Ovid, and the epigrammatists had already been given.
Surrey had translated two books of the *Aeneid;* Chaloner tried
an epistle from the *Heroides* and a fragment of the *Metamorphoses,* and there were a few epigrams in Tottel.

The new age ventured on long books and kept at them until
they were finished. Surrey had been unable to do more than
give a sample of Vergil; Phaer never abandoned his labors on
the *Aeneid,* working hastily indeed, and only at intervals of
leisure, but persistently, until he had translated more than nine
books; and the work left incomplete at his death was carried
through by his friend, Thomas Twyne. The *Eclogues* and
Georgics followed by other hands. Golding began with the
Metamorphoses in 1564 and did not finish till 1567. Turbervile
completed the *Heroides.* Seneca occupied the leisure of a
group of translators until all his plays were extant in English.
The new translators brought to completion ample works of
history, working boldly and steadily until they finished the
known works of Livy, Caesar's *Gallic War,* Diodorus Siculus,
Aelian, Appian, and Plutarch's *Lives.* The most extraordinary
single achievement was the translation of the whole of Euclid's
Elements, done direct from the Greek, and by a man who later
became the Lord Mayor of London.

To speak first of the verse. It is a commonplace that Vergil
was the leading classic poet of that age, as he had been
throughout the medieval period. He was studied in early
youth; he was consecrated by unbroken tradition; he was at
once known, loved, and honored above every other poet. At
the head of the translations of the day, by common consent,
stood Phaer's *Aeneid.* Thomas Phaer, first a student of the
law and then a physician, was blamed by his friends for his
too discursive mind and scattered interests. There was certainly a cultivated amateurishness about everything he did.
In his dedication to Queen Mary, in whose service he had
been, he lets his readers know that the translation had been the
pastime of his vacations; and he notes at the end of the book the
number of days actually spent upon the work. They were not
many, and at first, especially, too few;—two hundred and two
days for nine books. The first seven books were printed in
1558; the first nine books and part of the tenth in 1562. Phaer,

as we learn from the dedication of the 1562 edition by William Wightman to Sir Nicholas Bacon, meant to revise his work and dedicate it to Sir Nicholas; but he was cut off by death. Eleven years later (1573) Phaer's work was reprinted, the rest of the *Aeneid* being added by Thomas Twyne, and after another eleven years (1584) the joint translation was again printed, with the addition of a translation by Twyne of Mapheius Vegius's "thirteenth book." The later editions follow the 1584 copy. All the editions were accompanied by notes and arguments, and Twyne added Donatus's life of Vergil.

Phaer's conclusion contains the first suggestion of "defense" of the English language, the word and the idea both, of course, coming from the French Renaissance.

> Thus far fourth good readers, as well for defence of my countrey language (whiche I haue heard discommended of many, and estemyd of some to be more then barbarous) as also for honest recreation of you the nobilitie, gentelmen and Ladies, that studie not Latine, I haue taken some trauayle to expresse this most excellente writer, as farre as my simple abilitie extended. And if God sende me life and leisoure, I purpose to set forthe the reste, vnlesse it maie like some other that is better armed with learning, to preuente my labours, whereof I assure you, I woulde be righte gladde, contentyng my self sufficiently with this, that by me firste this gate is sette open. If now the yong writers will vouchesafe to enter; they may finde in this language, both large and aboundant Campes of varietie, wherein they maie gather innumerable sortes of most beautifull floures, figures, and phrases, not onely to supplie the imperfection of me: but also to garnishe al kindes of their owne verses with a more cleane and compendious order of meter then heretofore commonly hath ben accustomed. . . . (Text of 1558)

Phaer's Vergil is the most considerable of the enterprises in its field, but it is typical of them all. It is, in the first place, a tentative work. There were no masterpieces to suggest the possibilities of the language, or to create any standard of style. There was no abundant body of metrical achievement to guide the translator to a worthy form. The time was not ripe for the assimilation of those literary qualities which are preëminently classic: proportion, measure, the harmonious relation of substance to expression, in a word of high literary unity,—unity of outline, of texture, or of style,—the blossoming of thought into form.   All that the writers of the day could give was a rough and boisterous expression of the rich and varied substance of classic story.   This they perceived, and this they communicated, like eager amateurs, as they were.

The translator, in the time of Phaer, had first of all to decide on a verse-form.   He had no tradition to guide him, and the experiments already made were not decisive.   Should the translator of Vergil's or Ovid's hexameters make use of quantitative hexameters, as Ascham had somewhat vacillatingly suggested, or of Alexandrines, like some of Grimald's, or of the unrhymed ten-syllable line which has since become our standard "blank verse," as Surrey and Grimald had done in their experiments, or of the heroic couplet, like Gawain Douglas, or of stanzas, like Burgh, or finally of the long line, the fourteener, then the most steadily approved by long tradition in English? Experiments were tried in every form, but the great number, and the most successful, of the translations were in the fourteen-syllable line, the meter of Phaer and Golding and Chapman's *Iliad*.

The fourteen-syllable line is our most ancient meter, and seemed in the middle of the sixteenth century the most natural one.   It is the meter of Orm, of Robert of Gloucester, and of the ballads, and it is the "common meter" of hymns.

> An other kynd next in length to thys [sixteen-syllable verse], is, where eche verse hath fourteene syllables, which is the most accustomed of all other, and especially vsed of all the translatours of the Latine Poets for the most part thus.

> My mind with furye fierce inflamde of late—I know not howe, Doth burne Parnassus hyll to see, adorned wyth Lawrell bowe.

> Which may likewyse [as the sixteen-syllable verse into equal parts] and so it often is deuyded, eche verse into two, to [Arber conj. *the*] first hauing eyght sillables, the second sixe, whereof the two sixes shall alwayes ryme, and sometimes the eyghtes, sometimes not, according to the wyll of the maker.

> > My minde with furye fierce inflamde,
> >   Of late I knowe not howe:
> > Doth burne *Pernassus* hyll to see,
> >   Adornd wyth Lawrell bowe.[1]

----

[1]Webbe, W., *A Discourse of English Poetrie*, ed. Arber (English Reprints, No. 26, 1870) p. 59.

The verse, as Webbe says, is nearly always broken by a pause after the eighth syllable, and without that pause tends to become too indistinct to be recognized. In a long poem, therefore, the verse is likely to be monotonous if the pause is strictly observed, and clumsy if the pause is neglected, so that the translations which excited so much enthusiasm in the days of Webbe are pretty hard going for a modern reader. All translations require some padding, especially if they are in rhyme; but the fourteener is especially liable to dilution, the shortness of English words making it difficult to fill fourteen syllables with the material of one classic line. In expository passages, it is difficult to keep the fourteener from prosaic commonness, not to say from doggerel jog-trot, as in any page of the sober-minded writers of the first part of the reign of Elizabeth. The verse can be noble and moving, as in South-well's *Burning Babe;* but it cannot fall from this height without flatness, and hence is most effective in short lyrics. The verse can be tender, as in a number of ballads, but again lacks flexibility in changing its mood, and therefore in gentle as in noble emotion is best suited for lyric composition. Its characteristic is motion; its special quality is energy. A story of action can be told vividly and forcibly in this meter; Keats touched its quality when he tells how he heard

> Chapman speak out loud and bold.

Whatever obscurity or excessive ingenuity of phrase there may be in these Elizabethan narratives, they let you know what happened. Phaer's best is not good; at most it gives hope and promise of something better. Still, suppose that one knows no Latin, and has heard no English blank verse, and an active passage in Phaer may speak to him with no little power.

> There Hecuba and her doughters all (poor soules) at the altars side
> In heapes together affrayèd them drew, like doues whèn doth betide
> Some storme them headlong driue, and clipping fast their gods did
>   hold,
> But when syre *Priam* thus beclad in armes of youth so bold
> Espied: what made alas (quoth she) O wofull husband you
> In harness dight: and whither away with weapons run ye now?
> Not men nor weapons vs can saue: this time doth axe to beare
> No such defence, no not if Hector mine now present were.
> Stand here by me, this alter vs from slaughter all shal shelde,
> Or die together at ones we shall. So said she, and gan to welde

Him aged man, and in the sacred seate Him set, and helde.
Behold where scaping from the stroke of *Pirrhus* fiers in fight
Polites, one of *Priam's* sonnes, through foes and weapons pight,
Through galleries along doth run, and wide about him spies
Sore wounded than, but *Pirrhus* after him sues with burning eyes
In chase, and now welneare in hand him caught and held with spere,
Til right before his parents sight he came, then feld him there
To death, and with his gushing blood his life outright he shed.[2]

It will be noted that in this passage the pause is absent in
several lines, and uncertain in some others; though the general tendency is to set off the eights and the sixes. This metrical freedom is characteristic of Phaer, who thus departs
from the tradition of the form.

There is a hill whan out the towne ye come, and temple old
Of *Ceres* long vnused, there beside ye shall behold
An auncient *Cipers* tree to grow, that for religions sake
Our fathers there did set, and there long time did honor make.
In that place out of diuers waies we all shall seeke to meete.
You father take your countrey gods in hand, our comfort sweete.
For mee, that from the battels fresh am come and slaughters new,
I may not them presume to touche, till waters drew
With floods hath washt me pure.
Thus said I, and on my shoulders broad and thwart my necke I kest
A weede, and in a lions skin full read my selfe I drest.
And vnder burden fast I fled, my child my right hand kept
Iule, and after mee, with pace vnlike in length, he stept.
My wife ensued, through lanes and crookes and darknes most we past.
And mee, that late no shouts, nor cries, nor noyes, nor wepons cast
Could feare, nor clusters great of *Greeks* in throngs agast could make
Now euery winde and puffe doth moue, at euery sound I quake,
Not for my selfe, but for my mate, and for my burdens sake.
And now against the gates I came, which out of danger found,
I thought I well escaped had, when suddenly the sound
Of feete we heare to tread, and men full thicke my father scared.
Flee flee my son (he cried) loe here they come, loe here at hand,
Their harness bright appeares, and glistring sheeldes I see to shine.
There what it was I not, some chaunce or God (no friend of mine)
Amazed than my wit, for while through thick and thin I pas,
And from the accustomed waies I drew to seke to skape (alas)
My wife from mee most woefull man *Creusa* beloued best,
(Remaine she did, or lost her way, or sat her downe to rest,
Vnknowen it is) but after that in vaine her all we sought,
Nor of her losse I knew, nor back I looked or bethought:
Till vnto *Ceres* temple old and auncient seate, each one

[2]Sig. Dii *v.,* edition of 1584 (one of the most clearly printed).

Was come, and there togethers met we all, but shee alone
Did lacke, and there her friends and childe, and husband did beguile.[3]

Dr. E. J. W. Brenner,[4] in his minute examination of Phaer's style, finds it marked by expansion and generalization, and deficient in elevation, plastic imagination, and rhetorical resourcefulness. All these comments are just, as the passages cited abundantly show. Phaer seldom fails to get the general meaning of his original; but his diction practically always misses the definiteness of Vergil, especially in passages having to do with physical impressions. Thus he is commonplace in thought and vision. In language, he permits himself the use of colloquialisms which are seldom out and out vulgar, but which are mean and unworthy. For example:

> . . . . it lose from ground
> We shogd, and with the shog for heft, with ratling noyse and fall
> Down ouer along the *Greekes* it light . . . [D ii *recto*]
>   . . . other vpsteps . . .
> With bounsing thick and larums lowd   [Dii *recto*]
>   . . . . twibles tall
> To grub . . . .   [D iv *recto*]
>   Within my parlour flores
> Mine enmies I must see to kill my folkes within my dores?
>   [D iv *recto*]
> My child Iule shall go, my wife shall trail aloof behinde.
> You seruantes what I say take heede, imprint it well in minde.
>   [D v *recto*]
>   . . . trembling wiues in long aray
> Were stowed about and wept.   [D vi *recto*]
> Polidore of[f] chops   [D viii *recto*]
> And *Coribantes* beat their brasse the moone from clips to cure.
>   [E i *recto*]

Phaer in all his defects is typical of his age; he is in fact more dignified and effective than most of his contemporaries.

Twyne's continuation lacks even the moderate fluency of Phaer's verse, and is more clumsy in the structure of the sentences.

---

[3]Sig. D(v).

[4]*Thomas Phaer, mit besonderer Berücksichtigung seiner Aeneis Uebersetzung etc.* in *Wurzburger Beitr. zur englischen Literaturgeschichte.* (Heidelberg, 1893).

They blow alarme. *Aeneas* first the rusticke sort sets on
For happy hansils sake, and Latines layes the ground upon.
[P vi recto]
. . . Sir Tarquitus . . .
Whom *Driope Nimphe* sumtyme had borne to *Faunus* siluane god,
With him thus raging meetes, who with his lance in length full od
His breastplate, and his shield of hugie weight he breakes in twaine.
[Q i recto]
And thoundre out thy twatling talke [R iii *recto*]
And *Rutils* run amoapt. [S ii *verso*]
Forth his vease he fet withal [T vjii *verso*]

Phaer's version is the sincere work of a superficial and hasty
dilettante, who though he lacked talent, had the honest purpose
of interpreting his author without uncouth pedantry and without the desire to exploit fantastic theories.

About him there gathered a rout of pedantic experimenters—
Fleming and Fraunce and Stanyhurst—who made Vergil the
victim of their misdirected zeal. Stanyhurst is the best known,
and legitimately so, for he is the most energetic and assertive
of them all, the most eccentric and the most grotesque. Fleming is perhaps the most gently and stupidly pedantic.

Abraham Fleming published a translation of the *Bucolics* in
1575, "which labour I attempted, partly for my priuate practise (vsing it as a perseruative against idlenes [Elizabethan
translators greatly feared this vice] rather than a preparatiue
to gaine and profit) & partly for the benefit of young learners
of the latine tongue." This version is in the fourteener couplet.
In 1589 he published a version of the *Bucolics* and the *Georgics*
together, though with separate title-pages, in unrhymed fourteener. Each of the translations is dedicated to Archbishop
Whitgift.

At the end of the *Bucolics* Fleming gives the following statement of his purpose, and defense of his methods:

> Now, forsomuch as there be three kinds of writing or speaking
> by art (according to *Tullie*) the first homelie and base, the second
> meane and indifferent, the third statelie and aloft; the poet therefore
> very aptly doubtlesse hath vsed these three kinds of art: for his
> Pastoralls are written in a base, his ruralls in a meane, and his
> Martialls in the loftie style. Wherfore such as meane to be acquainted
> with poetrie, let them begin with these Pastoralls, as the *Italians*
> doo, whose youths or Grammar boyes doo learn these said Pastoralls
> perfectly, and thereby prooue learned youngmen, wittie and rare

poets, deintie in deuise, abounding in matter, neat in words, and curious in order. As for the fondlings of our time, they make it a heinous matter to meddle with poetrie at all; without the which I am of opinion (let who list thinke I mainteine a paradox) none can become learned indeed; none can vnderstand these ancient diuines, diuines I call them, and I wot well why; none can avoid offence in pronunciation &c: they that know anything will confesse no lesse than I say.

Wherfore I, for the profit and furtherance of English youthe, desirous to learne, and delighted in poetrie, haue (by the gracious assistance of almightie God, from whom euery good gift procedeth, & without whom we can doo nothing (no not in meere naturall actions) assaid, trauersd, and finished the translations of Virgils Bukoliks or Pastoralls, not in foolish rime (the nise obseruation whereof many times darkeneth, corrupteth, peruerteth, and falsifieth both the sense and the signification) but in due proportion and measure; plaine I confesse, and easie withall (for so I desired and stroue with my wits to answer my will) that yoong Grammar boyes, may euen without a schoolemaster teach themselues by the helpe hereof. For these Pastoralls (the beginning of Poetrie) being vnderstood and learned, the entrance and proceeding in greater matters will haue the lesse hardnesse. As for enuie, I defie it; and to findfaults I wish silence, whose only worke it is to barke at other mens painful labours, themselues in the meane season more barren than ferne, and bringing foorth nothing (if at any time they fall in trauel) but what they are conceiued withall by the vse of other mens books; and (which is a fawlt vnsufferable and ouersawcie) they read and learne nothing but what they can controll, and cannot correct, whom I haue sowsed in their follie, or rather malice, as men vtterly vnworthie of the words already written; of more, amending their maners but first renewing their mind, which is the worke of Gods onely spirit obteined by praier, the meane wherby Gods maiestie will vouchsafe to stoope & talke with the vilenesse of mankind, and graunt their petitions that pray in true beleefe, which he giue vs that made vs. Amen.

In the dedication to the *Georgics* Fleming again shows his angry uneasiness under criticism:

The translators intent considered (namely to do some good for Grammar schools) the lesse checke should redound to this honest and painefull translation . . . . For mine owne part as I set light by the foule mouth of the one, so I passe not for pleasing the fine ear of the other . . . .

In the address to the reader Fleming makes plain that his main object in the translation is to give assistance to school-boys;

and it is of course unfair to expect that a translation written with such an object should have any high merit.

> The translators meaning is, when occasion serueth, to make this interpretation of his run in round rime, as it standeth now vpon bare metre; partly to discharge his sufficiencie, and partly to please the readers fantasie: desiring them to beare with such shifts as they shall bee vsed here and there for the conveiance of the poets sense in plaine words applied to blunt capacities, considering the expositors drift to consist in deliuering a direct order of construction for the releefe of weake Grammatists, not in attempting by curious deuise and disposition, to content courtly Humanists, whose desire he hath been at this time to suspend, because he would in some sort satisfie such as need the supplie of his trauell, remembering the old metricall prouerbe, *Deficit ambobus, qui vult seruire duobus.* Elisions are sometimes vsed, so are sections or diuisions of whole words in the conclusion of a verse and line; which being ordinarie among Latine poets, is the more sufferable in English, how vnsweet a sound so euer they seeme to make in the eare.

How unsweet a sound they make in the ear!

> His wife also refreshing hir long labour with a song,
> In the meane-time runs through hir web with whurling shuttle
> [swift][5]
>
> Or els she boils with fire the li-quor of sweet must [new wine]
> And skums away with leaues the run- ning ouer of the brazen kettle
> lukewarme [on the fire seething a gentle pase].[6]
>
> .   .   .   .
>
> Oft haue I seene the battels all of windes to run together,
> When as the husbandman should bring a reaper to the yellow fields
> [in haruest when the winds annoy the ripened corne].[7]
>
> And enter thou the way of te- ming them, whiles that the natures of
> the yoonglings gentle be, and trainable their age.[8]

But such extreme liberties in dividing words are rare. Though it is difficult to perceive that the pause is really a fact in the structure of the verse, there is a hyphen in every word that straddles the fourth and fifth feet.

The following passage is better than most of the work of Fleming:

---

[5]Square brackets are used by Fleming to indicate a word not in Vergil.
[6]Georgics, bk. i, p. 11.
[7]*Ibid.*
[8]Georgics, Bk. iii, p. 42.

The boies saw *Silen* lie asleepe in caue, his veins puft vp
With [swilling] wine but yesterday, as alwaies he is woont,
His garlands only fallen from his head did lie far off,
And neere him hoong a mightie kan with eare [or handle] worne,
These boies setting on *Silen* cast vpon him binding bands,
Made of the very garlands, for old *Silen* oftentimes
Had both these boies beguiled with [vaine] hope of [promis'd] song,
Aegle the fair'st of waternymphs hir self companion ioind,
And cometh in the nicke [to helpe and succour] them afraid.
Aegle she paints old *Silens* browes, and temples of his head,
With bloudie [colour] mulberries, he being now awake,
And laughing at the subtill iest said [to them] To what end
Knit you these knots and bands! O boies loose me, it is ynough
That you haue beene seene of you [being seene but when I list:]
Know sons of me now what you will, songs to you [I will sing]
[But] to this *Aegle* shallbe [giuen] another [due] reward.[9]

The following extract more fairly represents the average
of his achievement:

And when as *Proteus* went away out of the floodes, going
Vnto his woonted caues: the wa- terish nation [tribes] of
The sea so huge leaping and skip- ping sprinckled far about
Him bitter dew [sea water which is bitter in the taste:]
And sundry sea calues lay themselues along vpon the shore
A sleepe [For as they vse the sea, so doo they haunt the land]
Then [Proteus he] himselfe sat downe full in the midst [of his
Great troopes of fishes] on a rocke, and reckons them by number:
Euen as the keeper of a herd sometime dooth count [his beastes]
Vpon the hills, when th'euening star dooth bring the bullock home
Vnto the house from feeding, and when lambs being heard of wolues
Doo whet or set their teeth on edge with bleatings [that they make].[10]

The only challenge to Phaer's place as the translator of Vergil during the century came from Richard Stanyhurst—one of
the Englishry in Ireland, a man of important family connections who became a Roman Catholic, apparently under the influence of Campion, and who printed in Holland, whither he
had gone into exile, his famous version of the first four books
of the *Aeneid,* with a fragment of the eighth. This, the first
edition, appeared in 1582; a second edition was printed in London in 1583.

The completeness of Stanyhurst's genius for being absurd
and the bustling self-assertion that caused his absurdity to be

[9]Eclogue vi, p. 17.
[10]Bucolics, Bk. iv, p. 71.

conspicuous have made the comments of the critics from Thomas Nash to Mr. Whibley one long competition in the rhetoric of ridicule. The rhetoric is brilliant; Stanyhurst had a power of kindling men by contraries. But merely to cite Stanyhurst is enough. The humorous roar of Nash and the witty comment of Hall are pale beside the absurdity of the translator himself. Irishmen are charged with absurdity, but the first historical examples come from the Englishry of Ireland more than from its Irishry; and Stanyhurst is the supreme example.

Venus, while addressing Jupiter on behalf of Aeneas, her child, asks:

What sin hath Aeneas, my brat, committed against the?

and is favorably answered:

Thee prince of mankind, father of Gods, mirrelye simpring,

. . . .

Bust his pretty parat prating.

Phisnomye is a favorite word (Stanyhurst is short of dactyls). Jove calms the tempest with *cheerful phisnomye,* Sichaeus' ghost appears with *pale wan phisnomye staring,* Dido has a *down cast phisnomye.* Cupid takes the *phisnomye* of Ascanius; Dido *thrusts in couch her phisnomye cheerless;* Aeneas fears that tears *shal bayne his phisnomye deeply;* the Trojans have a staring *phisnomye.*

The caitif Trojans are "with storms ventosity mangled." The south wind is a "sootherne swashruter huffling." Cupid is "cockney Cupido"; Queen Dido falls to him and "smackly bebasse him," and "lyplicks sweetlye she fastneth." The queen could not die: "Proserpina would not . . . her ding to damnable Orcus"; but "Rainebow" "snipt'" her locks; and her "liefe too windpuf auoyded."

Dido, when she sees Aeneas departing, cries: "Shall a stranger giue me the slampam?" The Trojan horse when struck resounds "with clish clash busing." Jove sometimes clattereth a clapping firebolt to the ground "with rownce robel hobble," with the sound of thunder—

Of ruffe raffe roaring, mens herts with terror agrysing,
With peale meale ramping, with thwick thwack sturdelye thundring.

Cupid playing Ascanius's part is a "dandiprat" and a "princox."

What *ruter* of Dolopanes?—What *karne* of canckred Vlisses?—*blind hodipecks*—*kim kam* sectes—*luskish* approaching—a *doly* chance.

Pack, trudge, tug, cog, frisk, flounce are favorite words. Dido goes to *church;* the priest carries holy *relics;* Priam bootless belted *Morglay* to his sides.

The object of Stanyhurst was to set the example of an extended piece of work in classic meter in English, as he says to his brother-in-law Lord Dunsany in his dedicatory letter.

> Hauing taken vpon mee to execute soom part of master Ascham his wyl, who in his goulden pamphlet intituled *thee Schoolemayster,* dooth wish thee Vniuersitie students too applie theyre wittes in bewtifying oure English language with heroicall verses: I held no *Latinist* so fit, too geeue the onset on, as *Virgil,* who for his peerelesse style, and machlesse stuffe, doth beare the prick and price among al the Roman poets.

The principles upon which Stanyhurst in common with his contemporaries constructed his quantitative verses are simple. In the first place, he strove, not quite successfully, to be thoroughgoing and entirely consistent; his intent was to write verse truly quantitative, not accentual. His first difficulty was the temptation to be guided by the Latin derivation in his judgment of English quantity; but of this danger he was aware, and he succeeded in avoiding it. But his distinctions of long and short are simply those of the Latin which he was adapting to English usage. They seemed to him to be founded on the realities of pronunciation. Vowels long by nature and diphthongs were of course long. Length by position was as important: a syllable formed when a vowel, long or short, is followed by two consonants is a long syllable. Thus *if, in,* and *of* are long when followed by words beginning with a consonant. Short syllables are formed by short vowels followed by single consonants. Final vowels Stanyhurst regarded as in general common, that is, as capable of being uttered abruptly or with extension.

In towne/ you deni/ sons I do/ make let/ nauye be/ docked/

---

[11]From the address *To the learned reader*, prefixed to his translation.

Serious modern efforts in this kind are not thoroughgoing.
Most are purely accentual. Such works are embarrassed by
the difficulty of finding English words with approximately
equal stress on two successive syllables, "spondees," as they
call them. Some writers pay some attention to quantity, without making it fundamental. For example, in the hexameters
of Coleridge, praised by Swinburne, and beginning:

Earth thou/ mother of/ numberless/ children the/nurse and the/
mother/,

even an untrained ear cannot fail to hear the last syllable of
numberless as long. *Of* is not so clear. In truth, the Elizabethans were embarrassed not by excess of dactyls, but by excess of spondees. In point of fact, nearly all syllables in English are long. Our vowels, even our "short" vowels, are nearly all diphthongal, especially in open syllables. In closed syllables, the concluding consonant tends to be spoken with the
preceding vowel as well as with the succeeding one, and pro
duces length by position. Hear a Frenchman say *agilité* and
an Englishman say *agility*. The Englishman's first and second syllables are certainly long: his *g* is two consonants in itself, and his *i* and his *l* are united by a glide. His *y* may be
long or short. Stanyhurst in his preface lays down certain
principles which display some acuteness of observation. Final
vowels are all common; final closed syllables are all short, except those ending in *c* and *k,* and in *As, Es,* and *Os.*

> *Moother* I make long. Yet *groundmoother* most be short. *Buckler*
> is long; yet *swashbuckler* is short. And albeyt that word bee long
> by *position,* yeet doubtlesse thee natural dialect of English wyl not
> allow of that rule [i.e. of length by position] in middle syllables,
> but yet must bee of force with vs excepted, where the natural pro-
> nunciation wyl so haue yt. For otherwise wee should bannish a
> number of good and necessarye wordes from oure verses. [Certainly
> this admission gives up the case; it is a practical admission that
> quantitative verses cannot be written in English.] And soothly too
> my seeming, yf the conjunction, *And,* were common in English, yt
> were not amisse although yt bee long by *position.*

It is difficult to select from Stanyhurst a passage in which
the eccentricity of the diction does not attract the attention so

much that it is hard to keep the mind on the meter solely.   But try the following lines :

1   When that he/ percea/ued thee/ coast to be/ cleere, then he/ summond
Oure men/ too ship/board, thee/ camp we/ swiftly re/mooued
Foorth we take/ oure pass/adge, oure/ sayles ful/winged vp-/ hoysting
Thee stars/ are darck/ned, glitt/ring Au/rora re/shined

5   Wee do se/ swart moun/tayns, we doe/ gaze eke at/ Italye/ dymmed.
Italye/ loa yoon/der, first/, Italye,/ shouted A/ chates
Italye/ land na/ming, lyke/wise thee/ coompanye/ greeted.[12]

Attention is given to quantity by position throughout: the final *-ed* in *perceaued,* 1.1, and *darckned,* 1.5, are long.   *We* is long before *swiftly,* 1.2, short before *take,* 1.3.   Some syllables are certainly long by nature: loa, 1.7.   But in the main the variations permitted are purely conventional, and destroy any naturalness of expression.   The treatment of final vowels is an example: "*E* common: yf yt bee short, I vvryte yt vsualy vvith a single E.   as *the, me.* yf long vvith tvvo, as *thee, mee.*" *Wee do se,* 1.6, is accordingly a good dactyl, though the abused English language cries out that *se* must be long.   The truth is, that with the best of will, and in spite of an occasional illumination, Stanyhurst could not hear quantity.   His longs and shorts are longs and shorts to the eye and not to the ear.   It is true that he enters his caveat against misinterpreting his spelling; . . . "althogh I vvould not vvish thee quantities of syllables too depend so much vpon the gaze of thee eye, as thee censure of the eare"; . . . yet in practise *the* (article or pronoun), *we, be, to,* even *a,* are short or long not because they are really spoken short or long, but as they are spelled.   If Stanyhurst had really heard quantity, soft *g* would of course have always made position; it is spelled as one letter, but it represents two consonantal sounds.   But *g* in Stanyhurst usually does *not* make position, but may be made to do so, in which case *d* is written in; . . . "soomtyme long by position vvhere D may be enterserted, as *passage* is short, but yf you make it long, *passadge* vvith D would be written, albeyt, as I sayd right novv, the eare not ortographie must decide thee quantitye, as neere as is pos-

---

sible." It was not at all possible for Stanyhurst, as the quotation makes evident. It was to the eye, not the ear, that he appealed, as is shown by his monstrous spellings of *huge* as *hudge,* age as *adge* (*adgemate*), in order to make the syllables long.

Attempts have been made, with little success, to ascertain Stanyhurst's pronunciation from his spelling, which is peculiar, and evidently deliberate. His diction has some value to the lexicographer, for some of his vulgar words are provincial, and supplement the dialect dictionaries; but the body of his odd vocabulary throws light only on itself. But his proverbial expressions are of more importance. Professor Arber collected some thirty in turning over only a few pages;—"wild as a march hare,"—"cock sure,"—"not worth a bean,"—"hit the nail on the head,"—"certain for knauerie to purchas a Tyburne," —"blind bayards."[13]

A milder eccentric, a child of "gentle Dulness," is Abraham Fraunce (the second Abraham-man of poetry!). Abraham Fleming offered his dreadful version of the *Eclogues* and the *Georgics* to poor schoolboys as a specimen of the "plain style"; Abraham Fraunce made the debates of the shepherds a vehicle for the principles of Ramus's logic. Ramus had enlivened and illustrated his logic by applying it to Ovid's *Epistles;* Fraunce began his experiments by similarly applying the logic to pastoral poetry, including the new poetry of the day, namely, the *Shepherd's Calendar.* When he determined on the law as a profession, he applied his logic to his cases; and then in making up his book on *Lawier's Logike* he used some of his "old examples." One of these is a version of the *Alexis,* Vergil's second eclogue. The version is in English quantitative hexameters, verse for verse, and is evidently a contribution to the experiment in classic meters made by the Cambridge group of which Spenser was a member and Fraunce a younger satellite. *Lawier's Logike* appeared in 1588; and in 1591 Fraunce used the translation of the *Alexis* again, in *The Countess of Pembroke's Ivy-Church.*

Lawier's Logike brings the *Alexis* into quaint company:

I haue for example sake, put downe a Logicall Analysis of the second Aegloge in Virgill, of the Earl of Northumberlands case in

---

[13]Arber, p. xxiv.

Maister Plowdens reportes, and of Sir William Stamfords crown pleas. For the Aeglogue although the verses of Virgill be better known in Latine than I can make them vnderstoode in English (especially obseruing the same order of verse) yet I haue attempted the interpreting of the same by a poeticall *Paraphrasis,* for the contentation of such as vnderstand no Latine: & withall inserted the Latyne verses, for their pleasure, that disdayne the English.[14]

The Ivy Church is largely made up of material which had already been printed: paraphrases in English quantitative hexameters of Tasso's pastoral comedy *Aminta,* of Thomas Watson's pastoral elegy on the same subject, and of the *Alexis.* A few lines from the beginning of Heliodorus's *Aethiopica* in the same meter are added, from Underdowne's English. Fraunce's hexameters are not disfigured by eccentricities of diction, and move more rapidly and smoothly than Stanyhurst's; but they are utterly weak.

O let this be thy will, to frequent my rustical labours,
And simple cotages, sticking in forcks to vphould them,
And driue on forward our flock of Kidds to the mallowes.
We wil amidst wylde woods contend *Pans* song to resemble;
Pan is good to the sheepe, and *Pan* is good to the sheepesman.

The passage from Heliodorus is an exercise in the most insipid verbal rhetoric:

But, good God, what a sight, what a strange sight, yea what a sweet sight,
And yet a woeful sight to the theeues vnlookt for appeared?
There was a maide so made, as men might thinck her a Goddesse,
There was a sweete-fac't maide, that sate on a rock by the sea-shore,
Sate on a rock full sad to behold this desperat outrage,
Sad, yet not dismaid to behold this desperat outrage,
For that a maiden's face was there well matcht with a mans-hart.
Lawrel crowned her head, but her head gaue grace to the lawrell:
Left hand arm'd with a bow, and back with a quyuer adorned,
Right hand held vp her head; her thye was a stay to the right hand:
Head neuer mouing, eyes euer fixed on one thing,
Fixed on one yong man sore wounded by the sea-shore.

William Webbe's *Discourse of English Poetrie* bears witness to the confusion of mind and to the seeking for a standard in this era. He has the sense of poetry to welcome the *New*

---

[14]Fo. 120 *v*.

Poet, to be finely enthusiastic about the new formative poem which at last found the way; but he is blind to the gradual but certain formation of a definite norm of meter established by Grimald, Gascoigne, Sackville, Turbervile, and Spenser himself. He still had faith in the adaptation of classic meters:

> I am fullie and certainlie perswaded, that if the true kind of versifying in imitation of Greekes and Latines, had been practised in the English tongue, and put in vre from time to tyme by our Poets, who might haue continually beene mending and pollyshing the same, euery one according to their seuerall giftes: it would long ere this haue aspyred to as full perfection, as in anie other tongue whatsoeuer. . . . I my selfe with simple skyll I confesse, and farre vnable iudgment, haue ventured on a fewe [classical verses], which notwithstanding the rudeness of them may serue to shewe what better might bee brought into our speeche, if those who are of meete abilitye would bestowe some trauell and endeuour thereuppon.[15]

The experimental verses are the first two eclogues of Vergil. Webbe gives some of his rules for quantity. In the main he strives to follow actual English practice; but he in effect gives up his case from the first. He recognizes the fundamental difficulty.

> For indeede excepting a fewe, of our Monasyllables, which naturally shoulde most of them be long, we haue almost none, that wyll stande fitlie in a short foote: and therfore if some exception were made against the precise obseruation of *Position,* and certain other of the rules, then might we haue as great plenty and choyse of good woordes to furnish and sette foorth a verse, as in any other tongue.

In other words, since classical rules will not work in English, abandon them.

> Indeede most of our Monasyllables I am forced to make short [contrary to what he has said with truth as to the nature of English] to supply the want of many short words requisite in these verses. [More accurately than Stanyhurst] The particle *A,* being but the English article adioyned to Nounes, I always make short, both alone and in composition, and likewise the wordes of one sillable ending in *E,* as *the* when it is an article, *he, she, ye,* etc. *we* I thinke should needes be alwayes long because we pronounce continually *VVe. I,* beeing alone standing for the Pronowne *Ego,* in my iudgment might well be vsed common; but because I neuer sawe it vsed but short I so obserued it . . . The myddle sillables which are not very many,

---

[15]Edition of 1586, in Arber's *English Reprints,* no. 26 (1870), pp. 70-71.

come for the most part vnder the precinct of *Position,* whereof some
of them will not possibly abide the touch, and therfore must needes
be a little wrested: such are commonly the aduerbs of three sillables,
as *mournfully, spyghtfully* and such like words, deriued of this
adiectiue, *full*: and therfore if there be great occasion to vse them,
they must be reformed by detracting onely (*l*) and them stand metely
currant, as: *mournfuly.*

Though this last remark sounds as if Webbe wrote his
dactyls and spondees to the eye,—printer's-devil meter,—yet
he is not really quite so bad as that. He knows that the first
syllable of *pretty* is short, and that *th* does not make position.
Yet his verse gives no more warrant of success than that of his
colleagues; it has the essential faults of its kind: uncertainty
of form on account of the frequency of common syllables, and
the compulsory shortening of long syllables.

Happie/ old man. In/ shaddowy/ bancks and/ coole prettie/ places/
Heere by the quainted floodes and springs most holie remaining.
Heere, these quicksets fresh which lands seuer out fro thy neighbors
And greene/ willow/ rowes which/ Hyblae/ bees doo re/ioice in/
Oft fine whispring noise, shall bring sweet sleepe to thy senses.[16]

Webbe tells us also that he spent some time on a translation
of the *Georgics* into the "same English verse, which other such
workes were in," that is, of course, fourteeners.

The tale of Vergil translations is completed by Spenser's
Virgil's Gnat—a version varying from close literality to a very
free paraphrase of the Culex. The chief interest of this early[17]
poem of Spenser's is in the use of *ottava rima* in a version
from the Latin hexameter. Spenser makes a not ungraceful
English poem of the Latin trifle—a lavishing of mythological
learning by the gnat in a dream, like the humor of the cock's
learning in the Cock and the Fox—but carried to unreasonable
length. Spenser employs the unhappy fate of the gnat slain
by the shepherd allegorically to convey to his patron Leicester
his grief at some unlucky turn in his relations with Leicester,
apparently caused by too great frankness on the part of the
poet. He expands four hundred and twelve lines to six hundred and eighty-eight.

---

[16]*Op. cit.* p. 75.
[17]Riedner, W., *Spensers Belesenheit,* pt. 1, in *Münchener Beitr.* No. 38;
Spenser, *Poetical Works,* ed. Dodge, R. E. N., (Camb. Mass. 1908), p. 79.

To turn:

> cui cuncta paranti
> paruulus hunc prior umoris conterret alumnus
> et mortem vitare monet per acumina: namque
> qua diducta genas pandebant lumina gemmis
> hac senioris erat naturae pupula telo
> tacta levi.

into:

> Whom thus at point prepared, to prevent
> A little noursling of the humid ayre,
> A Gnat, unto the sleepie shepherd went,
> And marking where his ey-lids, twinckling rare,
> Shewd the two pearles which sight unto him lent,
> Through their thin coverings appearing fayre,
> His little needle there infixing deep,
> Warned him awake, from death himself to keep.—

this is not to make as Warton says a "vague and arbitrary paraphrase."[18] It is inexact as to the Latin original, but precise as to the action represented; and it is not arbitrary but in a style harmonious with the form chosen and the effect intended. Spenser was not concerned to render his original with precision, but to express his own discontents through an elegant allegory. No doubt he found amusement in finding a classical original so pat, and using it so cleverly.

Ovid naturally came next after Vergil. His glory, like Vergil's, had continued without interruption throughout the centuries. Caxton had prepared to print an Ovid moralized as well as a Vergil mutilated. There was a bit of Ovid in Tottel's *Miscellany,* and Chaloner's fragment bears testimony to the interest in his poems. Ovid was an author in whom his readers took a more intimate delight than Vergil. He was the favorite poet of Goethe's[19] and it would seem of Milton's youth. Shakespeare's abundant classical mythology practically all comes from Ovid, who contributes to give Shakespeare's writing its peculiar atmosphere of romance.

---

[18]Haz. War. iv, 290.

[19]*Dichtung und Wahrheit,* bk. X, 99 (*W. A. Werke,* vol. XXXVIII, p. 381) "[Herder] hatte mir den Spass an so manchem, was ich früher geliebt, verdorben und mich besonders wegen der Freude, die ich an Ovid's Metamorphosen gehabt, auf's strengste getadelt. Ich mochte *meinen Liebling* in Schutz nehmen . . . ."

Ovid's more superficial temper, his narratives complete in briefer space, his more consciously decorated style, his unflagging interest and variety, his abundance made him easier to translate and easier to enjoy than Vergil. As with Vergil, so with Ovid, there was in this era one leading translation of his greatest work, while a number of fragments and minor works were Englished by men of inferior talent. Golding's *Metamorphoses* stands out above all the verse translations of the period. Arthur Golding or Goldyng was a man of letters,— not an amateur giving his vacations to the work of translation, —but a diligent workman, who devoted his main energy to providing English readers with those Latin authors whom he thought it most important for them to know. The *Metamorphoses* was his largest and most important work, but the bulk of his translations were histories and geographies, and his primary object was to afford knowledge rather than delight.

Golding finished four books of the *Metamorphoses* late in 1564, dedicating the work in a prose letter as a New Year's gift to his patron the Earl of Leicester.

> If this woorke were fully performed with lyke eloquence and connyng of endyting by me in Englishe, as it was written by thauthor thereof in his moother toonge, it might perchaunce delight your honor too bestowe some vacant tyme in the reading of it for the nomber of excellent deuises and fyne inuentions contriued in the same, purporting outwardly moste pleasant tales & delectable histories, and fraughted inwardly with moste piththie instructions and wholsome examples, and conteyning bothe wayes moste exquisite connynge and deepe knowledge. Wherefore too counteruayle my default, I request most humblye the benefyte of your L. fauor, whereby you are wont not onlye too beare with the want of skill and rudenesse of suche as commit their dooinges too your protection, but also are woont to encourage them to proceede in their peynfull exercises attempted of a zeale and desyre too enriche their natiue language with thinges not heretoofore published in the same . . . Thassured hope and confidence wherof, (furthered by the priuiledge of the new yeere, which of an auncient and laudable custome, licenceth men too testifye their good willes, nor only too their friendes and acquaintance, but also too their betters and superiours, by presentes though neuer so simple,) giueth me boldnesse too dedicate this my maymed and vnperfect translation of the firste fower bookes of Ouids Metamorphosis vntoo your honor, and too offer it vnto you for a poore Neweyeres gift, I confesse not correspondent too your worthyness, or my desyre, but yet agreeable too the state of the giuer. The whiche if it may please you too take in good part, I accompt my former

trauell herin sufficiently recompensed, and think myself greatly enforced to perseuer in the full accomplishement of all the whole woorke. And thus beseeching God too send your Honor many prosperous & ioyfull Newyeres: I cease too trouble you any further at this tyme. At Cecill house the .xxiij. of December, Anno. 1564.

Your good L. most humbly too commaund
Arthur Goldyng.

When Goldyng completed the *Metamorphoses,* in 1567, he prefixed a dedicatory epistle in fourteener couplet, addressed to the same nobleman, and giving a philosophical interpretation to the whole. The chief stories of the books in succession are allegorically interpreted, a theological defense of Ovid is given, his cosmogony is harmonized with that of Moses, and the epistle ends with a caveat that the book should be used as a guard against vice. In a similar verse addressed *Too the Reader*, Golding strives to reconcile the book with a Christian temper. He urges the reader not to be shocked to find gods named in a heathen book: the true God permitted the little seeds of light in man's darkened mind to grow into this superstition. Would that Christians indeed worshiped not their sins but their God! The heathen gods stand for types of human life; and the metamorphoses represent the change of moral natures by which men become beasts. These poems give an image of all kinds of human nature, and multifarious information. If you cannot digest the book, avoid it.

There is an interesting account of Golding's work in Court-hope's *History of English Poetry,* but Professor Courthope errs in implying that Golding is at all responsible for the allegorizing interpretation of Ovid, or of any heathen poetry. The spirit of this reconciliation of profane literature with sacred is as ancient as the effort to amalgamate the two which was made in the great formative era of Christian civilization by the learned fathers of the fifth century. Allegory, of course, grew and flourished during the middle ages, so that in the discussion of the treatment of classical authors, an allegorical interpretation is taken to be a mark of the medieval as distinguished from the renaissance spirit in regard to them; but the obtaining of a critical and direct view of a classical writer was a gradual and slow process and an allegorical spirit about antiquity continued to be long held and was only slowly thrown off.

Ovid had been systematically interpreted into a teacher of ethics by the method of moral allegory,—"moralized,"—by Pierre Berchoir in the fourteenth century, and the standard editions of the early Renaissance passed on the tradition. In the edition of the *Metamorphoses* printed at Lyons in 1527 by Guillaume Boulle, the reader is told that the "Reverend father, Master Peter Lavinius, philosopher, poet, and theologian," teaches that Ovid's account of the creation, fall, and flood are so accordant with the narrative of Moses that the poet must have read the Pentateuch or the books of those who had read it; he teaches simply what Golding put into English rhyme in his letters dedicatory and addresses to the reader.

> Dum canit in varias homines migrasse figuras
> Quam sint peccati damna timenda refert.
> Fabula quos doceat ficto velamine mores
> Quod damnet vitium: dat tropus ecce tibi.

> And when the people giue themselves to filthie life and sinne
> What other kinde of shape thereby than filthie can they winne?
> So was Licaon made a Woolfe: and Ioue became a Bull:
> The tone for vsing crueltie, the toother for his trull.
> So was *Elpenor* and his mates transformed into swine,
> For following of their filthie lust in women and in wine.
> Not that they lost their manly shape as in the outward show:
> But for that in their brutish breastes most beastly lustes did grow.

Golding's version is less inadequate than Phaer's; he is a better verse-writer, and succeeds in uniting unity of form with variety. His verse, it may be remarked, grows looser as he advances in the work, either from haste or because of increased facility. He dilutes his original, partly for the sake of rhyme and meter, partly like so many authors of the time, to explain allusions. He lacks both elevation and grace. And yet his translation is the best verse translation in English before any original masterpieces existed to set a standard which the versions of the next generation were to attain. The *Rape of Proserpina* is a fair example of his work.

> Neare *Enna* walles there standes a Lake Pergusa is the name.
> Cayster heareth not mo songs of swannes then doth the same.
> A wood enuirons euery side the water round about,
> And with his leaues as with a Veyle doth keepe the Sunne heate out.
> The boughes doe yeelde a coole fresh ayre: the moysture of the
>   ground

Yeeldes sundrie flowers; continuall spring is all the yeare there
 founde.
While in this garden *Proserpine* was taking hir pastime,
In gathering eyther Violets blew, or Lillies white as Lime,
And while of Maidenly desire she filled hir Maund and Lap,
Endeauoring to outgather hir companions there. By hap
Dis spide her; loude hir: caught hir vp: and all at one well nere.
So hastie, hote, and swift a thing is Loue, as may appere.
The Ladie with a wailing voyce afright did often call
Hir Mother and hir waiting Maides, but Mother most of all.
And as she from the vpper part hir garment would haue rent,
By chaunce she let hir lap slip downe, and out hir flowers went.
And such a sillie simplenesse hir childish age yet beares,
That euen the verie losse of them did moue hir more to teares.
The Catcher driues his Chariot forth, and calling euery horse
By name, to make away apace he doth them stil enforce:
And shakes about their neckes and Maynes their rustie bridle reynes.
And through the deepest of the Lake perforce he them constreynes.
And through the *Palie* pooles. the which from ground doe boyle
And smell of Brimstone verie ranke: and also by the soyle
Where as the Bachies folke of *Corinth* with the double seas,
Betweene vnequall Hauens twaine did reere a towne for ease.[20]

Golding, though not praised so highly as Phaer by his contemporaries, is mentioned with encomiums by Puttenham,
Webbe, and Meres, and was as is well known familiar to
Shakespeare. The reprinting of his Ovid in 1575, 1587, 1593,
1603, 1612, and 1675, shows that he maintained an important
place for the "mere English" reader, as the agreeable pur-
veyor of the Greek mythology at a time during which it was the
accepted adornment of verse, and the typical enrichment of the
imaginative view of life.

Thomas de la Peend began a translation of the *Metamorphoses,* but gave up the work, as he tells us in his dedicatory
letter to "M. Nycholas Sentleger Esquyer," when he learned
that Golding had undertaken it. He published, however, his
version of Salmacis (*Metam.* IV, 287-388) in 1565. It is in
fourteener couplet, rigidly cesural, and is followed by a moral
interpretation. Hermaphroditus typifies a young man just
past boyhood, Caria the world full of temptation, Salmacis
"each vice that moueth one to ill," the spring "the pleasant
sport that doth content the will," the metamorphosis, the change
of nature and weakening due to sin, etc. Notes explaining al-

---

[20]Vol. ii, p. 139 (1903).

lusion for "the unlearned reader" are added; and there is a
roll of "the mad desires of women." The version is insipid;
the diction flavorless from generalization, and the whole diluted
by nugatory expansion.

> But now thys sonne of *Mercuryes*
>   in *Ida* mounte was fed,
> And fostred; thear full fyftene yeres
>   hys lyfe also he led.
> And then desyrous for to know
>   the state of countreyes straunge,
> All *Licia* land, by trauayle great
>   to Caria he dyd range.
> Wheras vppon a tyme, what wyth
>   his trauayle that was great,
> And eke the weather being hote
>   he weryed then wyth heate,
> And redy for to rest hym selfe,
>   by chaunce he dyd espye
> A well wyth water fayre and clere
>   as Chrystall to the eye.
> Whych neyther bushe at any tyme
>   nor wede it ouer grew.
> Much lyke the well it was
>   wherto *Acteon* drew,
> When that *Diana,* and her Nymphes
>   al naked in the same
> He saw, by chaunce as he did seke
>   his lately coursed game.
> About thys sprynge an idle Nymphe,
>   fayre *Salmacis* dyd vse:
> Whych euen as soone as wyth her eies,
>   the yonge man fayre she vewes,
> Strayght set on fyre: the moldrynge heate
>   doth strike vnto her harte,
> And thorow persed by the dynte,
>   Of cruell *Cupydes* darte,
> She straight desyres with him to ioyne,
>   her luste for to fulfyll.
> She tryms her selfe, & goes forthwith
>   for to declare her will.

The *Narcissus* (*Metam.* III, 342-510) printed by Thomas
Hackett, [ca. 1560] and of unknown authorship, is moralized
after the traditional manner. Indeed, it is more thoroughly
moralized than most of the Ovidian poems. It begins with a
moral motto, and is introduced by a moral address by the

printer, and a moralizing poem some five times as long as the
version, interpreting many of Ovid's narratives allegorically.

> I meane to shewe, accordyng to my wytte
> That Ouyd by this tale no follye mente
> But soughte to shewe, the doynges far vnfytte
> Of soundrye folke, whome natuer gyftes hath lente,
> In dyuers wyse to vse, wyth good in tente
> And how the bounty torneth to theyr payne
> That lacke the knowledge, of so good a gayne.

The moralization is given of Tiresias, Lycaon (that God pun-
isheth for sinne), of Pyrrha (that God preserueth the Juste),
of Daphne (a prayse of verginite). Phaeton is a good warning to young people. Narcissus is a sermon against pride;
pride marreth all; a proud heart cometh to confusion, as is
shown by the examples of Lucifer, Lazarus and Dives, "Cres-
sus, the welthy kinge of Lide," Golias, Samson, Milo, Sena-
charyb, Darius, Philomela, Absalom, Clytemnestra, and Cleopatra. In truly medieval manner the author has emptied upon
the page his store of commonplaces on the subject of pride;
and he proceeds to empty also his store of commentary learning. "Bocase" thought Ovid meant to write against the giving up of fame, for pleasure; "Ficius" teaches the meaning
of the tale to be a parable against placing body above mind;
and an English and an Italian writer had opinions which the
writer gives, "leaste anye wryter I may seeme to spare."

The verse is a rhymed distich composed of an Alexandrine
followed by a fourteener, which Gascoygne called *poulter's
measure,* because like a poulterer it gave something more than
twelve to the dozen. The only verse in English which is more
awkward is the inversion of this one, in which the Alexandrine follows the fourteener. The translation is loose and
crude, as might be expected from its date. It is amusing to
find *resonabilis* translated *dobbeler of skreeche,* and Echo
denominated *the callynge Ympe,* but the chief value of the
work is to illustrate anew how great and how sudden was that
"bettering of the time" of which the later years of the reign
of Elizabeth were justly conscious.

> So feblyd by loue, to waste he doth begynne
> at length and quyte consumed, by heate of hydyng fyre wythin,
> And nether hath he nowe, hewe of red and whyte

no lyvelynes nor lusty strength, that earste dyd eyes delyte
  Nor yet the corpys remayes, that Ecco once had loued
whyche tho wyth angry mynd she vewed, to sorow she was moued.
  And loke howe ofte alas, out of hys mouth dyd passe
so ofte agayne wyth boundyng wordes, she cryed alas alas,
  And when that he hys sydes, wyth rechles handes stryke
she also then was hard to make, a sounde lamentying lyke
  thus lokyng in the well, the last he spake was thys
alas thou ladde to much in vayne, beloued of me a mys,
  Whyche selfe same wordes agayne, this Ecco streight dyd yell
and as Narcissus toke hys leue, she bad hym eke fayre well
  Hys hed that hym abused, vnder the grasse he thraste
And deth shut vp those eyes, that on there master mused faste
  And when he was receyued, into that hyllye place
He yeke wythin the ogly stype, beheld hys wretched face.

The Stationers' Registers contain the titles of a number of ballads on Ovidian subjects, and the narratives of the *Metamorphoses* were much imitated.

The *Heroides* of George Turbervile (first edition, 1567) was in its day a not unimportant book. It was reprinted again and again, and was heartily praised. The *Heroides* appealed by the interest of dramatic situation, and by satisfying the current curiosity about classic story. Phaedra, Oenone, Dido, Canace, Hero and Leander, Helen and Paris were made the more actual by them. And though Turbervile is not vigorous, he is not wholly inadequate. He had applied himself to acquiring (and improving) the art of verse; and the material with which he had to deal tended especially in his blank verse translation to repress that tendency to diffuse expansion which is his besetting weakness. About half the letters are in "poulter's measure," and about a quarter each in fourteener couplets and blank verse. The blank verse of Turbervile is worthy of attention in the history of English prosody. Up to the time of the first edition of Turbervile's *Heroides* there had appeared Surrey's experiment, Grimald's two attempts, *Gorboduc,* and *Jocasta.* Turbervile's heroics are wooden enough, stiffer, indeed, than his fourteeners or his verses in the poulter's measure; but he had got beyond the scansion of the verses line by line, and a follower of greater talent might have gained from him the idea of a verse better suited for the stage than that of either of the dramas named.

[Medea quotes Jason's pleadings:]

> But [By?] my sinister haps (which lies in thee
> For to redresse) and by thy noble race,
> And Grandsire, that all mortall thinges suruayes:
> And by the triple form of Dian, and
> Her priuie sacred rites. this country Gods,
> (If any here within this soyle doo raigne)
> Rue on my Mates and mee, (O Queene) I pray
> And oblige me vnto thee by thys boone,
> And so a Greecian thou not seeme to scorne.
> (But how might I the Gods so freendly finde?)
> Sooner my soule to weightlesse ayre shall waste,
> Than any (saue your grace) with me be linckt
> In spousall bande, and bridely knot be tyde
> Let Iuno witnesse be, that hath in charge
> The marriage rites: that holy Goddesse too
> Within whose Marble Church we stooden haue.

Most of Turbervile's blank verse is less free than this; yet always he shows a certain skill in forming a verse-period with a vigorous close. The letter of Acontius to Cydippe gives an example.

> Abandon dread, for to thy louer thou
> Shalt frame no farther hest ne sweare again;
> Thy once ingaged faith I recke enough.
> Reade and suruaie my lines: so may this griefe
> And languor leaue thy corps, which is my tene
> When anie limme of thine sustaineth smart.
> Why blush you? and why with vermilion taint
> Be flecke your cheekes? In Dian's temple so
> I deeme thy face with Scarlet hue infect.
> Marriage and plighted troth, no crime I craue:
> I loue not as a Letcher, but a spouse.

His fourteeners are in point of mere sound as good as any up to his time, but the form encouraged his fatal tendency to wordiness. The following passage seems to me to exhibit some imaginative realization of the tone of the original—a rare quality in the versions which have been considered. The passage is from Leander's letter to Hero.

> When I by night directed course,
>   amid the yeelding Seas,
> The water glistered with
>   rebound of Phoebes rayes:

And night for cleernes might compare
    euen with the brightest dayes.
No voyce I heard with eare,
    but euery thing was husht:
Saue whilst my bodie brake the waues
    the troubled water rusht.
Alcyones alone
    did vse a pleasant note:
And did record Ceycus loue
    with sweete and warbling throte.

Thomas Churchyard's version of the *Tristia* (1572) is a perfectly characterless work, in a monotonous fourteener couplet, not so abject as for instance Hall's Homer or so spirited as Golding's *Metamorphoses*. The interest in Ovid must have been strong to cause this version to be reprinted as often as it was. In his dedication, "To his most assured and tryed Friende Maister Christopher Hatton Esquire, Thomas Churchyarde wisheth continuance of Vertue." He regrets the delay in the publication of his whole works, which by high direction he is to write again (when they are done he is only going to call them *Chips,* they are such trifles and so miscellaneous); and in the meantime he issues the translation, for which the name of Ovid alone would suffice to gain a good report.

His translation of Ovid's account of the spring break-up in his dreary Pontic exile, and of the poet's eagerness for a word from Rome, which bade him seek the company of the simple seamen that visit the port, is as well done as anything in Churchyard's version.

The fertile fields do florishe now, with flowers of sundry hewe,
And babling byrdes w' tongue untaught, do chaunt with notes so newe.
The Swallow eke a mother vile her cruel deedes to hide,
Her neast by beames she maketh close, and buildes by houses syde.
The growing Graine in Plowed fieldes, with Furrowes lai'd unsene,
With slender spiere through tender Earth apper'th with ioyfull greene.
The Vines also (whereas they be) their buds from braunches lowe
Do now bringe out: in *Scythia* for, no Vines at all do growe
And whereas lofty woods be set, the Bowes do spread from tree,
(For nere to coast of Geta Land, no Trees deserned bee)
Lo there this is the vacant time, for sport and pleasaunt playes,
And taulkinge tongues in iudgment haules, do cease for certaine dayes.
On hinneyghinge horse with Armour light, they bravely now disport;
And some to Ball, and some to Toy, with mery minde resort.
The lusty youth annoynted longe with thinne and sliding Oyle,

Their weary limmes with water washe, and rest from former toyle.
Now triumphes are: with soundinge voyce, the Lookers on do crye,
From three fould stage the factions three, their favouring words let
    flie.
O foure times blest, and blessed more the [n] number can make plaine:
That mayst the Citty free enioy, and in the same remaine.
But I with snow with Sunne consum'd O wretch do here approve,
And frozen Sea the yse whereof no force might them remove.
No yce the same doth now congele, as wont it was to do,
Nor herdsmen way by *Ister* make to *Sauromathia* go.
Yet if by happe that any shippe, arrive within this coast,
Or any stranger hap to be, in *Pontus* Hauen at'hoast,
In hast I seeke the shippemen out, and saluinge them before
What shippe or whence she come I aske, or from what happie shore.
Then they (unless it marueile be) from some nere ioyninge Land,
Do aunswere make: from Nations farre, to sayle few tak'th in hand.
And seldome from *Italia* seas do any passage take,
Nor in these ports from hauen so wide, no shippe his bydinge make.
But if that any come that speake, the Latin or the Greeke,
Hee is for that more welcome much, such language I do seeke.
It lawfull is from mouth of Sea, and from *Propontus* longe,
That men may saile with Northren winde these *Scythian* Seas among.
Who so hee bee may happely make, some whispering rumour lowe,
Whereby a past occasion gev'th, more fame thereof to growe.
Then do I pray him make discourse of *Caesars* triumphe braue,
And eke what vowes that duty driu'th the *Latin Ioue* to haue.
Or els if that *Germania* land, which still rebell'th in fielde,
With carefull minde at Captaines feete, al prostrate now do yelde.
Who doth (which would my selfe had seene) of these things haply
    tell,
I pray him vse as welcome ghest, the house wherein I dwell
But well away is *Nasoes* house, now set on Scythia's ground?
Or shall to helpe my payne withall, a place therefore be found?
God graunt that Caesar may commaunde, not this my house to be,
But rather for the time a place, wherein to chastise me.[21]

Even the *Ibis* did not fail of a translator. Thomas Underdowne, whose almost famous version of *Theagenes and Chariclea* illustrates well how much more successful a man not of
real genius can be with prose than with verse, made a version
of *Ibis,* dedicating it to "Thomas Sackuyle, lord Buckhurst,"
who seems to have been a patron of Underdowne's family.
If it were not for Buckhurst's reputation of courtesy, says Underdowne, he would not have ventured to proffer the translation to his "excellent honour," . . . "not for the unworthinesse

[21]1580 ed., Fo. 26, 27.

of the worke which is very wytty, but for the simplenesse of
the translation which ill besemeth the same." The familiar
"hauty Persian king" and "the cuppe of troubled water"
(*troubled* is a new touch) make their appearance, an anecdote of Philip of Macedon follows, and the dedication con-
cludes with a reference to "the good affection your honour had
to my deere father Steuen Vnderdowne."

In the "Preface to the gentle Reader," Underdowne says:

> I haue translated . . . a lyttle peace of Ouyd . . . It is very hard
> . . . and that the obscurity of it should not be displeasant to the
> (which I know must needes haue bene) I, haue added thereunto a
> breefe draughte of all the storyes and tales, that are contayned
> therein, by reason whereof the reading of it no doubte, wylbe very
> pleasant, & perhaps not without profit. For therein shall you see
> all maner of vices punished, all offences corrected; & all misdeedes
> reuenged. There is neither story, nor tale almost, from the beginning
> vnto hys time, wherein any ill luck was noted, to happen to any
> man but the Poet wisheth the same to light vpon his aduersary.

There follows a narrative of the circumstances calling forth
the poem, including a digression upon the subject of friendship, stuffed with classical examples, and rhetorical commonplaces such as:

> There is no poyson to the poyson of a Serpente, no strength, to the
> strength of Gunpowder, no sting to the sting of the Aspe, no malyce
> to the malyce of a woman, nor no euill to the euill of a fayned
> friende, and a dissembling louer.

The rhythm in general is sweet and graceful, in spite of the
excessive dulness of the substance, and lack of distinction in
the words.

The verse is a cesural fourteener, freely broken in upon by
the explanatory notes, with which the poem is printed continuously, so that sometimes one distich stands in two pages of
comment; and then another distich follows, with a similar mass
of explanation. We are told who Nictymene was, and what
nameless sin she wrought, who were Plereta and Tideas, and
in brief we read nearly all the horrible stories of ancient mythology. To the ending of the poem:

> These things in sodain mode thus pend to thee directed are
> That thou neede not complayne that I vnmindefull am of thee.

Underdowne adds the note:

> In deede he were much to blame, that woulde thinke Ouid had forgotten Ibis, if he haue read but this over.

I cannot forbear quoting the following reference to Underdowne in a modern edition of the *Ibis*.

> Sed ne mei quoque laude sua careant, non est praetereundus Thomas Vnderdown, qui totum carmen Anglice versibus reddidit ediditque cum adnotationibus a. 1569. Qui si cum aliis comparetur qui Ouidii scripta in nostrum sermonem transtulerunt, inter quos fecit poeta summus Christophorus Marlowe, cuius extant Ouidii Amores Anglicis versibus sed inprospere expressi, prope unicam gloriam consecutus est. Libellus est rarior, dignissimus tamen qui perlegatur; adeo in toto opere perlucet rudis et uernacula simplicitas, adeo acri et ardenti et poene Anglico odio fertur. Lectitabantque Ibin Angli eo tempore discebantque, si quidem poematio quo in Mariam Scotorum reginam inuectus est scriptor ignotus in Froudii Hist. Angl. c. 48 et ipsum carmen nominatim citauit et multa ex eo imitatus est. Legerat hic Ibin ut docent versus cius Tamburlaine iv. 3 *A sacred vow to Heaven and him I make confirming it with Ibis' holy name. Now all the woes that Ovid in Ibin Into his pretty little book did write,* etc. Hoc mihi indicauit amicus Balliolensis, W. H. Forbes.[22]

This delightful note expresses, I fear, rather the enthusiasm of the scholar who edited *Ibis,* at finding another sincerely interested in his darling little hidden corner of the poetic field than any real critical judgment. Ovid, no doubt, disliked Ibis, and had cause to; but his poem is inspired not by hate, but by the pleasure of getting together ingeniously all the learning of Ovid's mythology about misfortune; and Underdowne's temper is one of a Herculean humour and quite genuine amusement, as his last note shows. *Anglicum odium* is not very *acer et ardens;* the English are not a fierce people; they are humorous, and usually mild As for Underdowne's verse, it is smooth and accomplished, but necessarily monotonous because of the complete absence of variety in the cesura. There are some passages which show a neat ingenuity in the phrasing of a fairly difficult passage. But the main reason for the reading of the poem in the age when it appeared is that it was a

---

[22]*P. Ovidii Nasonis Ibis ex novissimis codicibus edidit scholia vetera commentarium cum prolegomenis appendice indice addidit R. Ellis collegii Trinitatis apud Oxonienses socius, Oxonii e typographeo Clarendoniano. MDCCCLXXXI;* Praef. xi.

treasure-house (especially with the interesting notes) of information about classical, especially mythological allusions, and thus supplemented the other works of Ovid.

> Let not the Sun shine bright·on thee
>   nor glistering Moone by night:
> And of thy eyes let glimsing starres,
>   forsake the wished sight,
> Let not the fire graunt thee his heate
>   nor Ayre humiditie:
> Let neither earth nor yet the Sea
>   free passage graunt to thee,
> That banyshed and poore thou mayst,
>   straunge houses seeke invayne:
> That crauing to, with trembling voyce
>   small almes mayst obtayne.
> That neither sound of body, nor
>   thy mynde in perfect plight:
> This night be worse than passed day,
>   and next day than this night.
> That thou mayst still be pitiful,
>   but pitied of none.
> And that no man nor woman may,
>   for thy mischaunces mone.
> And that thy teares may hatred moue,
>   thou iudged worthy to,
> On whom (though many mischefes light)
>   yet worthy many mo.
> And (that that seldome commes to passe)
>   I wishe thy whole estate:
> All wonted fauour for to want,
>   and be replete with hate.
> And that thou want no cause of death,
>   but mayst be voyde of powre:
> And that thy lyfe be forste to flye,
>   of death the wished houre.
> And that thy soule with troubles tost
>   constrayned styl to stay:
> May leave thy wery limmes at length,
>   tormented with delay.[23]

Among the large undertakings of the generation between Tottel's *Miscellany* and the beginnings of great Elizabethan work, the fourth in importance (next after Golding's Ovid, Phaer's Vergil, and North's Plutarch) was the translation of the ten tragedies attributed to Seneca. This version was the

---

[23]Ed. 1577, Fo. 7, 8.

work of five hands, and occupied a score of years. Jasper Heywood seems to have given the impulse and done the most important work. His *Troas* was printed in 1559, *Thyestes* in 1560, and *Hercules Furens* in 1561. Two other young students followed his example with a translation of a single play each. (Alexander Nevyle translated the *Oedipus* in 1560, though his work was not published until 1563, and Thomas Nuce the *Octavia*, translated in 1563, published in 1566.) John Studley then pushed on the work in earnest, translating the *Agamemnon* and *Medea*, printed in 1566, the *Hippolytus*, licensed to Henry Denham in 1566-67, and the *Hercules Oetaeus*, apparently first printed in the collected edition of 1581. Finally, all these translations were collected and reprinted in 1581, Thomas Newton rounding out the collection with a version of the *Thebais*.

The general influence of Seneca on the English drama has been carefully investigated and abundantly discussed by scholars. That Seneca contributed an important influence to the formal aspects of the serious drama is beyond dispute, and it is equally certain that he had a direct influence upon the whole dramatic method of Kyd, and hence upon the work of Shakespeare, and upon the content of some later writers, such as Marston, Chapman, and Jonson, and others. Professor H. J. C. Grierson[24] even credits Seneca with being the source not only of the formula of Elizabethan drama, but also of the spirit which inspired it; the formula, namely, of crime and the nemesis that overtakes it,—too often degenerating into mere revenge,—and the spirit, the sense of sin, calling for retribution. It is also maintained that the violence, the bloodshed, the terror, and the descriptive element of English tragedy owe much to Seneca.[25] To my mind, this credits too much to the Latin writer. The raw energy of the native drama makes Seneca seem quiet; and the special form of the English reformation, the turmoil of questing minds, the desire for violent effect, all tended to the lower, the exciting drama of crime and punishment, instead of the higher, the more penetrating drama of the noble soul solving erroneously the problem of the insoluble universe.

---

[24]*Cross Currents in English Literature of the 17th Century* (1929), p. 100.
[25]Manly, J. M., In essay introductory to F. J. Miller's *The Tragedies of Seneca* (Chicago, 1917).

In particular, no case has been made for the influence of
Seneca on Marlowe, who is not Senecan in his fundamental
ideal of tragedy, the nature of his tragic magnificence or terror, his rhetoric, or the formal aspects of his writings. He
has long speeches, but they are not Senecan, since they are
not specimens of ingenious rhetoric but of imaginative exuberance, and he has supermen, but they are not Senecan, since
they are not perverts, but visionaries, inspired by a glowing
imagination, radically different from the introspection of Seneca. And though Senecan phrases are frequently to be met
with in the English drama of the age, many of the parallels,
particularly those with Shakespeare, are accidental. They are
such natural coincidences as would easily occur in dramatists
dealing with similar situations.

Be the influence of Seneca what it may, the 1581 translation contributed little to it. To most of the authors who most
exhibit the obvious influence of Seneca the Latin was entirely
familiar; and the researches of Professor Cunliffe give no
evidence of any abundance of borrowing "of manie good sentences, or whole Hamlets, I should say handfulls of tragical
speeches from English Seneca" in the plays of the time. There
was indeed no little borrowing of *sententiae,* but the English
versions generally dilute them, while the borrowings strive
for Senecan pithiness. Hence on the whole the Senecan bor-
rowers, so far as their plays are extant, do not warrant the
gibe of Nash. Indeed *direct* influence of the versions is quite
impossible to trace. Miss Searing calls attention to the fact
that Heywood translated the *Troas* freely, adding notable passages on his own, that he is more exact in the *Thyestes,* and
that he ends by endeavoring to translate the *Hercules Furens*
line for line, not improving his work by his care. Studley, as
she makes clear, is homely and popular in his style, heavy and
inadequate in the more ambitious passages, but interesting from
quaintness and exuberance, while Nuce's language "has fewer
Latinisms than Heywood's, and is slightly less colloquial and
more archaic than Studley's." Nevyle's rendering of the
Oedipus, printed in 1563, was exceedingly crude, and Nevyle
revised it thoroughly for the edition of 1581.[26]

All the versions are in fourteeners, except Nuce's *Octavia,*

---

[26]M L R iv (1909), p. 437 ff.; xv (1920), p. 359.

which is in clumsy heroic couplets, not systematically closed. The verse of most of the translators is heavily thumping, made more thumping by unintelligent alliteration, and the diction is undistinguished. The best translator, because his verse is more fluent and his style less colloquially mean than that of others, is Jasper Heywood.

The *Jocasta* of George Gascoigne and Francis Kinwelmersh (or Kinwalmarsh) is interesting as the only English translation coming however remotely from a Greek play during the entire era covered by this book; and it is all the more interesting in that all its features show how alien the art and ideals of the Greek drama were from the temper of the age. The very name gives evidence. The play of Euripides which the translation represents at fourth hand is the *Phoenissae,* named from the chorus of Phenician captives; the English version is *Jocasta,* named from the personage whose character is the most fully and subtly developed. The chorus and the choral odes were from the first a stumbling-block to the Renaissance reader. When Erasmus, for example, translated the *Iphigenia in Aulis,* he permitted himself, he says, to deal somewhat freely with the meter of the choruses. And he declares that if his graver studies should give him time to translate any more tragedies, he would not hesitate to go further and would alter the style and the topics of the choruses, preferring to treat some "locum communem," some theme of accepted human interest, or to leave the straight road (*expatiari*) for some attractive by-way ($\pi a \rho \dot{\epsilon} \kappa \beta a \sigma \iota s$), to spending his energy on high sounding trifles—*canoras nugas,* in the words of Horace. For nowhere did antiquity seem to him to show more ineptitude than in this sort of choruses, in which by aiming at too great originality of expression the writer spoils his style, and by hunting for wonders of words fails in the judgment of things. And in the preface to his version of the *Hecuba,* he calls the choruses so obscure as to need an Oedipus or the Delian god to divine them, rather than a translator to interpret them. It is no wonder, then, that Dolce, the Italian translator of the Latin translation of the *Phoenissae* paraphrased the choruses, and that the English translators reduced them to the blank verse in which the rest of the play was written. This is true even of the *Phoenissae,* the play of Euripides most abounding in "effects," and filled with incident; how much less could the men of the Renaissance find satisfaction in the clear simplicity and strong lyric quality of Sophocles, to say nothing of the stark architectural outlines of Aeschylus. Aeschylus, indeed, was not until 1663 provided with a Latin version.

The Italian was translated probably from R. Winter's version (1591) of Euripides: loosely, inaccurately, and poorly, doing little justice to Euripides' close-wrought and subtle manner, but maintaining the general course of the action. Gascoigne and Kinwelmersh held close to Dolce. The stichomythia and the formal rhetoric of Euripides appears even in the translation, but the power and energy of the Greek have vanished.

Though Latin comedy was a real influence in the development of the native drama, the English translations are very few and unimportant.

The translation of Plautus's *Menaechmi* (1595) by "W. W.," probably but not certainly conjectured to be William Warner, is easily accessible, having been frequently reprinted in the various collections of Shakespeare's sources. The printer's introduction gives a fair and clear view of the translator's purpose in making the version, and of his standard of what a translation ought to be. His version is intended to give pleasure to the general reader, but it does not aim to do either of the two things which the translator regards as the higher aims of serious work in this field, namely by free additions and substitutions to create a practically original work on the foundations of the original, or to hold so close to the original as to give not only its substance but its form so far as the difference of languages will permit. The title-page makes clear that the humanists who objected to the "bold baudrie" of medieval romance hesitated to venture upon the grosser indecencies of classic comedy. Plautus's obscenity was not so tolerable as Ovid's voluptuousness. For one thing it could not be interpreted allegorically. For the *Menaechmi* was "chosen purposely from the rest, as least harmefull and yet most delightfull," and no more Plautine comedies were printed.

The translation, in prose, is simple and direct in style, without any effort to give the play vivacity by clever turns or slanginess of phrase. The little changes and additions introduce, mildly and appropriately, a few allusions to contemporary manners, or simply abbreviate long speeches or make the dialogue move with more liveliness than a literal translation of the original.

Kyffin's *Andria* is essentially a school-book and is therefore treated with those translations intended primarily for the help or guidance of beginners. (p. 223.)

Vergil and Ovid easily became familiar and almost popular poets in their English versions, because of the attractive narrative contents of their poems, which could spare adequacy of style and yet be understood and enjoyed. Horace because of the reflective and detached character of his content could not attract in the same way; and again the Horatian spirit could not be communicated without some English equivalent for the Horatian style. The Elizabethan version of Horace by Thomas Drant is a libel on Horace; it never even began as a translation, because the spirit of the author is actively opposed to the spirit of the original, and it has no qualities of its own to compensate for its imperfections as a version. Drant himself, to his horrified amazement, learnt from a bookseller that his book was not likely to awaken general interest. ". . . as I was aunswered by a prynter not long agone, Though sayth he (Sir your booke be wyse, and ful of learnynge, yet peraduenture it wyl not be so saileable) signifying indeed that flim flames, and gue gawes, be they neuer so sleight and slender, are soner rapte vp thenne are those which be lettered and Clarkly makings." Drant proceeds to inveigh against the corrupt taste of his time, which would prefer an amorous pamphlet, no better he suggests than a tale of a cock and a hen ("as for example let them be cawled Sir Chauntecleare and Dame Partilote"), to good books of learning; "for good thyngs are hard, and euyl things are easye."

As for the other side of the work, the adequacy of the translation, Drant has to the full the current defects—the clumsy form of the fourteener, incapable of the subtle and gentle shadings of Horace's delicate humor or sentiment, and the diction, generalized from its original, and made emphatic by a vulgarly familiar manner. Drant's manner was indeed uncommonly coarse and heavy. He was quite incapable of approaching Horace's tone. He was an ecclesiastic, Archdeacon of

Lewes, a theologian and an earnest man—something of a hot gospeller. If he had once really apprehended Horace's keen, detached, kindly, sympathetic worldliness, he would have told Horace (as Carlyle told Sir William Vernon Harcourt when he betrayed indifferentism) that he was headed straight for perdition. To Drant sin was sin, which Jeremiah, as was fitting for a sacred writer, rebuked with tears, and Horace as was fitting for a secular writer, rebuked with laughter. But Drant laughs little, and if at all with scorn. As Professor O. L. Jiriczek remarks,[27] the impression that he produces upon a reader through his sermons and prefaces is that of an atrabilious scolder; I think we must add a man of heavy conceit and clumsy mind. Horace, then, in his hands becomes vituperative rather than satiric—still less is he a satirist that plays about the midriff with his jest. The earlier of Drant's versions are paraphrastic and expanded with an excess of crude means of literary effect, such as alliteration, which give a strangely antique look to his verse.

> Th' unwyldye warryer waste with toyle
>   wyth grouelyng elde for spente,
> O makelesse marchaunte mumbleth he,
>   O state with blysse Y blent.
> The fearefull marchaunt he again,
>   When waltryng wyndes amayne
> With plunging puffes from Sothren coste,
>   And hydiouse hissing rayne
> Torments the Sea, hoistes vp the waues
>   that doth surmounte the sayle,
> Saunce pere doth deme the souldyers guyse,
>   . . . .
> The chubbyshe gnof that toyles, and moyles,
>   And delueth in the downe,
> If happlye he a suertie be,
>   so sente for into towne;
> Who gapes, who gawes, who pores, who pries,
>   who progges his mate but he?
> Perfaye (saith he) here all things ryfe,
>   there people blessed be.[28]

---

[27]Jiriczek, O. L., *Der elisabethanische Horaz* in *Jahrb. d. deutschen Sh. G.* xlvii (1911), 42. Drant's prolegomena and long extracts are reprinted with scrupulous accuracy, and accompanied by a valuable discussion.
[28]Jiriczek, *op. cit.*, pp. 55-56.

The later work of Drant is more accurate, less diffuse and less violent, but utterly without that union of frank and fresh reality and finished elegance, that urbanity which makes Horace so much the favorite of "gentlemen." An illustration may be drawn from the *Ars Poetica.*

> Let things be formall of one kinde
>   and do not chop it vp
> To make tone part a gallon potte,
>   and tone a prittie cup.
> The more deale of vs Poets. both
>   the olde, and younge most parte,
> Are ofte begylde by shewe of good,
>   affectinge to muche arte.
> I laboure to be verye briefe,
>   it makes me verye harde.
> I followe flowinge easynes,
>   my style is clearely marde
> For lacke of pith and sauerye sence,
>   Write loftie, thou shalte swell:
> He creepes by the grounde to lowe, afrayde
>   with stormie vayne to mell.
> He that in varyinge one pointe muche
>   would bringe forth monstruous store,
> Would make the dolphin dwell in the wooddes
>   and in the flud the bore.
> The shunning of a fault is such
>   that now and then it will
> Procure a greater faulte, if it
>   be not eschewde by skill . . .[29]

Drant, however, was not content with translating Horace, however freely. "I have done as the people of god were commaunded to do with their captiue women that were hansome and beautifull: I haue shaued of his heare, and pared of his nayles (that is) I haue wyped away all his vanitie and superfluitie of matter. Further, I haue for the moste parte drawen his priuate carpyng of this or that man to a general moral. I haue englished thinges not accordyng to the vain of the Latin proprietie, but of our own vulgar tongue. I haue interfarced (to remoue his obscuritie. and sometymes to better his matter) much of myne owne deuysinge. I haue peeced his reason, eekede, and mended his similitudes, mollyfied his hardnes, prolonged his curtall kynd of speches, changed, & muche altered

---

[29]*A Medicinable Morall.*

his wordes, but not his sentence: or at leaste (I dare say) not his purpose."[30] He substituted for Horace's satire on prevailing licentiousness (Sat. i, 2) a composition of his own on the fashions of the day. He omitted the *Iter Brundisinum* altogether, as uninteresting to an unlearned, mere English reader, and replaced it with a long-winded defense of himself as a theologian for occupying himself with profane authors.

The problem of presenting Horace in a modern dress is indeed insoluble. The necessity to effective satire of concrete reference to current events, of being steeped in the ordinary life of its own time, makes it essential to accompany a version of Horace with interpretative notes. To incorporate the explanation into the translation destroys the vigor and pungency of the latter, and to append it makes the commentary outweigh the text.

Professor Jiriczek very clearly expounds Drant's method of dealing with this problem, which is to dodge it. He evades difficulties as much as he can by generalization; sometimes he substitutes English for Latin ideas. But he does not recast the setting, and on the whole he does not include annotation in his verse. Altogether his version is tame and lifeless.

There is no evidence that Drant's version had any importance for its age. Webbe mentions the translation, without naming the author.[31] Meres refers only to Drant's epigrams— compositions in Latin, Greek or English, purely occasional, and of the slightest nature. It has been suggested that Shakespeare probably read Drant, because of some resemblance between the phrases at the beginning of *A Midsummer Night's Dream* and Drant's version of Epist. I, i, 11, 20 ff. but Shakespeare hardly needed to borrow from Drant a reference to a stepmother's unkindness.

Drant took some steps toward making a translation of Homer, probably direct from the Greek, a language which he knew well enough to write verses in it. He did not complete the work, and what he did is lost. The first serious effort to give the English an Iliad in their own language was undertaken by Arthur Hall. Hall was no scholar (the phrase in the Dictionary of National Biography describing him as *proficient in*

---

[30]*Op. cit.*, p. 49.
[31]Arber, p. 34.

classics is unfortunate, considering that he knew no Greek), but a well-educated and wealthy gentleman, a dependent of the Cecils, a man of riotous and misdirected energy, who wasted his fortune and plagued himself with his outrageous actions and violent language. His Homer was printed in 1581.

Hall's *Epistle Dedicatorie,* addressed *to Sir Thomas Cicill,* speaks of having begun his *Iliad* many years before, when Hall was a scholar with Cecil in Cecil's father's house: and of his anxieties during the work because of lawsuits against him and his "carefull turmoyle to preserue somewhat to my poore house, in a manner overthrowne by my vngouerned youth." He was discouraged from getting on by the superiority of the work of other translators, especially of Phaer. "But as it is a propertie of euerie man soone to finde a reason to will him proceede with his owne humour, be it neuer so vnreasonably grounded, in like case fell it with me: for these were my Arguments against these sound persuasions obiected to staie me. First I remembered that about. 18. or 19. yeeres past walking with *M. Richard Askame* (*sic*: of course for *Roger*), a verie good Grecian, and a familiar acquaintaunce of *Homer,* & reciting vpon occasion of talke between vs, certaine verses Englished by me of the said Authour, he animated me much, with great entreatie to goe forwarde with my begun enterprise. The like did also about that time the erst named *M.* Iasper Heywood, a man then better learned than fortunate, and since more fortunate than he hath well bestowed (as it is thought) the giftes God and Nature hath liberally lent him. [Referring to Heywood's conversion to Catholicism.]"

The translation is in rhymed fourteeners, from the French of Hugues Salel, except the Catalogue of Ships, which is filled in from the Latin version. The relation of Hall to his original is made clear by the following passage. Salel's version is mean and creeping; but Hall's bolsters it out and vulgarizes it by the effort to give concrete vivacity to the diction. Compare for example Salel's and Hall's version of the beginning of the second book.

Les dieux haultains et les hommes aussie,
Toute la nuyct dormirent sans souci

Juppiter seul, records de la promesse	Iuppiter ne
Qu'il avoit faicte à Thetis la Déesse	peult dormir

Fut sans repos, ne cessant de penser   pour le
Quelque moyen, pour Achillés haulser   soing qu'il
En grand honneur et mouvoir quelque noise   a d'Achilles
Au grief danger de l'armée Gregeoise.
Si fait venir vers soy le Dieu des songes
Pernicieux, et porteur des mensonges :
Auquel il dict. Songe malicieux
Laisse soubdain le manoir des haultz cieulx,
Et t'en descends promptement au nauire
D'Agamemnon, auquel tu pourras dire
Que de par moy bien exprés luy commandes,   Iuppiter
Qu'il face armer toutes les Grecques bandes.   parle au
Car a present conuient que son emprise   Dieu de
Soit acheuée, & que Troie soit prise :   songe
Veu que les dieux diuisez & partiz
(Quant à ce point) ores sont conuertiz,
Persuadez de Iuno, qui souhaite
De veoir en brief ceste Cité deffaicte.

The Heauenly sires and mortal folke passed the night as tho
In pleasaunt sleepe, yeelding to it ful fre of care and wo.
But Ioue sticking with tooth and nayle stil vnto hys behest
To Thetis made, with irksome cheare bereft was of his rest,
Casting how he Achilles fame vnto the starres might raise,
And moue some broyles in the Greeks Campe to their losse any
          ways.
Iohn dreaming God[32] he callde to him, that God chiefe God of il,
Common cole carrier of euery lye, thus saying him his wil:
Thou cankerde dreme thinke on thy charge, & leaue thy seate
          nowe here
And straight to *Agamemnons* ships this message sée thou beare,
Without abode that he do arme eche Gréekish crue and bande,
His enterprise to ende, my selfe wil put an helping hande.
For now the Gods do all agrée that *Troy* to ruine goe,
Among them though hath bene great tug whether it should be so
Throughly hath Iuno brought thereto, whose wil and whole desire
Is both the Troyan towne and folke to daunt with sworde and fire.

Compare the following phrases :

            (Salel)   (Hall)
Bk. I   Phoebus ioua de la harpe.   Phoebus he his doulced Harpe
                                     doth strike.

---

[32]Ms. note in B. M. copy: "The God of Dreams was Morpheus. The
imaginary Being that caused Dreaming was stiled by our Ancestors, John-
a-Dreams."

Bk. II . . . ayant la charge   Who hath the charge of such
        De tant de gens . . .   a crue of knights and army
                                                big.

        Car le soucy lui doibt   For not throughout to sleep
        donner matiere   a night the care of them
        De ne dormir ainsi la   would twig.
        nuit entiere.

Bk. IV Sur le printemps   When Prime time first forth
                                                leaps.

        Honteusement   Dastardlike with shame
                                                enough.

Bk. IX . . . sont venus droite aux   Unto the vessels straight they
        vaisseaux et tentes   come and tents of Myrmi-
        Des Myrmidons, tres-   dons,
        belles et patentes.   In compasse wide and gay to
        Et ont trouue Achilles,   Achilles where he runnes,
        qui chantoit   And on the Viole Ditties
        Sur la viole   sings.

Bk. II Bryseis his tricke and gal-   [this word seems to be so
        lant trull at the gates   commonly used by all trans-
        doth light   lators that it almost loses its
        Of Priam King, where in   character, likewise *church*.]
        a plumpe consult both
        yong and olde.

Bk. III   She riseth up and deckes her selfe with gorgeous attire,
          And out she goes, distiling teares, as they wel saw
            stood by hir.
          The aged dads theer closely sit, the scorching heat
            they dout.
          O graunt that he for whose default now this accord
            shal stay,
          (As rebel vnto your decrees) with brayning to be sped,
          And for his gilt, let of his ympes the braines be absorbed.

Bk. IV   —curteous Venus she
          againe with finger in hir eye.
          [Juno to Jupiter] ; I am as well as you,
          A God, a Saturne Impe.

Bk. V   Venus on her maribones thus prayes him earnestlye.
          Diomede that rebel (quoth she) hath given me the gelpe.

Bk. VI   His son the pretie leefe,
          A little pretie bulchion fat. [Astyanax]

Bk. VII   These peruke Greekes.

Bk. VIII Now like a hartlesse fem, thou shalt be led in prison
wise, [*fem* or *feme* cannot have looked so very odd to
the Elizabethans.]
Make hast thou gay and glorious freke, dreadful with
flaming eyes.
Where is the kilcow chatte become in Lemnes which
you had
Upon your Alebenche, where you were so impudent
and mad?
                    and like the growing Poppy,
As wel for fruit as Aprill showres, doth leau[n?]e his
head so loppy.
In gardens fat: Gorgythion hurte loden with steele
did helme him,
On shoulder layes his head, and dies with weaknesse
which did whelm him.

Hector a coggd beaver.

Bk. X   Of Leinster woll the best it was.

Yes sure, I am, but your quick sprite is neuer dull
nor ydle,
Sound freend (quoth Hector) what you say as true is
as the Byble.

Of far more significance than these minor translations of
important authors were the versions of classic epigrams. The
appearance among Tottel's *Songs and Sonettes* of a few brief
poems coming originally from the Greek Anthology has been
remarked. They are mostly reflective or gnomic verses, reaching their writers more probably from Erasmus's *Adagia* than
from any collection primarily devoted to epigrams in verse.
That English collection of moral dicta, Baldwin's *Moral Philosophy,* contains, as has been observed, several "epigrams" in
verse, collected from English writers. But the earliest English
writer to translate any considerable number of classical epigrams, and to treat the form as sufficiently important to deserve
a place to itself among literary categories was George Turbervile, who did so many minor things worth doing, that it is a
great pity he could not do any of them well. It is observed
with surprise by several students of the Elizabethan era that
the Elizabethan writers of epigrams seem to have no idea of
giving "point" or what nowadays would be called "epigrammatic
surprise" to their writings. Of course, the conception of the

epigram, so far as it derives from the Greek, involved no idea of smartness. The Greek epigram as the Elizabethans knew it from the collection first printed by Ianus Cornarius in 1529, or from the translations of selections which followed this edition, was a poem complete with a certain decisive unity within a small space; but it seldom ended with a "snap," and it was seldom witty in the modern sense. Originally, of course, the epigram was an actual inscription, commonly funereal or dedicatory; then later poets wrote imaginary inscriptions, and in that way the epigram, becoming more and more inclusive in character, came to be a poem of a few lines having in ideal something of the brevity and finish of a good inscription. Parody and weakening imitation were at work, also, and in the course of ages—the period covered by the Planudean collection runs over about two thousand years—very diverse compositions were gathered into the Anthology. It even included some brief narratives. But in general the epigrams of the Greek Anthology had in common brevity, the vitality that comes from concreteness of subject, and some energy of either mind or feeling. Much that in Greek would have been made into an epigram appears in Elizabethan literature as a sonnet, the conception of which as held by Petrarch was to develop an idea by a similitude or a series of similitudes to an elaborate completion. Shakespeare's magnificently built periods in *That time of year,* or *When in disgrace* are examples. Milton on Shakespeare, Dryden on Milton,—English brief epitaphs or dedicatory verses in general are not distinguished works. Shelley's shortest poems are essentially lyric; they are cries, they have so much of the divine madness that they approach mystic nothingness; one could not take time to carve them on stone. Landor's examples are more nearly like the Greek.

On Himself

I strove with none, for none was worth my strife;
  Nature I lov'd, and next to Nature, Art;
I warm'd both hands before the fire of life;
  It sinks, and I am ready to depart.

MARGARET

Mother, I cannot mind my wheel;
My fingers ache, my lips are dry;
Oh, if you felt the pain I feel!
But oh, who ever felt as I!

No longer could I doubt him true,
All other men may use deceit;
He always said my eyes were blue,

Later verses written under the influence of the conception expressed by Coleridge, who distinguishes poetry from prose in that the former should give pleasure in every part as well as in the whole, or Keats' declaration that he meant to load every rift with ore, or Poe's that only short poems are possible, has made English ideals approach more nearly to the epigram. Some of our late work after the Chinese is not wholly unlike a Greek epigram. Mr. Walter de la Mare's

Here lies a most beautiful lady,
Light of step and heart was she;
I think she was the most beautiful lady
That ever was in the West Country.

But beauty vanishes; beauty passes,
However rare—rare it be;
And when I crumble, who will remember
That lady of the West Country?

modern as it is (there are no *ladies* possible in Greek epigrams) approaches the epigram, but its pattern is too archaistic, too dependent on recurrent sound and phrase for the severity of the Greek serious epigrams on the dead.

The only collection known to the sixteenth century of course was that of the Anthology made by the monk Planudes in the fourteenth century, of which Professor Mackail says that "there is a marked tendency to select later and worse in preference to earlier and better epigrams,"[33] and the English translators showed a tendency to select from it, again, likewise the worse; the more abstract and gnomic epigrams because of their conscious and clear didactics, or those of coarse ridicule because of their superficial vigor and the ease of translating them.

[33]*Select Epigrams from the Greek Anthology*, 3d ed. rev. (London 1911) p. 23.

Though the earliest extant edition of George Turbervile's *Epitaphs, Epigrams, Songs and Sonets* dates from 1567, it must have been preceded by an edition which, however, must be later than March 1564.   There are in it some forty-two short poems which may be regarded as epigrams and of these thirty-one are translated from Latin translations of Greek epigrams, collected and published by Janus Cornarius in *Selecta Epigrammata Graeca Latine Versa, ex septem Epigrammatum Graecorum libris,* Basileae 1529.

In 1577 Timothy Kendall published *Flowers of Epigrammes, out of sundrie the most singular authors, as well auncient as late writers.*   In this work Kendall makes free use of Turbervile's epigrams, without acknowledgment; indeed he prints likewise without acknowledgment several epigrams by other English writers.   Professor Rollins speaks severely of Kendall's course: "Kendall's plagiarisms are almost unbelievably impudent"—and seems to suggest that Kendall falsified by attributing epigrams really by Turbervile to classic sources,— "Epigrams said by Kendall to be translated from Ausonius" . . . "Epigrams said by Kendall to be translated 'out of Greek'."[34]   This severity, I think, would have surprised Kendall and Turbervile.   The word *Flowers* in the title means the *pick, selected examples* of the best elegant extracts.   *The Anthology* itself, *Florilegium,* is a collection of flowers, plucked in the garden of poetry.   Thus there were *Flores Legum* often printed in the sixteenth century, *Flores Erasmi, Flores Terentii,* to which reference was made earlier.   Even in the nineteenth century *Flowers of Fable,* and *Flowers of Piety* were published.   Kendall's title therefore means *The Best Epigrams selected from Ancient and Modern Writers.*   And as is well known the rights of literary property had not been established in his day; and even on principles of decorum as then understood there was no obligation upon him to print his author's name in his anthology.   He draws epigrams from Grimald, Surrey, and Sir Thomas Elyot without acknowledgment.

---

[34]Rollins, Hyder E., *New Facts about George Turbervile,* in *Mod. Phil.,* xv (1918), p. 513 ff; Lathrop, H. B., *Janus Cornarius, Selecta Epigrammata Graeca and the Early English Epigrammatists.* M L N xliii (1928) p. 223; since this article was published I have found that Turbervile's indebtedness to Cornarius's selections was noted by Emil Koeppel in the appendix to his article, *Englische Tasso-Uebersetzungen,* in *Anglia* xiii (1891), p. 69.

The editor of the edition published by the Spenser Society is quite wrong in saying that the epigrams are the work of one author. On the contrary, as Kendall has been traced to his sources, it is evident that his collection is mainly drawn from the work of others.

In comparing his epigrams with the printed forms of his originals we find remarkable variations. Grimald's epitaph on Cicero, for example, appears as the epitaph of *Titus Liuius,* his second epitaph on Sir James Wilford is attributed to Beza and is said to be on Budaeus, and several of Turbervile's epigrams appear in a form nearer to their originals than that in the printed book. Did Kendall mainly edit these poems, restoring them to their sources, or did he have before him manuscripts differing from the printed text? In the case of the matter from Grimald it would seem that the latter is the case, for if he had known Tottel's *Miscellany,* it is almost certain, as Mr. Crawford suggests, that he would have used it more freely.

Kendall has fifty epigrams in the list headed "Out of Greek." All but one are in Cornarius' collection; that one is *There's many a slip twixt the cup and the lip* (Anth. Pal. X, 32) It might have come from Erasmus' *Adagia,* where it is the first adage of the fifth century of the first Chiliad. All the epigrams but three, moreover, are in the same order in which they appear in Cornarius, Timon's epitaph being placed at the end for evident rhetorical effect, and the others being only slightly misplaced. The first epigram in the *Flowers* moreover is *"Out of Pulix an auncient Poet"* and the first epigram in *Selecta Epigrammata Graeca* is headed *Pulicis Poetae antiqui.* Kendall, accordingly, seems to me to have probably worked directly from Cornarius' collection, but I believe he followed a manuscript. It is unlikely that he should have altered Turbervile's poems to bring in the original proper names, or in other respects to make them approach more closely to their originals. Kendall's epigrams include about a hundred and twenty from Martial, sixty recognized as coming from the Greek Anthology, two from Claudian, and nineteen from Ausonius, of which some half dozen were originally translated from the Greek by Ausonius himself.

About one third of the *Epigrams* (omitting T. Kendall's

Trifles at the end of the book) are from antiquity; the rest
are by learned men, mostly of the century: Politian, Beza,
Thomas More, Pontanus, George Buchanan, Stephanus, Walter
Haddon, John Parkhurst, Bishop of Norwich, Roger Ascham;
Pictorius, B. Dardanius, Michael Tarchamota Marcullus,—
strongly and controversially protestant.

They are coarse and vulgar, not licentious, in general miser-
ably done. From Martial Kendall draws epigrams of personal
attack, and tiny verses (as it were alphabet verses) on objects,
—leeks, peacocks, the book chest, tooth powder,—Martial's in-
decency is omitted intentionally. The epigrams from Ausonius are mostly on pictures and emblems and include several
translations from the Greek. The Greek epigrams are gnomic
verses on life and conduct, and the coarser type of personal
epigrams, harshly grotesque: *The Drowned Boy, Orestes killing his mother.* From Claudian come *The Boar and Lion,*
and *The Poor Man in Love.* After the *Flowers of Epigrammes* there follows a collection with a separate title-page:
"*Trifles* by Timothe Kendal deuised and written (for the
moste part) at sundry tymes in his yong and tender age."[35]
Among the trifles are half a dozen classical epigrams, including
the pseudo-Theocritean Idyll 19 (Cupid stung by a Bee) which
had somehow got into the Anthology and was included in
Cornarius's selections, with several Latin versions. The
pretty Moschus Idyll, *Runaway Cupid* in Turbervile, Col. 187,
came from the Anthology. It has been translated into Latin
by Politian, and by others (*Selecta Epigrammata,* pp. 55-58).

Upon these selections we may remark, first, that the selections made by Turbervile are indiscriminate, but include a certain number of the epigrams of the Planudean collection which
had charm or special energy. (*The pine to the mariner; Of a
covetous niggard; Amor Fugitivus*) as well as a much larger
proportion of the mere grotesque (*Of the cruel hatred of step-
mothers; Of a physician and a soothsayer; Of a deefe plaintiff;*
etc.) and a small number of sheerly didactic gnomes without
imaginative or concrete quality (*The open foe and fayned
friend*). Kendall's taste is shown by his faculty for selecting
altogether the last two types (*Great nose; Long beard; Few*

---

[35]Hutton, James, *Timothy Kendall's Trifles and Nicholas Bourbon's
Nugae* in M L N (1929) xliv, 19; *cf. England's Parnassus, compiled by
Robert Allot, 1600, edited by Charles Crawford* (Oxon. 1913), note on p. 484.

teeth; It matters not where a man die; Nothing is hid from God.) He adds to the types selected by Turbervile a good many of the conceits on statues. (*Myron's cow, Venus seen by Praxiteles,* etc.) The saving quality of such things is evidently perfection of form, lightness of touch, deftness and elegance. But Kendall has a natural gift of loutishness of style; and if Turbervile is not so bad he only is so because he has no positive quality at all. Chalmers[36] seems to hold the poor man responsible for his flat jests and gives him the importance of passing on the tradition, ". . . his occasional strokes on large noses and other personal redundancies or defects, descended afterwards to Shakespeare, and other dramatic writers." I think it is too much to credit Turbervile with passing on the classic tradition to Bardolph and Falstaff.

Considering the importance of the pastoral in English literature during the Elizabethan age, alike as a type and as a spirit affecting the lyric, the drama, and the romance of the era, it is somewhat strange to observe the complete insignificance of the versions of pastoral poems. Mention has already been made of Webbe's, Fleming's, and Fraunce's translations of Vergil's *Bucolics* and *Georgics* between 1586 and 1591. In addition there were the anonymous translation of *Six Idillia* of Theocritus, 1588, (*dedicated to* E. D., not *made by* E. D., and hence not by Sir Edward Dyer, whoever E. D. may be), a "Dialogue betwixt two Sea nymphs . . . out of Lucian," by Giles Fletcher, the elder, in *Licia,* 1593, and the first (in modern editions numbered *second*) Idyl of Moschus, by Barnabe Barnes, in *Parthenophil and Parthenope,* 1593.

The *Six Idillia* of Theocritus are: Idylls 8, 11, 18, 20 (wrongly numbered 21), and 30 (wrongly numbered 31). The translation is in various meters, but mainly in the fourteener couplet. The eighteenth is the most interesting.

> In Sparta long agoe, when Menelaus wore the crowne,
> Twelve noble Virgins, daughters to the greatest in the towne,
> All dight vpon their haire in Crowtoe garlands fresh & greene,
> Danst at the chamber doore of Helena the Quene,
> What time this Menelay, the younger Sonne of Atreus,
> Did marry with this lovely daughter of Prince Tyndarus.
> And therewithal at eve, a wedding song they iointly sung,
> With such a shuffling of their feete, that all the Pallace rung.

---

[36]Life of Turbervile in *Chalmers' English Poets.*

Of the idyl of Moschus in Barnes's *Parthenophil and Parthenope,* the first two-thirds are gracefully and cleverly turned; the last part is awkward. Sir Sidney Lee (*Cambridge History of English Literature,* Vol. III, p. 265) has been misled by the numbering into speaking of it as "what *purports* to be a translation of Moschus's first Eidullion." Modern editions, indeed, number the idyll second; but the translation is exceedingly exact. In general Barnes lacks restraint, condensation, energy; he has facility without artistic conscience, but his writing manifests a direct contact with the late minor Greek writers; the Anthology, the Anacreontics, and the Alexandrians. In consequence his writings have the hot, musky quality of his models, not relieved or refreshed by the English pastoral reality.

The madrigal "Rest thee desire," by Robert Greene is from the pseudo-anacreontic poems, (Anthologia Lyrica, no. 31). It is the familiar poem in which Cupid begs protection from the storm and wounds his host. Though Greene's version does not correspond with any known French version, it is unlikely that he went direct to the Greek. "It would be absurd to call Greene a scholar," as Professor Collins says;[37] all his poems have the background of French or Italian belles-lettrists: "They remind us sometimes of Bembo and Sannazzaro, and sometimes of Desportes and Ronsard." But besides this, it was Greene who first made the magic union of Italian or French grace, delicate, but lacking in vitality, with the blithe and brisk rural and sylvan tradition of English life. This Greene does most effectively in his plays, but no less really in his romances and his songs.

The chief value of the verse translations made in this era of obscure growth before the great burst of the end of the century was that they made it easy for the English reader to become acquainted with the body of ancient poetical story: the tale of Troy in the *Aeneid,* the marvels of Greek mythology in Ovid, the most horrible aspects of Greek tragedy in Seneca. The other verse, the clumsy epigrams, the insipid pastorals, gave nothing to excite the imagination, or to arouse thought, or to call forth emulation. The few translations of any effectiveness are graceful trifles.

---

[37]Greene's *Works,* ed. J. Churton Collins (Oxon. 1905), Vol. I, p. 16.

The prose is more important. Translators threw themselves as heartily upon narrative fiction in prose as in verse; their work was almost as enthusiastically welcomed and has proved to be even more enduring. Some of these versions, the first in our study, unless Caxton's *Aesop* be reckoned, have continued to interest by their own charm and to be reprinted for their own sake down to our own time. The Greek and Latin tales are characteristic productions of a decadent era,—learnedly voluptuous, or quiveringly chaste, or elaborately simple, or comic with a sudden gruesome twist. They were eagerly received by the public, which took pleasure in violent effects, and indeed proved more hospitable to post-classical than to classical Greek and Latin works. The prose style of a school of writers, pleasantly rhythmic in movement, and characterized systematically by that colored and colloquial diction which has been noted as a fault in several of the verse translations, proved to be well suited to this kind of material, in so much that two of our English minor masterpieces—Underdowne's *Aethiopica* and Adlington's Apuleius—are Elizabethan translations of late Greek and Latin tales.

Apuleius in his Latin dress has been a popular author ever since he was first printed (1469); the *Asinus Aureus* had been translated into French by Guillaume Michel and again by George de la Bouthière; Beroaldus supplied an illuminating commentary; and the Latin writer, in spite of his difficult style, took his place, not quite at the head, but near the head of the group of popular Wanton Masters.

His evident purpose is to put his reader into the highest possible state of agitation. He deals in elaborate lewdness not merely frankly but enthusiastically, sets forth horrors almost as hauntingly terrible as the Japanese imaginings recorded by Lafcadio Hearn, shocks his reader with sheer disgust, mauls him with sheer physical terror, touches him with eerie sweetness, and awes him and consoles him with the mystic powers of imposing religious ceremony. The robber's cave, the witch's dimly lighted place of incantation, the soubrette's bedroom, speaking ghosts, gods seen in visions, invisible servitors, seeming beasts that are men, moonlight on the waters, and an oppressed maiden restored to her lover—everything is there that can work strongly upon the reader's nerves. Nearly all this

certainly, even the Isis part probably, is Greek in origin, so
that Apuleius gives us a knowledge of what may be called the
late Greek lower superstition as typical as Ovid's learned as-
sembling of the mythology.

But Apuleius is determined that his style in itself shall be as
exciting as his matter: swiftly moving sentences, with strong
concentrations and alterations of emphasis, and vivid brief
rhythm, but with no effort for consecutive flow, abstract words
for concrete, and extraordinary metaphors, old words, new
words, queer words; he is as conscientiously astounding in his
manner as a reporter of sporting news. It is a pity that the
best modern editions of Adlington's version suggest that all
this ingenuity may be due in part to the fact that Apuleius
wrote Latin not as a native tongue. It is not true that ". . .
he was a typical Romano-African, speaking a somewhat mixed
tongue which had to be clarified when he settled as a lecturer in the capitol."[38] Apuleius was no more and no less a
foreigner than other provincials, than Seneca the Spaniard,
or Ausonius the Gaul. Africa was as completely Latinized as
any other part of the Western Empire, and there is no more
reason for thinking that Apuleius spoke a barbarian or half-
barbarian tongue at home, than to think the same of other
great Africans, such as St. Augustine, or Tertullian. He
wrote—though in an extreme form—the fashionable style of
baroque rhetoric.[39]

Thomas Adlington, in his translation, pretty consistently
and apparently of set purpose avoided the extravagance of
Apuleius's style, retaining nearly always the agitating substance, usually securing an appropriate, or even a powerfully
sympathetic tone, but expressing himself more simply and normally than his original. His own remark in his introductory
letter to the reader is that "the author had written his woork
in so darke and highe a style, in so straunge and absurde
woordes, and in such newe inuented phrases, as he seemed
rather to set it foorth, to shew his magnificency of prose, then
to participate his dooinges to other": and for my part I think
the translation better than the original, for I am unable to
read Apuleius without having my attention drawn so constantly

---

[38]*e.g.* Seccombe's edition (1913) p. xi.
[39]*Cf. Apulei Apologia*, Butler, H. D., and Owen, A. S., edd. (Oxon. 1914),
p. xiii.

away to the oddity and difficulty of the language that I lose
the thrill of the situation, and thus the language comes into
conflict with the substance. As Adlington says toward the end
of his letter: "I haue not so exactly passed thorough the Auth-
or, as to pointe euery sentence accordinge as it is in Latine, or
so absolutely translated every woord, as it lieth in the prose,
(for so the French and Spanish translators haue not done)
considering the same in our vulgar tongue would haue appeared
very obscure and darke, and thereby consequently, lothsome to
the Reader, but nothing erringe as I trust from the giuen and
naturall meaninge of the author, haue vsed more common and
familiar woords (yet not so muche as I might doo) for the
plainer settinge foorth of the same."

Adlington was in part led to this very free treatment of his
original because he did not understand him, and relied on a
French translation. Mr. Whibley has proved the connection
between the two versions neatly and amusingly in his Introduction. Adlington refers also to a Spanish translation; but the
only Spanish translation antecedent to his of which I find
record is that of Lopez de Castegana. Careful examination
fails to bring out any connection between the two. It is true
that like Adlington Lopez chose a simpler style than Apuleius,
and that in the most scabrous situations, he has the same regard
for decency; but he gives the sense of Apuleius nearly always.
If Adlington had paid any attention to this version, he would
not have followed his French guide every time he went into the
ditch.

Briefly speaking, Adlington not only modifies his original
intentionally, but often quite misunderstands him; and he leaves
out details which he does not understand. These changes are
unintentional; but in the main his modifications are with distinct design. He modifies and omits freely for the sake of decency and he reduces Apuleius' high-flown language where
there is nothing in it but the attempt to make a show of words.
For example Apuleius always makes a display about sunrise,
and Adlington always cuts him down to the sober fact.

Vt primum tenebris abiectis dies inalbebat (Just as soon as
the darkness was cast off and day began to whiten) becomes
"assone as the night was paste" (VII, I); *Vt primum nocte
discussa, sol novus diem facit* (As soon as night was shaken

off, and the new sun brought day), "As soone as night was passed, and the day began to springe" (II, I); *commodum pernicantibus phaleris aurora roseum quatiens lacertum coelum inequitabat, et me secura quiete reculsum, nox diei reddidit,* (as Aurora with her jewels glowing red rode up the sky shaking her rosy arm, and night snatching me from careless quiet gave me back to day), "when morninge was come and that I was awaked from sleepe" (III, I).

Three features of Adlington's style may be remarked: he substitutes for the abrupt and chiming rhythm of Apuleius an ample and flowing manner, using connectives and filling up omissions, and balancing large groups unostentatiously but harmoniously. His diction is habitually a little raised above prose without being extreme and strange, and now and then flowers into imaginatively exquisite phrase. There is a bright picture of the gay Fotis, as she was shaking the sauce-pan, (II, 9) "girded about her bodie vnder her pappes with a swathel of redde silke." There is a gentle vision of "poore Psyches left alone wepyng and tremblinge on the toppe of the rocke . . . and carried from the hill, with a meke winde, which retained her garments up, and by little and litle brought her down into a deepe valley, where she was laide in a bedde of most sweete and fragrant flowres" (V); and a grim one of the slaves: "O good Lorde what a sort of poore slaves were there, some had their skinne black and blew: some had their backes striped with lashes, some weer couered with rugged sackes, some had their members only hidden some ware such ragged cloutes that you might perceave all their naked bodies, some were marked on the forehedes with hote yrons, some had their heare half clipped, some had lockes on their legges, some were ugly and evill favored, that thei coulde skarse see, their eies and faces were so blacke and dimme with smoke, like those which fight together in the sandes [i.e., the arenas], and knowe not where they strike by reason of duste, and some had their faces all mealey." (IX. 39).

Even more important in the history of literature through its influence upon a long line of works inspired by its principles of composition is the *Aethiopica* of Heliodorus. Praised by Cervantes and Tasso, a source for Calderon and Sidney, quoted by Shakespeare and Burton, Heliodorus is now forgotten.

The truth is, he was the first master of a tiresome style, and gave rise to tiresome imitations. When the learned Abbé Huet said of him, "if Homer was the source of all good poetry, Heliodorus was so for all good fiction in prose,"[40] he was writing in the spirit of the time before Boileau demolished the heroes of Romance. The long-winded novels, alike of shepherdry and gallantry, all spring from Heliodorus. The *Arcadia* of Sidney, the *Arcadia* of Montemayor, *L'Astrée, Cassandre,* and so on to *Ibrahim or the illustrious Bassa,* all adopted its ideals and its plans and through them, though at a distance, the effect of this novel upon the ideals of Richardson may be perceived.

The narrative of Heliodorus is. well characterized by the heroine Chariclea in her midnight lament near the beginning.

> And when all was whiste in the marish, and every man at rest, the maide tooke that occasion, and absence of men, to be a fit time, to lament and waile, and the rather for that in the night, shee coulde neyther see or heare anie thing, that might comfort her, but contrariwise move her to sorrowe: when therefore with her selfe secretlie shee had wailed alone (for she was by the Captaines commaundement separated from companie, and laide in a simple bedde) and wept very bitterly, Apollo (said she) how much more grievous punishment doest thou take of us then we have deserved? Hast thou not beene sufficientlie revenged on us for that that is past? For as much as wee are farre from our frendes and kinsfolkes, and that wee were taken by Pyrates, and subject to six hundred daungers more by Sea, but that nowe againe wee must on the Lande fall into the handes of theeves and robbers: beside, who knoweth whether any thing worse is like to light upon us? when wilt thou make an ende? if in death, that shalbe voide of injurie. Oh that death woulde like me wel: but rather then any man shoulde filthilie knowe me, which Theagines never did, truelie with haulter I woulde ende my life, reserving my selfe pure and chaste (as hitherto I have done) even unto death, and thereby gaine a beautifull Epitaph for my singular virginitie, and no judge shall bee so cruell as thou.[41]

Written long after the Greek theatre had disappeared, by a Syrian who delighted in the reading of plays, it is made to combine as much as possible of theatric with epic narrative fiction. An exotically striking or pompous setting is provided —in the reedy fastnesses of the Egyptian bandits; at the great feast of the Aenions at Delphi; at the sacrifice in Aethiopia.

[40]*Essai sur l'origine des romans* (1670).
[41]Whibley, Charles, ed., in *Tudor Translations* No. V (1895), p. 15.

And the chief actors come upon the scene in striking fashion, magnificently costumed, Chariclea rising up and awing the brigands in the first act; Theagenes on horseback, leading the procession in the second; in the third Chariclea leaping into the fire.

The most marvelous and sudden events, melodramatic coincidences, so many that it is not worth while to reckon them up, and as many hair-breadth scapes, chase each other rapidly through the book.

But this brilliant excitement is all external; the author, being destitute of imagination, cannot create a character; he cannot produce even a logical unity of cause and effect. His one talent is ingenuity of handling. He is resolved that Chariclea shall be saved a virgin for Theagenes, and that Theagenes shall keep himself a virgin for her until the recognition and the marriage at the end. He plunges *in medias res* to get a hold on the attention, and he brings the story up to date by instalments of parenthetical narratives.

Of course all this is quite unchanged in Underdowne. And I must admit that in his pages the story is so tedious that I cannot read it continuously. But in the style there is a great alteration, and I think with Mr. Whibley a great improvement. The style of Heliodorus is full of ingenious conceits, drawn especially from stagecraft, but lacks color and various rhythm. It is poor and thin. But Underdowne is rich and full-bodied. He has the gift, like Adlington, of an ample rhythm; but unlike him, having a tamely written original, he heightens and gives spirit to the diction. The translation is made from the Latin of a Polish gentleman, Stanislas Warschewiczki, who in no way enriches his original, but passes on his errors to Underdowne.

A few examples will illustrate Underdowne's heightening of his original:

> ventus iam et nimio impetu languescebat et paulo post remissus, inefficaciter et molliter in vela incidebat, concutiens magis quam promouens aut protendens lintea.

> The vehement winde began to waxe caulme, so that within a little while it was almost downe, and blewe softly to no purpose on our sayles, whereby it rather huffed them together, then made any way for our ship. (Bk. v, p. 73.)

. . . . tradebat annulum quendam regium, eximiam rem et diuinam, quod ad circulum attinet ex electro confectum, caeterum in pala amethysto Aethiopica relucentem, tanta magnitudine, quanta oculus virginalis circumscribit et occupat: pulchritudine autem longe Ibericum et Britannicum superante. Haec enim inerti, et cui nullus adest splendor, flore rubet: similisque est rosae, quae primum ex baccis in folia finditur, et tum radiis solis rubescere incipit. At amethystus Aethiopica valde et ex profundo rutilat. Quod si tenens illam circumuerses radium proiicit aureum non obscurantem asperitate visum, sed gratia et puritate singulari illustrantem. Atque et vis ipsi inest genuina prae occidentalibus. Neque enim falso sibi vendicat appellationem, sed vere arcet ebrietatem ab eo a quo fertur, sobrium illum in conuiuiis retinens. Ac eiusmodi quidem est omnis Indica et Aethiopica amethystus.

. . . . he deliuered him a princely ringe, a passinge heauenlie thinge; as touching the hoope, it was of Iuorie, wherein was set a brighte amethyst of *Aethiopia* as great as a maydens eye, in beauty farre better then those of Iberia or Britaine. For those haue but an ill couler, which shines not at all, but are like to the rose budde at the firste, which after with the heate of the sunne waxe perfecte redde. But the *Aethiopian amethyst,* hath a perfecte orient colour, and shineth throughout, and if you turne him aboute, as you holde him, he casteth forth a golden beame, which doth not hurte or dimme the sight but maketh it much better and clearer, and he hath a naturall vertue, more then the westerne stones: for it hath not his name without effecte, but will not lette him be drunke in deede, that weareth him, but kepeth him sober at all feastes: and of this qualitie is euery *Amethyst* of *India,* and Aethiopia. (Bk. v, p. 67.)

The first edition (1569?) has a dedication to Edward De Vere, Earl of Oxford, and *The Contentes* of all the books follow, preceding the translation. The second edition (1587) has been revised with no small care, and improved in detail, not with reference to fidelity in translation, but to clearness and rationality in expression. The arguments are placed before each chapter. The *sundry additions* said to be contained in it consist of new prefatory matter, an epistle *To the gentle reader. Of the author out of the Latine.* A third edition (1602) is identical with the 1587 edition and in a fourth edition (1622) with a new dedication, by W. Barret to Sir John Sidley, Bart., and no other prolegomena, Underdowne's language has been somewhat modernized.

James Sandford translated Book IV from Warschewiczki (printed in 1567) omitting the Ethiopian origin of Chariclea, and the compact of the Phenicians to carry her away, and in brief as nearly as possible leaving the book complete in itself. The translation is crude, particularly in sentence-structure, and careless, being so vague in its diction as to leave no distinct impression on the mind of the reader. The translation is intended to fill the pages of a little book comprising first of all the *Amorous and Tragic Tales* of Plutarch, and dedicated to Sir Hugh Paulet. The preface is stuffed with classical examples of the evils of hot love and fleshly lust.

Plutarch's few and short narratives have little enough of the erotic in them, but are grim illustrations of the cruelty and violence which have never ceased to curse the Balkan peninsula. Sandford has translated from the elegant Latin of Politian. Even with the Heliodorus the book was so tiny that he appended some of the sentences of the Greek Philosophers, translated from the French to make up the measure of his gilt cup.

Even so we are not done with Heliodorus. Abraham Fraunce included at the end of *The Countess of Pembroke's Ivychurch* (1591) the opening scene and the taking of Theagenes and Chariclea to the brigands' pool, in quantitative English hexameters, already quoted (p. 122).

Daphnis and Chloe, though in itself a more interesting and perfect work than any of the other erotic romances and an even more potent influence than they, was much more unfortunate than *Theagenes and Chariclea* in its English translator. Indeed it has qualities of tone, a certain delicacy, in spite of its frankness, or even wantonness, a certain fitness of style, that made it the more difficult to translate. Amyot's French version, which was the original of the English translation of Angel Day (1587) is not one of his most successful: his loose and picturesque method was not suited to his material; and he was constrained by modesty to omit the erotic lessons of the original, which are essential to the action. Day found this turning point of the narrative quite inadequately dealt with, so he excised it wholly and filled the evident gap with *The Shepheard's Holiday,* a foolish and inappropriate pastoral scene in honor of Elizabeth. He also inserted clumsy amoeboeic verses in every episode, I suppose to give a true pastoral flavor. The translation, negligent from the first, grows looser and looser as it advances.[42]

William Painter's (or Paynter's) *Palace of Pleasure* (tome i, 1566; tome ii, 1567; revised and enlarged edition, 1575) receives the credit of having introduced into English literature the fiction of Italy with all that that implies of exotic color and interesting evil. It is true that two-thirds of his tales are drawn from Italian collections and their imitations—the *Decameron,* the *Heptameron, Il Pecorone,* Bandello, Cinthio, Straparola. But Painter began, as he tells us, with the intention of giving the English readers a group of narratives not from Italian sources, but the Roman historian Livy, and never altogether lost sight of the classics as a source of interesting anecdotes. Though his classical stories are mainly drawn from historians and biographers, they are selected for their picturesqueness and piquancy, for a human and imaginative, not for a historical and informative value, and hence the *Palace of Pleasure* takes a place among the translations of imaginative creation rather than of instruction and useful learning. Indeed he has translated chiefly myths or mythologized anecdotes: the tales of the Horatii and the Curiatii, Coriolanus, Candaules, Solon and Croesus, Cyrus and Panthea, Abdolominus, King of Tyre, Timon, Faustina; of virtues and vices on the heroic scale; of constancy, of monstrous lust, of overweening pride, of majestic self-control in kings, of genial generosity, of treachery scourged, and love triumphing in death.

Among Paynter's one hundred and one narratives, thirty-seven are directly or mediately from Greek or Latin authors; thirty-two are direct translations; seven tales are directly translated from Livy; a group of these narratives, mainly the heroic traditions of the days of the kings and the early republic in the first two books, begins his first volume and gives the tone of the whole. Next to them come twelve anecdotes, mostly dramatic stories of notable personalities, from Aulus Gellius. The first volume contains in its earlier parts two anecdotes from Herodotus, three from Aelian, three from Quintus Curtius, two from

---

[42] A thorough discussion of the bibliography and the translators' methods is to be found in Wolff, S. L. *The Greek Romances in English Prose Fiction* (N. Y. 1912), p. 234 ff.; see also Greg, W. W., *Pastoral Poetry and Pastoral Drama* (1906).

Plutarch, and one from Xenophon. In brief, the first twenty-eight of the sixty-six tales in the first part, or about five-twelfths, are Greek or Latin stories, nearly all of them translated quite accurately from the original Latin, or from Latin translations of the Greek. A few are taken from Italian versions. In the second volume, nine of the thirty-five tales, or about a quarter, are drawn from Justin, Quintus Curtius, Plutarch, Livy, the *Historia Augusta,* Strabo, and Diodorus Siculus. Of the thirty-seven tales which retell the ancient stories pretty accurately, thirty-two are direct from the originals, or from the current Latin versions; five from Italian sources, particularly from Bandello. Whether translated directly or from intermediate versions, the originals are presented substantially without modification in contents, tone, or language. Paynter renders his Latin freely and in general accurately, his errors looking like signs of haste rather than of ignorance. His style is painstakingly heavy.[43]

Paynter, beginning with the intention of giving to the English public a selection of dramatic classical anecdotes, had gradually submerged them among his Italian narratives, of which they almost took the color and became a part. George Pettie in *A petite Pallace of Pettie his pleasure*[44] took another step. He employed the names and the general situations of classical stories for eleven of his twelve tales, but made the tone, the language, and even the incidents anew; his stories are romantically erotic in spirit, Italianized in setting, and euphuistic in style, and as he tells us abound in covert allusions to occurrences in the lives of his private friends. His Admetus, Eriphile, and Minos make love in the fashion of the imitators of

---

[43]Koeppel, Emil, *Studien zur Geschichte der italienischen Novelle in der englischen Literatur des sechzehnten Jahrhunderts, Q. u. F.* LXX (1892), corrects Jacobs's inaccurate references to Italian sources; Bush, Douglas, *The Classical Tales in Painter's Palace of Pleasure,* J. E. G. XXIII (1924), p. 331, corrects those to classical sources: Bush's notes may be supplemented by the following memoranda. The twelfth narrative of the first tome (Abdolominus),—Jacobs' reference, "Quintus Curtius VI.: 19-16 (sic)" should be "Quintus Curtius, IV, iii, 1-4. The classical origins of the first narrative of the second tome (Amazons) are to be found in Justin II, iv; Strabo, *Geog.* XI, 503-595; Diodorus Siculus, II, 45-46. The classical original of the tenth and fourteenth narratives of the second tome is the *Historia Augusta* (Faustina, x, 1, 5; Zenobia xxii, 4, 5; xxiii, 10, 15, 30; xxvi, 22-23).

[44]1576; three editions, n.d.; repr. in *The King's Classics,* ed. Gollancz, Sir I. (1908), with a good introduction; and see Koeppel, E., *Studien zur Geschichte der italienischen Novelle; Q. u. F.* LXX (1892), p. 21 ff.

Petrarch, his Amphiaraus quotes the Bible, and his Progne chatters Euphuism before Euphues existed,[45] as readily as an Elizabethan maid of honor. The work of Pettie, accordingly, is in place here only as an illustration of the fact that conversance with Greek and Latin authors had no influence in the age of Elizabeth as a make-weight or a correction of the dominant tendencies of the age toward color, excitement, sentiment, exuberance, and excess.

The translations of the prose of use create as baffling an impression of strangeness, of a certain perverseness, as those of the prose of imagination. The judgment of the classics had ceased to be medieval, but it had not even yet become critical. As by a kind of instinct the translators reached out for late works of large scope and ample incident, in verse, in story, in history, and of general prudential wisdom in thought. To begin with history, and its handmaid, descriptive geography. The dedications and prefaces of the scholars who edited or translated into Latin for the benefit of educated men the historians of antiquity abound in dissertations on the value of history to the man of affairs, and especially to rulers and their agents, or as they were called, "courtiers" and "gentlemen." French princes were early supplied with a library of ancient history, translated into simple language, and supplied with clear explanations of allusions and the background of life. But the English translators lagged far behind their continental predecessors. Golding did indeed give his contemporaries that living book Caesar's *Commentaries on the Gallic War,* but he did so because of its special interest to English readers as dealing with France and Britain. Before that he translated Justin's abridgment of Trogus, and followed the Caesar with Pomponius Mela's general geography and Solinus's natural (and unnatural) history. Another summary work, Eutropius's *Breviary* was translated by Nicholas Haward (1564), and Appian's *Roman Wars* (1576) by a certain W. B. Finally, North's Plutarch (1579) gave a lively knowledge of the greatest warriors and statesmen of antiquity. Only these historical and geographical works were completely translated. A few books of Diodorus were done, but of recognized historians of importance only a book of Polybius and two books of Herod-

---

[45]*Euphues,* ed. Landmann, Heilbronn (1887), p. xxi.

otus. Why was this? Thucydides and Tacitus may well have daunted any translator by their austerity of thought and the difficulty of their language. Moreover, they dealt with subjects of quite limited range. But Herodotus was general in his scope and was accessible in Latin; Polybius was as important and interesting as Appian, and Livy and Suetonius would certainly have proved richly entertaining. Only on the threshold of the next period did Savile begin upon Tacitus. Why were Justin and Eutropius preferred; why were Solinus and Mela and Dionysius Periegetes translated, and Aelian, and Eunapius? Because the translators desired to give their readers the largest amount of information about the facts of history. Just as in poetry what was needed and welcomed was abundance of mythic story, a supply of material for the imagination —not quality, not realized poetic conception flowering in the perfect work, so in history and the works dealing generally with the life of man, it was not the energetic seizing of life by a great mind, not the intense vision of Thucydides or the ample picturesqueness and humanity of Livy that was wanted, but a ready, swift, and abundant communication of accessible and important fact.

Among the prose translators Arthur Golding stands out, as he does among the translators of verse. First of all, he put into English Justin's abridgment of Trogus Pompeius. This book, not indeed a universal history in conception or substance, was yet as near such a thing as the classic languages had to offer. The estimate of Justin was, in Golding's words, that "it may be doubted whether he be more brief of sentence or copious of matter." The book was for Renaissance scholars the sole compendium of non-Roman ancient history, and it came into the Renaissance sanctioned by long-continued prestige, maintained especially in northern Europe.[46] Golding's dedication, addressed to "Edward de Veer, Erle of Oxenford," then a youth under the wardship of Lord Burleigh, urges the accepted grounds for the reading of history; it is an exhortation to him to read histories, so that encouraged by the example of great men who have learned much from study he may run in the renowned footsteps of his famous ancestors, in such

---

[46]Rühl, Franz, *Die Verbreitung des Justinus in Mittelalter* (Lpz. 1871), p. 50.

sort as he may be able to do acceptable service to his prince and his country.

The second edition (1570) was a revision of the first (1564) casting out unnecessary synonyms, rejecting superfluity, slightly modernizing the idiom, and increasing the accuracy of details. Thus "oth and fidelity" becomes "oth"; "security and safeguard," "security"; "obteined to diuine honors," "obteined diuine honors"; "at the length," "at length." In the first edition a passage reads: ". . . began to encourage them when they were vanquished, affirming that they were superiour as toch013ing their prowesse & puissance they should see their ennemies be faine to sue to them for peace. As for the losses and domage whereby they thought themselues so much vndone, were but two thousand women, & a few children and bondmen, the which they might better recouer by getting the victory, then by forsaking the victory for want of courage." In the revision of 1570, this becomes: ". . . began to encourage them *after their losse,* affirming that they *had the upper hand in* prowesse and puissance they should see their ennemies *sue* for peace. As for the *domage* whereby they thought themselues so much vndone, were but two thousand women, & a few children and bondmen, which they might better recouer *following* the victory, than by *shrinking from* it." The edition of 1578 is a reprint of that of 1570.

Golding's style is well illustrated in the following passage:

> The Scithians in their third viage into Asia, when they had bene a seuen yeares from their wyues and chyldren, were welcomed home with warre by their owne seruauntes. For theyr wyues beyng weryed wyth longe tarieng for theyr husbandes, supposynge that they were not so long diteyned with warres, but rather all slayne maryed them selues to theyr slaues whom theyr maysters had lefte at home to look to their cattell. The whyche hearyng of their masters returne with conquest, met them in order of battell well appoynted and harnessed, to kepe them out of their country as if they had bene straungers. The *Scithians* perceiuing that by battell they lost as much as they won, aduised themselues to vse another kinde of fight, remembring that they had not to do with their enemies but with their slaues, who ought to be ouercom not by the law of armes, but by the law of masters, against whom it was more mete to bring whippes into the field then weapons, and laying a side swordes, euery man to furnish him selfe with rods and whips, and such other kind of stuffe, wher of slaues and bondmen are wont to be afraid. This counsell was well alowed, and therfore euery man being furnished as was before ap-

poynted, when they approached to their enemies, sodenly they shoke
their whippes at them, wherwith they so amazed them, that whome
they coulde not ouercome by battell, they ouercame with fear of
beating & made them run away, not like enemies ouercome by battell,
but like runnagate slaues. As many of them as were taken were
hanged vp. The women also that knew them selues gilty of the
matter, partly by wepon, partly by hanging, wilfully dispatched them
selues. After this the Scithians liued in peace, vntill the time of
Lanthine their kinge, to whome *Darius* king of Persie (as is before
mentioned), because he woulde not geue him his Daughter in mar-
iage, made warre; and with seuen hundred thousand men in armor,
entring into *Scithia,* when he saw his enemies would not come and
geue him battel, fearing that if the bridge ouer the River of *Danow*
should chance to be broken, he shuld be enclosed. From retourning
home againe, fearfully retired ouer the water with the los of four
score and X.M. men. The which neuerthelesse was counted as no
losse, for the exceeding great nombre of men that he had in his host.
Afterward he conquered Asia and *Macedonie,* and vanquished the
Ionians vpon the sea. Finally vnderstanding that the Atheniens had
aided the *Ionians* against him, he tourned the whole brunt of the warre
vpon them.[47]

Golding in his prose is as superior to his contemporaries who
translated history as he is in his verse to his contemporaries who
translated poetry, and for much the same characteristics. His
work, it is true, is not of even quality, being in no small degree
dependent on the style of his original, but it all tends definitely
toward a certain type. He loosens and breaks up the long periods of his original, with an approach to the analytic type of
sentence normal in English idiom. Thus although many intol-
erably sprawling sentences can be found in his work, they are
not typical; he has some sense of the easier flow and clearer
outline of the shorter period. His diction is manly and vigorous, presenting an attractive mean between the sheer dryness
of Sandford or Stocker, and the slangy and picturesque freedom of Underdowne. It should be said, however, that at
best the praise to be given is qualified praise—a norm of good
writing for practical purposes had not been attained in his
day, but he contributed his part toward developing it.

Golding's version of Caesar's *Commentaries on the Gallic
War* was an important book, both on account of its subject-
matter and its execution. It gave in clear and spirited English

[47]Ed. 1564, Fo. 11-12.

the whole of a central work of history; it gave direct contact with a master personality recording (with whatever concealment or evasion) something of his own work at a crisis in history. Thus it stands out above the scraps and the versions of pedestrian chronicles which most of the translations of history provided for English readers.

In his dedication, addressed to Sir William Cecill, Golding says that he had hesitated at first because of "want of experience not only in matters of war, but also in divers other things wherof this history entreateth." Finally considering the need of the work, and encouraged by Cecil's former favorable reception of his labors, he undertook it. Brende's version of the first four books, the manuscript of which he had received from Cecil, he finally laid aside at the advice of friends, not because he thought himself "of more skill or experience than Maister Brende (which I confesse mi yeres geve me not) neither bicause I wold in defacing his glorye (which were a point of lewdnesse) go about (as the Latin proverb sayth) to pricke out the crowes eyes. But I have done it, partly . . . because I was desirous to haue the body of the whole Storye compacted vnyforme and of one stile throughout."

It is a subject of regret that we have not Brende's Caesar. His Quintus Curtius was so admirably done that it became by far the most esteemed of the earlier versions of history, having been many times reprinted; but questionless Golding acted wisely in rejecting a work at least obsolescent in style in order to make his version harmonious throughout.

The account of the last conflict at Alesia is a good illustration of Golding's somewhat abrupt but manly rendering of Caesar.

> . . . For the Galles knewe that theyr good dayes were past, if they brake not through oure fortifications: and the Romanes yf they gate thupper hand, loked for an ende of all theyr travels. The greatest daunger was at the vpper fortifications, whyther we told you that Vergasillaunus was sent. The grabbedness of the top of a place to a falling grounde hath in it great advauntage. Some threw dartes: some cast theyr shieldes over their heades and preased vpward: freshe men succeded in the roumes of theym that were tyred: the Rampier being cast down by them all into the trench, did bothe make waye for the Galles to get vppe, and also didde couer such thinges as the Romans hadde hidden in the grounde: and nowe our men had neyther weapons nor strength to helpe themselues wyth. Cesar hauing knowledge herof, sent Labienus wyth syxe Cohortes

to rescowe such as were in peryll: and commaunded that yf he were not able to susteyne hys ennemyes, he shoulde issue out wyth his Cohortes and feyghte wyth them abroade: but he warned hym in any wyse not to doe so vnlesse there were none other remedye. He him selfe goeth to the reste, and hastened theym that they shoulde not faynt in theyr travell. He tolde theym that the frute of all theyr former encounters, consisted altogether in that daye and in that one howre. More that were wythin, despayryng to do anye good at the champion places, bicause of the Longenes of oure fortifications, attempted to get vp to the stepe places, and thither they caried all theyr prouision. There wyth the multitude of dartes they beate the defendantes from the towres: thei fil vp the dikes wyth earth and hurdles: and wyth theyr hookes rend downe the Rampyer and the Vamure. Cesar sent thither fyrst yonge Brutus wyth six cohortes: and afterward hys Lieutenant C. Fabius wyth other vii. and last of all. when thencounter waxed somewhat to whot, he himselfe brought fresh men to their succor. Whereby renewing the battell and driuing his enemies backe, he went thither as he had sent Labienus. He toke wyth him iiii. Cohorts out of the next bulwarke, and commaunded part of hys horsemen to folowe him, and part to fetch a circuit aboute the vttermost fortifications, and to set vpon hys ennemies behind. When Labienus saw that neyther Rampiers nor dikes were able to hold against the violence of hys enemies, he assembled nyne and thirty cohortes whych he met by chaunce comming out of the next Bulwarks, and sent woorde by a messenger vnto Cesar, what he thought was to bee done. Cesar hervpon made hast to be present at the feight. Assone as he was perceyued to be come by the color of hys garment, (the which he vsed in battels as a mark to be knowen by) and that the cohortes and troopes of horsmen which he had commaunded to folow him, were sene (as they might earlie be perceyued from such highe groundes being so steepe and falling,) his enemies gaue him battell. A greate shoute was raysed on both sides, and lyke shoutinge was heard agayne from the campe and from al our fortifications. Our men discharging theyr dartes, came to hand strokes. Sodeinly appeared our horsmen behind them, and other Cohortes came vppon them. Then our enemyes turned theyr backes, and our horsmen meting wyth them made a great slaughter of them. Sedulius Captaine and Prince of the Lemanikes was slaine: Vergasillaunus of Auverne was taken aliue in the chase: threescore and fowrescore banners and ante-signes were brought vnto Cesar: few of that great number recouered sauf into their campe. The Townesmen beholdinge oute of the Towne the flight and slaughter of theyr companye, castinge awaye all hope of welfare, wythdrew their armye from our fortifications. Immediatly vpon the receit of this heauyetidings, the Galles fled out of theyr camp: insomuch that if our souldiers had not bene fortrauelled wyth rescowing of so many sondrye places, and wyth the toyle of that daye, all the whole power of our enemyes might haue ben distroied vtterly. Our horsmen beyng sent out after midnight, ouertoke theyr rerewarde, and slewe and toke prysoners a great number of them: the rest scaped out of the chase into the next cityes.[48]

The Caesar, as was appropriate in translating a work dealing with the military conquest of a great region, shows a deep interest in geography. Golding strives to indicate the modern equivalents of Caesar's geographical names; the very hesitation expressed in his preface proves how seriously he felt that a translator should prepare himself for his work, in special knowledge as well as in language.

The feeling for the importance of geographical information led him to translate Mela, as a basis for a general knowledge of geography, and to supplement the book by "a briefe discourse, in which the partes of the Earth, perticulerlie (according to the late obseruations of the best cosmographers in our age) are exactly described . . . ."

Golding mentions, in the preface to the 1585 edition of the Mela a version of Solinus, "*Of the Noble Actions of Human Creatures*" (*Collectanea rerum memorabilium*) which he intended to print as an appendix to the *Mela*. I have not found it with the 1585 Mela, but it appears in 1587, and in 1590, in an exact reprint, down to the number of words on a page and the register, of the 1587 edition. Solinus borrows much from Pliny, and may well have been the immediate source from which the rhetoric of Elizabethan days got its fauna: the Hyrcan tiger, the Numidian bear, the Gryphon chased by the Arimaspian, the sweet-breathed panther, the Boeotian partridges that lie on their backs and take up clods in their claws to hide under. Solinus is rich in the geographical names that Milton delighted in. Golding's service in this version, therefore, may have been quite as much in contributing to the romantic setting of life in a world full of eccentric mystery, which the writers of the time drew from antiquity, as in the mere prosaic and direct purveyance of information which he intended. Golding's notes may almost all be found in the edition of the Italian savant who called himself Joannes Camers, dedicated to *Stephen Verbeucio Pannonio, locum tenenti* of the king of Hungary, [i.e. the palatine, Istvan Verboeczy] (1st ed. Vienna Pannoniae, 1520). I have read them in the Basle edition, 1557.

[48]Fo. 234 ff.

From all this it is plain that Golding was a conscientious and well-equipped worker, who knew how to acquaint himself with the best learning of his time before setting about any version.

Among the general geographical works translated during the period is Dionysius Periegetes, *De Situ Orbis,* translated by Thomas Twyne, 1572. Dionysius was a natural associate of Mela, with whose work his was published by Stephanus. Twyne dedicated his version to "the ryghte worshipful master William Lovelace Esquire, Serjeant at Law."

In his preface, "To the frendly Reader," Twyne indicates his dependence, obvious in any case, upon Latin versions. ("It is long sythence he wrote in the Greeke tongue, and hath bin translated into Latine of late yeares by dyuers.") He praises Dionysius, "for so muche as he is accompted of all antiquitie, the olde [*old,* the *finest of its kind,* "old swearing," "old turning the key"] writer, for compendiousnesse and breuity in that he took in hand." Like Golding, Twyne strove to give the modern equivalents of the ancient geographical names:—"And for thy commoditee adioinyng to the names.—countreys and other places in olde tyme frequented, the vsuall names also wherby they are knowne by all trauailers at this day, not omitting certaine woordes, whiche were always Latine, and so vsed, to make them Englishe for orders sake, not knowing any cause to the contrarye. as . . . . Europa, Europe, Asia, Asie, Africa, Afrike, with suche lyke what euer . . ."

The geographical names are largely Spanish or Italian in form (*"fennes Maeotides,* now el mar negro; Helespontus, now el far de Gallipoli and Brachium S. Georgi; The Hill Atlas now called Maiust; Hesperia now Bernie; Gades, now Cadiz; Liguria now Terra de Genoua; the Sicilian Sea, now el far de Mesina; Syrtes nowe Baxi or Banqui de Barbaria; Neapolis now Mahometa; Lotophagi now Los Chelbens.")[49]

They are to be found in *Petri Ioannis Olivaris Annotationes in Melam,* published with Stephanus's edition of Dionysius Periegetes. I have not seen an edition earlier than 1577. Twyne's English has the charm of a sweet unstudied rhythm in its prose, in curious contrast with singular clumsiness of his verse. Can it be, one asks, that the man responsible for the

---

[49]Sig. A i.

monstrosities in the completion of Phaer's Vergil is also the author of this charming prose?

> . . . The mounts of Mysia out of which the riuer Cius yeldeth forth his pleasant water: wher it is said, *that* the nimphs in time past stole away the beautiful child Hylos being then attenda*n*t vpon great Hercules. From thence there lieth open a great vent into Hellespontus, in Phrygia *th*e lesse. The one is situate farther wi*th*in a great deale & is farre larger, neere to the riuer Sangarius. And thys, which is the larger, and lieth forth to the east, is very fruitful for corne & grasse, & bringeth vp great store of good horses. The other which looketh to the west, is descried at the foote of the renoumed Ida, hauing at the one syde the noble and famous citie of Troy, called also Ilium, so muche spoken of, so large and so wyde, the nourse and brooder of many a valiant Gentleman, buylded (as it is thought) by Neptunus and Apollo but afterward destroyed by the aduise of Iuno and Pallas: planted faste by the riuers Xanthus and Simois of Ida. Hereto lyeth Aeolia, nigh aboue Hellespontus, towardes *th*e shore of the sea Aegaeum, in which also *th*e Iones be included: and the memorable riuer Meander glyding through with his gentle streame, parteth also Miletus and wide Prienas wherof that whiche is in the middle, and lyeth moste to the north, al that wholly Ephesus doth possesse, lying to the sea syde, sometyme the glorious citie of quiuered Diana, & to her dedicated. Wher (as fame telleth) in old time the Amazones buylded a temple of wonderful w*o*rkma*n*ship vpon the stock of an Elme tree, and for that cause was had in greate admiration amongest all people, & all ages. From this next forth to the East, lieth Meonia, vpon a steep rock vnder the side of the Mount Tmolus, out of which the Riuer Pactolus runneth with his sande all of golde, and maketh therwith the whole countrey to glitter. Vppon whose bankes when once the spring tyme of the yeare is come, there are Swannes herd continually singing, which feede there commonly raunging on the riuers side, with such harmonie, that nothing can be more pleasant to the eare, their foode dayly encreasing vpon the shoare. And the Riuer also Gnister spryngeth vp, and bestoweth his water plentifully in diuers places of the countrey. Moreouer it bringeth foorthe very faire women, who many time according to their custome, hauing their loynes girded with girdles of gold, do make pastyme among them selues, leadyng straunge formes of dauncing, cast round into a ring or circle, cheefly whe*n* they celebrate their accustomed feastes of Bacchus, once euery yeare in daunces, and other myrthe: when wenches of flourishing yeres, being mingled with them lyke wanton kiddes and lambes dance and play togither, & raise no small pleasure (while they be dauncing) to *th*e beholder. For the winde sometime huffeth vp their garme*n*ts, & their order in dauncing ingendreth a certain plesant noyse, much deliting *th*e minds of the hearers.[50]

---

[50]Fo. Dvi, vii.

Eutropius is an author exactly meeting the desires of the Elizabethans—extensive in scope, convenient in form, summary in method, and for a compiler accurate and trustworthy, and intelligently making use of the best sources. Nicholas Haward's version (1564) takes a very respectable place among the works of information translated from the classics at this time. Haward dedicated his translation to Master Henry Compton, a young man, not far from his own age. The loquacious address to the reader, in an elaborate "conceited" style, contains one interesting passage:

> And where as some theyr be whyche obiecte that through these translatyons, the affectynge and desyre of the attaynynge of the Greeke, Latyne, Italian and other tonges dooth decay, and is the lesse sought after, who seeth not howe friuolous and vaine that theyr saying is. For as it is very absonant to say, that anye man hauing ones tasted the pleasaunte puritye of the Greke and Latine tounges, woulde (forsaking the same,) fal to the barbarousnesse (in respect) of thys oure Englyshe tounge . . . . some must neades contente themselues to wade only in the troubled streames of Translators: for that they are not able to attayne to the well spryng it selfe.

The version substitutes the English for the Latin idiom, is substantially accurate, and shows some feeling for dignity of rhythm and freshness of vocabulary:

> After that Julianus was Emperoure, who wyth greate preparation made warre vpon the Parthians, at which viage I my self was present, diuers towns and holdes were peasibly yelded vp, and other some won by hym. And when hee hadde despoyled Assiria, hee pytched his tentes, and entrenched them, and soiourned there for a season. And retournynge from thence a conqueroure hee was slain by his ennemies, as hee pressed somwhat vnaduisedly into the battailes, in the .vi. of the kalends of July, in the .vii. yere of his raign, when he had liued .xxxi. yeres, and was cannonized. He was a notable man, and suche one as would passinglye well haue gouerned the weale publique, if desteny woold haue permitted him to haue liued. He was exceedinglye wel sene in all the liberal sciences He did excell in the Greke tounge, in so muche that his knowledge in the Latin tounge was nothing to be compared with that which he had in the Greke tong. He was very eloquent, and of a very redy and prompt memory. In manye thynges, hee resembled muche a Philosopher. He was lyberall to his frendes, but not all together so hedefull aboute hys affayres, as it was fittinge and fitte for so mightye a Prince: whyche fault dyuers obiected to hym, whereby hys fame and glorye was somedele stayned in that behalfe.

He delt very uprightly with thinhabitauntes of the Prouynces, whiche were vnder the Romaynes. He charged hys subiectes to paye as few taxes and tributes as mighte be. Hee was very ciuil and curtuous to all men. He sought litle to augment hys own tresure. He was very desirous to attaine glory and renoum: In so much that he did affect it sometimes wythout measure. He was an exceadinge great persecutor of Christian religion, but yet in such sorte, that he abstained from sheding their bloud. He was not muche vnlyke to Marcus Antoninus, whom he did also earnestly endeuor himselfe to immitate and folowe.[51]

Besides the competent and systematic translations of Golding, four other large works of history and biography were brought to satisfactory completion in this period: Aelian, by Abraham Fleming; Appian, by "W. B."; Plutarch's *Lives,* by Sir Thomas North; and Tacitus's *Histories,* by Sir Henry Savile.

Aelian was interesting because of his wide range, and abundance of savory anecdote. Abraham Fleming's translation of the *Variae Historiae* (*A Register of Histories,* 1576) is from the Greek, with the constant assistance of the Latin of Justus Velleius Wetteranus (Lugd. 1588),[52] and is accurate and natural, if undistinguished. It is the characteristic work of a gentle and simple pedant, one of a group of pedantic friends.

---

[51]Fo. 123 *v.,* 124 *r.* and *v.* (Sig. Si and Sii).

[52]The following passage (fo. 34) will suffice to indicate Fleming's expansions, and his dependence upon the Latin version.

Of the wine bibbing of the people *Bizantii.*

The people *Bizantii* are so·prone and addicted to drinking of wine,
Byzantii vero, quoniam procliues et propensi sunt ad vinum,

Βυζαντίους δὲ δεινῶς   οἰνόφλυγας   ὄντας ἐνοικεῖν τοῖς

that they forsake their owne mansions and tenements, which they ought to
rejectis suis aedibus et domibus

καπηλείοις   ὁ λόγος ἔχει, τῶν οἰκιῶν τῶν ἰδίων   καὶ τῶν δομάτων

inhabite, setting and letting them for rent to strangers, and they
peregrinis eas mercede locant

ἐξοικισθέντας καὶ τοῖς ξένοις   τοῖς ἐπιδημοῦσι τῇ πόλει

them selues in the mean season, haunt vittailing houses
transmigrant in cauponas, ut fama est.

ἐπιμισθώσαντας αὐτὰ

and Tauerns; Neither do they set ouer their dwellings to sale,
neque solum haec

    καὶ οὐ μόνον ἐκείνων

but also (which is a most execrable abuse) deliuer their wiues
sed etiam   uxores

ἀλλὰ καὶ   τῶν γυναικῶν

to aliens and forriners to hyre as hackneys.   By the meanes
illis   relinquunt   Itaque

αὐτοῖς   ἀποστάντας   ὡς

Seven Cambridge scholars contributed a vanguard of prefatory verses, in Latin, Greek, and English, to his version,—testimonials at once, and exhibitions of learning. Fleming's Latin dedication to Dr. Goodman, Dean of Westminster, is in accord with this display. It is diffuse, highly ornamented with affected balance and antithesis, strained figures, trite illustrations, and a vocabulary of uncommon words; terribly loquacious but in substance merely complimentary and painfully apologetic. His very enthusiasm for Aelian, who is certainly an amusing and useful but by no means a great author is in character:

> Pulchrum hoc pandochaeum, cum politicarum tum physicarum rerum cognitione cumulatum, apophthegmat ὧν et stratagemat ὧν varietate, ubertateque locupletatum, sententiarum sale conditum, verborum delectu exornatum, aromaticis eloquentiae odoribus perfusum, orationis nitore puritateque decoratum, viatorem non solum inuitat, lenociniis suis illectat inescatque, verumetiam affluentia ita permulcet, ut effascinat, ut vel reluctantem renitatemque retardet, atque remoretur.

The address "To the Courteous Reader" repeats these praises in English with the same verbose ingenuity in elaborating an obvious metaphor:

> This booke replenished with varietie & chaunge, (Courteous Reader) may be compared to a greate & stately building, which is not altogether outwardly voide of beauty, but inwardly also, gaily decked & finely furnished with all sightly and sumptious implements. It is lyke vnto an inestimable Iuell, or precious pearle, which although

---

of which dissolutenes, they entangle them selues in a reprochful
              duorum criminum   calumnia
ἐν τ' αὐτῷ   τοὺς Βυζαντίους διπλῆν   αἰτίαν
labyrinth of two detestable offences, namely, drunkenness, and baudrie.
eodem facte sese implicant Byzantinii, temulentia et prostitutionis.
   φέρεσθαι   καὶ οἰνοφλυγίας καὶ προαγωγείας.
Furthermore, because they have planted the perfection of al their
Quoniam vero ebrietate vinoque diffluunt, delectantur
ἅτε   δὲ   ὑπὸ τῆς μέθης καὶ τοῦ οἴνου   διαρρέοντες
pleasure in tippling and quaffing of wine, they

intermingle this delight with musical disportes, as

with the sound ofth flute, the viole, the harpe,
                       tibiarum sono, et tibiis maxime
                    αὐλοῦ μὲν ἀκούοντες χαίρουσι, καὶ
the lute and such like tuneable instrumentes. But the
valiant   and
δ'ἔργον αὐτοῖς αὐλεῖσθαι ἐστὶ,   σάλπιγγα δὲ

yt be inclosed in a homly wodde*n* box, and shut vp in a simple casket, litle or nothing worthe in comparison, yet is it neuer a whit the lesse in vallue notwithstanding, but reserueth his price vndiminished. Wherefore (Courteous Reader) in consideration of thine owne profit, and vauntage, pleasure, and harts ease, enter into this princely pallace, view euery roome circumspectly, behold each seuerall chamber and lodging aduisedly, and vse the benefite of euery thing liberally, to thine owne contentation. Open this base boxe, and lifte vpp the lydd of this course casket, wherin so riche and costely a Iuell is inclosed, wey yt, and weare it, the commodity issuing from the same is singular, so is the delight redundant and plentifull. Take all, and possesse all, thy title is substantiall, and thine interest sufficient.

Farewell,

Abraham Fleming.

The translation of Appian, by a certain W. B., (1578) is more important in itself and better done. The dedication of the first part declares: "How worthy the Writer is to be redde, I referre it to the witnesse of one worthy Prelate of this lande," *i.e.* as a marginal note indicates, "T[homas] C[ooper]," in the dictionary of proper names at the end of his *Thesaurus linguae Latinae et Britannicae, s.v.* Appianus;—"A noble historian,

---

shrill sound of the trumpet they cannot abide to heare in any case,
tubae frenitu primo auditu etiam non sustinent.
οὐδὲ   ἀρχὴν   ὑπομένουσι.
Which is an euident argument & a plaine demonstration, that this
Ex quibus liquet, quod ab armis belloque gerant
καὶ ἐκ ἰούτων ἔξεστι νοεῖν   ὅτι καὶ
peeuish people haue holow harts, and can away neither with warre nor
alienissimos animos Byzantii.
πρὸς ὅπλα καὶ πρὸς πολέμους ἀλλωτριώτατοι   διάκεινται Βυζάντιο
warlike weapons. For this cause the captaine generall of their army,
that is
Propter hanc causam Leonides dux militaris ipsorum
διὰ ταῦτά τοι, καὶ Λεωνίδης ὁ στρατηγὸς αὐτῶν
to say, lusty *Leonidas* in a very fearce and sharp assault
in acerrima   urbis oppugnatione
ἐν   πολιορκίᾳ   ἰσχυρᾷ
against the citie, when the enemies adventured vpon the walles, and
cum hostes moenia adorirentur,
ἐπεὶ τῶν πολεμίων τοῖς τείχεσι προσβαλλόντων,
they neglecting watche and warde, consumed whole dayes, from the rising
illi relictis excubiis   totos dies
ἐκεῖνοι γέ τὰς φρουρὰς ἐκλιπόντες   διημέρευον
of the sonne, to the falling of the same, in their usual and accustomed
hospitalles:
in consuetis diuersoriis tererent,
ἐν ταῖς   συνήθεσι   διατριβαῖς
Leonidas commaunded that the victualling houses which they frequented
should

borne in Alexandria, wrote excellent woorkes of the Romains ciuile warres, which bookes I counsayle a[l] theim that bee studious in Tullius woorkes, to reade diligently, whereby they shall vnderstand many thinges, that els they can not wel vnderstande." The dedication of the second part cites Stephanus's addition to the preface of his Greek edition, to the effect that Dionysius of Halicarnassus is best to read down to the Carthaginian war, Dion for the history of the empire, and Appian for racial history.

The dedication of Part I, to Sir Christopher Hatton, signed by the printer, H. Binniman, does not fail to make the usual comment introductory to ancient historians, in support of autocracy . . . "How God plagueth them that conspire against theyr Prince, this Historie declareth at the full. For of all them coniured against Caius Caesar, not one did escape violent death. The which this Author had a pleasure to declare, bycause he would affray all men from disloyaltie toward their Soueraigne." It is, indeed, the narrative of the civil wars more than the general view of the relation of the conquered races to Rome that gave Appian his interest; and Shakespeare gleaned from this translation several passages which added to the dramatic effectiveness of his Julius Caesar.[53] The translation is from

---

mandavit ut cauponae ipsis in moenia transferrentur

προσέταξε τὰ καπηλεῖα   εἰθὶ τῶν τειχῶν διασχηνωθῆναι

be remoued to the citie walles, by which subtile slight and politicke
                        quo sophismate
                        καὶ αὐτὸ τὸ σόφισμα

deuise, he perswaded them not to forsake the army, each colourable

sero tandem, eis persuasit, ut aciem ne desererent, cum

            ἀνέπεισεν αὐτοὺς ὀψὲ, καὶ βραδέως τὴν τάξιν μὴ καταλιπεῖν,

pretence, and reasonable occasion why they should so do, being

praetexta   et causa quamobrem obvient, non esset.

ἄτε τῆς προφάσεως   αὐτοῖς περιηρημένης

utterly dashed and remoued. These things concerning them doth *Daemon,*

            Haec affirmat de ipsis Damon.

            λέγει δὲ ταῦτα ὑπὲρ αὐτῶν Δάμων,

manifestly affirme to whom *Menander* alludeth saying: *Vinolentos*
                        negotiatores facit Byzantium, totam

Hic astipulari videtur Menander, cum dicit: Vinolentos nego-
                        tiatores facit Byzantium, totam

ὁμολογεῖν δὲ τούτοις   ἔοικε   Μένανδρος, ὅταν λέγῃ   μεθύσους τοὺς

noctem perpotat. Byzantium maketh winebibbing and drunken
noctem perpotat.

ἐμπορίους ποιεῖ τὸ Βυζάντιον, ὅλην ἐπινε τὴν νύκτα.

merchantes, and consumeth whole nights in swilling and gulling.

[53]Extracts from Books ii and iii have been reprinted by the New Shakespeare Society: *Transactions*, (1876), pt. II, Appendix iv, pp. 427-439.

Stephanus's edition of the Greek, and the translator comments
intelligently on the first Latin translation, by P. Candidus, and
the Italian of Bracio. The style of the translation is poor—
the sentences are long and involved without salience of emphasis, and the diction is tame.

> *Brutus* perceiuing what wayte his enimies made for him, and hauing
> no more but foure legions, wherewith he was wel warded, desired the
> chiefe of his host, whiche now were ashamed and repented of their
> act, to sende to see, how they might make way to passe the traynes,
> and to recouer their owne that was kept in the aba*n*doned tentes.
> They being unwilling, and now considering more than they did, and
> that God was agaynst them, tolde their Generall they had giuen him
> euill counsell, and they hauing tried fortune so oft, woulde not now
> put any more hope in their matter. Then *Brutus* sayde to his
> friendes : I am no longer profitable to my Countrey. He called one
> of his moste trusty friendes, named *Strato* of *Epire,* and wylled hym
> to kyll hym out of hande, who entreatyng hym to take better aduice,
> called one of hys seruauntes, and sayde: O *Brutus,* in thy laste,
> commaundement thou shaltè not wante, neyther thy friende, nor thy
> seruaunt. And hauyng thus sayde, he thruste hys sworde into *Brutus*
> side, neyther resistyng nor helpyng.
>
> Thus *Cassius* and *Brutus* died, moste noble and worthy *Romanes,*
> and but for one facte, euer folowed vertue.
>
> .   .   .   .
>
> *Brutus* (they say) celebrating hys birtheday in *Samo* vpon the
> sea, beyng nothyng mery aboute it, without caste forth this verse.
>
> But me cruel destinie, and *Latones* sonne doth destroy. Goyng
> with his army between *Asia* and *Europa,* and watchyng in the night
> when lighte fayled, a fearefull shape appeared to hym. Whome hee
> boldly asking what man or God hee was, the vision answeared: I
> am *Brutus,* thyne euill lucke, and at *Philippi* I will appeare agayne
> vnto thee. And they say he sawe hym there before the laste fight,
> and when the armie wente out of the campe, an *Ethiopian* mette
> them, whome as an euill token, they killed.[54]

In the year 1591, practically at the point which has been
marked as the end of the third period, Sir Henry Savile, ward-
en of Merton and later provost of Eton, began with a version
of Tacitus' *Histories* and *Agricola* that group of translations
from Silver Latin prose carried on so valiantly by Holland and
Lodge. His work is so closely connected with these later
translations that it will be discussed along with them, in the
next chapter.

Finally, we come to the version of Plutarch, by Sir Thomas

---

[54]Pp. 301, 303.

North—a book which of its own right holds its place as one of the great works of English literature. As Plutarch was for the English translators of the school of Erasmus the epitome of antiquity, and the most effective agent in communicating Greek ideas to their readers, so it was a translation of Plutarch in which the versions of the earlier Elizabethan period found their culmination. The work done on Plutarch in each period is strikingly characteristic. The translations of the time of Sir Thomas Elyot are from the *Morals;* they render deliberate and direct instructions for conduct: how to educate children; how to take profit of an enemy; how to care for the health. They present small essays and parts of large books, and are modest in their efforts and their ideas of their own importance. Sir Thomas North's translation of Plutarch's *Lives* (1st ed. 1579), like Phaer's Vergil and Golding's Ovid, indeed like Golding's work in general, boldly undertakes a vast enterprise, and this with a firm confidence in the value of the work itself for their age and in the powers and importance of the English language. The age of Elizabeth could not reach to the conceptions of large historical forces or extensive movements. Its ideals of rule were simple and naïve, though practical; its theological and national prepossessions sincere but unanalyzed. The personal and incidental view of history held by Plutarch was therefore the more acceptable. Thucydides and Tacitus were out of the reach of the time. This is not altogether unsound. The historian of social and economic movements too readily abstracts his men from life, and the figures of history grow to be conventional mosaic figures indistinctly seen in fixed attitudes against a flat background. To come to cases and people is a good corrective. The view of abstraction is all too easy in historical study, and to come to see the great movements in and with men and incidents is intellectually healthy. It is necessary to abstract in order to understand, but it is well sometimes to be compelled to see the past made whole by the imagination, to know the concrete thing, to know Pompey as adored by his wanton mistress, and Caesar as uncomfortable about his bald head. General forces and large movements are not the whole of essential reality; it is a fundamental fact that individuals are important in history, and that even the weaknesses of great men are important.

Again, though the *Lives* of Plutarch were valued as works of information, they worked upon the age more by their imaginative power in the presentation of forceful, individual characters than by the communication of useful knowledge. They formed no mere chronicle or storehouse of encyclopedic reference, like Appian or Eunapius, but a book which by its point of view and its creative power raised and deepened the conception of manhood and of the possibilities of human achievement. It enriched the sense of personality, and made men more ardent in being themselves. On the other hand, the translation is not the work either of an amateur young scholar, keeping up his literature while at the Inns of Court, or of an elderly pedant, but of a cultivated mature man of affairs who wrote after years of practice with the skill of a finished artist.

It is fitting that Plutarch's *Lives* should signalize the height of achievement in the translations of the classics in the sixteenth century, as the *Morals* marked the beginning. These lives, the tragic narratives of the careers of great men who conducted the affairs of state, fed the interest of the time in the mutability of fortune, manifested in the careers of statesmen and warriors. The *Mirror for Magistrates,* the popular chronicles, the serious popular drama, are all concerned with this same theme; and Plutarch is the father and guide of the tragic literature defined by Chaucer's Monk.

Mr. George Wyndham in his interesting and valuable introduction to the edition of North's Plutarch in the *Tudor Translations,* calls attention to the fact that when the text of Plutarch is purged of the accretions added in the Renaissance, his preoccupation with the men of public affairs in the tragedy of Greece, destroyed by factious particularism, and of the Roman republic, dying in its own too much, becomes obvious; and he traces this preoccupation mainly to the political temper of Plutarch and Plutarch's time. No doubt. But from the point of view of the writer of effective narrative, the careers of warriors and statesmen, and especially of conquerors, tyrants, and their opponents, in the critical periods of history, when states were formed, defended, and ruined, offered more interest, more of dramatic contrast, more vivid personalities, a more tragic interest, than the narratives of private men, heroes of thought, and artists, or even of emperors and generals in less critical periods. The Aristotelian principle of striving to develop in each type its most complete and characteristic manifestations directs Plutarch's writing. Marius in the cave; Demetrius in purple robes insulting his humble suitors and in a black gown fleeing by night from his own soldiers; Antony in the matchless life and in Cleopatra's tomb, Caesar passing the Rubicon and weltering at the foot of Pompey's statue, these make telling scenes in dramatic narratives on the theme of mutability. And behind them is the shadow of the fate of mighty states. Moreover, Plutarch conceives of his subject as a dramatic narrator. His men are individuals with a character, manifested in small actions as in great, lovers, homely jesters, fat, thin, vain, gross, vascular or thin-blooded, seen in daily life and action; and at the same time they are great men engaged in great and important actions,—carrying with them the cloudy burden of their own destruction. It is no wonder that Shakespeare paid him the compliment of adopting his characters and their treatment, of using Plutarch's detail and his very words, for the underlying spirit and the artistic ideals of Plutarch are those of the tragic drama.

It is a commonplace that North follows faithfully the French translation of Amyot. The reader, turning page after page of the two versions, not only discovers no essential departure in North from Amyot, but must be astonished to find the general form, the rhythm, and the color of the two practically identical. Most striking of all, this closeness is greatest in the best passages. North at his height is Amyot at his height, as in the voyage of Cleopatra on the Cydnus, and in the deaths of Antony and Cleopatra. Yet after a time a difference equally notable becomes gradually apparent. North's method of translation was not word by word, or even phrase by phrase, but in a large way, idea by idea, mass by mass. He fully apprehended the meaning of Amyot, and then expressed it in his own way, without being studious either to follow or to avoid the phraseology or the forms of his original. His own style is indeed close to Amyot's, perhaps formed upon it, noble, simple, gracious, musical, ample, clear, warm, and valiant. But he constantly varies from Amyot slightly in the direction of colloquialism, and at passages of excitement or climax is likely to use somewhat more energetic terms than his French guide.

The high points of this difference have been often noted. Mr. Wyndham, for instance, cites as an illustration of the outstanding energy of North at the points of crisis the passage in the *Themistocles* in which is declared the confidence of the Greeks in coming to close conflict with the Persians. Amyot's assertion is "que la grande multitude des vaisseaux, ny la pompe et magnificence des parements d'iceulx, ny les cris superbes et chants de victoire des Barbares, ne servent de rien à l'encontre de ceulx qui ont le cueur de joindre de près, et combattre à coups de main leur ennemy, et *qu'il ne fault point faire compte de tout cela, ains aller droit affronter les hommes et s'attacher hardiment à eulx.*" Mr. Wyndham points out that "North follows closely for a time, but in the last sentence he lets out his language to the needs of a maxim so pertinent to a countryman of Drake. The Greeks saw, says he, 'that it was not the great multitude of shippes, nor the pomp and sumptuous setting out of the same, nor the prowde barbarous showts and songes of victory that could stand them to purpose, against noble hartes and valliant minded souldiers, that durst *grapple with them, and come to hand strokes with their enemies: and that they should make no reckoning of all that bravery and bragges, but should stick to it like men, and laye it on the jackes of them.*'" But if we put side by side the whole passage which culminates in these vivid words, we see all along small deviations from Amyot, each of little consequence in itself, but all together giving the style of North a perceptibly different tone from Amyot's, a tone which is accentuated in the passage just cited. "Ces premieres rencontres, qui se feirent dedans le destroit de l'Euboe entre les Grecs et les Barbares, ne furent pas de grande consequence pour la decision finale de toute celle guerre; mais ce fut comme un essay, qui servit beaucoup aux Grecs, leur faisant veoir par experience, et au danger mesme du combat, que . . ." is in North, "these first fights in the straite of Euboea, betweene the Greecians, and the barbarous people, were *nothing to the purpose* to end the warres between them. For it was but a *taste,* geven unto them, which *served the Greecians turne* very much, by making to see by experience, and the manner of the fight, that . . ." North likes to speak of a youth as "whotte-headed", (*ardent,* Themistocles II), of a "ragged" colt (*les plus rebours et les plus farouches poulains,* Themistocles III), of "cruel" wars (*grosse,* Themistocles VII), "out of all speache" that they alone should fight (*il n'y falloit pas penser,* Themistocles XVII), "bleating, mowing, and howling out alowde" (*avec hurlements et significance de regret,* Themistocles XX), "on a marvelous steepe highe hill" (*en un lieu hault elevé* Themistocles XXV), "two good whirts on the ear" (*un couple de soufflets,* Brutus X) "drunken soppe" (*yvrogne,* Brutus V), "all of a goare bloode" (*une grande effusion de sang,* Brutus XIV), "a multitude of rakehells of all sorts" (*une tourbe de gens ramassez de toutes pieces,* Brutus XVII) "all that he could rappe and rende" (*tout ce qu'il pouvoit avoir,* Aratus VII; *tout ce qu'il en peut finer* Brutus XXXVII), "it ranne for good payment among all the Graecians" (*en coura de rechef bien grand bruit entre les Grecs* Aratus XLIV), "a bedlem and frantick motion" (*avec une impetuosité et une furieuse et passionée affection,* Brutus XLII) "when a mad moode or toye tooke him in the head" (*à quoy que ce fust que sa passion l'incitast* Brutus XLII).

Now this steady but slight variation affects the general tone of the writing perceptibly, and the energetic phraseology at crises confirms and points a difference which pervades the whole style of North.

Amyot, I think, would not quite have approved of his translator. North's colloquialisms would have seemed to fall short of due dignity, his vigorous words to smack of *emphase,*— to be striving for an external effect of manner not required by the subject. Be that as it may, the styles of the two, alike as they are, have a shade of difference characteristically national, Amyot's French in its reserve, North's English in its tinge of colloquialism and its frank energy of diction. In this North shows the tendency of his period. Not so boldly as Underdowne, or even as Golding, he still constantly animates his writings by the use of colloquialisms, picturesque concreteness about familiar things, and proverbial phrases.

The minor works of history and biography include a book of Polybius, a book of Herodotus, several books of Diodorus Siculus and Eunapius's lives of the philosophers. These less important works are in general poorly translated.

A youth, Christopher Watson, translated the first book of

Polybius (printed in 1568). He dedicated the work to his patron "the right worshipful Thomas Gaudy, Esquier," writing "from my chamber in your house at Gaudy Hall." To the reader he apologizes for his boldness in undertaking the translation—"being yet in my nonage—" and speaks of his work as his "freshmanly enterprise." Bound up with the Polybius is an abridgment of the life of Henry V, in a letter to the "Questioners" prefixed to which Watson declares that having read in Hall's Chronicle the oration of "the right honorable Lorde Rafe earle of Westmerland" in answer to Chichele, Archbishop of Canterbury, he was moved by it to read histories, and especially "that Historie intreating of the warres made by the Romans for Sicilie, and the Citie of the Samnites, out of the which he hadde collected the most firme and infringible arguments of his Oration." Then Watson says, "I was so rapt and pleasured . . . that I vowed 'to apply my vacant howres in reducing it to our maternal and vulgar tong." (Westmorland's speech, of course, is a literary exercitation of Hall's; and no knowledge of Polybius was necessary to draw the parallel between the Roman policy of first conquering the Samnites before attacking Carthage, and the policy urged in the speech of first conquering the Scots before attacking France.)

The translation, from the Latin (Basle, 1529), is loose and vague, and studded with manifest errors. It is full of ink-horn terms, not in the Latin, and dilutes the original by doubling synonyms. Thus *dicta* becomes "inculcate of many"; *res gesta* "facts perpetrate"; *novitas ipsa* "the noueltie and strangeness"; *instituimus* "determine and deliberate"; *satis superque* "of efficacie and force enough"; *ad hanc nostram historiam* "to the reading and diligent digesting of this my worke"; *refugiat* "eschue or auoide"; *domitae et intra trium et quinquaginta annorum subiectae* "vanquished, subdued, and in space of three and fifty years made subject and obedient." Watson is also at times unidiomatically literal: "a coniunct commemoration of things done vniuersally" (coniunctam rerum gestarum commemorationem)—"the original of this profection"—"impleat with inestimable treasure"—"when the war was protracte"—"Fabius in the diameter quite dissenting."

Watson's work is a good example of the raw Latinization of the English language against which the genuinely learned humanists such as Elyot, Ascham, and Cheke had set their faces.

The more important the author, the less attention was attracted to the translation.   Thus a certain B. R.[55] translated books I and II of Herodotus (lic. 1581, earliest known edition 1584), and in his preface "To the Gentlemen Readers" puts forward his translation as tentative, and is hopeful though uncertain of being able to continue it.

To the Gentlemen Readers.

Right courteous Gentlemen, we haue brought out of *Greece* into *England,* two of the Muses, *Clio* and *Euterpe,* as desirous to see the lande as to learne the language; whome I trust you wil vse well because they be women, and you can not abuse them because you be Gentlemen.   As these speede so the rest will followe, neyther altogether vnwilling to forsake theyr owne Countrey, nor yet ouerhasty to arriue into this, reposing the ende of theyr counsayle in the proofe of your courtesie.   If you lyke them not for the attyre they weare, yet bid them welcome for the newes they bring, which I confesse are in many poyntes straunge, but for the most parte true. . . . Neyther of them are braued out in theyr colours as the vse is now adayes, and yet so seemely, as eyther you will loue them because they are modest, or not mislike them because they are not impudent, since in refusing ydle pearles to make them seeme gaudy, they reiect not modest apparell to cause them to go comely.   The truth is (Gentlemen) in making them newe attyre, I was fayne to take example by theyr olde array, cutting out my cloth by another mans measure, beeyng great difference whether wee inuent a fashion of our owne, or imitate a paterne set downe by another.   Whiche I speake not to this ende, for that my selfe coulde haue done more eloquently in englishe then our Authour hath in Greeke, but that the course of his writing beeying most sweete in Greeke, conuerted into Englishe, looseth a great parte of his grace. . . . .

The translation seems to have been carried no further.

B. R. translates in the main from the Latin version of Laurentius Valla (of which Stephanus had published an edition in 1566), sometimes helping himself by a note from the margin.   He enlivens and amplifies the style of his original, striving to make the general terms of the original specific.   An example illustrates his dependence on Valla, even reproducing the errors of that writer, and exhibits B. R.'s manipulation of the language.

Neither were the Carians onely destitute of the glorye and renoune of noble dedes [Valla quite literally from the Greek, *nullum ediderunt,*

[55]Probably not Barnabe Rich; *v.* Andrew Lang's reprint of the second book (London 1888).

"did no deed of note"] : but the rest also of the Grecians there about lurked in silence and had their name darkened with obscurity [V. *nec Graeci quot quot illam regionem tenebant*, "nor any of the Graecians thereabout"]. There kept resiantes [V. *tenebant*; Herod. οἰκείουσι; "dwelt"] and in those places aswel others, as also the *Corydians*, which were a remnaunt of the Lacedaemonians thither drawen and deriued, [V. *coloni*; Herod. ἄποικοι, "colonists"] whose region wyndeth [V. *declinat*, "slopes"; Herod. τετραμμένης, "is turned toward"] to the sea called Tryopium [so Valla; the original means the country is called Tryopium] and is almost on euery side hemmed in by the sea. The North part beyng limited with the salte waues of *Ceraunium* ["salte waues" is an addition]; the southside by the Rhodian and Limanian sea. The rest which is a very narow strayght, not passinge fiue acres in breadth: the people of *Corydus* (whyle *Harpagus* was busied in *the* affaires of *Ionia*) thought to have digged a way, & in so doyng to haue brought ther countreye into the forme of an Iland geuing free course and passage to the sea on euery syde ["geuing free course etc." is an addition]. For their whole territory was within the broken circle of the Sea ["the broken circle of the Sea" is an embellishment]: ioyninge to the mayne or firme lande in that strayght where the waters almost mette, which space they were in mind to have trenched throughout, wherby the sea in manner of a circle mighte haue his full scope and issue about the Ile, [V. *eratque hic isthmus quem perfodere statuerent, ea parte qua continentem spectat Cnidia;* i.e. the isthmus which they were in mind to have trenched throughout is on the side where Cnidia looks toward the main land] whereto employing their whole force and indeuour [V. *multa manu*] it chaunced them in the middest of this toyle to be taken in manye partes of the bodye, and chiefly with an extreme smarting, and soreness of the eyes [V. *praecipue oculos infectante petra,* the stones hurt their eyes] wherupon resoluinge to send to *Delphos* [V. *Delphos;* Herod. Δελφούς] to Apollo, they inquired of him what it might be that so greatly hyndred them to proceed in their enterprise.

To whom *Pythia* made answere in certayne verses consysting of sixe feete after this maner.

> Seeke not to saue your seate
> by trenche or heaped pyle.
> If mighty Ioue had pleasde
> Your land had bene an Ile.

. . . . More then this [margin: *Porro*], some what about *Halicarnassus* in the region dwell the Pedaceans: with whom at the shew or appearance of any daunger or misfortune either to themselues or their neighbours, it falleth out that *Mineruas* [margin *Minervae;* text *Palladis*] Priest hath continually a longe [margin: *prolixa;* text: *sacra*] bearde: which happened vnto them three sundry tymes.[56]

---

[56]Fo. 54, 55.

B. R. pretty frequently gives his version a free colloquial turn.

Bk 1.
[Helen:] one silye dame of *Lacedonia* fo. 3 *v*.
[Gyges to Candaules:] for a woman, you know, the more in sight lesse in shame. 3 *v*.
Gyges, take hart at grace. 3 *v*.
Pull vpp thy spirites, and leaue al to me. 3 *v*.
[Candaules' queen to Gȳges:] There is no remedy *the* one of you both must to the pot. 4 *v*.
[Croesus] mynding to haue a fling at the *Grecians* 7 *v*.
to gleike the one other syde 7 *v*.
I deeme her not happy but fortunate till the last gaspe 9 *v*.
[illustrates a frequent type of fault—not quite slangy, but common]
When all was hush at the sepulchre 12 *v*.
[Pisistratus] came flyngyng amaine 16 *r*.

The Persians are a croked generation, and of nature peruerse and stubburne: yet neuertheles, very base and beggerly, whom if in this sort thou securely permit to ryg and ransacke cities, ... I feare me that as euery one groweth to greatest aboundance, hee will soonest sllpp the coller, and become of a true subject, a trayterous rebell. 27 *v*.

....

The result is a warm and vivid piece of writing, in the somewhat heightened manner characteristic of the period.

In 1564 there appeared a version of part of Diodorus Siculus, with a little Plutarch similarly fragmentary and similarly inaccurate; it was by Thomas Stocker, and bore the title, "A History of the Successors of Alexander." Of its four books the first three are Diodorus, books XVIII, XIX, and XX to Cap. cxiii (with many omissions); and the fourth is from Plutarch's Life of Demetrius. It is for its time archaic, being translated from the French of Claude de Seyssel, itself translated from J. A. Lascaris's Latin version. The proper names are in their French form—Lucie Fury and Dece Juny (fo. 1 *verso*); Lisimache and Leonate; the traitor Lipodore (fo. 5 *verso*); Pantharite (fo. 148 *verso*). Stocker, then, is satisfied with scholarship old-fashioned in his own day; and he follows the bad old fashion of needlessly repeating synonyms (*exhortaient*: prayed and exhorted; *leur solde*: their salary and wages; *quarante galires subtiles*: fourtie excellent tall, long and flete gallies; etc.) His sentences are sprawlingly awkward; his diction lacks individual character.

The dedication, addressed to Ld. Ambrose Dudley, Earl of Warwick, speaks of the vicissitudes of fortune among the great in the same spirit with the *Mirror for Magistrates,* praising the History of Diodorus,

> wherein is shewed the vncerteintie of fortune, whiche maruellously may serue and helpe to read, and consider the worldly happes heretofore, to great Kings, Princes, and Nobles chaunced, who sometime were in great dignitie and had high authoritee and wonderful prosperitie. Wherby in seeing (after great felicitie and maruellous prosperitie) the straunge aduersitie and miserie whiche happened them, and the continuall chaunge of their estates and aduentures: may more and more be vnderstood the instabilitie and imperfection of worldly matters. And chiefly in those great and honorable personages, the successors of *Alexander the great,* by whom is most declared the inconstancie of all things subject to alteration and chaunge: and where Fortune (to speake after the vulgare opinion) hath best shewed the power, and auctoritie. . . . [Here we may learn something of the art of war, and get instruction in general conduct] . . . And chiefley, that whiche is moste meete and becomming a noble personage, whereof he is called *magnanimous,* that he shoulde not for any prosperitie whiche happeneth him, be ouer high minded nor yet for any aduersitie he hath or might chaunce him, lose hys hearte, courage or hope, whiche things wholly seruing to the perfection of man in this present life, and consisteth in the habitude and operation of Morall vertues: and also to the perfection of the soule, ordering and appointing the latter ende and intention to the euerlasting blisse; which god of hys infinite goodnesse and grace graunt your honour, and vs al, after the course of this present life.

Stocker reproduces the monotonous chronicle of Diodorus without light and shade, or skill in the massing of narrative details. His sentences are awkward and his diction is tame and characterless. The Plutarch has a livelier choice of words, following the original, but the sentences have neither rational definiteness, nor the cadence which may serve in place of it.

An anonymous version of Eunapius (1579) translated from Hadrianus Junius's Latin version (Antwerp, 1568) is perhaps the most discreditably inaccurate piece of work done in all this time. For example, take the account of Sopolis. Sopolis, the original tells us, tried to bring back the *style* of antiquity (Dicendi genus ad prisci saeculi characterem et formulam adnixus est affingere); the translator affirms that he was "desyrous to attayne to a sound *doctrine.*" The original declares that he did not knock at the doors of the goddesses rashly or

carelessly though he seldom found them open, but that if sometimes the hinges squeaked, and a faint little particle of divine
inspiration slid inside through the crack the auditors were
overwhelmed, and did not carry the little drop squeezed and
wrung from the spring of Castaly very far. (. . . haud temere
aut otiose dearum fores pulsauit, sed raro apertas: quin si
quando versi cardines striderent, exigua quapiam et teneri
diuini flatus particula intro allapsa, auditores percellebantur,
neque ferebant expressam ipsam et extortam Castalii latius
guttam). The translator makes this: "He knocked at the door
oft enough, but it was open but syldome. A soft and weak
sound did crack from thence. A lytle diuine breath issewed,
which pleased the audience. But dyd not beare away the flowing streame of the fountayne at Delphos."

Such then, are the versions of classic historians. Leaving
the Plutarch aside, which has its unique quality, they are in
the main summary and encyclopedic, useful to the practical man
who desires sketches or diagrams of the general features of
the past, and is little concerned with that scrupulousness of detail or that philosophical insight which mark the great historian.

Thomas Wilson's translation of the Philippic and Olynthiac
orations of Demosthenes (1570) is of peculiar interest because Wilson, alone among the translators, directly applied the
substance of his original to contemporary conditions, for patriotic propaganda. Wilson's translation is also the only version of a Greek orator within the whole era covered by this
book, and is one of the few translations direct from a Greek
original. The book, a scholarly performance, at the same
time strives to give the reader full information about Demosthenes and the political situation in Greece when the orations
were delivered. It contains a large amount of illustrative material and is fully annotated with comments on the substance of
the orations. A stately array of commendatory Latin verses
introduces the work, which is dedicated—inevitably—to Sir
William Cecill as "Chancelor of the Universitie of Cambridge."
In the Latin introductory verses, from the translator to the
reader, Wilson solemnly declares that it is at the monition of
God himself that he has labored upon the translation of Demosthenes for the good of his country. England has still time
to take warning before it goes down in ruin; to make Demos-

thenes an Englishman is to do England a service. Rude though
the version be he urges the reader to accept it (in time our
rude speech will grow more facile) ; for a patriotic citizen will
bid Demosthenes welcome. Wilson leaves no doubt what he
means by making Demosthenes an Englishman. Demosthenes
insisted that the Athenians must spend their wealth upon the
war with Philip, must go themselves to fight, must be active
and foresighted, anticipating their enemy's moves, and must
make war upon the enemy's frontier without waiting to be at-
tacked. Their enemy was a Philip, a tyrannical king, and the
aid of Athens was asked by a people to be reached by sea,
whom he oppressed. At the end of *The Bounding of Greece-
lande,* Wilson declares that all this is meant to apply to the
England of his day:

> And nowe most gentle Reader thinke that when I was occupied
> about this worke: to make Athens and the gouernment thereof to
> be knowne to my Countrie men: my meaning was, that every good
> subiect according to the leuell of his witte, should compare the time
> past with the time present, and euer when he heareth Athens, or the
> Athenians, to remember Englande and Englishmen, and so all other
> things in like maner incident thereonto, that we may learne by the
> doings of our elders howe we may deale in our owne affayres, and
> so through wisedome by our neighbours example auoyde all harme
> that else unwares might happen unto us.[57]

It is difficult to imagine an appeal to history more effectively
devised to gain English support for the Dutch in the conflict
with Philip of Spain.

Wilson's dedication to Cecil is of interest from its references to Cheke, as well as for its comments on Demosthenes.

> . . . . . . being solitarie of late time from my other studies, and
> musing on this world, in the middest of my books: I did then (as I
> have oftentimes else done) deeplye thinke of Sir John Cheeke
> Knight, that rare learned man, and singular ornament of this lande.
> And as the remembrance of him was deare unto me, for his mani-
> folde great gifts and wonderfull vertues: so did I thinke of his
> most gentle nature and godly disposed minde, to helpe all those with
> his knowledge and understanding, that anyway made meanes unto
> him and sought his fauour. And to say for my selfe amongst
> others, I founde him such a friende to me, for communicating the
> skill and gyftes of his minde, as I cannot but during my life speake
> reverentlye of so worthie a man, and honor in my hart the heavenly

---

[57] Sig. Bi *v.*

remembrance of him. And thinking of my being with him in Italie
in that famous Vniuiersitie of Padua: I did cal to minde his care
that he had over all the Englishe men there, to go to their bokes:
and how, gladly he did reade to me and others, certain Orations of
Demosthenes in Greeke, the interpretation whereof, I and they had
then from his mouth. And so remembering the rather this world
by the very argument of those actions: I did then seeke out amongest
my other writings for the translation of them, and happily finding
some, although not all: I was carried straightway, (I trust by Gods
good motion) to make certaine of them to be acquainted so nigh as
I coulde with our Englishe tongue, as well for the aptnesse of the
matter, and nedefull knowledge now at this time to be had: as
also for the right notable, and most excellent handling of the same.
And here must I saye, confessing mine owne weakenesse and imperfection, that I never founde in my life any thing so harde for me to
doe. Yea, the more I looke upon this Orator to bring his sentences
and wordes knowne to our common speach and language: the more
doe I finde him harde and unable to be translated, according to the
excellencie of his tongue. And manye times I have bene ashamed of
my selfe, when I compared his Greeke and my English together.
And no marueyle neyther. For the Laten translatours being otherwise most excellent men, have not alwayes satisfied themselves, much
lesse aunswered to their charge and enterprise in the opinion of
others that compared their doings and the Greeke together . . . .
[so Wolfius, Hegendorphius, Melanchthon, Clobardus, Carre have
not seldom failed to express the sense of the Greek, and even Maister
Cheeke himself cannot be said to have been absolutely successful]
. . . . And then what shall I thinke of my self, after the naming
of so manye excellent learned men, but only submit my doings to
the fauour of others, and desire men to beare with my weaknesse.
For this I must needes confesse, that I am altogether unable to
doe so in Englishe as the excellencie of this Orator deserveth in
Greeke. And yet the cunning is no lesse, and the prayse is as
great in my iudgement, to translate any thing excellently into Englishe, as into any other language. And I thinke (although there
be many doers) yet scant one is to be found worthie amongst us,
for translating into our Countrie speach. Such a hard thing it is
to bring out of any one language into another. And perhaps it
may be that even those who take themselues to bee much better
learned than I am (as what is he that is not, hauing any name for
learning at all?) will finde it an harder peece of worke than they
thinke, even to make Greeke speake Englishe, if they will make
proofe thereof as I haue done. Whose labor and trauayle I woulde
as gladly see, as they are lyke now to see mine, that such an Oratour
as this is, might bee so framed to speake our tongue, as none were able
to amende him, and that he might be founde to be most like himselfe.
The which enterprise if any might have bene most bolde to have
taken upon him, Sir John Cheeke was the man, of all that ever I
knew, or doe yet know in England. Such acquaintance had he with

this notable Orator, so gladly did he reade him, and so often: that I thinke there was neuer olde Priest more perfite in his Porteise, nor supersticious Monke in our Ladies Psalter as they call it, nor yet good Preacher in the Bible or testament, than this man was in Demosthenes. And great cause moved him to be so, for that he sawe him to be the perfitest Orator that euer wrote for these two thousand yeares almost by past (for so long it is since he was) and also for that he perceiued him to have before his eyes in all his Orations the aduauncement of vertue as a thing chiefly to be sought for, together with the honor and welfare of his countrie. Besides this, Maister Cheekes iudgement was great in translating out of one tongue into an other, and better than any else had that I have knowne. And often he would englyshe his matters out of the Latine or Greeke upon the sodeyne, by looking of the booke only without reading or construing any thing at all: An vsage right worthie and verie pro- fitable for all men, aswell for the understanding of the booke, as also for the aptnesse of framing the Authors meaning, and better- ing thereby their iudgement, and therewithall perfiting their tongue and utterance of speach. Moreover he was moued greatly to like Demosthenes aboue others, for that he sawe him so familiarlie apply- ing himselfe to the sense and understanding of the common people, that he sticked not to say, that none euer was more fitte to make an English man tell his tale praiseworthily in any open hearing, either in Parliament or in Pulpit, or otherwise, than this onely Orator was . . . . . Thirdly, the Oratour himselfe hauing bene a Counsellor in his Countrie as you now are in this Realme, he is your glasse I am wel assured whereopon you do often loke, and compare his time, with this time: Countrie with Countrie: neighbours with neighbours: and King with King . . . .

The version itself is creditably plain, direct, and unaffected.

The books dealing with philosophy—that is to say with principles of conduct—hold a relatively less important place in this era than in the previous one, but are still far from insig- nificant in number and weight. They are predominantly trans- lations of Latin authors, the traditional Seneca and Cicero, not of Greek ones. Plutarch has a trifling place, being repre- sented only by a few poor versions in slight pamphlets. Epic- tetus (Arrian's *Enchiridion*) is for the first time made known to English readers; indeed in Seneca and Cicero as in Epictetus the translations of the day have a strong Stoic bias.

In the field of ethics, the most important achievement of the era was the rounding out of the translations of Cicero's philosophical treatises. Grimald's *De Officiis* held its own as a standard and model for such work, and the translators of

Cicero set themselves to completing what he had begun. First
of all John Dolman translated the *Tusculan Disputations.*
Dolman, a contributor to the *Mirrour for Magistrates,* dedicated his translation to Bishop Jewell. Like many another
young scholar, he somewhat regretfully bade farewell to liberal studies before beginning the study of law ; and he speaks
of Cicero in the same spirit with Erasmus and many others,
as a spiritual guide and inspiration only next to the Scriptures
in profit and delight.

> Right honourable : when as, partly, by the counsel of them that
> might commaund me, and partlye, by mine owne consent, I left the
> vniuersity : and began to apply my selfe to the studye of *the* com-
> mon lawes of this realme : I felt my selfe chiefelye hindred
> therein, with the entermedling of those studies, the which, not with-
> out great delight, I had afore time vsed. The whych, because I was
> lothe to continue, to the defrauding of the expectation of those, with
> whom to trifle had bene impietie : I minded, to take my farewell of
> some such part of philosophye, as, both might be most profitable
> to the quiete leading of my life, to whatsoeuer trade I should giue
> my selte : and also should be so pleasaunt, that it might euen cloy
> me with delight. Whiche my desyre to satisfye, when I had sought
> many bookes : yet found I none more meete, then this. Whiche
> whiles I redde, I must needes confesse, that I was neuer more
> delighted with any worke, excepte it were the sacred volume of the
> holye Scriptures. Wherefore, when I had perused it ouer, and
> founde suche profyte, and pleasure therein, as it were not possible
> to find the like in anye Ethnike Wryter : I wyshed all men the lyke
> delyght, as the reading of it brought vnto me.

In his preface to the reader, Dolman, after excusing himself
for undertaking such a work in youth, gives an intelligent
statement of his purpose to avoid affectation of diction, and
explicitly recognizes as his public reasonably intelligent people,
above sheer ignorance, but not learned.

The preface to the Reader :

> [He defends himself for undertaking such a work in youth.]
> Then as for lacke of eloquence. First, this (I thinke) they wil
> al graunt. That, it is not possible for any man, to expresse the
> writinges of Tullie, in Englishe, as eloquently : as he hath vttered
> the same in latine. Then, for mine owne translation : forasmuche
> as it must of necessity be either more simple then, the stile of Tullie,
> or els more foolishe, and ful of croked termes (for Tullies meane
> none can attaine) I had rather to be partener of the fauour, due to

simplicity, and plainenes: then, with foolyshe and far fet wordes, to make my translation seeme more darke to the vnlearned, & more foolishe to the wise. By which my playnenes, withoute counterfaite eloquence, if I have gotten no other commoditye: yet, thus much I am sure of, that I haue thereby escaped, the iust reproofe, that they deserue, whiche thinke, to cloke their ignoraunce, wyth inkehorne termes. For, vnlesse it were in such thinges, as the Lodgicians terme names of arte, for the whych, we haue no proper Englyshe words: I haue vsed none but the playne and accustomed termes. Now: as touching the second objection, which containeth the vnprofitable disclosing of the mis[t]eries of lady Philosophye (as Mayster Grimoalde termeth her) I thynke, that besides the raskall multitude, and the learned sages, there is a meane sort of men: which although they be not learned, yet by the quicknes of their wits, can conceiue al such points of arte, as nature coulde giue. To those, I saye, there is nothing in this book to darke.

Dolman's reference to Grimald is significant. Like Grimald he translates idiom for idiom, with a sincere effort to render the sense, but without sacrificing naturalness of expression to an anxious care to reproduce the very words of his original, and without expansion or striving to raise his style by artificial means. His inadequacy is mostly in the failure to indicate delicate connections of thought, and sometimes in oversight or omission.

An example of his style follows:

Wherfore I desire all such as are able to do it, that they woulde helpe to take this prayse also from Greece, that is already taynted, and bring it into this our citye, as our auncesters haue already done by al the rest, that were with any payne or trauayle. And truly, the prayse of Oratoures encreased from a lowe to such perfection, that nowe (as natures course doth worke in all thinges) it beginneth to waxe aged, and within this shorte space is lykely to come to nought.

Wherfore, nowe let philosophy, begin to be spred in the latine tongue: and let vs helpe the encrease thereof, although that for the same we be reproued and refuted. Which trulye they cannot abyde, which bynde them selues to anye certayne opinion, as men wholye gyuen to the same, so that sumtymes they are constrayned, & get theym opinion of constancie, to maynteyne such thynges, as otherwise they would not alowe. But I who in al thinges folowe probabilitie, and can go no further then likelyhode, am readye both to wryte agaynst others without any stubbornes and also to be writen agaynst, without anye anger. If so we may brynge this kinde of exercise, from the Grecians to our countreymen, we shall not wante the helpe of the Greke libraries, which are stuffed with an infinite company of bookes, wryten of the same matter.

For manye haue wrytten the same in effect that some others haue done afore them. So that the noumber of books is infinite. The which shal in likewise happen to vs, when many geue themselues to writynge. But I will assaye chiefly to prouoke them to write, who being wel learned, and instructed with perfect eloquence, can endyte philosophye with a good trade and order. For there is a certayne sort of men, whych wyll needes be counted philosophers, that are reputed to haue written manye latine bookes, whiche surely I do not despise, because I neuer redde them: but inasmuche as the aucthours them selues, do playnely confesse, *that* they can wryte neyther distinctlye, orderlye, eloquently, nor trimlye, I assuredlye neglect the readyng of that, which shoulde nothyng at all delyght me, inasmuche as they care not, what they write: I know not why anye man shoulde be bounde to reade them, but suche as are of the same opinion that they be.[58]

Goddard Gilby's translation of Cicero's letter of advice to his brother Quintus (Epis. ad Quin. i, 1) belongs to this group of writings on conduct. It is the inexpert work of a not very intelligent youngster.

Gilby's *Preface to the reader* is not to be taken too seriously.

Where as men are now a days here in England glutted as it wer with gods worde, & therfore al most ready to vomit vp again *that* which thei haue receyued, lothing *the* sermons & despising the preachers, some turning to curious arts, & som contemning all artes & sciences, som Epicures, som atheistes, & few or none do stand forth as fathers to vs yonglings to byd vs folow their fotesteppes in vertues and godlines: We the youth of this realme are drawen into diuers and sundrye doubtfull wayes and wandering bypathes, and many of vs by pouerty and other calamities are oppressed at our first breathing & either know not which way to directe our studies or els want helpe to go forwarde and are cut of in the fyrste herbe accordyng to the Prouerbe. . . The world is full of oppression and the abuse of justice by officers. Therefore not seyng wherevnto in this my good youth I could direct my studies yet nether wherin I cold be better occupied both for mine own learning, and for the instruction of such politike men as wil vochsafe to read heathen writters, though they regard not the scriptures: I haue translated as I could into our natiue language, the notable epistle of that famous wise and politike man M. Tullius Cicero vnto his brother Quintus, wherein iustice and the right vse of an office is so wel and politikely described that the politike heades may learne therby to put good things in practise & nede nether to be ashamed of the authour who was a man of singuler wisedom & great experi-

<hr>

[58] Lib. ii, Cap. 2, 5, 6.

ence, nor of the matter which is an instruction of the magistrate meete for all ages: Yf God grant me any abilitie to expresse it. Take the first fruits of mine infancie in good part, so & you shal encourage me to farther trauails. My father commandeth to folow labour and to suffer others to seke for honours. Fare you wel in the Lorde. At London the vii. of July, the yere of our Lord 1561.

Gilby's version is too closely literal for ease. Its sentences by striving to reproduce the Ciceronian periods become heavy. Unimportant in itself, this version is interesting as another example of the ideal of closer linguistic accuracy which in this era of slowly advancing scholarship challenged the looser methods which had prevailed hitherto.

And yf I dyd see that thy dominion and authoritie had ben prolonged to thee whilest *thou* wast occupyed by some great and dangerous warre my heart woulde quake: to consider that the power of Fortune at the same tyme also should be prolonged agaynste vs. But nowe *synce* [the insertion *since* is an error] *the* parte of the common wealth is committed to thy charge in the which Fortune either hath small or els no parte of rule at all: euen that which semeth vnto me wholly to consist in thy vertue & moderation of minde. I thyncke we nede not feare any priuie traynes of enemyes, any open war, any rebellion and falling away of our felowes and confederates, any lacke of wages or prouision for corne, nor finally any sedicion of the army, which haue often chaunced to moste wise men: that as shypmasters be thei neuer so connyng can not resist the force of *the* tempest so they cold not withstand the violence of fortune [marginal note—the magistrate is compared to a shipmaster.] But to these is geuen the greatest peace and tranquillitie that can be, so that it is [*ita tamen*] of force inough to ouerwhelme a shypmaister that slepeth but a wakyng gouernour would be delited therewith.

Thomas Newton's contributions to the tale of Ciceronian versions was the most important of all, next to Grimald's. He began with the *Paradoxa* and the *Somnium Scipionis* (1569) and added *De Amicitia* and *De Senectute* in *Fowre Seuerall Treatises* (1577). The loquacious dedications (of the earlier *Paradoxa* and *Somnium Scipionis* to Sir Walter Mildmay and of *Fowre Seuerall Treatises* to the Earl of Bedford) contain nothing of interest, except a hope expressed by Newton in the earlier dedication that he will be able to go on with other larger and more difficult works. ". . . I will thinke . . . my trauaile much encouraged to procede in workes of greater volume and paine, already begonne and in part perfourmed by me, if my glassie health may be at any reasonable truce with his feuerous maladies and continuall atrophies."

Newton at his best has dignity, and understands his Latin and English. He lacks rhythm and elevation, fervor, flow, and charm. The 1569 version of the *Paradoxa* is one of the old-fashioned versions, in which the original is expanded by doubling synonyms and in which explanatory notes, developing every allusion and every figure of speech, are written into the text. In 1577 Newton published in one volume versions of the *Paradoxa, Somnium Scipionis, Laelius,* and *Cato Major.* In this work the earlier translation was carefully revised. As Newton says in his dedication to the Earl of Bedford of the second edition [1577]:

To the Earl of Bedford.

Eighte yeeres agoe (Right Honorable) some part of these my poore labors escaped my handes, and rashly (by peecemeale) passed the Printers Presse, not without some blemishes and Eyesores: which, as my meaning was then to haue repolished and brought into order, so the boastinge speede and shufling vp of the same, without my presence, consent, and knowledge, quight defeated my purpose and dashed my determination. But sithens things passed be irreuocable, I have thought good (vpon request) to take that direct course in the second edition thereof, which seemed best to breed the Readers profit, and soonest to salue myne own credite. And thereupon haue I pulled all asunder agayne, and aduentured the same anew, adding thervnto one Booke more [*Laelius*]. Then [i.e. than] before I had done because *the* whole VVorke beeing by that means fully supplied, should come foorth vniforme, and in one manner of style and order.

Newton strove in the new version to keep closer to Cicero's actual language, and to excise the diluting verbiage of the 1569 edition. A comparison of the two is interesting, for it illustrates the establishment of a new conception of the translator's duty, and new ideas of excellence in style. It is obvious that by this energetic striving to keep the English close to the original, to avoid expansions, dilution and explanation, a better discipline is given the translator, and a higher standard enforced for English. The resulting influence on the standard of English prose was certain to be salutary, though the actual translations thus written are often sacrificed, their style becoming stiff, clumsy, and heavy of cadence, while the looser versions have sometimes much grace and attractiveness.

The ethics of Cicero, though professedly eclectic, is essentially Stoic; and the ethical translations of the period are mainly likewise Stoic. The Stoic philosophy, indeed, had been largely accepted and embodied in current Christian ethics. Here, too, as in poetry and history, Arthur Golding rendered useful service. His version of Seneca's *De Beneficiis* shows his usual competence; it is characterized by skilfully idiomatic ease of subordination, without confusion or rigidity, and reproduces Seneca's pointed antitheses without making them too consciously ingenious. Golding's diction is pithily characteristic of the usage of his day on its more vigorous and less artificial side, but is only occasionally very familiar, as for example in satirical passages. His book is therefore important not only in the development of a standard prose English, but in lexicography. The specific and idiomatic definiteness of his use of words is exhibited in the following quotation:

> After so many examples, there is no dout but a Maister maye receyue a freendly turne at his Bondmannes hand. Why should the persone rather imbace the thing, than the thing innoble the persone? All men haue one beginning, and all spring out of one Rocke. Noman is more Gentleman than another, sauing he that hath a better disposed nature, and more apt too good actes. They that setfoorth their Pedegrees & their aunceters on a long rowe interlyned with many braunches of Collaterall descentes on the forefrunt of their houses, are rather notorious than noble. There is but one parent of all men, euen the world, whether it bee by famous or base descent, euery man conueyes his first Pedegree from him. There is no cause why these that keepe tale of their auncetres should beguile thee. Whersoeuer the world hath made any man renowmed, byandby they feyne him to bee a God. Despize no man though his Pedegree bee worne out of remembraunce, and smally furthered by vnfrendly fortune. Whether your aunceters were freemen, or bondmen, or Aleantes: bee of good corage hardily, and whatsoeuer bacenesse lieth in your way leape ouer it. Greate noblenesse abydeth for you aloft. Why should pryde puffe vs vp into so great fondnesse, that wee should disdeyne to take a good turne at our Bondmennes handes: and looke so much at their degree, that we should forget their desertes? Callest thou any man Slaue? being thyself the bondslaue of Lecherie and Gluttonie, and the comon Kickhorse, not of one Strumpet but of manye?[59]

---

[59]Lib. iii, Cap. 28.

The following passage (an exceptional one, it should be noted) exemplifies the importance of *On Benefiting* to the lexicographer:

Some men, bycause they haue dishonested other mens wiues, (and that not priuely but openly) are content too lend their own wyues vnto other men. If there bee anie man that wilnot suffer his wyfe too setfoorth hirself too sale [*prostare*] in hir Coche, and too be iaunced [*vehi*] [Murray finds of the verb with this spelling the form *jauncing*, and the meaning to prance; of the form *jounce* with the meaning to jolt there are many cases, but the first case cited of the transitive use is from Mulcaster's *Positions,* 1581] from place to place as a gazingstock [*vulgo admissis inspectoribus*] for all men to toote at: [*undique perspicuam*] he is a Rudesbie, a Cloyne, and a cankred Carle, yea and a hatingstocke [nonce-word] among greate Ladies. If there bee any that hath not blased himself by some louer, or lent his Ring too another mannes wyfe: [wyse: corrected in errata to *wyfe*] him doo the braue Dames call a Hodipeake, a sorie Leacher, and a singlesoald louer. Heeruppon commeth it too passe, that whoredome is counted honest wedlocke: and in the opinion of vnwyuing Bachelers noman hath wedded a wife, but he that hath inuegled hir from hir Husbond. Furthermore, they onewhyle striue to waste whatsoeuer they can rap and rend: and anon with like couetousnesse they stryue as fast too scrape toogether agein the things they haue scatered. They set all at six and at seuen, disdeyning other mennes pouertie, and dreading their owne: and as for other harme, they feare none. They spare no wrong, but make hauocke of the weaker sort, and keepe them vnder with force and feare. For, that Prouinces are pilled, and offices [*nummarium tribunal, audita utrinque licitatione alteri addici,* as a friendly exchange?] chopped and chaunged with louing and boding [making bids? if so the only instance noted in southern English] from man too man: it is no wonder, considering that by the Lawe of al realmes, a man may sell that whiche he hath bought.[60]

Beneficium, good turne, *passim*

foedissimum, the foulest shame that can be, fo. 1 *rec.*

non . . . facultatibus sed anima, not wealth but will, fo. 1 *rec.*

longis sermonibus et de industria non invenientibus exitum, long and endlesse bytalke, fo. 1 *ver.*

malignis et vix exeuntibus verbis, with murmuring wordes scarce vttered from the lippes, fo. 1 *ver.*

Quid ille consortis manibus in se redeuntium chorus, Why walkes that knot [of the Graces] in a roundell hand in hand? fo. 3 *ver.*

nequitiam, lewdnesse, fo. 7 *rec.*

petulantiam et audaciam, malapert behauour and flat Ruffianrie, fo. 7 *ver.*

maledictum non munus, A Corzie not a Courtezie, fo. 8 *ver.*

---

[60]Bk. I, Cap. 9; Fo. 7 *r.*

lente et diu cogitati, slow and long breathd vpon, fo. 12 *rec.*

Aequiore quidam animo ferunt praecidi spem suam quam trahi,
  Somme can better beare a flat nay, than too bee foaded of, fo. 13
  rec.

remotis arbitris, in hudther mudther, fo. 22 *rec.*

submisse, underlinglike, fo. 22 *ver.*

libertini, Franklinges, fo. 23 *ver.*

tam miseram, tam sordidam, so very a Wretche or so very a Puzzle,
  fo. 35 *ver.*

confusione captae civitatis, hurlieburly at the taking of the citie,
  fo. 38 *ver.*

transfugas, runnagates, fo. 38 *ver.*

stipem aeris, a vile Dodkin, fo. 60 *ver.*

pronepotum, childers children [Murray cites Coverdale Esther ix.
  28—1535], fo. 61 *ver.*

Allobrogum cohortes, the Armies of *Sauoy* and *Delphynois,* fo. 76 *ver.*

sorites inexplicabiles, the insoluble Kreeper whiche is hard too
  restreyne bycause it stealeth vp and neuer leaues kreeping, fo. 79
  ver.

paulatim, by inchmeale, fo. 79 *ver.*

talum torsisse, sprent your ancle, fo. 81 *ver.*

esecta ossa, splitters of bone pikt out, fo. 82 *rec.*

non . . . tuum munus, no Godhamercie to thee, fo. 90 *rec.*

Potis inire gratiam, It is worth Godhamercie, fo. 95 *rec.*

Demetrius cynicus, doggish *Demetrius,* fo. 104 *rec.* (and *passim*)

sacrilegos, churcherobbers, fo. 108 *rec.*

imperator, Graundcapteine, fo. 108 *ver.*

. . . quo illud in plures nodos arboris infelicitas torsit, as the war-
  rinesse of the Tree hath wrythed it intoo mo knurres. fo. 109 *ver.*

moliunt, they meeken, fo. 120 *rec.*

The translation is dedicated to Sir Christopher Hatton, in
the following terms:

Vnder hope of your honorable fauor & good likyng, I preace now
intoo this court ageine after long discontinewance, attendyng as an
interpreter vpon the worthy Ph[i]losopher *Seneca,* sometyme a
courtyer, and also a Counseller of the greatest state in the worlde.
The matter whiche he is too speake of, is the true maner of bene-
fityng or doyng of good turnes; a thing of all others most profitable
for mans life, and whiche maketh men like vntoo God.   In the
declaration whereof, he sheweth what a Benefite is; why, how, when,
too what ende, and on whom it is too bee bestowed; what reward
is too bee looked for in the dooing of it, and what frute it yeeldeth
again.   Likewise at whose hande, with what mynde, and when a
benefit is too bee receiued: how and when wee should requite, or
remaine still detters for it; and by what meanes a man maie be either
beneficiall or thankfull, euen without cost or peine.   His principles
and preceptes are in substaunce, Diuine; in forme, Philosophicall;

in effect, frutefull. His sentences are short, quick, and full of matter; his wordes, sharpe, piththie, and vnaffected; his whole order of writyng graue, deepe, and seuere, fitted altogether for the reforming of mennes myndes, and not too the delyghting of their eares. But great is the libertie of truthe emong wise menne, and yet greater is the prerogatiue therof emong good men. For wise men knowe that the wholsemost meates are not alwaies best in tast, nor the moste souerein medcines alwaies pleasauntest. And good menne being desirous too haue their faultes rather cured than couered, doo finde as well in infirmities of mynde, as of bodie, that the first step to helth is too discerne the diseaze, and the next is too receiue the right medicine for it: Onely too the vnwise and wicked sorte, truthe is troublesome and odious; because they cannot abyde the bryghtnesse of her countenance, nor the power and maiestie of her presence. I haue therefore thought this woorke not vnmeete too bee put intoo our Moothertung, that the mo myght take benefyte by it; nor yet vnexpedient too comme in Courtyers handes, who shalbe so muche the greater Ornament too themselues, and too the place whereof they take their name, as their Courtesies and Benefytes bee mo and greater towards others. And how woorthie it is too bee embrased of Counsellers; I referre mee too the iudgement of suche as shall voutsafe too read it. Of this I am fully perswaded, that you will thinke it a verie fit present for mee too offer vnto you in respect of the place wherintoo you are called; and a sufficient Argument and Witnesse of my duetyfull good will towards you. And thus recommending this my trauell too your good and honourable protection, I humbly take my leaue. Written at my House in the Parish of all Hallowes in the Wall of London the xvii day of March, 1577. Most humbly at your commaundement,

Arthur Golding.

Miss M. St. Clare Byrne has found a translation of selections from Seneca,—from the *Epistolae, De Tranquillitate Animi, De Brevitate Vitae, De Consolatione, De Providentia,*—bound up without a separate title-page as an appendix to a translation of De Mornay's *Excellent Discours de la Vie et de la Mort* (*The Defence of Death*). The work was probably printed in 1577, and in Miss Byrne's view "E. A.," the translator, is probably Edward Aggas, the publisher of the work. She characterizes the translation as being faithful to the sense and spirit of the original, vigorous and natural in expression, and as showing a fine feeling for rhythm,—a better translation than Lodge's.[61]

[61] *An Early Translation of Seneca*, in *The Library*. Ser. 4, vol. IV, no. 4 (1924), p. 277.

Another important Stoic treatise is Epictetus's *Manuell* (1567) translated by James Sandford. This is Arrian's brief aphoristic statement of Epictetus's moral teachings—the *Enchiridion, i.e.* "Handbook" or "Manual." It was translated "Oute of Greeke into French [by Antoine du Moulin, printed with some sentences of the Greek philosophers, Lyons, 1544, and with the Epistles of Phalaris, Antwerp, 1558] and now into English, conferred with two Latin translations [those of Politian and Hieronymus Wolfius]." The form *Manuell* is due to the French translation. The commentary, which deals with the substance and general interpretation is drawn from Wolfius; the marginal summaries are taken from Politian. The style is more flowing and easy than is usual in translations from the Latin. Sandford, in his dedication to Queen Elizabeth, speaks with a well justified, modest, but firm confidence of his work, the fruit of "paynfull practize ioyned with diligent studie," and praises the author, since "although he were an Ethnicke, yet he wrote very godly and christianly."

This body of Stoic works, I think there can be little doubt, did something to lay the foundation for the secularization of ethics, and even for the rationalization of religion, which was carried on during the seventeenth and early eighteenth centuries largely under the influence of classical writers. From the praise of ethnic writers as "godly and christianly," from thinking of St. Cicero and Holy Socrates, it was a natural step to raise the question whether revelation were necessary to teach men the way to God and good living. Thus Lord Herbert of Cherbury is a Ciceronian, and the Deists had the foundation of their doctrines laid in Stoicism.

Plutarch, Lucian, and Isocrates were not quite forgotten in this period, though they did not hold the central place which they held in the school of Erasmus, only a few minor translations representing them. The important place of Isocrates in the mind of the soberer classicists has already been explained. In 1585 R. Nuttall's *Ad Demonicum* was printed, and in 1580 Thomas Forrest's more important version of the three main compositions of Isocrates on the conduct of life, the letters to Nicocles and Demonicus, and the oration on Nicocles, with the title, *A Perfecte Looking Glasse for all Estates.* The translation is made from the Latin of Hieronymus Wolfius.

Wolf dates his preface to the first edition 1547, the second
1551. Forrest has the old-fashioned expansive ideal of translation. The commentary, which is only in part drawn from
Wolf, mainly illustrates the text from ancient history, but
a few of the notes have a contemporary flavor. The temper
best known from Ascham's comments in the *Schoolmaster*
was common among the scholars of his type. So Forrest in
his note on a passage in Isocrates to the effect that writers to
be popular must be entertaining and not serious, says, "As is
seene by many in these dayes which doe rather buy riming
Sonets, and Pallaces of pleasure, then any booke containing
wise Sentences and godly instructions." And later in the same
page, where Isocrates praises the inventors of Comedy, Forrest remarks, "But not such Commodies as are plaide in these
daies, containing onely toyes and bables as are the lyues of
rogues and Idiots, with Poeticall inuentions appertai[ning
thereto] you may come to a playe now, and neither vnderstand
the beginning nor ending, for it containeth not any example of
well liuing, but onely a fardell of gibes cobled togither by a
ignoraunt Idiot."

The dedication, to Sir Thomas Bromley, Lord Chancellor,
is conventional, but the preface contains a passage of some interest.

> . . . . And where as now beholding the magnificencie and singuler
> liberalitie of this renowned king with the great good will he shewed
> himselfe to heare towardes those which are studious in the knowl-
> edge of good literature I might iustly bewaile the want of such
> men in these our dayes, respecting not onely the infinite number of
> liuinges at the first allowed for the maintenance of studentes, but
> nowe remaining in the handes of those whom we may rightly call
> worldlinges, but also that horrible and most abhominable selling and
> craftie conueying of spirituall benefices, nothing respecting nor
> waighing the conuersation of the man on whom they bestowe them,
> so that they may haue eyther present money by him or his friends,
> or the personages themselues in pawne, vntill the income bee payde
> because I knowe it is but labour lost, in that it is so commonly cried
> out vpon, by most graue and learned preachers euen euery day, and
> yet not one to be founde whose couetous heart relenteth his former
> wretchednesse, I will rather returne to my authour as one with silence
> signifying my griefe, then sharpely in wordes to prosecute that,
> wherein I shall seeme so litle to preuaile, wherefore my onely
> request is that all true Christians would not forget euen in their dayly
> prayers, to beseeche the Lord our God among a number of other
> mischiefes, as especially to redresse this so horrible an infection.

The translations of a few of Plutarch's essays from the *Morals,* and of one trifle of Lucian's have little significance; they simply carry on the tradition of the beginning of the century, of Budaeus and Erasmus, without leading it further or giving it new force. Between 1500 and 1520 a number of the little disquisitions of which the *Moralia* are composed had been translated into Latin by various scholars, and published in scattered pamphlets or miscellaneous collections. In 1521 Josse Bade brought together a lot of these versions (*Opuscula Plutarchi chaeronensis undequaqua collecta etc.* . . .) and printed a second edition in 1526. From the same collection Blundeville took several opuscula and gave them an English form, beginning with "The Frutes of Foes" in four line stanzas of simple 4-stress verse, (*De capienda ex inimicis utilitate*), which found a not unfavorable reader in Queen Elizabeth.

> My morall muse, for that, yet had no dread,
>
> .   .   .   .
> Presuming of the fauor which [s]he founde
> When that she sang, what fruites of foes might rise;
> And that your Grace, gaue ear vnto the sounde,
> Of such rude rime, as she did then deuise.

The paradox of *De capienda* makes the antithetic gnomic verse from *The Fruites of Foes* not unsuitable to the material; though of course Plutarch's diffuseness and amplitude of illustration do not lend themselves well to the pithy conciseness which such verse should have as an ideal.

> If thou be sicke, or much in det.
> Falne out with wife, with maide, or man:
> Yea, no mishap can thee beset,
> But that they foes eft soone know can.

> Like rauening birdes, that carrion fleshe,
> And not the sound, far off can smell:
> So they thy illes, to spie be fresh,
> And all thy griefes, with eie full fell.

> What greater gaine may be than this,
> Hereby to learne, in such a sort,
> Our life to lead, as none there is,
> That ill thereof maie once report?

For as sicke men that warie bee,
In meates and drinkes, that may offend:
In wordes and déeds, euen so doe wée,
Take héede that they the best pretend.

Whereby we come in schoole to dwell,
Of customes good, and excellent:
For reason rules th' affections fell,
Whereto our mindes be alwaies bent.

Yea, though long time and exercise,
It breedes in vs such stedfastnes,
That learne we can none other guise
But aie to liue in holines.[62]

The little version was introduced by commendatory verses from the pen of Roger Ascham "Secretarie to the Queenes Maiestie, for the Latine tongue," in praise of the book.

Of English bookes, as I could find,
I haue perused manie one:
Yet so well done vnto my mind,
As this is, yet I haue found none.

The wordes of matter here doe rise,
So fitlie and so naturallie:
As hart can wish, or wit deuise,
In my conceit and fantasie.

The wordes well chosen, and well set,
Doe bring such light vnto the sense:
As if I lackt, I would not let,
To buie this booke for fortie pense.

Blundeville next turned *The Learned Prince* into similar verses ending naturally with some seven stanzas in honor of Elizabeth:

How happie than is Britan land,
Which doth enioie so noble a Queene,
As reasons rule doth vnderstand,
Whereby no vice in hir is seene?

Finally he turned the essay *De Tranquillitate* into English prose, under the title *The Porte of Rest*, dedicating it to "John Asteley, Maister of the Queenes Maiesties Ievvell House, and John Harington Esquier."

---

[62] Stanzas 29-34.

Instead of helping me the seas to pas
Of worldlie ioies, amongest the happie sort,
In ship full fraught, with fortunes gifts: as was
Hir vow, when first my state she did support.

The restles Muse, had made my feeble braine
The forge of care, and therein dailie wrought
Such dolefull dumps, and dreadfull dreames as cleane
From mirth my mind, vnto despaire had brought.

That booke did yeeld such glistring beames (I saie,)
Of comfort great, and ioifull quietnes;
As draue those dumpes and sorrowes all awaie,
My heauie heart which held in great distres.

.   .   .   .

Which comfort though, it gratefull was to mee,
In my conceit, yet did it not suffise,
Vnlesse that you, may faithfull freends might bee,
And partners of, the same some kind of wise.

.   .   .   .

Into our tongue, therefore this little quaire,
I turned haue, and termd *The Port of Rest,*
And wish each wight, thereto for to repaire,
With troubled spirit, that feeles himselfe opprest.

.   .   .   .

Budes workes, in all this treatise still I followed haue,
(I hope) most faithfullie.
Whose stile I found to be more graue than gaie, and hard
to turne, into our vulgar speech, ...

Budé's Latin expands even the expansive Plutarch, by the doubling of synonyms, and by explanation, so that Blundeville's English represents his original only in reproducing its general ideas, which it does in readable and easy English.

A sicke man (as *Ion* saith) is a verie vnpleasant thing, for he cannot abide his wife, he blameth his Physician, and is angrie with his bed. If his freend commeth to visit him he doeth but trouble him. And if he depart from him, he doeth again offend him. But after that his disease beginneth to asswage, and to be somewhat more temperate: then commeth health by litle and litle, making all things delectable and pleasant. In such sort, that whereas the daie before he did loath new laide egges, daintie brothes, and the finest bread that might be gotten: the next daie after, can hungerlie eate a peece of common bread, with a few cresses. Of suche importance is a good discourse in all changes of the life, the onelie force whereof procureth the happie life.

It is said, that when Alexander heard the Philosopher Anaxarcus, affirming in disputation, that there were innumerable worldes: he wept for sorrowe. And being demanded by his freendes what iust cause he had to weepe, he answered: *Haue we not iust cause* (quoth he) *to weepe: sith there be so manie worldes, and we be not as yet Lordes of one?* But *Crates* the poorelie clad Philosopher, contrariwise consumed all his life to the last daie in sport and laughter, as though they were all festiuall daies. *Agamemnon* likewise King of the *Micens* was not a little troubled, for that he had the rule of so manie men. Of whom *Homer* talking saieth thus:

> *Thou knowest right well* Atreus *son,*
> *That cleped is* Agamemnon,
> *Whom most of all with labor great,*
> *Ioues pleasure is, to vexe and freat.*[63]

A youth by the name of John Clapham later tried his hand on the *De Tranquillitate,* translating as he tells us from Amyot. His version is full of errors, inexcusable in one who ventures to give his work to the public.

Lucian's *Toxaris,* translated by A. O., 1565, I have not seen.

William Barker's translation of Xenophon's *Cyropedia,* of course, belongs most naturally with these moral works. It is dedicated to "Wyllyam Earle of Pembroke ... President of the Kynges hyghnes Counsell in the marches of Wales," and therefore was completed between 1551 and 1553. Barker says in the additional dedication (1567) to Philip Earl of Surrey, then nine years old, that the translation was done before he went into Italy. (Philip's father, the Duke of Norfolk, to whom Barker was a secretary and who was compromised by Barker's confession in 1571, called him "an Italianified Englishman".) But Barker adds that when he returned, he found six books already printed (1560), "not by my desires but onlye by the curteisie and good will of the Printer, a furtherer of good learninge."

In the original dedicatory preface to Pembroke, Barker says:

Those authors be chiefly to be red, which have not only by fines of wit, and diligence of study attained to an excellencye, but also have had the experience of manners of men, and diuersity of places, and haue with wisdome and eloquence, ioyned those two together. For as generall thinges and ordre of nature canne not be perceaued, but by them whose natural sharpnes of wit is holpen with earnest and continual painfulnes of study, priuate doynges and dispositions of men only knowen by dayly use and tryall of them. And there be many skilful in the one that be in the other kind verye symple,

---

[63]Sig. Ev r.

and can say much of generalityes, but in particularityes be utterly ignorant, and others again, . . . etc. [The praise of practical experience was likely to be acceptable to Pembroke, who could indeed write his name but only in capitals, according to the article in the Dictionary of National Biography. Xenophon, Barker says, sanely combined experience, learning, and eloquence.—He] understoode not only the natures of men, the usages of ordres, the deuices of councel, the engins of war, but also the sportes and pastimes most convenient for a leaserfull lyfe, and hath sorted with skill, that was engrossed by experience, and hath gyuen rules of peace and war, no learned man more, and furnisheth a gentleman with much goodlie knowledg so much more to be commended then the other, that his rules be in practice for common life and not sought out of the depth of nature, whose perfectnes as it is more commendable, so can it not agree with the common use of life.

Barker writes to Pembroke as to one "whose vertues are better knowne unto me, then you yourselfe are." He has heard that he has gotten his children a good schoolmaster: and to them this book may be of use for its substance and as a basis for English exercises. The book then was sent in manuscript.

Barker's translation is not literal, but substitutes idiom for idiom, not pedantically but effectively. It shows no signs of the influence of the Latin versions of Poggio or Filelfo, and looks as if it were made direct from the Greek: ταξιάρχων, "captains of crews"; λοχαγῶν, "bandleaders" (II. I, 30); οὐραγούς, "tayleguides" (III, 3, 41) are expressions that would much more naturally occur as equivalents for the Greek original than for any Latin intermediary form.

The errors are slight, and the language is lively:

Cyrus also hadde regarde, that when they made merye, suche talke shoulde bee mynystred, as was pleasant, and myght styrre them to manhood. And on a tyme he chanced to talke on this wyse. Frendes (quoth he) dooeth other men seeme inferiours to us, bycause they bee not trayned after our sort? or is there no dyfference at all beetwixte theym and us, neyther in behauyour, nor in thynges appertaynynge to the trade of warre? Hystaspes answered and sayd: What they be in warlyke matters, I can not tell, but in behauiour and company, there be some (by my fay) rude inough. For of late Cyaxares sent to every band and company sacred meate, and we had iii dyshes of fleshe euery man or more. The cooke began the fyrste mease at me. And whan he came the second tyme, I hadde hyme begynne again at the hyndermost. Wherefore one of the souldyours that sat in the myddest, cryed out and sayde: By god this geare goeth not indifferently, yf no man shall begynne at us that be in the middest. Whiche when I herd, I was greued, that he should thynke he had to lyttell, and called hym vnto me. He very modestly obeied me. When the meate came at us, and the lowest had taken theyr parte, there was, I thynke, but lyttell lefte. Whereat he was agayne greeued, as he did playnly expresse. And sayd to hym selfe: What yl lucke had I to come hyther, when I was called? And I said, Take no care for the matter, for he shall streight begin at us, and you shalbe first and take the moste. And with that he brought in the thyrde and laste course. And this felowe tooke nexte vnto me. Whanne the thyrde manne had taken, and seemed to take more than he, he layde asyde that he hadde taken, entendynge to take an other. The cooke, thynkynge he hadde no lyste to meate, bore it awaye before he coulde take an other peece. Thanne he was greued at hys euyll chaunce, bycause that that he had taken, was eaten up. Wherefore, beeying in a rage and furye for so euyll fortune, he ouerthrewe the sauce that was lefte hym. Whyche when the band-leader that satte nexte vnto me, sawe, clapped his handes, and laughed hartily. And I made as I hadde the cough, for I coulde not refrayne from laughter[64].

The classical writers of moral treatises were highly regarded for their influence in the formation of the character of the "gentleman," as is clearly put by Laurence Humfrey, in his discourse on *The Nobles or of Nobilitye* (1563): "To become therefore fyrste *Ethike* and morall, reade he [the nobleman] of the greekes Isocrates, chiefly *To Demonicus* and *Nicocles, Epictetus* and other like . . . Furthermore nexte *Artistotle* of maners, reade he *Cicero* dutyes, which he ought neuer laye from him, and peruse hee whatsoeuer that heauenlye wight wrote."

To his own treatise Humfrey appended *The Lytle treatyse of Philo a Jewe, concernynge nobilitye,* effectively translated from the Latin. The ethical idealism common to Greek, Jew, and Christian is well expressed in the following passage:

Sith therefore, the nobilitye of a cleared conscyence, is the peculyer enheritaunce of the good and perfecte: onely the temperate and iust, though borne of niefes and villens, must be adiudged nobles. Contrarywyse, of the euell, though descended of the best, unentred bee the holde of Nobilitye. For exyle from hys home and countreye is, who so is noughte. Wanderyng as a straye, from vertuc his true home, the natiue soyle of the wyse. And necessarilye must dishonoure accompanye, whoseo (though borne of blameles syres; and graundsyres) swarueth from theyr vertues and farthest twynneth bothe in worde and deede from Nobilitye. A i; *verso.*

[64]Bk. II, Cap. ii, 1-5.

Similar to the collections of proverbs and *apophthegmata* of which there were so many in the second period was Edmund Elviden's *Closet of Counsels* (1573). The sayings are drawn mainly from classic sources, and are in rough septenary couplets.

So far as these translations show, the Renaissance had come to England in two waves or streams of thought and feeling, the first grave and ethical, concerned with the refinement and elevation of ideals of conduct and with the development of efficiency, and presenting to English readers especially some of the moral writers of the past; the other eager for enrichment and color, expansive rather than controlled, and bringing into English amorous and tragical tales. Neither ever destroyed or drove out the other; and the two streams flowed on, sometimes mingling, sometimes apart.

Every type of version in this era had a fringe of freak performances; as poetry had its share of trivial and silly verses, history and geography their grotesque collections of pseudo-science, so philosophy had its version of Synesius on the Praise of Baldness, translated by the industrious cheese-mite of letters, Abraham Fleming. Synesius's jest had been brought into fashion by Erasmus's praises, and a Latin version by "I. Phrea" (John Free) was printed with Erasmus's *Encomium Moriae* (ed. Beatus Rhenanus) Basle, 1532. The Greek text was first printed at Paris in 1533. Fleming depends entirely upon Free, in whose version are many lacunae, and evidently used Beatus Rhenanus's edition of the *Praise of Baldness* bound up with the *Encomium Moriae*.

The Schoolemaster or *Teacher of Table Phylosophie* (Thomas Twyne; 1571, 1583) is in fact little more (if any more) than a translation of *Mensa Philosophica,* an anonymous book, telling what you ought to eat and drink, and what you ought to say in company, relative to the people you meet at table, giving questions and problems of the table, and finally containing a collection of anecdotes fit for the table. Macrobius is often cited, but is not translated, and is not the sole authority. Avicenna, Isaac, Rhasis, as well as Galen and Hippocrates, are drawn upon. The seventh book of Macrobius gave the author hints for the plan of his work.

Versions of Greek works of science include Sir Henry Billingsley's Euclid—all things considered the most remarkable of all the translations of the period. It is remarkable as a complete version of a central and original Greek book, as a scholarly translation direct from the Greek, as the work of a man not a professed mathematician, who gave himself to business and became Lord Mayor of London, and in its printed form as a beautiful and noble volume. Euclid at the time was known to European scholars, first, through the quite imperfect Latin version of Johannes Campanus, made in the thirteenth century from the Arabic, and based upon an earlier translation, likewise from the Arabic, by Athelhard of Bath, secondly, through the Latin version of Zamberti, printed in Venice in 1505, and thirdly, through the Greek text itself, from an inferior manuscript, printed in 1533. There were also a number of commentaries. The article on Billingsley in the Dictionary of National Biography, unfortunately, says carelessly that Billingsley's translation is from Campanus. This assertion is little less than a slander. As is shown by Professor G. B. Halsted, Billingsley carefully compared Campanus and Zamberti with the Greek text, which he could read intelligently, and utilized the commentary of "Flussas" (François de Foix-Candale.) Within the compass of a few pages one passage will be found the expression of which shows that it was translated direct from the Greek, another in which Zamberti is preferred, another in which Campanus is preferred, another which is indebted to Flussas. Billingsley's copies of the *Editio princeps* of the Greek text, 1533, and of Campanus's and Zamberti's versions (1558) with Proclus on the first book, bound together, are extant (in the library of Princeton) with copious notes comparing them, in Billingsley's handwriting. Billingsley gives also some historical account of the authorities; cites Iohannes de Sacro Busto, Theodosius and Galen,[65] and in speaking of Theodosius's *De Sphericis*,[66] calls it "a booke very necessary for all those who will see the groundes and principles of Geometrie and Astronomie, which also I haue translated into our vulgar tounge, ready to the presse." Dr. John Dee provided a preface, and some of his notes and comments appear in the book, with due acknowledgment. This has given rise

---

[65] Fo. 315, v. (Bk. XI, def. 12).
[66] Fo. 315 *v*.

to the idea that the translation is Dee's, supported by the false impression that the dignified portrait of John Day, the printer, is Dee's.[67] A consideration of dates shows that Billingsley could not have received into his family "the eminent mathematician called Whytehead" so early as the time "when Whytehead was put to his shifts after the demolition of his house in the latter end of Henry 8," for Billingsley entered St. Johns as Lady Margaret Scholar only in 1551; though it is possible enough that he did indeed study with Whytehead, that he later gave him an asylum, and that Whytehead gave him "all his mathematicall observations that he had made and collected together with his notes on Euclid's Elements that he had made and digested together." In any event, the existence of Billingsley's Euclid with his own manuscript notes is clear evidence that the Euclid as it came from Billingsley's hand was the work of an independent scholar, and not a mere transcript of what Billingsley had received from his master.

After the appearance of the Euclid, Billingsley gave himself wholly to business; he became a member of the Haberdashers' Company, amassed wealth, and was a busy man of affairs, collector of the Port of London, a member of Parliament, and in time (1596) Lord Mayor.

A few translations from classical writers on medicine deserve only a brief reference. They are of significance as forerunners of the composition of serious medical works in the vernacular, and as part of the intellectual side of nationalism, characteristic of the age. They are in general bound with other and later works, to which they are supplementary and include only parts of their originals.

Humphrey Lloyd's version of the Aphorisms of Hippocrates was appended to his translation of the *Treasuri of Helth,* compiled by Petrus Hispanus (Pope John XXI). It is possible that the first edition appeared as early as 1550; but the second edition is certainly dated 1585.

Though Lloyd translates Petrus, he complains of his "barbarous and arabicke terms." He intended his book, he says, only as a useful popular work, not as a substitute for the professionally trained physician's skill.

---

[67]D. N. B. XIV, 279; *v.* McKerrow, R. B., *Printers' and Publishers' Devices in England and Scotland, 1485-1640.* Bibl. Soc. Illustrated Monographs, No. XVI, (London 1913).

To the Gentilharted Reader, Humfrey Lloyd . . . . . .

. . . I dyd also translate and adde herunto the aphorysmes of Hipocrates redacted vnto such an order that as the membres of mannes body be disposed to receiue some one disease and some another, so the aphorismes, which entreate of eueri disease that may happen to that membre be gathered together into one chapiter begynnyng at the head and soo in order to the fette. . . . I and al other which intend anye such worke, ar muche beholden to Mayster Wyllyam Turner, ... vnto whose iudgment and correccion and all other lerned in the most necessary scyence of Physycke, do I submyt thys lytle worke and treatyse, desiring them most hartly to take in good worthe thys my fyrst labour & to accept my good wyll, not thynkyng it to be done to hurt any man, knowynge what a perylous thynge it is for them that be not lerned both in the complectyons of men, Age, Regions, and tyme of the yere, wyth the knowledge of the Orygyne and causes of the diseases, to take vpon them the cure of any pacient & that rather they shall do hurte then good wyth the sole and onely practyse therof except they do therunto adde great knowledge and perfyte iudgment had wyth paynfull study and long practyse, therfore I wold that all such rash & temerariouse persons shuld perfectly knowe, that it was neuer my mynde or wyll that thys worke shoulde be set furth to mayntayne there fylthy lucre and blind boldnes, but chefely to be a tokin and sygne of the entyer desyre I haue to set furth the thyng whych shuld be acceptable and pleasaunt to the Reader, & also I wold that it shuld be for the use and profyte of suche honest persons as wyll modestly and discretely (eyther in tyme of necessyty when no lerned Phisicion is at hande, or else conferrying wyth some lerned man and vsynge his councel) mynyster the thinges herin conteyned.

Galen's *Methodus Medendi* was translated from Linacre's Latin by Thomas Gale (1586).

George Baker appended to his translation of *Oil of Oleum Magistrale* (1574) a translation of Book III of the epitome of Galen, *De compositione medicamentorum per genera*, by himself, and added to a translation of Guy de Chauliac's medical catechism (*Guido's Questions*, 1579) a revision of Copland's version of Book IV (1st ed. 1541, v.p. 51). The preface has some interest in view of the humanistic endeavor to replace Arabian by classic, and especially Greek authority.´ In the *Epistle Dedicatory* Baker says:

It is not vnknowene to any (right honorable) which haue beene but meanly conuersant in good learning, how far the Gretians did surmount all the nations of the world in renown of vertue, learning, politique gouernment and noble victoryes. For what nation doth not reuerence their sages? what people dooth not imbrace their studyes? what Cittie dooth not desire their gouernment? what prouince was not subiect to their Empire? yea was not Grecia the Theatre, Spectacle and light of the whole world? were there not in it many famous Citties whose peple & inhabitants for ciuilitie, whose lawes for policy, whose edifices for magnificence might seem Angelicall, deuine, and celestiall? as Athens and Thebes & c. [Of all these cities Sparta was the greatest, whereof the downfall only befell when the citie deserted the wise laws of Lycurgus—a notable example to all noble families & famous cities that by virtue a state is saved. This I say not by way of exhorting you, whose honorable mind and vertues are well known. As for myself, nothing yet able to add to the perfection of the art of medicine] I haue adventured to interpret one small work of the fatherly both Phisition and Chirurgion Galen. . . .

In the same year (1574) with the publication of the *Oil of Oleum Magistrale* John Jones printed a version of the *Elementa* of Galen, bound up with *A Discourse of Living and Growing Things*.

The demand for manuals of the art of war was as practical and immediate as for elementary works on medicine. Neither barber-surgeons nor subaltern officers could be required or expected to be trained Latinists in order to prepare themselves for the actual exigencies of their occupations. And the classic writers on military matters were not merely conventionally authoritative but were regarded as practically useful. So Onosander was translated (1563), neatly and clearly, by Peter Whytehorne, the translator of Machiavelli on the *Art of War* (1560), and Vegetius (1572) by John Sadler. Sadler in his dedication to the second Earl of Bedford declares that the author is important to be known by Englishmen in their own tongue as by other nations. As to the literary quality of his translation he says,

> . . . . to speake vnfaynedlye my owne labour and trauayle can loke for no manner of prayse at all, excepte peraduenture the onlye commendation of painfull and faythfull dilligence, whiche as Vegetius sayth himselfe, is here more requisite, then elegancye and finenes of wordes. not addinge there vnto anye thinge of mine owne, after the maner of a Paraphrast to dilate the matter more at large with a curious and eloquent stile: but vsinge onlye the office of a translatour, plainlye and compendiouslye expressing so neare as I could, the true sense and meaning of the Authour. . . .

There is a genuine satisfaction to be got from these business-like versions of the military text-books, entirely free from pretentiousness and manipulation of style, and intent simply on the practical end in view. On the whole, they create a favorable impression of the "bookish theoric."

Perhaps Pliny's *Natural History* may be mentioned appropriately at this point; it was the great miscellany of entertaining misinformation, which was for the Renaissance as it had been for the Middle Ages directly and mediately a stock source of literary decoration and a means of envisaging the world under an interesting and picturesque guise. The original would probably at this time have been too large and daring an undertaking for printers; and indeed long stretches contain details of fact of little value except for reference. A French abridgment, however, made by Pierre de Changi, already had been printed at Lyons in 1551, and reprinted with slight abbreviations in 1559. A certain I. A. (perhaps the printer John Alday) translated the first French edition into English. His version appeared first in 1566, and excited some interest, having been reprinted in 1585, with the omissions of some leaves at the first and last of the book, as if the printer's copy had already been worn out in use, and again in 1587. The translation is studded with errors: *quand ils sont decrepites* [I.A. *dead*] *ils se sont jettes en la mer,—qui n'ont nez ne narrines, mais le visage tout plain* [I.A. *full*],—*boiuent avec un tuyaue et plume* [I.A. *with an oten straw*]. For the most part the book is dull and commonplace, but there is one interesting passage.

> Towards the west there is a people called *Arimaspi,* that hath but one eye in their foreheads, they are in the desert and wilde Countrey. The people called *Agriphagi,* liue with the flesh of Panthers and Lyons: and the people called *Anthropomphagi* which we call *Canibals,* liue with humaine fleshe. The *Cinamolgi,* their heades are almost lyke to the heades of Dogges. *Affrica* aunciently called *Libia,* doeth containe the *Moores,* and the pillers of *Hercules,* (among the floudes) there is *Onylus* that doth ingender Cocodrils. There are goodlye Forrests with vnknowen trees, some of the which trees beare threades, of the which is made clothing of cotton. Cyrenes and Syrtes, make their houses of salt stones cut out of the mountaines, there is the mountaine of *Ciry,* the which doth ingender and bring forth many precious stones. In *Libie* which is at the end of the *Ethiopes,* there are people, differing from the common

order of others, they haue among them no names, and they curse the Sunne for his great heate, by the which they are all black sauing their teeth, and a little the palme of their handes, and they neuer dreame. The others called *Troglodites* haue caues and holes in the grounde, & haue no other houses. Others called *Gramantes,* they make no mariages, but all women are common. *Gamphasantes* they go all naked. *Blemmyis* is a people so called, they haue no heades but haue their mouth and their eyes in their breastes.[68]

Here are brought together the marvels which Othello refers to in his account of his experience: the Antars vast, the Caves of the Trogloditae; the desarts idle, the rough quarries and rocks, the Canibals that each other eat, the Anthropophague, and the men whose heads do grow beneath their shoulders. Everything is here except the hills whose heads touch heaven, and everybody knew that Mount Atlas was in the country of the Moors. Years ago, when I first saw this passage, it seemed to me that almost certainly Shakespeare had read Changi's abridgment, and plucked out of it its one striking passage.[69] However that may be, the fact that all the wonders of Othello's narrative, scattered in Pliny's book VII, are here brought together brings forward strikingly the fact that it was the classic past that in unexpected quarters enriched the imagination of the Elizabethans, and filled the corners of the earth with wonders. It is true the new discoveries played their part,—even in Changi *Anthropophagi* is glossed by *Canibals,* the wonders of antiquity and of the new world being thus amalgamated, as in Othello. But the main stamina are ancient. Shakespeare had no need to go out of his way in compliment to Sir Walter Raleigh in order to bring in such wonders as the headless men, the cannibals, and the vast caves and rocks and mountains of Africa.

After Pliny's pseudo-science may well follow the pseudo-science of Artemidorus. Thomas Hill in 1576 published a work entitled "The moste pleasaunte arte of the interpretation of dreams." About a quarter of the book is a summary, with many omissions, but literal as far as it goes, of Artemidorus' *Oneirocritica,* Latin by Janus Cornarius, Basle, 1544.

Interesting evidence of the growth in the consequence of the

---

[68]Sig. Biii and Biv.
[69]Lathrop, H. B., *Shakespeare's Anthropophagi,* in N. Y. *Nation,* C (1915), 76.

vernacular in the conduct of important business, and of the constant reference to classic sources as practical guides is to be found in the printing of a body of model letters, based upon ancient collections and translated into English. There had been many such collections in Latin just before Fleming's day, beginning with a collection of letters by divers Greek philosophers, orators, and teachers of rhetoric ("sophists") printed with a Latin version by Aldus in 1499. This collection, Diogenes Laertius, Pliny, and Cicero, with some letters of modern Latinists ([Paulus] Manutius, Haddon, and Ascham) are Fleming's sources. It seems to me likely that the labor of collection had been mainly done before him; though in the many Latin collections of exemplary letters before his day which I have examined, I have not found any which exactly correspond with his collection.

[To the learned reader this book will give pleasure; to the unlearned a useful equipment and armor of knowledge.] As it is not for a naked and vnarmed soulder, to encounter his enimie being harnessed at all pointes, and to the proofe prouided, except his intent be, wilfully to incurre daunger of violence: so it is not for any man to tye the vse of his penne, to the vanities of his owne imagination, which commonly be preposterous & carelesse in keeping order, vnlesse his meaning be, of set purpose, to reape repprehension for his securitie and negligence. Hee therefore that is to play the part of a warriour, ought with his force and valliauntnesse, to ioyne substantiall furniture, that the seruice of his naturall abilities, and the vse of his instrumentall powers, may concurre and goe together, making him the more venturous to withstand his enimies assault, and fuller of force also to giue him the discomfiture. So he in like manner (that I may rather shewe myselfe a *Mercurialist* than a *Martialist*: for I have not to deale with war, nor yet with warlike weapons, otherwise then by way of application.) that loueth orderly to indite, & plausibly to occupie his penne in diuising and disposing as well both meete matter, as also fit wordes, in any kinde of letter, (for of letters there be sundrie sortes) [marginal note giues 17 of the 21 kinds—"reade Libanius sophista, De epistolarum characteribus"] must make meanes and prouision for him selfe in this case, that those wantes and imperfection of Art & cunning may be supplied. To such a one I giue counsell to passe and repasse, to view & review, to take down and put on, to exercise and vse, such weapons as he shall find in this our Panoplie or house of furniture, & he shall feele him selfe in short space, fenced and strengthened to the purpose against ignoraunce that ougly monster of many heades, an enimie to order, and a friend to confusion. For there shall be no kinde of letter, but in forming the same, thou shalt (though the gifts of nature, wherewith thou art indued, be but weake and slender) haue knowledge, cunning, iudgement, and experience sufficient: be the person to who*m* thou writest neuer so princely, neuer so learned, neuer so woorthy, neuer so noble neuer so friendly . . . finally be his qualities of this kinde or that kinde, what so euer . . . . What should I say more? wilt thou write grauely, wilt thou write wise, . . . wilt thou write angerly? wilt thou complaine, wilt thou accuse . . . . wilt thou intreate? [22 wilt thou's] . . . . what so euer thou art disposed to do by letter, eyther to thy friend, or to thine enimie, thou hast this Panoplie to guide thy head in deuising, and thy penne in disposing. . . . . .

There follows: An Epitome of Precepts whereby the ignoraunt may learne to indite, according to skill and order, reduced into a Dialogue between Maister and Scholer.

Master: What is an Epistle or letter? . . .
          To what end was it deuised? . . . . .
Maister.   Deliuer vnto me the partes or circumstances of an epistle demonstratiue?
Scholer.   An epistle demonstratiue consisteth in these two points, namely commendation and dispraise.
So we are taught for what things and in what work to praise & dispraise persons,
namely of the (Basenesse of byrth   )
              (Waywardnesse in infancie   )
              (Euill properties in childhode)
              (Lewdnesse in youthfull yeares)
              (Slouthfulness in perfect age)   All which touch
              (Beggerie in old age   )   the person.
              (A wicked life   )
              (A shamefull death   )

We are taught to praise deeds and places, to support our propositions by examples, and especially for what circumstances regions, cities, and buildings are to be glorified, (*e.g.* for goodly galleries, pleasaunt parlours, braue bed chambers, commodious closets comfortable prospects, . . . gorgeous gates or entrances . . .) We learn how to address Kings, Dukes, Earls, Knights, aediles, Judges, praetors, Poets, Logicians, Father, Mother, wife, matrones or good auncient women, maidens well disposed, young men of good inclination, Soldiers, Craftesmen.

All this of course is the familiar material of the schools of rhetoric, coming ultimately from the Greek sophists, who digested the topics of practical composition into commonplaces.

Fleming's method of inflation may be illustrated by the following examples:

conantem. purposing and attempting.

deterruit pudor. perceiuing my selfe restrained and stil drawne back by. . . shame fastnesse.

audacius. and therefore supported with the more boldnesse

nomen ut nostrum scriptis illustretur et celebretur tuis. to have our name made famous by your pen, and with your workes to win euerlastynge worthynesse.

factorum. accomplishe and fulfill.

ignoscas velim huic festinationi meae. I pray you dispence with my much haste, and suppose my speedinesse in this point pardonable.

illa cupiditas, ut vel auctoritate testimonii tui vel indicio benevolentiae vel suavitate igenii vivi perfruamur—the earnest desire where-with I feele myself all kindled: *that* we may inioy whiles we be aliue, to our full expectation, either the absolute authoritie & credite of your testimonie or else the signification of your bene-uolence, or else the sweetnesse and pleasantnesse of your flour-ishing inuention & excellent wit.[70]

Ἐι μὲν νεώτερος ἦν, οὐκ ἂν ἐπιστολὴν ἔπεμπον ἀλλ' αὐτὸς ἄν σοι πλεύνας ἐνταῦθα διελέχϑην. If I were in the pearle of my youth, and had in my bones marrow; in my limmes and ioynts strength, and in the rest of the parts of my body, desired ability, I would not make writing the instrument to speake vnto your maiestie.[71]

In 1588 Maurice Kyffin published a translation of Terence's *Andria* in prose. His version was frankly intended to assist in an understanding of the Latin;—"To all young Students of the Latin tong (for whose only help and benifit this comoedie is published) Maurice Kyffin wisheth encrease of knowledge and final perfection." If one may judge by Kyffin's "Preface to the curteous Reader," Terence had lost something of the place which he had so long and so tenaciously held as a source of idiomatic and elegant Latin. Reference has been made to the medieval use of Terence for pithy gnomic passages and familiar phrases, to Valla's exploitation of his works, and to the employment of Terence in the Renaissance schools. It was the *Andria* which was most familiar and most employed; the *Andria* as has been said was the one imaginative work com-pletely translated before 1557. So Kyffin's preface is a bit plaintive and a trifle apologetic.

---

[70]P. 53.
[71]P. 154.

A Preface to the curteous Reader.

Among all the Romane writers, there is none (by the iudgement of the learned) so much available to bee read and studied, for the true knowledge and puritie of the Latin tong, as Pub. Terentius: for sith the cheefest matter in speech, is to speak properly and aptly, and that we haue not a more cunning Crafts-master of apt and proper speech than Terence, well woorthy is he then, euen with all care and diligence, to be both taught and learned before any other. And surely, great is the pity, that Terence were not more used of maisters in teaching, and made more familiar to schollers in learning, than commonly it is: being (as I haue knowen my selfe) by dyuers men, in diuers sentences, diuersly misvnderstood: for, the Author in many places, vsing abbreuiations, and figuratiue speeches, aswell in regard of his verse, as also that such maner of writing, was very eloquent and familiar in his tyme: doth thereby cause the sence seeme very doubtful, to such Readers as are not fully acquainted with him: which comes to passe, by meanes that this booke, is not so frequented in schooles, nor laboured in studie, according to the woorthines of it: but other base and inferior bookes, commonly preferd before it, to the vtter marring, and maiming of Scholiers both in stile and iudgement.

Though this Comoedie, now englished, perhaps seeme not altogether so pleasant, as could be wished, neither in matter, nor manner of handling: yet is it to be considered (besides that it leeseth his natural grace, being turned into another language) that the tyme when, and the place where, it was first published in Latin, affoorded no other sort of Comoedies than this is. And therefore, it was no part of my meaning to translate the same, as a thing either pleasant to be played, or very delightful to bee read: (Notwithstanding that this Author was most excellent, and most learned, of any that wrote in this kinde:) but especially, for that the Latin is pure & eloquent, much commended by Tullie himselfe, & right requisite to be studied, & understood of all such, as would attaine to the knowledge of right speaking, and readines of wel writing, in the Latin tong: for whose only sakes (and also at the earnest request of some, whom I was desirous to satisfy) I haue aduentured the englishing hereof: wishing, that as I haue thus boldly begoon with the first, so some other hauing more leisure, and learning, would go thorough with the rest of the Comedies. I haue vsed (as neere as I could) the most knowen, vsuall, and familiar phrases in common speech, to expresse the authors meaning, as (to my thinking) best agreeing therewithall. Neuertheles, I make account my doing herein, shall be carpt and caueld at by some, from whose malicious censure, euen the best writers can not escape vntouched, and therefore no marueile if they spurne at me. Of which kinde of men, I haue knowen by experience, & noted for memory, twoo sorts: One sort pretending a shew of learning, & being indeed but very dunces, loue to be speaking they wot not what, to disgrace they care not whom, and yet not rendering any reason why, but onely to feed their

owne bad humours: In whom, true iudgement, being altogether sup-
prest, what with affection, or ignorance, or both: as either mooued
by fond lyking, to commend that is bad: or stird with fowle hatred
to dispraise that is good: are thus commonly carried along, with
the vaine tyde and winde of their willes, without any regard of
right, or due respect of wrong. An other sort (whereof I knew
some good schollers, the more the pity) blinded with ouerweening
of themselues, and mislyking al other mens dooings (how wel soeuer
they deserue:) like onely of their owne, be they neuer so mean:
neuer geuing any man his due, fearing, by like, whatsoeuer commendation is attributed to others, that the same must needs be a
derogation from themselues: wherin they are far vnlike Tullie,
the welspring of wit and learning: who alwaies praised, all men of
desert, euen in those things, wherein he both desired, and deserued,
most praise himselfe: This is read of Tullie, to his great praise,
and remembred of others to their iust reproch. And here, least
perchance I be mistaken more than I would, & misconstrued otherwise than I meane, though my woords before doo sufficiently declare
my meaning: yet (to auoyd all dowt) it shall not be amisse, if
I ad a few more in this place. To disalow the iudgement of such, as
by learning can, and by reason know, where, when, and how, to
finde fault, as iust cause and matter shall lead them: were to be
wilfully blinde, and obstinately foolish: God forbid I should be so
vnreasonable, or that men should iudge of mee so vnrightly.

Of the curious Carper I looke not to be fauoured, and yet if my
labour may be equally compared with my Authors words and meaning, I doubt not but it will appeare vnto him, an easier matter to
finde fault with part, than to amend the whole.

Onely, I submit this poore translation vnto the vew & iudgement
of the learned: who lyking the Truth, and louing to speake Truth,
will both allow what is well don, and amend that is amisse: As for
others, I see not but that they ought first to learne, before they
take vppon them to Controll.

Farewel.

Kyffin, who was a tutor in the family of the earl of Dorset,
dedicated his little version to "Maister William Sackeuille,"
who was killed in battle in 1591, and wrote a pleasant introductory letter to "Maister Henry & Maister Thomas Sackeuille," in the course of which he says:

It is now full .7. yeeres (as you can well remember) since I first
attempted the translation of *Andria* into English verse . . . . But
afterward . . . . I playnely saw, that such manner of forced translation must needs be both harsh and vnpleasant to the Reader, and
also not halfe seemely befitting the sweete style and eloquence of
the Author. So as hauing thus translated the whole comoedie in
verse (sauing the two last leaues) my paines bestowed therein did

> so much mislike me, as that euer sythens yt lay by me, vtterly neg-
> lected . . . now of late . . . I haue . . . indeuored to turne it into
> Prose, as a thing of lesse labour in show and more libertie in sub-
> stance, seeming withall, most accordant with this Comicall kinde of
> writing . . . .

His work is intelligent; his style in the translation free from affectations, sometimes a little violent in its colloquialism, natural, but lacking in ease, grace, and delicacy. The translation gives fairly early but not the earliest examples of a number of interesting familiar expressions; *Daying* ("Why should I make any more daying for the matter?") cited in Murray from Bernard's Terence, 1598, originates here. Bernard in fact carried out Kyffin's wish that some other scholar might go on where he left off, and finish a version of Terence, and began by borrowing the whole of Kyffin's *Andria*.

Kyffin wrote an intelligent discussion of special passages, scrutinizing and rejecting erroneous translations, and also analyzed the construction of the drama, the conduct of the action, and the merit of the dialogue.

Finally there are three school-books of some interest.

Two are the work of Corderius—*Principia latine loquendi*, based upon the letters of Cicero, with a characteristically ample commentary, and with a step-by-step construing of the text (1575) and *Cato Construed*, a similar edition of Cato's *Distichs*. Corderius did much to establish the method of instruction in Protestant schools, and his text-books held a place in English schools even into the nineteenth century.

His Latin letter to Stephanus, the printer of the first edition of his Cato (1534) speaks vividly of his own gentle devotion, and of the conditions in schools before text-books became common in the lower classes. A translation follows:

Mathurin Cordier to Robert Estienne, Printer, Greeting:

Last year I dictated to our beginners in letters some childish trifles, that is to say Latin and French interpretations, on those distichs on morals which bear the name of Cato. This I never would have done, if it were not that I saw this little book customarily everywhere put into the hands of beginners at the very outset of their studies. And so far as I am concerned I do not think this custom deserves to be wholly condemned, especially since the little work has always been approved by the judgment of the learned. And I used to hope it would turn out to be enough at least in our school to have dictated it once for all, and for the boys themselves, as they went on up the grades, to receive it from each other, as it were passed on to them. But it has turned out to be the case that by being written down over and over nearly everything has got wrong, for some of the boys not knowing how to write, and others writing negligently, they have left scarcely a single word accurately written, so that when we come to reading aloud, it takes more trouble to correct than to dictate. So I thought I should save no little labor if I should revise the whole systematically, and should have it worked out once for all by your art, especially since our pupils themselves seemed to wish nothing better. Hence I have sent you the little work, and will ask you to get the advice of friends; and (if you think it will be for the good of the boys and to your own advantage) to print it with your types, with your usual accuracy. But if you do not think so, just suppress the thing permanently. I have no doubt that if you print the booklet, a good many people will laugh at me; but I do not care a bit about such laughers. I should only hope the thing would be to the advantage of the boys. I have devoted myself so completely to their good that for their sake I would not hesitate to descend to the very lowest of things. In my little commentary I have followed the learned notes of Erasmus very closely, very seldom departing from their sense. As for the text, I have supported the older reading as far as possible, though Erasmus has changed it in many places. I have prefixed as it were epitomes to a number of distichs, not to add a summary to the poem, than which nothing is more succinct, but to make it easier for the boys to grasp the sense immediately. I have not added them every-where, as I judged some distichs to be unchristian, or inferior, or too difficult for childish minds. At the end I have added some brief sayings of the wise, as being as worthy to be known as the Cato, and of the same type. But I see you wrinkle your brow because I am keeping you so long from your urgent affairs with this wordy letter. So good-bye; and in your work think (as you do) of the good of this generation and of those to come.

Nevers, *postridie Liberalium* [March 18] 1534.

The preface of the English printer "To the freendly reader" is of interest:

> The occasion that moued that famous Schoolemaister *Maturinus Corderius* to make this familiar interpretation vpon Catos preceptes, was: for that thei were approued of most men, & thought very necessarie to be taught, and also forbecause euery where euen at the firste, this booke is receiued into Schooles: and for that by experience he did perceiue that his Scholers through ignorance in writyng erred, and through negligence were forgetfull, and for lacke of readie instruction learned muche, and profited little, so that when the scholer should come to repetition, the Maister should haue more labour to correcte, then he had before to teache.

Now, the occasions that moued me herevnto, were not onely those of *Corderius,* but also the good allowing of the same, by the learned Printer *Robertus Stephanus,* and also the Translations of this Booke into diuers languages, whiche, occasioned me (for that our Englishe youth should not want those aides, which foraine countries haue, for the easier obtainyng of the Latine tongue) to cause this booke also to be made Englishe.

But paraduenture some will saie, if the scholler haue his Lesson construed, and Englished to hym in his Booke, what shall he doe at Schoole? To them I aunswere, (who I thinke are afraied that scholers should haue too muche for their money) that after he hath learned perfectly *ad vnguem* his construction, then he shall pars it as perfectly, whiche I am of opinion, he will not be able to doe at the first, without this helpe, For firste, to a yong Scholler, the readyng of the Latine tongue is harde, construyng harder, and pars-yng hardest, so that by this helpe, the yong Scholer shalbe able to reade interprete, construe, and pars his Lesson well, whereas the moste parte of Scholers (I meane in the first Booke thei learne) dooe neither read well, construe a right, nor be able to pars one worde of their Lesson.

And thus muche I haue thought good to saie, vnder correction of good schoolemaisters, whiche I thinke will bee content, to bee eased of some of their paines, and glad to bryng forward their scholers in learnyng. And that learning maie increase in all to the glorie of God, and profite of our Englishe commonweale. GOD graunte.

AMEN.

William Bullokar printed in 1585 a little book containing versions of Aesop's *Fables* and the *Distichs* of Cato.

Bullokar's primary object was the reform of the perplexing orthography of the English language on a phonetic basis, and in a practical way, without requiring any more new symbols than could be avoided.[72] As Plessow says,[73] his efforts had arisen from his many years of experience as a teacher. He had learned by painful experience how great an obstacle to progress in the mastery of the language is the confusion of the accepted spelling of English, not only for foreigners but for native children, and had slowly developed his own system. To give currency to his projects he went to the expense of printing a number of books in his special types, among them the translations of two Latin elementary school-books: Aesop's

---

[72]Plessow, Max, *Geschichte der Fabeldichtung in England bis zu John Gay (1726). Nebst Neudruck von Bullokars "Fables of Aesop" 1585, "Booke at large" 1580, "Bref Grammar for English" 1586, and "Pamphlet for Grammar" 1586.* Palaestra lii (1906); Booke at Large, p. 3; Plessow, p. 239.

[73]Plessow, Max, *op. cit.,* p. cxlviii.

Fables, and the *Distichs* of Cato. The secondary object of the translations was to be helpful to young pupils in interpreting the original, and hence his versions are as literal as practicable, and are without literary interest. As he says himself in the preface [neglecting his peculiar orthography] :

> . . . I haue translated out of Latin into English, but not in the best phrase for English, though English be capable of the perfect sense thereof, and might ben used in the best phrase, had not my care ben to keep it somewhat near the Latin phrase, that the English learner of Latin reading ouer these Autors in both languages might the easilier confer them together in their sense, and the better vnderstand them the one by the other: and for that respect of easy conference, I haue kept the like course in my translation of Tully's offices out of Latin into English to be imprinted shortly also. But if God lend me life and ability to translate any other Autor into English hereafter, I will lend myself to follow the excellency of English in the best phrase thereof, more than I will tie it to the phrases of the langage to be translated: knowing this withal, that euery good conceit hath his best beauty in his primitive langage, if it proceed from the best users of such language.

So far as I can learn the poor, devoted man never succeeded in getting the Tully printed, or in translating any other excellent author. He reaped obloquy for his efforts, and has become important only because of his evidence as to the pronunciation of his time.

The Aesop is as ample a collection of all the current fables as he found in his authorities, including the additions to the traditional fables made by Abstemius, Valla, Rimicius, and Poggio. Its exact source has not been determined, but coincides with Thomas March's Latin collection printed in 1580, and is in the line of descent from the Strassburg Collection of 1515.[74] The Aesop is in prose; the Cato in crude verse.

It was the translations of this period, of the formative years of the reign of Elizabeth, of the time of groping experiment in literature, of obscure gestation preceding the great birth of the great age, which counted for most in English thought and letters. The verse translations made classic mythology and the tale of Troy, especially the story of Dido, familiar to the "mere English" reader, so that a poet imbued with their romantic interest could enrich his writings freely from their

---

[74]Plessow, p. lx-lxiii.

abundant store. The ethical writings became genuinely a part of English thought, and contributed to establish a body of principles defining the responsibilities of men which rested on a high and generous view of human nature, and which was a seminal force in English reflection upon moral questions. The histories and biographies helped to fill the imagination with great pictures from the past, and to encourage reflection upon the problems of statecraft. They contributed to a high sense both of the responsibilities and of the possible achievements of individual men, and they presented the tragic outcome of over-weening ambition and the destructiveness of faction in the commonwealth.

Professor C. H. Conley in his useful and informing book, *The First English Translators of the Classics,* sees in this efflorescence of translation a deliberate and even organized effort on the part of the translators, under the patronage and to some extent at the initiative of leading personages in the state, to strengthen the government of Elizabeth by contributing to the enlightenment and liberalizing of English thought. His main reasons are as follows: The translators, especially of histories, in their prefaces avowed their patriotism and pointed to history in proof of the evils and dangers of faction and rebellion against a lawful prince. The nobility encouraged the translations, nearly all the dedications being to members of the Privy Council or their near relatives, prominent supporters of the Protestant cause and the new government. Books on the art of war played their part in the translations. And the whole body of translations breathe a spirit of opposition to all types of medievalism. Moreover, the translators appeal constantly for protection against detractors, opponents, and dangerous enemies; and their only conceivable enemies were those wedded to the cause of conservative medievalism, to the overthrow of Elizabeth's government and to obscurantist reaction. "In view of the intimate relations of the renaissance Protestantism and the new political regime, is it not possible that after the period of Spanish domination under Philip and Mary ending with the loss of Calais, the new nobility who had brought about the revolution in Edward's and Elizabeth's reigns, and the translators, both groups advocating much the same radical political, religious, and philosophical principles, had combined

with 'Youth' as a slogan, for the improvement and enlightenment of the nation? This theory seems plausible from several
considerations."[75]

I think Professor Conley goes too far in seeing so self-
conscious and organized a "Youth Movement," or so distinct
a political bias in this mass of translations. The detail of his
facts is certainly accurate: a great proportion of the translators were young; they dedicated largely to those in power
under the new government; they solemnly disserted on the evils
of faction and rebellion; some works on the art of war were
published; and the writers of translation were energetically
anti-medieval. But if all these phenomena are to be interpreted in relation to English politics, they should have been
primarily English. Now, in point of fact, they are European.
They appear in Italy, in France, and to some extent in Germany.
Italy had an earlier and a more complete body of translation
than England.[76] The Italian despots were as ready to patron-
ize an effective translation as the so-called liberal government
of England—more so than the Queen. French translators
had begun translating history and ethics for royalty in the
fifteenth century. Francis I of France energetically encouraged the translation of classic literature at large, and especially of histories as forming useful public servants.[77] France,
like Italy, had more and earlier translations than England. The
truth is, that this enthusiastic activity in translating from the
classics was an aspect and a symptom of the growing consciousness which for want of a better word we may call *national*—
strongly felt in Germany and Italy, though they were as yet
but inchoate nations, and clearly enunciated in France. This
spirit was in a sense *liberal,* in that it tended to free the mind
from traditional medieval restrictions, and in course of time
even from the reverence for the classic past in which it originated. The English translators and their patrons, indeed,
sincerely desired to spread enlightenment among their countrymen; but not otherwise than the translators in other countries,

---

[75]P. 34.

[76]Argelati, F., *Biblioteca degli Volgarizzatori* etc. (with supplement by
Villa, A. T.), Milan, 1767.

[77]Chamard, Henri, *Les Origines de la Poésie française de la Renaissance* (1920), p. 276.

and apparently not so self-consciously as in France, for in England the *defense and illustration* of the English tongue was far from being at first a definite impulse of the translators.

Again, it seems to me a complete misreading of history to regard the government of Elizabeth as desiring to strengthen its position by the subtle method of spreading liberal principles among the population through the critical study of history. Elizabeth's government was an autocratic one, in which a monarch gave unity to a nation in sympathy with its ruler. It was necessarily, by the pressure of circumstances, Protestant; but it was not liberal. The patriotic prefaces of the translators who cry out against sedition, no doubt, tended to strengthen the government; but they differ in no essential respect from the prefaces and protestations of translators in other countries. What else could the translators have said? If they had indeed submitted government to an unbiased criticism, to a truly liberal view, they would have been severely punished or perhaps executed. It is little likely that Burleigh would have welcomed a glorification of Athenian democracy, which was implicit in Herodotus, or the critical study of the complicated political forces present in Thucydides.

Moreover, if the members of the Privy Council desired to support a "Youth Movement" of translation they would have rewarded the translators; they had ecclesiastical and public offices in their gift. No English translator was recognized as, for instance, Amyot in France; and there is no evidence that the translator got more than the gratuity usual for any literary work. If they had, they would have done more; and most of them stopped with a single book. Golding alone made translation his central activity, and he alone received some recognition from authority, by obtaining the right of sale of his own writings. All these facts tend to make credible the statements of many of these young men; that in their translations they were bidding farewell to the engaging pursuit of letters before settling down professionally to graver things. Scholars did not generally engage in translation—they had more scholarly business to attend to. Wilson, Drant, and Savile are the only men really distinguished for learning who occupied themselves with translation. Active and energetic, loyal and patriotic, as the group of translators were, they were not banded together under Burleigh and his fellow-counsellors to carry through a self-conscious campaign.

They were at the Inns of Court—where young men went to finish their education for practical life; it is where you would expect to find amateurs of letters. And as for their fear of detractors, the "carping critic" is a familiar figure in dedications of all kinds of literature. There were indeed, opponents of translation. Many scholars must have felt that "translation is the enemy of exact scholarship." There is reason enough for finding few translations emanating from the universities. And it is true that Catholic scholars would be likely to be among the most conservative. But it is hard for me to understand how with the examples, of Catholic Italy and France before us, we can hold that Catholicism as such was wholly unfriendly to translation into the vernacular. This rich, abundant, and fruitful body of translation was a natural, unorganized response to the needs and interests of the time, under the example of other nations, and particularly of France.

CHAPTER IV: PROFESSIONAL TRANSLATORS

1593-1620

The translations of the fourth period—the last ten years of Elizabeth and the greater part of the reign of James—are in a soberer spirit than those of the third. The prose works are seriously instructive. They include the ethical writings of Seneca, Epictetus, Cebes, Boethius, Xenophon, and Plutarch; the *Politics* of Aristotle, the *Characters* of Theophrastus; a large number of histories dealing mainly with Rome—Tacitus, Livy, Caesar, Justin, Ammianus Marcellinus, Josephus; Pliny's *Natural History,* and Aelian's *Tactics.* The most important achievement in verse was Chapman's Homer, and this too was a grave work, in a spirit of lofty devotion, moral and mystical, even religious. To the *Iliad* and the *Odyssey* Chapman appended the other works associated with the name of Homer, and Hesiod's sober *Works and Days.* The miscellaneous verse translations—Persius, Lucan, Musaeus, the *Ars Poetica,* parts of Ovid, a satire of Juvenal—are of relatively little importance in themselves, but are interesting in their form. The heroic couplet took the place of the fourteener as the normal verse for translation, and was somewhat slowly beaten into clear and graceful shape. The medical works and the translations for school use have an interest of their own in the history of the use of the vernacular for the purposes of science and of the methods and ideals of teaching.

The most important translators of the period were skilled writers, mature men, and so far as such a class existed in that age, professional men of letters (professional, that is, in their practised mastery, not necessarily in their way of earning a living): Lodge, Holland, and Chapman. And the most important writings undertaken were chosen by the individual preference of the author, and not in accordance with a fashion or a tendency of the time.

To begin with the prose, which exceeded the verse in amount, and (always excepting Chapman's Homer, which stands by itself) in substantial value and in the skill of the writers.

Toward the end of the reign of Elizabeth, the temper of English literature as of English thought changed from exuberant enthusiasm to a grave and even bitter tone, a change evinced in turning from Ovid and Vergil and frivolous story-tellers to the stern authors of the Silver Age. Ben Jonson is the leader of the movement; and his works wide as is their range in ancient literature draw particularly upon Juvenal and the Senecas, Tacitus, and Suetonius. The professed translators busied themselves especially with the prose of the Silver Age; and as has been said Sir Henry Savile set the example with his translations from Tacitus (1591).

Savile was one of the very few distinguished scholars who translated any classic writer into English. He thoroughly understood the difficult Latin of his original, and could elucidate his version with intelligent explanations of customs and incidents referred to in the text. His commentary, drawn from the sources by original investigation, was copious and learned, yet free from pedantry and genuinely valuable; it set an example for Holland's thorough annotations. Yet Savile's version affords proof that the highest scholarship does not suffice to produce even a tolerable translation. His work is dry and bald at its best, and commonly does harsh violence to the English idiom. Occasionally the Latin is necessary to translate the English. (Who would understand that "matter enough for invocation, though not greatly in favor of any yet prepared for him that would venture," means "plenty of fuel for a revolution, heaped ready not for some one person to whom favor inclined, but for any one that dared to make the venture"?) Yet in general the meaning is clear to a patient reader, but clumsily and somewhat confusedly delivered, so that the central ideas do not stand out; the facts are given, but the point is obscured. The following, from the account of the siege of Vetera, is a typical sentence:

> And as some were now clammering up, they were beaten down head-long with swords and pash of pike, and so with clubs, and darts overwhelmed, being men otherwise hot in the beginning, and too too couragious when fortune favoureth, but then for desire of prey

they tolerated all hardnesse also; yea and that which with them is unusuall, they endeavoured to prove with engines, whereof they had of themselves neither experience nor skill, onely some fugitives and captives taught them to frame timber in manner of a bridge, and to drive it forward on wheeles, whereon certain standing above might skirmish with them on the walls, as it were from a mount, and others within secretly undermine the foundations.

Savile translated the *Histories* and the *Life of Agricola;* Richard Grenewey carried on Savile's work by translating the *Annals* and *Germania* in the same style, though without the learned commentary. Thomas Gordon's remarks on his predecessors in the preface of his translation (1728) are marked by the usual arrogance of the Augustans in speaking of Elizabethan writers, and they demand too much, for who could reproduce the turns of Tacitus's style? And yet they are not substantially unjust:

> I am going to offer to the publick the Translation of a Work, which for wisdom and force, is in higher fame and consideration, than almost any other that has yet appeared among men; a Work often translated into many Languages, seldom well into any, into ours worst of all. The first was done in Queen *Elizabeth's* reign, the Annals by one *Greenway,* and four books of the History by *Sir Henry Savill,* a man exceeding learned, and esteemed for his critical notes upon *Tacitus,* as well as for those upon *St. Chrysostom,* of whose works he has published an elaborate edition. But tho' he was an able Grammarian, and understood the antiquities in *Tacitus,* and his words, his Translation is a mean performance; his stile is stiff, spiritless, and obscure; he drops many of his author's ideas, preserves none of his fine turns, and starves his meaning even where he best conveys it. 'Tis a mere Translation, that rather of one word into another, than that of a dead tongue into a living, or of sence into sence. The Roman idiom is forced and wire-drawn into the English, a task altogether impossible; and not adopted and naturalized, a thing possible enough; and out of a Book profuse in eloquence, fine spirit and images, he has drawn a work harsh, halting and barren. *Ogilby* is not more unlike *Virgil. Greenway* is still worse than *Savill;* he had none of his learning; he had all his faults and more: the former has at least performed like a schoolmaster, the latter like a schoolboy.

The references to Philemon Holland in Fuller and Pope create an impression that he is dull, plodding, and somewhat absurd. Fuller's good-tempered jest at the voluminousness of his translations, "sufficient of themselves to furnish forth a country gentleman's library," makes the books seem as if they must be heavy mentally as well as physically. The books of the country gentleman described in fiction and by smart city writers must, it seems, have been stodgy if not gross. And Pope's smart line in the *Dunciad,* taking full advantage of Philemon's quaint name,—"And here the groaning shelves Philemon bends,"—puts Holland with cool finality on top of the heap of rubishy books fit only to be burnt as a sacrifice to Dulness,—"the classics of an age that heard of none." Of course, as everybody knows who knows Philemon's work, the words of the clerical jester and the satirist produce an entirely false view of this admirable writer. Philemon's books may bend the shelves with the weight of their pages, but they do not load the mind with a burden of stupidity. Philemon is the master of a picturesque, rich, and lively style—the last of those Elizabethans who combine sweetness and homely force; and the substance of the books he chose to translate is rich in human interest and human wisdom. If indeed the country gentlemen of the seventeenth century read them attentively, their intellectual curiosity and energy were above those of most business men of the twentieth century. Philemon translated not so many books as big books. And big books are not a big evil, as the cowardly epigram declares; for the necessary means of understanding great matters are thoroughness and amplitude of detail, which require space.

Philemon's main labors covered about ten years. To quote the commendatory verses of "Thomas Farneby, Armiger," prefixed to Holland's version of the *Cyropedia*:

> Hence hath our Language Natures mysteries;
> Moralls, Domestique, foreine Histories:
> *England* knowes *England,* For the thankes is thine
> That *Pliny, Livy, Plutarch, Marcelline,*
> *Suetonius, Camdens Britaine, Xenophon,*
> Speake English, now can stand alone.

Livy, with Florus's *Epitome* and the *Topography* of Marlianus, appeared in 1600; Pliny in 1601, Plutarch's *Morals* in 1603; Suetonius in 1606; and Ammianus Marcellinus in 1609. After completing a translation of Camden's vast *Britannia,* printed in 1610, Holland enjoyed a well-earned rest from his labors as a translator. Then in 1621 the *Cyropedia* was completed,

recast in 1629, and published in 1632. A revision of the Pliny
was printed in 1634, of the *Britannia* in 1637, the year of
Holland's death, and of the *Morals* in 1653. His method is
the same in all the translations, and may well be illustrated
from his Livy. He took pains to obtain the help of the best
scholarship of his time, not only by using the edition provided
with the most complete and accurate commentary, but by considering versions in the French and Italian. His main reliance
for Livy is upon the edition printed at Paris, 1573, which contains practically all the commentary and all the supplementary
matter present in Holland's edition or referred to by him: the
Breviaries (epitome) of Florus, the *Chronologie* of Verrius
Flaccus, compiled by Ioachimus Grellus, the introductory
Epistle to the Reader prefixed to the Florus, excerpted from
Grellus, the *Topography of Rome* by Bartholomew Marlianus,
the *Table of the Orations* and Erasmus's dedication to Charles
Montjoy of the five books discovered by Grynaeus. In his
discussion of his authorities (p. 1234) Holland says "neither
hee that translated Livie into the Tuscane language, nor they
who have done him into French (as farre as I could ever see)
have taken that paines [to translate Florus]." The "Tuscane"
translation is presumably that of Jacopo Nardi, first printed in
1540, and several times thereafter. Holland speaks of Livy as
"twice enfranchised" among the French. It seems probable
that he refers to the medieval translation of Pierre Bercheure
or Berchoire (printed at Paris in 1486-7) and that of Antoine
de la Faye (Paris 1583). There were also French translations of parts of Livy by various authors; but so far as I
have been able to ascertain no others which covered the whole
body of the extant remains of the history. The Italian translation had no influence on Holland; I have not compared Holland's work with the French.

Every English translator from the Latin is compelled to do
two things, first, to frame anew the sentences, bound together
by the synthetic Latin syntax, in the articulated structure of
English analytic syntax, and secondly to replace the somewhat
general Latin words by more exact English ones, the Latin
vocabulary being comparatively small, and the words acquiring definiteness by skilful combination, the English vocabulary
being larger, and the words more definite in themselves. The

conscientious translator runs the risk of a hard mechanical precision alike in structure and diction; the genially loose translator of missing the point of his original from failing to deal adequately with the logic of his structure, and of vague inefficiency from failing to get a fair English equivalent for the energy of the Latin words. Most of the sixteenth-century translators neglected entirely the accurate relationship of thought, the juncture of ideas, being content with rendering the general meaning of the author; Brende and Grimald are noteworthy exceptions. Holland is scrupulous to indicate with precision the transitions and connections of thought, never sparing words, in order to leave no doubt of the sequence of ideas.

Livy's sentences follow what may be called the order of discovery, or revelation; details succeed each other as they would be perceived by an eye-witness. Thus his style combines picturesqueness with activity. The complete period builds up a total impression, but it is not static, it moves constantly onward. Holland strives—not unsuccesfully—for definite effectiveness by the use of concrete, homely, and picturesque diction; but, though vivid, is sober and restrained, not overcharging or heightening the style. He constantly, one might say systematically, doubles synonyms in the translation of important words. A fair illustration is his account of the battle of the Trebia (Livy, xxi, 55-56), beginning just after the Balearic islanders had opened the battle by throwing their darts and putting the Roman cavalry into confusion. The very first sentence exhibits Holland's method. The Latin is: *Ad hoc elephanti eminentes ab extremis cornibus equis maxime non visu modo sed odore territis fugam late faciebant.* This sentence, brief though it be, is thoroughly Livian. The end is foreseen from the beginning, the details are as it were clamped into the structure of the sentence, and at the same time the sentence proceeds naturally and vividly from detail to detail in the order of perception. Holland "resolves" the compact syntax, but is careful to maintain Livy's natural order, to make the form of his English sentence adequately express the course of thought in his original, to retain Livy's connections and transitions, and to find clear and vivid equivalents for Livy's words, striving to be idiomatically definite (*eminentes,—appeared aloft*), changing the abstract (*fugam faciebant*) to the concrete and personal (*made them flie everie way*), and not hesitating to expand a phrase (*from the hinmost ends of the wings*), to repeat an idea (*straunge—uncouth*) or to double a synonym (*sent and savor*) in order to be sure of his effect. "Mooreover the elephants which appeared aloft from the hinmost ends of the wings frighted the horses especially, & not onely with the straunge sight, but also with as uncouth a sent and savor, made them flie everie way." The result is a style of warmth and vigor, picturesque ease and graphic vividness. On the other hand, Holland uses more words than enough, and has not the faculty of concentration or the energy which comes from terseness. Livy, too, is generally ample in manner, but is so by the accumulation of detail, being skilled in the economy of words. Partly on this account, Holland's rendering of the speeches, though vigorous, is not so satisfactory as his narrative. But to return to the account of the battle of the Trebia.

Pedestris pugna par animis magis quam viribus erat, quas recentis Poenus paulo ante curatis corporibus in proelium attulerat; contra jejuna fessaque corpora Romanis et rigentia gelu torpebant. Restitissent tamen animis, si cum pedite solum foret pugnatum; sed et Baleares pulso equite jaculabantur in latera et elephanti iam in mediam peditum aciem sese tulerant et Mago Numidaeque, simul latebras eorum inprovida praeterlata acies est, exorti ab tergo ingentem tumultum ac terrorem fecere. Tamen in tot circumstantibus malis mansit aliquamdiu immota acies, maxime praeter spem omnium adversus elephantos. Eos pedites ad id ipsum locati verutis conjectis et avertere et insecuti aversos sub caudis qua maxume molli cute vulnera accipiunt, fodiebant. Trepidantesque et prope jam in suos consternatos e media acie in extremam ad sinistrum cornu adversus Gallos auxiliares agi iussit Hannibal. Extemplo haud dubiam fecere fugam. Additus quoque novus terror Romanis, ut fusa auxilia sua viderunt. Itaque cum iam in orbem pugnarent, decem milia ferme hominum, cum aliter evadere nequissent, media Afrorum acie, quae Gallicis auxiliis firmata erat, cum ingenti caede hostium perrupere et, cum neque in castra reditus esset flumine interclusis neque prae imbre satis decernere possunt, qua suis opem ferrent, Placentiam recto itinere perrexere. Plures deinde in omnes partes eruptiones factae; et qui flumen petiere, aut gurgitibus absumpti sunt aut inter cunctationem ingrediendi ab hostibus oppressi. Qui passim per agros fuga sparsi erant vestigia cedentis sequentes agminis Placentiam contendere, aliis timor hostium audaciam ingrediendi flumen fecit, transgressique in castra pervenerunt. Imber nive mixtus et intoleranda vis frigoris et homines multos et jumenta et elephantos prope omnes absumpsit. Finis insequendi hostis Poenis flumen Trebia fuit, et ita torpentes gelu in castra rediere, ut vix laetitiam victoriae sentirent. Itaque nocte insequenti, cum praesidium castrorum et quod reliquum ex magna parte militum erat ratibus Trebiam trajicerent, aut nihil sensere obstrepente pluvia aut, quia iam moveri nequibant prae lassitudine ac vulneribus, sentire sese dissimularunt, quietis Poenis tacito agmine ab Scipione consule exercitus Placentiam est perductus, inde Pado trajectus Cremonam, ne duorum exercituum hibernis una colonia premeretur.

Mooreover the Elephants which appeared aloft from the hinmost ends of the wings frighted the horses especially, & not onely with the straunge sight, but also with as uncouth a sent and savor, made them flie everie way. The battaile of the Infanterie was egall in courage of heart, rather than in strength of bodie: which the Carthaginians (as having a little afore taken repast) brought fresh with them into the field: but contrariwise the Romanes were fasting & wearie, and for cold even starke and benummed. Howbeit their stomacks would have served to have held out & withstood to the end, if they might have fought with footmen onely. But both the Baleares, having disordred the horsemen, flanked them with their shot, and also the elephants by this time were entred into the middle battaillon of footmen: and withall, Mago and the Numidian light horse (so soone as this battaillon was unawares gone past their ambushment and lurking holes) start up and arose from behind, and put them in exceeding trouble and fright. Yet for all these inconveniences and disvantages (so many on everie side) the maine battaile a good while stood unmoveable and stirred not, but kept the array, and especially (beyond the expectation of all men) against the Elephants. For certaine footmen placed for the purpose, by flinging of darts forced theme to turne head: and when they were once turned fromwards, they followed hard upon them, pricking & gauling them under the tailes, in which place by reason of the tender skin they are soon wounded. Whom when Annibal saw thus feared & readie to turne upon their owne part, from the maine battaile to the flancks & outsides, he commanded them to be driven to the left wing upon the Gauls that came to aid, and presently enforced them to run away. The Romanes seeing their auxiliarie Gaules put to flight, were driven into a new feare. Whereupon fighting now as it were in a ring and round on both sides, there were among them to the number almost of ten thousand, who seeing no way else to escape, brake through the middle battaillon of the Africanes, which was strengthned with the aide of the Gaules, and that, with a great slaughter of their enemies: and seeing they neither could returne into their campe, (the river being between) nor for the raine well discerne how to succour their fellowes, the tooke the way straight to Placentia. After this, the rest brake forth in all parts. They that tooke the river either perished in the streame and whirlepooles: or such as made stay to enter, were by the enemie overtaken and slaine. But as many as here and there fled skattering through the fields, following the footing and tracks of the battaillon that retired backe, came to Placentia. Some for fear of the enemie, aduentured boldly to take the river, and being once over, recovered the campe. The raine and snow together, and the intollerable cold killed many as well men as beastes: and in manner all the Elephants. The Carthaginians followed the enemies in chase as farre as Trebia, and there gave over: and returned into the campe so clumsie and frozen, as scarcely they felt the joy of their victorie. By reason whereof, the night following, when as the gard of the Romane campe, and the remnant of the great companie of soldiors passed Trebia with floatboats and flat barges, the Carthaginians either perceived them not indeed for the noise the tempesteous raine made, or for wearinesse & sore wounds were not able to stirre, and therfore made semblance, as though they knew not of it. And so whiles the Carthaginians were at rest, the armie was by Scipio the Consull brought (in a still march) to Placentia: and from thence having crossed the Po, came to Cremona, because one Colonie alone should not be charged with the wintering of two armies at one time.[1]

Holland translates not like North, mass by mass with easy nonchalance, but point by point consciously and deftly. He is felicitous in his individual renderings, as in translating *curatis corporibus* by *having taken repast, animis* by *stomachs, circumstantibus* by *on every side, cunctationem* by *made stay*. But even more characteristic is his evidently intentional alteration of impersonal constructions and of abstract nouns of action into personal verbs. *Finis insequendi hostis Poenis flumen Trebia erat* becomes, *The Carthaginians followed the enemies in chase as farre as Trebia, and there gave over;* *Plures deinde in omnes partes eruptiones factae* becomes, *after this the rest brake forth in all parts*. Most notable are the expansions and duplications: *animis* "courage of heart," *viribus* "strength of bodie," *rigentia* "starke and benummed," *restitissent animis* "their stomacks would have served to have held out and withstood to the end," *latebras* "ambushment and lurking holes," *fodiebant* "pricking and gauling," *in orbem* "in a ring and round on both sides." Thousands of examples could easily be gathered from Holland's pages.

The Pliny is translated after the same manner as the Livy, the nature of the subject and the style of Pliny calling for a somewhat more colloquial diction than the Livy;—". . . to say nothing of the precedent given by the authour himselfe, who endited the same, not with any affected phrase, but sorting well

---

[1]P. 425.

with the capacitie of the meanest and most unlettered." The translation resolves the compact constructions, makes concrete the abstractions, doubles the synonyms, sometimes makes the diction more homely, and to some extent makes the metaphors literal. The result is that the translation is clearer, more flowing, and less artificial than the original, but is not heightened or made more graphic. Indeed Holland resists the temptation to spice his Pliny with colloquialism, and to modernize his allusions. "The land of Prester Jehan" (Lib. VI. Cap. 30) is quite exceptional in its introduction of a post-classical tone, and very few passages will be found as free as the lively one about fleas and lice: *Adeoque, nihil non gignitur in mari, ut cauponarum etiam aestiva animalia, pernici molesta saltu aut quae capillus maxime celat existant et circumglobata escae saepe extrahantur, quae causa somnum piscium in mari noctibus infestare existimatur*:[2]

> In summe, what is there not bred within the sea? Even the verie fleas that skip so merrily in summer time within victualling houses and Innes, and bite so shrowdly: as also lice that love best to lie close under the haire of our heads, are there engendred and to be found: for many a time the fishers twitch up their hookes, and see a number of these skippers and creepers settled thicke about their baits which they laid for fishes. And this vermin is thought to trouble the poore fishes in their sleep by night within the sea, as well as us on land.[3]

Here and there, indeed, Holland makes his version a little more homely than his original. Pliny says (Lib. XXXVI sec. 117): *ingenio . . . utendum suo Curioni,* Holland, "Curio was put to his shifts." *Nec fuit rex Curio . . .* becomes, "Yet was he neither *King nor Kesar.*" "*Qui nihil in censu habuerit praeter discordiam principum;*—"When the great men of the city, *Caesar* and *Pompey,* were *skuffling together by the eares,* he knew well how to *fish in a troubled water.*" (Lib. XXXVI, sec. 120). *Quacumque harena secare;*—"make no more adoe but take the first sand they come by . . . this serves their turne . . ." (Lib. XXXVI, sec. 53).

In the Plutarch, Holland closely followed Amyot, whose explanatory additions and turns of phrase he reproduced,

---

[2]Bk. ix, cap. 47.
[3]P. 264.

though he evidently compared the French with the original, giving the Greek forms for Greek names, separating proems from the substance of essays, as Amyot did not, occasionally marking verse as such, when Amyot translates it in prose. Being guided by Amyot, Holland gives his periods a somewhat ampler swing in the Plutarch than in the preceding translations, but otherwise the Plutarch presents no new features.

Several years passed before Holland returned to the labors of his well-worn and well-kept pen. Then, as he says in his dedication to Lady Harington, the pestilence in Coventry occasioned his translation of Suetonius. "For being altogether restrained then, from free practise of my profession abroad, and no [l]esse impatient of idlenesse at home, I could not readily thinke of a better course to spend that vacation, than in an argument having a reference to mine old Grammatical Muses, and according, in some sort, with my latter studies in Physick. What howres therfore, either the doubtful or diseased estate of my neigh[b]ours, together with the meditations of mine owne mortalitie would afford, I employed gladly in the said Su[b]iect."

The translation of Suetonius, the fruit of this period of leisure, appeared in 1606. Casaubon's edition of 1605, though used by Holland, was not at all slavishly followed. He himself says in his address "To the *Readers*: . . . considering that brevitie is many times the mother of obscuritie, may it please those among you, who are not conversant in such concise writings, as admit not one word superfluous, to have recourse, for the clearing of some doubts unto the margin, as also to those briefe Annotations which for their sakes, out of mine owne readings, together with the select observations of Beroaldus, Sabellicus, Torrentius and Casaubonus I have collected. Which will ease them of many difficulties that his succinct style and termes, not elsewhere obvious, interlaced, may breed." The difficulties explained, however, have to do much more with history, geography, and Roman customs than with obscurities of language; and the notes are specially full upon medical matters.

The Suetonius is the most successful of Holland's translations, not because it is better done than the others, from which it does not differ in method and quality, but because abounding in picturesque details it is more perfectly suited to Holland's leisurely, but graphic style. The description of the personal appearance of Caligula will repay a minute comparison with its original.

Of Stature hee was very tall, pale and wan-coloured: of body grosse and without all good making: his necke and shanks exceeding slender: his eyes sunke in his head, and his temples hollow, his forehead broad, and the same furrowed and frowning: the haire of his head growing thinne, and none at all about his crowne: in all parts else hairie he was and shagged. It was therefore taken for an hainous and capitall offence, either to looke upon him as he passed by from an higher place, or once but to name a Goate upon any occasion whatsoever. His face and visage being naturally sterne and grim, hee made of purpose more crabbed and hideous: composing and dressing it at a looking-glasse, all manner of waies to seeme more terrible and to strike greater feare. He was neither heathfull in body nor stoode sound in minde; Being a child, much troubled with the falling sicknesse. In his youth, patient of labour and travaile: yetso, as that ever and anone upon a suddaine fainting that came upon him, he was scarce able to goe, to stand, to arise, to recover himselfe and to beare up his head. The infirmitie of his minde, both himselfe perceived, and oftentimes also was minded to goe aside (unto Anticyra), there to purge his braine thoroughly. It is for certaine thought, that poysoned he was with a Potion given unto him by his wife Caesonia: Which in deede was a love medicine, but such an one, as crackt his wits and enraged him. He was troubled most of all with want of sleepe; For, he slept not above three houres in a night: and in those verily hee tooke no quiet repose, but fearefull; and skared with strange illusions and fantasticall imaginations: as who among the rest, dreamed upon a time that hee saw the very forme and resemblance of the sea talking with him. And heereupon for a great part of the night, what with tedious wakefulnesse and wearinesse of lying, one while sitting up in his bed, another while roaming and wandering too and fro in his Galleries (which were of an exceeding length) hee was wont to call upon and looke still for the day-light.[4]

The following examples illustrate Holland's expansions:

compescuit; stikled and repressed.
componendum; to compose the troubles against the state.
livores; blackish sweat spots.
virtutes; good parts & gifts.
formam et fortitudinem egregiam; for shew full of passing beauty, favour and feature; with strength and valour answerable thereto.

---

[4]Caligula, cap. 50.

In translating Ammianus Marcellinus Holland was rounding off the works on Roman history accessible to the English reader. Holland had himself translated Livy, Edmondes had translated Caesar's Gallic War, Savile and Grenewey Tacitus, Holland Suetonius, thus covering Roman history from the beginnings to the end of the first century of the Christian era. Marcellinus carries on the story through the next three centuries, the era of the decline.

The chronology which he prints appears in the Paris text of 1591. He cites largely from Pancirollus's edition of the *Notitia Dignitatum*, Pomponius Laetus, Sigonius, and Wotton *De Animalibus*, and a large number of well-known Renaissance geographers. It is likely that he drew mainly from a single edition of his author, but I have not been able to find it.

Holland throughout affords an interesting study to the lexicographer, but the Marcellinus abounds in colloquial terms and in words now obsolete.

pavoisado, p. 178; striving a vie, p. 227 (*certatim*); devant, p. 270; walmed, p. 229 (*vagaretur*); not unskilfull of holding the plough taile, p. 234 (*nec . . . stiuam ignorant*); hunger-bitten, p. 234 (*urgente inedia*); thirled a hole through, p. 244 (*forauit*); a cold swawme of feare, p. 255 (*frigore*); in a fell and cruell gare, p. 412 (*cruditate*); clunged, p. 423 (*fixi*); to the outrace, p. 426; weerish, p. 16 (*leui corpore*); stride-long, p. 16; tewed and gashed p. 20 (*sulcatis*); knurre and difficultie, p. 23 (*nodum et codicem difficillimum*); captaine of Smell-Feasts, p. 32 (*somniorum comes*); faiterous plot p. 36 (*insidiis*); whirle-puff, pp. 41, 136 (*turbo*); conflowed, pp. 46, 63, 119; resiant, pp. 43, 59; dissite, p. 77, demisse (adj.), p. 44; execrable oath, p. 93 (*execratione*); regible, p. 69; chevisaunce, p. 221; tregetour, p. 223; whither in that doubtfull braid, p. 106 (*quo dubius impetus trusit*); bug-beare, or grim-visaged Gorgon, p. 109 (*Vultus Gorgonei torvitatem*); not (as they say) with spret nor oare, p. 111 (*non contis nec remuleo ut aiunt*); this unhappy accident made us bestir our stumpes, p. 134 (*hoc conciti*); become fantome, p. 136 (*fatiscunt*); osse, p. 136 (*omen*); if all men were shrigged of their goodes, p. 137 (*adtenuatis omnium opibus*); a most puissant frie of young soldiers, p. 138 (*tirocinia validissima*); scrow [i.e. scroll], p. 158 (*volumine*); jurres and pushes, p. 161 (*adsultibus*); set agog, p. 206 (*elata*); forage and stoover, p. 56 (*pabula*); how to catch and not to latch, p. 56 (*rapere non accipere*); al' arme p. 61; shogged, p. 62 (*concuteret*); a fresh-water souldior, p. 68 (*rudis*); warde all venies, p. 75 (*vulneribus declinandis*); whirle-pits, p. 76 (*gurgitibus*); chawnes, p. 89 (*rimas*); a very lob and foole, p. 96 (*stolidum*); lither and heartlesse, p. 92

(*commarcuit*) ; a slow-backe and a coward, p. 93 (*segnem et timidum*) ; frampold, p. 94 (*ferocientes*).

Holland's version of the *Cyropedia* completed on the eighth of February 1620-21 (a recasting finished on the fifth of April 1629 "aetatis interpretis 77,")[5] was dedicated by Henry Holland, Philemon's son, to King Charles I, having been prepared by King James's direction for Prince Henry. The publication was delayed because of the prince's death, and now at the request of friends the work was revised and published. Philemon Holland, *"now an old man, full of yeares,* and living still in your Mediterranean City *Coventry* (named in former times *CAMERA PRINCIPIS*) farre remote from Court, could not himself present this last labour of his unto your Highnesse hands, but hath left it unto me so to doe."

The *Cyropedia* shows no influence of the French translations nor of the Latin of Stephanus or Leunclavius many times printed. Holland seems to have been helped by Filelfus's translation, finished at Milan in 1467, reprinted by Stephanus in 1581, but to have translated with fair independence from the Greek, utilizing Stephanus's edition, *Gr. et Lat.* 1581. He follows the Greek order and structure pretty closely and does not double the synonyms so much as in the earlier work. Although the vocabulary is not so full of oddities as that of the Ammianus Marcellinus, there are a good many words worthy of notice, and remarked on in the Dictionary of the Philological Society.

Clement Edmunds, Remembrancer of the City of London, gradually brought to completion a translation of Caesar's *Commentaries* on the Gallic and the Civil Wars. He began with *Observations vpon the five first bookes of Caesars commentaries, setting foorth the practise of the art military, in the time of the Roman empire, wherein are handled all the chiefest points of their discipline, with the true reasons of euery part, together with such instructions, as may be drawn from their proceedings, for the better direction of our moderne warres.* This title is an accurate description of the book. It contains not an exact version of Caesar's commentaries but an abridgment, or rather a translation with many excisions, omitting

<hr>

[5] P. 213.

many sentences or parts of sentences not essential to the understanding of the actual military operations, and sometimes drastically abbreviating the material.   For instance, the whole stirring narrative of the conflict with the Nervii at the end of Book V is cut down to the bare statement of the military maneuvers on both sides, with the tactical reasons for them. The translation was accompanied by Edmunds's observations on the principles of the art of war exhibited in Caesar's operations.   The work was dedicated to Sir Francis Vere, regarded in his day as the chief English master of the "art military."

Later Edmunds made a complete translation accompanied by his observations of Books VI and VII, and published in 1604, at first separately and then in a book made up by combining it with the earlier work.   (The bibliographical details of publication are somewhat complicated, and are dealt with in the appendix, p. 327).   The separate edition of the newly translated books and the entire work each bore the same dedication to Prince Henry.   It is not without interest:

> Hauing heretofore (most worthie Prince) published a part of this booke, describing the practise of former times, as a Paralel to the fashion of our modern warres: I was purposed after that essay not to proceed any further therein, but to leaue the rest to the gaine of euery priuate indeuour.   Yet when I found in his Maiesties princely pen, how much his Excellent wisedome doth value these Commentaries, for the worthinesse of the matter aboue all prophane Histories; judging the Authour worthie more honour, then any of of the Ethnicke Emperours or other great Commanders of the world; I was incouraged to adde that which remained and make the worke perfect with all his parts.   Which being brought to an end, I do in all humblenesse present to the Gracious Patronage of your Princely fauor.   And the rather, forasmuch as those maine principles of warre which his Maiestie has set downe by way of precept to informe you, are here confirmed by Caesars example, and proued at large from the true grounds of that art, according to the practise of the best discipline. . . . .

Edmunds continued to occupy himself with Caesar's commentaries, and in 1609 published the *Gallic and the Civil Wars* in one volume.   In this translation the whole of Book I and the end of Book V of the *Commentaries on the Gallic War* were revised, the *Commentaries on the Civil War* were translated *in toto,* and of course the observations of Edmunds ac-

companied the entire work.   This book, like the 1604 version
of the *Gallic Wars* was dedicated to Prince Henry.

> Hauing ended this taske of Obseruations, and according to your
> gratious pleasure & command, supplied such parts as were wanting
> to make up the Totall of these Commentaries: it doth return again,
> by the lowest steps of humblenesse, to implore the high patronage of
> your Princely fauour; Emboldened specially because it carieth *Caesar*
> and his Fortunes, as they come related from the same Author:
> which, in the deepe Iudgement of his most excellent Maiesty, is
> preferd aboue all other profane histories; and so, commended, by
> his sacred authoritie to your reading, as a cheefe paterne and
> Maister-piece of the art of warre.   And herein your admired wise-
> dome, may happely the rather deeme it capable of freer passage, in
> that it is not altogether vnproper for these happie dayes; as know-
> ing, that warre is neuer so well handled, as when it is made an
> argument of discourse in times of sweete and plentious peace.   The
> blessings whereof, may euer crowne your yeares; as the soueraigne
> good of this temporarie life, and the chiefest Ornaments of Princely
> condition.

The humblest

of your Highnesse seruants,

Clement Edmondes.

The book is honored by commendatory verses from the pens
of Camden, Daniel, Sylvester, and Jonson, congratulating Edmunds that without experience of war he should have written
so practically on the subject.

Edmunds' Caesar was highly regarded throughout the seventeenth century, having been reprinted in 1655, 1677, and 1695.
It has no literary quality, either the springing, elastic energy
of the original, or any compensatory power or grace.   It does,
however, do its pedestrian duty of communicating information
accurately and clearly, though clumsily.

The facile talent of Thomas Heywood was employed upon
a translation of Sallust's *Catiline* and *Jugurtha*, (1609)—a curiosity of misplaced ingenuity of style alike in the dedication
and in the translation itself.   The work is dedicated "To the
right worthy and valorous, Sir William Summerset, Maister
of the Horse to the Queenes most excellent Maiesty," as follows:

> Sir, hauing no fitter occasion to manifest my duty to your Worthi-
> nesse (though I haue often wisht matter more expressiue both of my
> loue & zeale) I haue aduentured rather to tempt your acceptance

in this small presentment, worthy (no man will denie) in its proper Ornament, of an Honourable Patronage; Then by perpetuall neglect to incur the imputation of Ingratitude, a vice amongest the Heathen punishable, amongest Christians, contemptible. Herein therefore (right Generous) let me in lieu of all my friends, make confession of your many and extraordinary fauours, from time to time vouchsafed vs. In acknowledgment wherof, sithence we want power to deserue, yet giue vs leaue with thankfull ouertures to remember. Protesting, that if you daigne to accept of this vnpolisht Translation, partly divulged vnder the shadow of your protection, for the pleasure of your vacant howers, but especially for the general good of all English Gentlemen, when eyther Time or better iudgment shall furnish me with a more desertfull proiect, to prostitute it soly to the approbation of your most iudicious censure. Thus far presuming, that if it passe your allowance, I will aduenture neither to feare the discourtesy of the Cinicke, nor the sole-conceit of the Curious. In assurance whereof, being constantly warranted by the generous carryage of your Heroycall disposition, I esteme it as rich in value as I account it happy in acceptance, hauing in it nothing so worthy as your fauour, wherevnto I wholie refer it.

Yours faithfully deuoted,
Tho. Heywood.

The introductory epistle "Of the choice of History, by way of Preface, dedicated to the Courteous Reader, vpon occasion of the frequent Translations of these latter times," as a marginal note *"Bodin"* indicates, is a translation from Chapter IV, "De historiarum delectu," of Bodin's *Methodus ad facilem historiarum delectum.* I have read it in the edition printed at Paris, 1566. It discusses the merits of the chief historians down to Guillaume du Bellay and Guicciardini.

The following examples illustrate Heywood's ingenuity, his freedom, or his undue striving for effect. Unlike Holland, for instance, he hesitates before no loss of dignity or excess of phrase in the desire to be striking.

> church-robbers, *Catiline,* p. 12 (*sacrilegi*)
> redargued of offence, p. 13 (*exagitabat*)
> any true, Gentleman, innocent of these mis-behauioures, p. 13 (*a culpa vacuus*)
> Knights of the Post, p. 14 (*testis . . . falsos*)
> he proceeded to points of higher doctrine, p. 14 (*maiora alia imperabat*)
> . . . the remaines of Sullas army, by liuing more riotously than the rapines of their late victory could warrant them (whereof a fresh memory yet boiled in their stomackes) did itch after a second civill Warre, p. 14 (*plerique Sullani milites largius suo*

usi rapinarum et victoriae veteris memores civile bellum ex-optabant)

euill education, p. 16 (*mali mores*)

to poast away, p. 16 (*mittere*)

broke the neck of the intended enterprise, p. 17 (*consilium diremit*)

Lord President, p. 17 (*quaestor pro praetore*)

any giddy straine of a running wit, p. 18 (*vana ingenia*)

as also for that it is now past dispute, that we are all like ingaged, and must of necessity all drinke of one Cup, be it good or euill, p. 18 (*Simul quia vobis eadem quae mihi bona malaque esse intellexi*)

a Woman that had committed many virile outrages, above the creation of her sex, p. 23 (*Quae multa saepe virilis audaciae facinora commiserat.*)

well seene, p. 23 (*docta*)

the recording of their glorious actions, did disperse such a *Bout-feau* of imitation in their spirits . . ., p. 3 (*memoria rerum gestarum eam flammam egregiis viris in pectore crescere*)

more curious-cunning, p. 23 (*elegantius*)

But upon the first budding of innovation, their prestinat prerogatives brought passed sorowes to remembraunce, p. 35 (*Sed ubi primum dubiis rebus novandi spes oblata est vetus certamen animos eorum adrexit*)

roytelets, *Jugurtha*, p. 9 (*reguli*) ;

Euen vnto this day, those vpland buildinges of the *Numidians*, which they terme *Mapalia*, Cottages, are a kind of building edgelong on top, and broad-wasted below, in manner resembling the bottomes of ouerwhelmed Shipping, p. 17 (*ceterum adhuc aedificia Numidarum agrestium, quae mapalia illi vocant, oblonga incurvis lateribus tecta quasi navium carinae sunt*)

The townesmen, who till now beleeued that they had bin out of gunshot by their inaccessible scituation, p. 72 (*oppidani, qui se locorum asperitate munitos crediderant*)

On the whole the diction of Jugurtha is less picked and curious and vivid than that of Catiline.

Thomas Lodge's translation of Josephus is a very different work, grave and sober in style, and entirely free from the artificiality of Lodge's style in his own earlier romantic writings. The sentences are long but clear, boldly recasting the original, and, like Josephus's own, monotonous in form; the diction is dignified and somewhat learned.   The work purports, as the title indicates, to be translated "out of the Latin, and French." It is based, in point of fact, mainly upon the Latin of Gelenius, printed at Geneva in 1595, with constant suggestions from the

French of Antoine de la Faye (Paris, 1597). The translation was in favor throughout the century, having been printed seven times by 1670. Lodge's dedication of the 1609 edition to the Earl of Nottingham praises Josephus "for dignitie and antiquitie of the subject, the elegance and puritie of the style, the choise proprietie and copie of words, the grauitie and varietie of sentences, the alterations and memorable events, and lastly for the birth and dignitie of the author." His preface, "as touching the vse and abuse of Historie," is drawn mainly from Grynaeus.

Golding's version of Justin had by this time become obsolete; and a new translation by "G.W." was printed in 1606. In a prolix dedication to Sir James Haies the author expounds the moral value of history as an example to virtue and a deterrent from vice, and its interest in satisfying curiosity about the habitable world. Grynaeus's preface on *The Profit of Reading Histories* is also prefixed to the text. The translation clearly reproduces the sense of the original, idiom for idiom, sometimes substituting flowery or redundant phrases for the simple original, but not multiplying synonyms or striving to add color and concreteness. The sentences are long and suspended, sometimes sprawling and slovenly, but the translation in general is vigorously written, and is a not unworthy pendant to the great body of Holland's work.

Another minor historical translation of the period is Edmund Bolton's version of Florus's *Epitome*, first printed in 1618. In the interesting preface *To the Reader* Bolton quotes Justus Lipsius's praise of Florus's manner of writing:

> *There is in him a sharpnesse of wit and shortnesse of speech, oftentimes admirable; and certaine gemmes as it were, and iewels of wise sentences, inserted by him with good aduisement, and veritie.* Thus farre that excellent master, and with him let iudgement goe, if thou wilt herein doe iustice, howsoeuer, with *Mathematicall Stadius,* Florus is but *a tumultuarie author:* for so it pleaseth that learned Critike to style him, ouer loading him with the comparison of incomparable *Liuie.* . . . . His generous, bright, and flowrie writings (the best memoriall) are aliue, and now translated into our vulgar, with as much proprietie as one Englishmans English could attaine vnto for the present; but euerywhere with a religious ayme to his meaning, howsoeuer it may bee many times mist, the diuersity of Copies, like a change of the marke, and the peculiar manner of his stile coming like a sudden blast comming betweene. For this is

true, that there are in *Florus* sundrie knots, not easy to vntie, while he, desirous to speake quick and close together, our vnderstanding in him wanteth roome as it were, and that scope which is, hath somewhat thicke in it, amounting to a clowdinesse:

.........................breuis esse laboro,

obscurus fio.........................

more perhaps in this author, through corruption of manuscripts, and Prints, or of our duller-pointed wits, then through his fault, whose writings are altogether as luminous, as acuminous. . . . .

What the translatour thinkes worthy of thy precious time, to know further, requires a large booke, rather then an Epistle, and that also will be but a briefe (vpon a briefe) of all the old *Roman* wisedome ciuill and martiall, as here thou hast of their facts . . .

Bolton is true to his original yet free in style, not diluted, and clear, and spirited. He sympathizes with Florus's celebration of Roman virtue and achievement. As he says in his dedication (to George Villiers, created Marquis of Buckingham January 1, 1618):

. . . . IIis scope, to kindle the valor of the old Roman world in the bosome of the new: though himselfe, an heathen man, and liuing vnder *Traian* the emperour, saw the proportion of valour wellmaintained: that being the most goodly, and most flourishing estate, which at any time vnder heathen princes, that monarchie enioyed. Those annotations, and collections, whose lights will lead your Lordship into the wise, and heroike secret of the most potent, grave, and honourable masters which euer mankind had, are fittest for your more leisure. . . .

Bolton deserves to be represented by a characteristic passage, and there is none better than his account of the Servile War.

Though wee fought with our associates (an hainous matter) yet were they free-men howsoeuer, and at *leastwise* generous persons. Who can patiently brook, that the soueraigne people of the earth should arme against their slaues? The first troubles of that base nature were attempted in the yonger dayes of *Rome,* & within the citie it-selfe, by *Herdonius Sabinus,* captaine, when the state busied with the quarrels stirred by the *Tribunes,* the *Capitoll* was besieged, and taken by the Consull. But this was rather an vprore then a war. But now the empire *being* mightily enlarged with diuers countreys, who would beleeue that the *Iland* of *Sicilie* should be more cruelly wasted in the warre against slaues, then in the *Carthaginian?* An excellent corne countrey, and as it were a purlieu of *Rome,* where the *Latine* people had their farmes, and granges; for furniture of tillage ther wer very many bridewels, & husbandmen kept in chaines, which ministred matter for warre. A certain *Syrian* called *Eunus* (the great mischiefs he did makes vs remember his name) faining himself inspired with a diuine furie, while hee vaunts the ceremonies of his *Syrian* goddesse, call'd bondmen to armes, and libertie, as it were by authoritie from heauen: and to get credit in that point, he iuggled a nut into his mouth, filled with brimstone, and fire, and blowing it softly, spat fire as he spake. This coozning wonder drew at the very first two thousand of such as came in his way, and eftsoones breaking vp the workeiails, or bridewells, by right of warre, he made vp an host of aboue fortie thousand: & that nothing might bee wanting to the euill, he pranckt himself vp like a king in royall ornaments, and made miserable spoile of castles, townes, and villages: for a last disgrace, the campes of our Praetors were taken by him; nor shames it to tell their names; the camps of *Manlius, Lentulus, Piso, Hysaeus.* They therefore who ought to haue beene fetcht backe by officers as fugitiues, pursued our *Praetorian* Generals, whome they had made to runne away in set battell. In the end yet we had the punishing of them, *Publius Rupilius, our captaine* General: For after he had vanquisht them in the field, and last of all besieged them in *Enna,* when hunger, like a plague of pestilence, consumed them, he bound the remaynes of those strong theeues, in chaines, and fetters, & trussed them on gallowses: and for this seruice contented himselfe with an ouation, lest he should dishonour the dignitie of triumph, with *carrying in the inscription,* the title of villaines. The Iland had scarce taken breath, when by and by wee came from the bondmen, and the *Syrian* to the *Cilician, Athenio,* a shepheard swaine, murthers his master, and freeing his fellowes out of the work-iayle, put them vnder banners into battel-ray: himselfe in a robe of purple, with a staffe of siluer, and about his head a royall wreath, pieceth together no lesse an armie than the former madman, but rageth farre more eagerly against masters, and bondmen, as if against fugitiues, and as if he would reuenge the *Sicilian bondslaues* cause, sacking castles, townes, and villages. This varlet also had the killing of *Praetorian* armies, the campe of *Seruilius* taken *by him,* and that of *Lucullus* in like sort. But *Aquilius,* vsing the example of *Publius Rupilius,* vtterly distrest the enemie by staruing, & they who were otherwise hard to ouercome by force, hee easily destroid by famine: it was their desire to haue yeelded, but through the fear of the pains of punishment, they preferred voluntarie death: nay, wee could not take vengeance vpon the ringleader himselfe, though he came *aliue* into our hands: for very many striuing together whose prisoner he should be, the prey was torne in pieces while they wrangled about that interest.[6]

With these histories may be mentioned John Bingham's translation of Aelianus Tacticus (1616). Aelian, as Delbrück

[6]Pp. 347-353.

says,[7] was an author of practical value in the seventeenth century, the tactics of the phalanx as he describes them being adaptable as the basis of the drill instituted by Maurice of Nassau, under whom Bingham served. The translation is clear and adequate, and Bingham's notes are intelligent.

The discussion of the histories with their strong practical and ethical bias, leads naturally to the discussion of the works of moral philosophy; Holland's work, indeed, includes both classes of literature translated in the same spirit and with the same object, and it is natural to treat his Plutarch and Xenophon in connection with his Livy, Suetonius, and Ammianus Marcellinus.

The enduring interest in Boethius is witnessed by the continuing succession of translations of the *Consolations;* Chaucer's version printed by Caxton appeared about 1478, Walton's in 1525, Colvile's in 1556. Elizabeth wrote a translation, and two translations were made in the first decade of the seventeenth century, one by John Bracegirdle dating from between 1604 and 1608, dedicated to the Earl of Dorset, but apparently never printed; the other by "I. T." (probably Michael Walpole, S. J.)[8] dedicated to the Countess of Dorset after her husband's death, and printed in 1609.

Bracegirdle's version is entitled *Psychopharmacon. The Mindes Medicine, or the Phisicke of Philosophie.* The prose is translated into metrically fluent but clumsy and characterless blank verse, each section concluding with a couplet; the metres are in various metrical forms, two of them in unrhyming hexameters. The notion of versifying the prose was an error. The scholastic ratiocination is difficult to deal with in verse; even Dryden would have found it hard to give it variety and energy; and the blank verse tempts the writer to an unaccented, slippery continuity in form, which fails to give point and definiteness to the expression of the argument. The stanzas are better than the prose; the distinct outline forces

---

[7]Delbrück, Hans, *Geschichte der Kriegskunst,* Berl. 1920, Pt. IV, pp. 179-185.

[8]Stewart and Rand in the introduction to their edition of Boethius's *Theological Tractates* (1918) suggest John Thorie; G. Bayley Dolson in *I. T.—Translator of Boethius, Am. Jour. Phil.* xlii (1921) 266, John Thorpe; Walter E. Houghton, Jr. in *Michael Walpole, Translator of Boethius' De Consolatione, Am. Jour. Phil.* li (1930), 243, makes an almost convincing case for Michael Walpole, a Jesuit.

the expression to be more reserved and more energetic than the blank verse of Bracegirdle, which is, moreover, full of awkward inversions, unmelodious, and somewhat pompous.

"I. T.'s" version is better than Bracegirdle's; it gives the Proses in prose, the Metres in verse.

Boethius employed a picturesque vocabulary, full of striving for effect, and had the faults which accompany ingenuity and elaborately wrought small decoration. He is not largely and serenely passionate, but eager and vociferous, almost shrill. The movement of his style covers this restlessness with a suave and elegiac manner, producing in the most characteristic passages an affecting pathos. "I. T.'s" translation is *dry;* it is not exuberant in figure as Boethius is, being sometimes intentionally reserved, but more often merely negligent or lacking in energy. The effect is too cool as well as too dry, and the elegiac pungency of the original has vanished. The style lacks smooth sweetness of flow, but is meritoriously definite and sound in logical structure. The words of the original are often inadequately though not incorrectly rendered:

> *mulier reverendi admodum vultus oculis ardentibus et ultra communem hominum valentiam perspicacibus colore vivido atque inexhausti vigoris.* Bk. I, prose i, *ad init.* "a woman . . . hauing a graue [*reverend*] countenance, glistering clear [*glowing*] eyes and of quicker sight than commonly Nature doth afford; her colour fresh and chearefull [her *bodily force inexhaustible*] I.T. (fo. 2, *r.*)
>
> *partes quos quisque potuit* (I, prose i, p. 5, 1. 23, Teubner's ed.) such pieces as they [*each one*] could get (fo. 3 *r.*)
>
> *torvis luminibus* (I, prose i, 1. 27) angry looks [savage eyes] (fo. 3 *r.*)
>
> *in virilis animi robur* (I, prose ii, 1. 4) to man's estate [to a man's full strength of mind] (fo. 4 *v.*)
>
> *contuleramus* (*ibid.*) given [got together, or contributed].
>
> *nisi prior abjecisses* (*ibid.*) if thou haddest not cast them away [if thou haddest not cast them away beforehand].
>
> *contracta in rugem veste* (do. 1. 16] with a corner of her garment [with her garment gathered into a fold] (fo. 5 *r.*)
>
> *certissimam sedem tibi deligeres* (I, prose iii, 1. 8) thou thyself hast chosen to sit in at my house [hast chosen to sit upon a fixed seat] (fo. 8 *r.*)
>
> *in imbecilli cuique fortunas impetum faciens* (I, prose iv, 1.30) Violently possessing himself with poor [defenseless] men's goods (fo. 9 *v.*)
>
> *astrui* (I, prose iv, 1. 60) "adde to". [heap up] (fo. 11 *r.*)

The verse is better. "I. T.," bred in the accepted school of the day, works out ingenious metaphysical comparisons in simple words, as Boethius did, and constructs his verses with clean-cut rhetoric.

What cause of discord breakes the bandes of loue?
What God betweene two truths such wars doth moue?
That things which seu'rally well settled be,
Yet ioyn'd in one will neuer friendly proue?
Or in true things can we no discord see,
Because all certainties doe still agree?
But our dull soule, couer'd with members blind,
Knowes not the secret lawes, which things doe bind,
By the drown'd light of her oppressed fire.
Why then, the hidden notes of things to find,
Doth shee with such a loue of truth desire?
If she knowes that, which shee doth so require,
Why wisheth shee knowne thinges to know againe?
If she knowes not why striues she with blind paine?
Who after things vnknowne will striue to goe?
Or will rash ignorant pursuite maintaine?
How shall she find them out? or hauing so,
How shall she then their formes and natures know?
Now she, though clouds of flesh doe her debasse,
Forgets not all that was her ancient due,
But in her mind some generall motions are,
Though not the skill of things particular.
He that seekes truth, in neither course doth fall,
Not knowing all, nor ignorant of all.
He marketh geniall things which he retaines,
And matters seene on high doth backe recall.
And things forgotten to his mind regaines,
And ioynes them to that part, which then remaines.

Here and there the lines are really vigorous.

Flesh hath not quenched all the spirits light,
Though this obliuious lump holds her opprest.[9]

And my loose skin quakes on my flesh halfe dead.[10]

All pleasure hathe this property,
She woundeth those, who haue her most.
And like vnto the angrie Bee,
Who hath her pleasant honie lost.
She flies away with nimble wing
And in our hearts doeth leaue her sting.[11]

[9]Fo. 82 r.
[10]Fo. 1 r.
[11]Fo. 64 v.

Lodge's Seneca, (1614), like his Josephus, is a grave work, done in the period of his maturity after his conversion, sober in manner as in matter. Lodge chose as the patron of his work the Lord ,Chancellor Ellesmere, and addressed his dedication to him in a tone appropriate to his work, as to one of the few able to perceive the higher beauty of a serious work on a serious subject, and as one of the chief among the wise and prudent in England. In his preface, "To the Courteous Reader," Lodge insists again upon the serious aim of his work, urging his readers who have wasted their time on vanity, to study now how to live and how to die well.

> . . . This shalt thou learne in our *Seneca,* whose diuine sentences, wholsome counsailes, serious exclamations against vices, in being but a Heathen, may make vs ashamed of being 'Christianes . . . . I could haue pickt out eyther an author more curious, or a subject more pleasant for common eares, to allure and content them. But seeing the worlds Lithargie so farre growne, that it is benummed wholly with false appearance, I made choice of this authour, whose life was a pattern of continence, whose doctrine a detection and correction of vanities, and whose death a certaine instance of constancy. Would God Christians would endeuour to practise his good precepts, to reforme their owne in seeing his errours; and perceiuing so great a light of learning from a Pagans pen, ayme at the true light of deuotion and pietie, which becommeth Christians . . . . My soule and conscience bearing me witnesse that my intent and scope was to drawe men to amendment of life, & to root out vain customes, that are too much ingrafted in this age; What care I for detraction? which rather barketh for custome sake, then baiteth at mee for fiercenesse . . . .

In his Latin letter to the learned, Lodge frankly defends the freedom of his translation. He strives to replace the Latin idioms with natural English idioms, but in the process of "resolving" the concise rhetorical structure of the original, he gives up any attempt to reproduce the pungent energy of Seneca's epigrammatic style. His diction is as concrete as Seneca's, without colloquialism, and with almost no expansion by the reduplication of synonym. The result is a straightforward and dignified version, free from strain, but without much color.

In 1620 Lodge issued a revision, dedicated to the Earl of Suffolk, whose career is in such striking contrast with that of Ellesmere, to whom the first edition was dedicated. Lodge says in his Epistle "To the Reader," "Gentle Reader I present thee once more with Senecaes Translation, if not so fully and exactly cleansed from his former misprisions and errours, as I wish; yet I hope, in such sort examined and perused, that the iudicious Reader shall finde lesse matter to except against, and the indifferent, better light to vnderstand him. My businesse being great, and my distractions many; the Author being seriously succinct and full of *Laconisme;* no wonder if in som things my omissions may seeme such, as some whose iudgement is mounted aboue the Epicycle of Mercurie, will find matter to carpe at though not to condemme." Look at my translation as a garden—pull out the weeds, but carefully. "What a Stoicke hath written, Reade thou like a Christian. If any doubts entangle thy iudgement, haue recourse to the sacred Synod of learned and pious Diuines; whose iudgement will select thee out that which is for thy Soules profit, and disswade thee from admitting that, which may either depraue thy iudgement, or corrupt thy Soule."

The revision is thorough, not so much in correcting errors as in making the English of the version more intelligible and accurate.

A fair example of Lodge's style is to be found in the twenty-ninth chapter of the second book of *De Beneficiis*:

> See howe vnindifferentlye Gods gifts are esteemed, euen of some that professe wisdomme. They fynd faulte that wee bee not as bigge bodyed as Elephantes, as swifte of foote as Hertes, as light as Birdes, as strong as Bulles: that beastes haue substancialler hydes than wee, that the falow Deere hath a fairer heare, the Beare a thicker, the Beuer a softer: that Dogges excell vs in smelling, Aegles in seeing, Rauens in longliuing, and diuers beastes in easie and happie swimming. And whereas nature suffereth not certain thinges to ioyne toogither in one, (as, that swiftnesse of bodye should bee matched with equall strength); they call it an iniurie, that man is not compounded of diuerse and disagreable properties: and they blame the Gods of neglecting vs, bycause they haue not giuen vs perfect health, inuincible strength and corage, and knowledge what is too comme. Yea and they scarce restreyne themselues from russhing into a shameless impudencie, as too hate nature for making vs inferiour too the Goddes, and not felowes with them and full as good as they. How much more meete were it for vs too returne backe too the beholding of their so many and so great benefites, and too yeeld them thankes, that it hat[h] pleased them too allot vs the second roome in this most beautiful house, and too make vs Lords of all earthly things? Is there any comparison betweene vs and those

bestes wherof wee haue the souereintie? Whatsoeuer is denyed
vs, could not be giuen vnto vs. And therefore whosoeuer thou art
that doost so vnderualew mannes Lot, bethinke thee how greate
thinges our souerein Parent hath giuen vs: how much stronger
creatures wee bring in subiection, how muche swifter creatures wee
ouertake; and how there is no mortall thing exempted from our
power. Consider how many vertues wee haue receiued, how many
artes, and what a mynd, whiche perceth through all thinges euen in
the same instaunt that it setteth itself vntoo them, being more swift
than the planettes, whose courses it foreseeth many hundred yeeres
before they come too passe. Finally marke what plentie of frutes,
what abundance of riches, what store of all things heaped one vpon
another bee bestowed vppon vs. Well: Take the vew of all thinges,
and bycause thou canst fynd no one whole thing that thou haddest
leuer bee: picke out suche seuerall thinges as thou wouldest wish
too bee giuen thee out of them al. So when thou hast well weyed
the louing kyndnesse of nature, thou shalt be forced too confesse,
that thou wast hir Dea[r]ing. And so it is indeede. The Gods
immortall haue loued vs and doo loue vs most deerly: and (which
is the greatest honour that could bee giuen) they haue placed vs
next vnto themselues. Greate things haue wee receiued, and greater
we could not take.

Some of Lodge's locutions are not uninteresting:

philologum aut grammaticum, p. 447, a humanist or pedant
onerat priore sequentibus, p. 4, redoubleth his benefits one vpon the
    necke of the other
si cohaeret et vices servat, p. 5, when they are vnited and hand-fasted
    together
in sella prostare et . . . vehi . . . undique, p. 9, to get vp into
    their Caroches and prance through the streets
supercilio, p. 19, crabbednesse of their lookes
pietas munus suum, p. 24, diuoire and paternall pietie
tutelam, p. 189, vnder our tutely and protection
pileatae turbae, p. 197, the round-cap multitude
voluptas autem non illa levis et fugax, p. 198, such pleasure which is
    fomie and fleeting.
stultorum divitum adrosor, p. 216, a smell-feast, and sharker of foolish
    rich men
minoris, p. 216, for less price, and better cheape
iacere ac deprimi, p. 232, the flame directly mounteth vpward, neither
    may be disnatured or depressed
solet magno cursu verba convellere, p. 233, continued (according to
    his custom in discoursing) to huddle vp his wordes with great
    volubilitie
vini minister, p. 243, skinking the wine
deversorium vitiorum, p. 250, the hostrie of vices
fortunam in aequum deducere, p. 251, to keepe Fortune at staffes end

non trepidabo ad extrema, p. 256, when I shall find my selfe at the
last gaspe, I will not be astonished

The use of ancient ethical philosophers and fathers of the
church without discrimination as moral guides is well illustrated in *"Six excellent treatises of life and death, Collected
(and published in French) by Philip Mornay, Sieur du Plessis;
and now (first) Translated into English."* (1607) Du Plessis-
Mornay, the most eminent of French protestants, and for no
short time resident in England, was well known and greatly
respected in that country. His own discourse on life and death
had been translated by the Countess of Pembroke. The *Six
Discourses* include the pseudo-Socratic dialogue the *Axiochus,*
extracts from *De Senectute,* extracts from Seneca's Letters,
a sermon of Saint Cyprian on mortality, Saint Ambrose on the
benefit and happiness of death, and extracts from Scripture,
with prayers and meditations. The translation has the ease of
movement common in translations from the French, but is
without distinction.

Among the most active of the translators in King James's
reign was John Healey, whose versions of Mornay's *Teares
for the death of his son,* and of Joseph Hall's *Mundus Alter
et Idem* were printed in 1609, Arrian's abridgment of Epictetus
with Cebes's *"Table,"* and St. Augustine's *City of God,* in
1610, Theophrastus's *Characters,* with a reprint of Epictetus
and Cebes in 1616, and a revision of St. Augustine's *City of
God* in 1620. Thomas Thorpe, the publisher of Shakespeare's
Sonnets, his dedication of which has given rise to so much controversy, published the 1610 editions of Epictetus and Cebes,
with the following characteristically enigmatic and sentimental
dedication by "Th. Th."; "To a true fauorer of forward spirits,
Maister Iohn Florio . . . Your poore friend . . . doth follow
you . . . that as his *Mecaenas* you would write to *Augustus* . . .
For his apprentises essay you procured (God thanke you) an
impregnable protection: He now prayes the same Patron . . .
for his iourneyman Maisterpeece . . ." The 'prentice-essay
seems to be the translation of *Mundus Alter et Idem,* a book
"light but not lewd," as Healey calls it. The *Mundus Alter et
Idem* was dedicated by Hall "To the True mirror of truest
honor, William Earle of Pembroke."

Thorpe in the dedication of Epictetus evidently took it upon him to speak for the author.

The versions of the Epictetus and the *Table* of Cebes show the influence of Hieronymus Wolfius's Latin translation, (Cologne, 1596) joined to the Greek text. Healey controlled the Latin by the Greek, sometimes failing to notice a discrepancy, and translated with great freedom, occasionally rendering a metaphor by a totally different one. The manner of the Epictetus is colloquial and is made more piquant than the studiously direct and unassuming original.

The following brief example illustrates Healey's freedom and bold colloquialism:

Φιλοσοφίας ἐπιθυμεῖς; παρασκευάζου αὐτόθεν, ὡς καταγελασθησόμενος, ὡς καταμωκησομένων σοῦ πολλῶν, ὡς ἐρούντων, ὅτι ἄφνω φιλόσοφος ἡμῖν ἐπανελήλυθε, καὶ πόθεν ἡμῖν ἡ ὀφρύς; σὺ δὲ ὀφρὺν μὲν μὴ σχῆς.

Sapientiae studium suscipere capis? Statim te para, quasi futurum sit ut deridearis: ut multi te subsannent: ut dicant te subito philosophum exstitisse: ut rogent, unde supercilium istud? Tu autem supercilium ne habeto.

Dost thou ayme at the attaynment of wisedome? Then first of alle, prepare thy self to bee the worlds laughing-stocke [lit. simply *to be laughed at*], to bee the common place of the multitude of mockers [*to have many mock at you*]. Then one will come with this gird [*to have people say*]: Oh here is a mushrump Phylosopher! Shotte vp since yesterday: [*we have a philosopher come back to us all of a sudden*]: and then with this [not in the original]: Lord sir where light you on this graue statelinesse [*where did we get this haughtiness*]? But let not statelinesse be found in thee!

All in all, Healey's lively but homespun style makes the little book pleasant reading, but is entirely out of the tone of the matter-of-fact practicality of the plain Stoic directions for life, as "close, naked, and natural" as a report to the Royal Society.

The Cebes, though as free as the Epictetus, is less colloquial in manner.

Healey's Theophrastus seems to have made curiously little impression on English literature in his own time or later. It came at a time when a collection of "characters" was becoming a form of real literary importance, and when the analytic character was supplanting the dramatic presentation of persons in action, alike in history, satire, poetry, and imaginative prose.

It would seem that a version of the founder of the genre would have been as welcome in English as La Bruyère's in French, but Healey's book apparently fell perfectly flat. It is not alluded to in its own day, and in later times it has remained all but unnoticed. It is hard to find in library catalogues; it is not even mentioned in the preface of Dr. Jebb's translation of Theophrastus, though not only Hall's, Earle's and Overbury's English characters, but La Bruyère's French version are intelligently criticized. Yet it is at least as accurate and as spirited as the French version. To be sure, it is not really a good translation. In it Healey is unconstrainedly free in manner as in his Epictetus and Cebes, and even, as in them, unhesitatingly adds passages of his own to his original. This is out of place in Theophrastus, whose method is to recite the characteristic actions of his typical personages, and thus to give us a coherent picture of the Athenian bore, or coward, or mean man, a picture of human permanence, typical in spirit, but in habit and surroundings belonging to his age, and not to be found anywhere else or at any other time. Healey by the addition of a few traits from the manners of *his* day creates a character which is not at one with itself, is neither Greek nor Jacobean, and by his colloquial jazzing of the style destroys the simple and unobtrusive humor of the original. Yet he does succeed in making a lively and pleasant impression, in arresting and amusing his reader.

A few examples will illustrate the point. Where his original —that is to say, the Latin of Casaubon's version (1592)—says *he spends his time purveying sometimes for himself, sometimes for the whole household,* Healey is not satisfied without a more vivid and complete account: "He grinds, caters, drudges, purveighs, & playes the Shutler, for all things belonging to a house-prouision." (p. 17). It is not enough for him that one should merely *listen,* if anybody knocks at the door: "he listens *like a Cat for a Mouse." Yesterday I vomited* becomes: "Yesterday I was wamble-cropt and (saving your presence) parbrak't." A man who *changes his use of costume,* "changeth and *Turkizeth his cloathes"* (p. 2). Where Theophrastus's character is not ashamed being sober to dance the *Cordax,* Healey's character is not ashamed, being sober, *in coole bloud,* to dance *Country dances* and *Matachines, as a*

Zanie or Pantalon. His cowardly man not only hides his sword in his bed;—"His two-heel'd sword [*i.e.* his runaway feet] is his best weapon." This piece of smartness, like every other piece of smartness in the book is Healey's own invention.

The preface contains interesting comments on previous translations.

To the Reader:

Gentle Reader, to be too seruile or too lice*n*tious, are alike amisse in a Translater for the one oftentimes darkneth the beautie of the worke, there being certaine properties almost in euery language, which cannot, word for word, in termes terminant, be expressed in another. And likewise to swerue too much from the Author, implieth a secret disabling, as if the Original might be bettered; which cannot but sauour of much self-opinion and singularity, yet if there were a necessity to erre in either, I had rather be ouerstrict then any whit too bold: hauing to Precedent, (it were contumely to say lesse) that great Magazine or Storehouse of all learning M. *Casaubon* who in the translation of this Peece, hath tied himself very precisely to his Text. From so learned a hand the Authour can lose little lustre, lesse vigour. Howeuer, by powring it out of the Latin into the vulgar, the great disproportion of Languages and abilities considered, it cannot but (by my unskilfulnesse) it hath taken some wind.

In this mention it commeth oftentimes into my minde to maruaile whence it should be that *Homer* [Salel-Jamin *vs.* Crispinus revised by Stephanus], Theocritus [probably scattered translations by Jamin and others *vs.* Eobanus Hessus], Plutarch [Amyot *vs.* Cruserius] Heliodorus [Amyot *vs.* Warschewiczki], with diuers others, are so lamely done in the Latin (be it spoken with supportation of better iudgements) and as happily in the French. Wee may not challenge the pouerty of the Latin, the negligence of the Translators, (hauing been all very learned) much lesse the Latin Idiom, as disobedient or refractory to the Greek. We should be almost as vaine as *Picardus,* to aduance the French before the Latin: who maintaineth after his Mountebank impudent fashion, that the French is more ancient & copious then the Greeke; and that they spoke Greeke in *Marselles* before they spoke it in *Athens.* The French is elegant enough, passably copious, happie in composition, and hath many Graecismes, which couch very aptly when they are cald for; yet in no degree comparable with the learned Languages. (The rest is almost altogether explanatory of terms in allusion to the characters.)

So deep and broad, so far out of the range and reach of the every-day thought of the age, are the really philosophical works of the great Greek masters that it is surprising to find a translator venturing upon them at all. Hence the translation of

Aristotle's *Politics* by I. D. (1598) deserves special attention. It is dedicated: "To the Right Noble and Renowned Gentleman, Sir Robert Sidney Knight, Lord Gouernour of the cautionarie towne of Vlissing and the castle of Ramekins."

"I. D." declares that since the "most barbarous and Gothish opinion" that learning and arms are contrary in their nature is abundantly refuted by many Greek and Roman examples, he hopes he shall not be condemned for choosing a military man as patron to this work of political science; indeed Sidney's public employments, like his private studies, bear witness that "as your noble brother (the true knight of Minerua) hath to his eternal honor augmented the number of those few who in this last age of the declining and degenerating vvorld, haue honourably emulated those auncient Worthies: so your selfe treading the same path of Vertue, haue by like desert purchased to your name & house, a second eternitie." The subject is noble; as for the author, "what Philosopher can in depth of knowledge equall *Aristotle* vvhose workes may be iustly tearmed, *The Treasurie of humane wisdome?* all which as they sauour of diuinenesse, so amongst them all, these his Discourses of Gouernment haue not the meanest relish thereof; especially vvhere hee handleth the changes and destructions of euery Commonweale, vvith their causes, and sets downe seuerall precepts for the upholding and preseruing of each: vvhich vvhosoeuer doth aduisedly read, can doe no other than say of him as *Cornelius Nepos* dooth say of *Tully, Prudentiam esse quodammodo diuinationem*: for what he so many yeares since did vvrite, hath bene in all points exactly verefied by Examples of following times, descending euen to our present age."

The Preface, "To the courteous Reader," sets forth at length the difficulties of the undertaking, and the circumstances under which the translation was made and published:

> . . . . . It shall suffise briefly to acquaint you with some thinges which being absolutely considered and the truth thereof vnknown, may seeme to yeeld large and iust occasion of reproofe: as first, the harshnesse of the phrase and rough conueiance of the stile, which if any doth dislike, as doubtlesse some will, I entreat them to remember (for I can hardly thinke they know not) that no translation is capable of Elegance as the originall, because the one hath full libertie of inuention, & the other is by necessity tied to obserua-

tion: next I desire them to consider Aristotles maner of writing, the obscuritie, compacting and vnusuall composition of his stile, which if they weigh vprightly, they needs must graunt that though *Tullies* honourable *Encomium* which he doth generally giue it, calling it *Aureum flumen orationis,* be in respecte to the puritie thereof, and of the excellencie of the matter most true, yet that they cannot with any reason looke for a fluent and flourishing stile in the translation of such a subiect, either out of the originall or any other language whereinto it hath ben since translated. I wish them farther to consider that manie places of the Comment (wherein are set downe whole discourses touching astrologie, Cosmographie, and other deepe points of the mathematicall sciences, lightly touched by Aristotle) are more obscure than the text it selfe. Touching the diuersitie that may be found in the translation, it is not to be meruelled at, sith some part of the booke was performed by another, before I vndertooke the rest. But I hope, that though wee differ in the manner, yet that we swarue not from the truth of the matter, howsoeuer the Compositors mistaking hath therein somewhat wronged vs, and the oft & thicke enterlining of copie, hastily written, deceiued him; but the cheefest of those ouersights are noted in the end. As for the difference of the English in some places from the French, I answere, that when vpon any obscuritie I resorted to the Greek, and found the rendering therof in French not so significatiue as might be, I haue been bold to follow the originall, vnlesse it did so depend on the Comment, that I could not alter it. And touching the difference of it from the Latin, I hope none will accuse me for not following that whereto I was not bound, and besides if they conferre the Latine with the French, and both with the Greeke, they shall (I doubt not) find that the French doth approoch far neerer to Aristotle. Lastly, touching the extraordinarie harshnesse that may in some places be found, I say thus much only, that the difficulty of the thing, wherin euen learned men themselues haue sometimes faild, with the small time and leisure which I had both to doe and reuiew it may suffise if not to excuse me, yet at least to purchase pardon. But sith my present post allowes me not sufficient time to touch euery particular, I will commit vnto your courtesies the further consideration both of this & whatsoeuer els may be obiected, humbly entreating you to measure my labour not by it selfe, for it is worthlesse, but by my good will and earnest desire to please, which is therefore the greater, because I feare that my former toies haue displeased, which were they againe to pen and publish, should rather sleepe in silence, than I through them be accused of time mispent.

LeRoy's notes are so full that under his hand the *Politics* becomes rather a text to be commented on than a book to be translated. He fully explains allusions, making up by the completeness of his annotations for the absence of convenient books of reference on classic mythology and biography, and not only telling who Amasis, Aristogeiton, and Dionysius are, but what particular thing about them is alluded to. He illustrates the ideas of Aristotle by citations from his other works, thus explaining the general trend of his thought. He supplements Aristotle by comparison with other philosophers, especially Plato. He illustrates the substance of the book by citing abundant examples from history, ancient and recent but seldom medieval, often bringing out interesting and apposite parallels to Aristotle's illustrations. He amplifies Aristotle's generalizations abundantly; if Aristotle says that the food of man differs in different countries, Le Roy specifies the differences in many regions; if Aristotle enumerates types of government, Le Roy compares the councils, estates, and parliaments of many modern countries. In the main his effort is to show the permanent significance of Aristotle's conceptions; but he makes a few acute critical comments on details, without having any fundamental contribution to make on any vital point. The book is a really important and useful one in assisting to create a modern political science, based on Aristotle's fundamental investigations. The translation contains nothing not in Le Roy though the English translator intelligently compared and corrected his version by the Greek text; the first five books are annotated fully, the last three summarily. "I.D.'s" part is adequately done; the first two books are by an inferior hand.

The *Problems of Aristotle* (1595) is really not identical with the Problems which go under his name, but is a medieval collection mainly of "Vulgar Errors."

Question. *Why are the Iews subiect vnto this disease* [the Piles] *very much?*
Ans. The Diuines do say, because they cried at the death of Christ, *Let his bloud fall vpon vs and our children.* And therefore it is sayd in the Psalm, *Percussit eos Deus in posteriora dorsi.*[12]
Question. *VVhether should he* [a hermaphrodite] *bee baptized in the name of a man, or of a woman?*
Answer. In the name of a man, because names are giuen *ad placitum*, and therefore he should be baptized according vnto the worthiest name, because euery man is worthier then a woman, because euery agent is worthier then his patient, as *Aristotle* doth say, 3 . *de anima.*[13]

---

[12]Sig. Dvi *r.*   [13]Sig. Eviii *r.*

Question *Why is the bloud red?*

["Why grass is green, or why our blood is red,
Are mysteries that none have reached unto."
            Donne, *Second Anniversary,* 11. 288-289]

Answer. Because it is like vnto the part where it is made, that is, vnto the liuer, which is red.[14]

Question. *Why hath a man which lieth on his backe horrible visions?*
Answer. Because then the passage or sinewe of the fantasie is open, which is in the forepart of the braine, and so the fantasie is destroyed, and then those visions followe.[15]

Question. *Why doe men become hoarse, by the looking of a woolfe?*
Answer. The answer according vnto *Aristotle* is, because a wolfe is a very cold beast in the brain, and thereupon hath a very heauie head. If then the spirit of the sight or beames be directed & goe towards the wolfe, it doth draw some coldnes from him to the breast, and then of that coldnes the breast is straightened, where the instruments are by which the voyce is formed: because a woolfe can not send foorth any other fumosities, and they are breathed out into the ayre, that ayre next vnto him is infected, and the next aire by that aire, and so another aire, vntill it come vnto the man: then that ayre being infected, is drawne in by man, and so doth make him hoarse, by closing the vocall arterie or windpipe. And it hath been alreadie sayd that a woolfe is a very rauenous and deuouring beast, and doth eate as much at once as will serue him for three days, and therefore by opening his mouth doth cast foorth rawe and grosse humours vndigested, by the which the next ayre vnto him is infected, and so the next vnto it, vntill it come vnto the looker on, and so dooth infect like the Basilisque, which dooth cast foorth venemous ayres, which infect men by the eyes.

Question. *Why is not a wolfe hoarse when a man doth looke on him?*
Answer. Because a man is not so cold as a wolfe, nor of so malignant a qualitie. And for the like reason this probleme is moued.[16]

Question. *Why haue men more teeth then women?*[17] . . . .

Question. *Why is raine prognosticated by the pricking vp of the asses eares?*
Answer. Because the Asse is a very melancholy beast, and it proceedeth from the melancholy that he doth foresee raine to come. In the time of raine all beasts doe pricke vp their eares, and therefore the asse perceiuing that it will raine doth pricke vp his eares before it come.[18]

In the seventeenth century began actively the movement all over Europe to make all learning and especially science and the

---

[14]Sig. Ev *r.*
[15]Sig. Dv *r.*
[16]Sig. Cv.
[17]Sig. Bviii *v.*
[18]Sig. Bvi *v.*

professions more easily accessible by using the vernacular in place of Latin. Thomasius first lectured in German at Leipzig in 1687; in 1558 Placotomus urged the publication of medical works in German; not till 1807 did the Berlin Academy begin to prefer German in its reports.

The higher products of thought were still published in the international language: Harvey, Torricelli, Grew, Leibnitz, all wrote in Latin; but the accepted works of fundamental information and basic principles were put within the easier reach of men not learned in the tongues and reaching out for information. The art of war was discussed in the vernacular, and the principles of classical strategy and tactics made accessible by such works as Bingham's Aelian and Edmunds' Caesar. Medicine likewise, to the annoyance of conservatives, began to have the veil of mystery lifted from it. Among the active agents was the eminent Scotch surgeon Peter Lowe, who after a very active and general experience on the Continent, retired to Glasgow, where he was instrumental in founding the Glasgow College of Physicians and Surgeons. He published in English his own *Discourse on the Whole Art of Chyrurgerie*, and subjoined a translation of the Hippocratic Oath and "Presages" *i.e., the Prognostics* (1597, 1611-1612, 1634). The translation is, indeed, inaccurate, diffuse, and diluted by the addition of much foreign matter.

The translation of the *Aphorisms* by S. H. (1610), is a much more creditable work, being accurate and intelligent, and not wasting words. The translator expresses his fear that his version, being the translation of a translation, will suffer in point of style;—"*To the vnderstanding reader* . . . . —the first translation cannot haue the grace of the originall, nor a second translation that of the first, but must needs seem more harsh and barraine than the first: So I feare me it will happen with these Aphorisms, which were first written in Greeke by the Authour, and after in latine, and now as thou seest in English . . . ."

The *"Flowers of Celsus,"* included in a medical hand-book (*Enchiridion Medicum*, 1619) are an intelligently made and translated set of extracts: but very brief and empirical;—"It is the part of a skilfull Physitian, not forth-with to take the Patient by the arme with his hand, to feele his pulse, but first to sit down by him with a chearfull countenance, and demand of him how hee feeleth himselfe, and if hee be discouraged with feare, to releive his spirits with some probable speech which may breed some hope: then afterward to put forth his hand to his body. " (p. 162.) —"It is superfluous to use medicines, but in vehement evils." (p. 166.)

As an appendage to these medical works may be mentioned the translation of "The interpretation of Dreames, Digested into five bookes by that Ancient and excellent Philosopher Artimedorus [sic] Compiled by him in Greek; and translated afterwards into the *Latine,* the *Italian,* the *French,* and *Spanish* Tongues, and now more exactly rendered into English." The translation by R. Wood (first edition, 1606; fourth edition, 1644) is entirely dependent on the French, reproducing all the French prolegomena and dedications. It covers only three books of Artemidorus's *Oneirocritica,* and Book i, Tit. 7, of Valerius Maximus ("a little Epitomy of Valerius Maximus concerning dreames.") The edition of 1644, which purports to be "newly corrected, by the French, and Latine Copy," is identical with the edition of 1606 except for some changes in spelling and punctuation. The work is of some interest in showing the continuity of minor superstitions, for Artemidorus filiates from very ancient sources, back to Assyrian times, and some of his intepretation may be found in the latest cheap "Dream books" on booksellers' stalls.

The prose fiction which constituted so important an element among the translations between 1560 and 1590 was represented in this period by a single translation, William Burton's version of Achilles Tatius's *Cleitophon and Leucippe* (1597), rounding out the *corpus* of Greek amatory romances. The short narrative of Achilles Tatius is a lively piece of melodramatic extravagance, altogether conventional in its theme and incidents, which moves along rapidly except for some expanded descriptions. Burton, who translates from the Latin of Cruceius, follows Cruceius, naturally, in his few errors, and adds some of his own; but his translation is written in the vigorous, melodious style characteristic of the best Elizabethan prose. His errors, on the whole, are not important, he does not attempt to add piquancy by any startling colloquialisms, and all in all his version does justice to its original.

Of the minor poetic translations of this period, none is of importance in literary history, and none can be called successful in itself except the *Salmacis* sometimes attributed to Francis Beaumont.

The most interesting, not for their success as translations or for their beauty as poems, but for their probable influence in the development of the poet's command of his art, are Marlowe's versions of the *Amores* of Ovid, and of the first book of Lucan's *Pharsalia*. Nobody has praised, and nobody can praise Marlowe's translation of Ovid's *Amores*. Swinburne with characteristic vehemence declares: "Had every copy of Marlowe's boyish version or perversion of Ovid's *Elegies* deservedly perished in the flames to which it was judicially condemned by a brace of prelates, it is possible that an occasional bookworm, it is certain that no poetical student, would have deplored its destruction, if its demerits could in that case have been imagined." I speak, perhaps, as a bookworm; but to me it seems that a poetic student more than anyone else would be solicitous and eager and hopeful about the first stammering accents of a great poet, and would search them carefully to learn whether they could show any steps of his progress to perfect powers of utterance.

The version is certainly not creditable to Marlowe's scholarship. It is reprehensible, of course, but not fatal, for a translator from Latin not to know that *manus* (I, 9, 27) may mean *troops* as well as *hands;* and that *gorges* is only a derivative meaning of *faucibus* (II, 1, 25) and that *jaws* is the natural sense. But it is a much more serious matter to construe *miti* a dative (II, 17, 5) as a masculine nominative. It is obvious that Marlowe had never been trained out of the common but vicious practise of reading Latin by the stems and putting the words together by guess without worrying about the endings. At the same time, even this method generally gives the sense; and Marlowe generally gives the sense of Ovid, though often clumsily and stiffly. Even Professor Tucker Brooke is obliged to say, "Judged by absolute standards, Marlowe's *Elegies* must be adjudged to be a failure, both as poetry and as a rendering of the Latin." However, as he adds, "when considered as a very early metrical exercise, the translation shows decided promise." He perceives the enthusiasm which the work manifests from the first line to the last, an occasional example of melody in the cadence of the lines, a prevailing richness of vocabulary and epithet, and above all an extraordinary facility in rhyming. But even Professor Tucker Brooke has not observed that the version is line for line, in rhyme. Swinburne himself remarks on the extreme technical difficulty of a line-for-line rendering into blank verse, such as Marlowe attempted in his Lucan. Much more severe is the hard anvil labor of beating each easy Latin distich into a firm English rhyming couplet. There is no room for expansion or dilution, rhyming words must be found and fitted to the sense, and at least (for Marlowe) some energy given to the expression. Of Ovidian ease and facility there is not a trace in Marlowe's version.

The Lucan must have been done not long after the Ovid, as Professor Brooke insists; it cannot be a product of the later part of his poetical activity as the *Dictionary of National Biography* and the *Encyclopedia Britannica* incautiously suggest. Marlowe could never have submitted to the trammels of translating Lucan line for line after tasting the freedom of paraphrase as in the *Hero and Leander,* still less of unrestrained original blank verse, as in his plays. The Lucan is translated more boldly, idea for idea, than the Ovid. It has the same mistakes in syntax (1. 40, it is Manda, not the battles, which are "dreadful"; 1. 79, 80, it is not Phoebe who will "full of strife dissolve the engines of the broken world," but the engine of the broken world which full of strife will dissolve all bonds of treaties). And many lines are stiff, rugged, or obscure, inexpert, if not boyish. In general Marlowe is quite unsuccessful in translating the epigrammatically sententious passages, which depend upon a purely intellectual energy for their force.

	summisque negatum	
stare diu (High seats quickly perish) ;		(11.70,71)
uictrix causa deis placuit, sed uicta Catoni		(1. 128)
(. . Caesar's cause		
The gods abetted, Cato lik'd the other)		
	Stat magni nominis umbra	(1. 13)
(And thought his name sufficient to uphold him		
	fecunda uirorum	(1. 165)
paupertas		(1. 166)
	(Poverty, who hatch'd	
Rome's greatest wits)		

On the other hand he is effective in the more emotional passages, ample in method, terrific in idea.

> Caesars renowne for war was lesse, he restles,
> Shaming to striue but where he did subdue,
> When yre, or hope prouokt, heady, & bould,
> At al times charging home, & making hauock;
> Vrging his fortune, trusting in the gods,
> Destroying what withstood his proud desires,
> And glad when bloud, & ruine made him way :
> So thunder which the wind teares from the cloudes,
> With cracke of riuen ayre and hideous sound
> Filling the world, leapes out and throwes forth fire,
> Affrights poore fearefull men, and blasts their eyes
> With ouerthwarting flames, and raging shoots
> Alongst the ayre and nought resisting it
> Falls, and returnes, and shiuers where it lights.   (11. 145-158)

From the first work to the second Marlowe has made a great advance in poetic skill. Not often, but sometimes he gives the energetic rhetoric of Lucan sonorous and brilliant expression in English. The ways by which a genius learns and trains himself are incalculable. It is indeed no doubt strange that Ovid's rather tedious erotic conventionality and Lucan's smoky rhetoric should have been selected to be the means of Marlowe's youthful poetical discipline. But such as they were, the one helped him to gain the flow and facility, the abundance, and the easy and pleasant rhyming of *Hero and Leander*, the other to form the mighty line of his plays.

The scattering versions from Ovid, of which there were some seven between 1598 and 1620, are insignificant. The earlier renderings of the long narratives of Ovid and Vergil did provide for English readers a knowledge of traditional ancient story which gave sustenance to the imagination; but the later crude renderings of the substance of the *Ars Amatoria* and the *Remedia Amoris* had no value for the reader, and were too superficially done to exercise the writer usefully in the craft of verse. Their only interest is as evidence that the creative writers of the age had caused the clumsy fourteener to be abandoned for eight and ten-syllable lines.

A version of the *Ars Amatoria* (1598), probably by Thomas Heywood, in heroic couplets, does not show a trace of the rhetoric of the original. It is blemished by a good many serious actual errors, still more inadequate renderings, a clumsy style, and a versification comparatively rude and halting for the period.

The first book of the *Remedia Amoris,* (*i.e.* through 1. 398), translated by an unknown F. L. (1600) in six-line stanzas of iambic ten-syllable verse (ababcc), is a little better. In the same volume were the spurious epistle of Dido to Aeneas, from the *Heroides,* and Aeneas's answer. The former is one of the stiff and clumsy translations of the Googe-Turbervile period, in "poulter's measure"; the latter in the same meter and apparently by the same hand as the *Remedia Amoris.* A paraphrase and expansion of the tale of Salmacis and Hermaphroditus in flowing and graceful couplets has been attributed to Francis Beaumont, but is not like his known work in tone or style. It decorates and exaggerates the poem with reference to half the stories in the *Metamorphoses,* and debases its spirit by making Salmacis purchasably lascivious.

The use made of Ovid in Thomas Heywood's *Troia Britannica or Great Britaines Troy* is quaint. The poem is a huge chronicle-romance telling as nearly as possible the story of the world: the narrative of the Creation, the whole body of classic mythology euhemerized, the tale of Troy to its fall,—all this in fifteen cantos,—the chronicle of England from Brute to William the Conqueror in one canto, and from William to the accession of James I in one canto. It brings together the heroes of antiquity, of romance, and of English history as all part of the tradition of Britain: Daedalus, Achilles, Aeneas, Arthur, Brennus, Edmund Ironsides, on down to Howard, Grey, Norris, Sidney, Essex, and Vere. Heywood dedicates his work to the Earl of Worcester.

> 'Tis fit those Lordes which we from Troie deriue,
> Should in the Fate of Troy remembred be.

In the "Epistle: To the two-fold Readers: the Courteous, and the Criticke" Heywood lays out the plan of the poem.

> . . . . Yet if you vnderstandingly consider this proiect, you shall finde included herein a briefe memory or Epitome of Chronicles, euen from the first man, vnto vs, the second time created Britons [*i.e.* by the union of the thrones under James], with a faithfull Register, not onely of memorable thinges done in Troy and this Island, but of many, and the most famous accidents happening through

the World, In whose raigne and what yeare of the world they chaunced.

In the fifth canto of the first book we read:

> From *Adam* and Euahs first *Creation*,
> It follows we deriue our *Brittish Nation*.

In Cantos V-XII a large part of the story is a rationalization or euhemerizing of the *Metamorphoses,* while the *Ars Amatoria* is drawn upon quite directly for a multitude of legends: of Mars and Venus, Pasiphae, Achilles and Deidamia, Calypso, Circe, Ariadne, etc. There are a few lines here and there from the *Remedia Amoris,* the Helen to Paris and Paris to Helen letters from the *Heroides,* and a free paraphrase of the Cephalus-Procris tale from the *Metamorphoses.*

There is some interest in the note Heywood appended to *An Apology for Actors* (1612), "To my approued good Friend, M. Nicholas Okes" [printer of this edition of the *Apology,* as W. Jaggard had been of *Troia Britannica.*]

Jaggard, says Heywood, would not print *Errata* after *Britaines Troy,* though the misprints were the printer's fault, being unwilling to "publish his owne disworkemanship." To Okes Heywood presents his congratulations on his efforts to "doe the author all the rights of the presse. Here, likewise, I must insert a manifest injury done me in that worke, by taking the two Epistles of *Paris to Helen,* and *Helen to Paris,* and printing them in a lesse volume [*The Passionate Pilgrim*] vnder the name of another [William Shakespeare], hee to doe himselfe right, hath since published them in his owne name: but as I must acknowledge my lines not worthy his patronage, vnder whom he hath publisht them, so the Author I know much offended with M. Jaggard (that altogether vnknowne to him) presumed to make so bold with his name. These and the like dishonesties I know you to be cleere of . . . ."

Heywood, of course, was a facile rhymer and has a nimble, superficial ease in telling his stories, but was quite without style or artistic responsibility. He writes in a rather rough enjambed heroic couplet, the heavy rhyme-words of which are uncomfortably emphatic in the reading, and does not hesitate at any clumsy expedient to hitch his verse along. *E.g.,*

Why should thy [ou] fly? Thy fore-sheets and thy Mizen
Why swell they with the wind? No Troy is risen
For thee again to sacke, here are no brals,
No man thy Mates, and thee to battle cals.[19]

Why could not his blind lusts *Aegistus* bridle?
Will you needs know, th' Adulterer was still Idle,
When others laboured *Islion* to annoy,
And lay strong siege about the wals of *Troy,*
Abroad he war'd not, nor at home he law'd,
His thoughts no nauall office could applaud.[20]

Sir Thomas Overbury's version of the *Remedia Amoris* (first printed in 1620) has the melancholy interest of all the few pages from the pen of that high-spirited and finely trained gentleman. It might well be companion to *The Wife* among Overbury's literary efforts to break up the connection between Somerset and Lady Essex. In the version Ovid's genial amplifications are remorselessly cut down, and his pleasant tattling mythology almost wholly omitted. The poem thus abridged has lost its humor and the charm of a heightened style, and taken on the dry hardness characteristic of Overbury. The translation is in heroic couplets, by this time become the recognized equivalent for Ovid's elegiacs, and a frequent form for reflective poetry in English. But several generations were to pass before the capabilities of the closed heroic couplet for this purpose were developed. It is a rigid undistinguished type of verse in Shakespeare, clumsy in Ben Jonson, and loutish in Marston. Donne, indeed, as paradoxical in his meter as in everything else, succeeded in giving a force of his own to his apparently careless versification. In spite of occasional graceful passages in *Hero and Leander* made up of closed couplets, and of some firmly minted and clearly ringing couplets in Bishop Hall's satires, the age had not yet learned the "excellence of rhyme" in pointing the couplet, and ease of manipulation in forming it. In such work as Overbury's and other forgotten Elizabethan and Jacobean writers of the closed couplet is to be found the justification for the complacence of Dryden and his contemporaries as to their achievements in versification—a complacence at first sight quite astonishing when the reader compares their work with the lofty blank

[19]P. 411.
[20]P. 412.

verse, the rich stanza-forms, and the magical lyrics of the Elizabethan age.

Leonard Digges's translation of Claudian's *Raptus Proserpinae* (1617) is the quite undisciplined work of a youth of talent. In his dedication to his sister, Lady Palmer, wife of Sir Anthony Palmer, Digges says the version "was intended as a Patterne for a piece of needle-work (I knew you were about;) for which purpose, I perswade my selfe, no Poeticall Authour will with more variety furnish you, then *Claudian.*" The translation, without losing its character as a translation, is freely amplified, having about twenty-five hundred lines to the thirteen hundred of the original. If not distinguished, it is not unpleasant. The diction is sometimes "low" without any gain in specific vigor: The rector of the damn'd . . . *bustles* to and fro to find a way to earth. (Sig. F2 *v*) ; his coursers are *foggy;* Aegaeon is long *cabb'd* up in *little ease* (Sig. C1 *r*) ; his coursers feel the *tarry* whip [merely *black,* because hell is dark] (Sig. F3 *v*) ; a *crew* of blest Elyzian saints thus sweetly sing (Sig. G3 *r*). The poem is interpreted in its Historicall Sense, its Naturall Sense, and its Allegorical Sense. That is to say, it is interpreted first, as the mythologizing of an actual event in history, when Orion King of the Molossians stole away the daughter of Ceres, Queen of Sicily; secondly, as symbolical of the burial and renewal of life in the seed in tillage; and thirdly as typifying moral doctrines: the insolence of the rich, and the justice of over-ruling Providence. The verse is in the enjambed couplet, the accepted verse of the day, and is very fluent and smooth.

On the title-page of the first edition of the *Batrachomyomachia* of William Fowldes (1603; 2nd ed. 1634) appear these words: "couertly decyphering the estate of these times." It is difficult to find in the poem any reference to the public affairs or to the social conditions of the time. There is apparently some definite allusion to a chancery case in which a connection of Fowldes's, by name Hargreves, was involved. Fowldes himself, as the title-page of his second edition informs us at length, was a cursitor of the court of Chancery. At the end of the poem is a letter in verse to a cousin, Master Ambrose Hargreves, in which the recent death of the cousin's father is lamented, and reference is made to a slander against the dead man, which no one uttered while he lived. The slanderers, shepherds in seeming, wrapped in sheep's clothing are described as in truth bears, wolves, vultures; a herd of swine led by a grunting boar. At the end of the poem, accented by quotation marks, appear the lines:

> "For if blacke *Crabs* do chance to part the fray,
> Small is their gaine that beare the best away."

The note is appended: *Hodie sub hominum specie, Cancri causas agunt.* The amiable pun on *cancri* and *chancery* is a jest such as would appeal to "gentle Dulness." And the *toz* may well have some cryptic allusion to Hargreves.

The version is enormously expanded in order to acquire the dignity aimed at by diffuse elaborate description. On the other hand, the monotonous style lacks pomp and the rhythm of magnificence, and the humor of the accumulation of adjectives at the end about the crabs is not even ventured upon. These are defects in skill; but the poem presents an inherent difficulty in the humorous names, not translatable, difficult to replace by equivalents, and deadly dull when explained by notes.

The version is in an eight-line stanza, not unpleasant, of which the following passage affords a fair illustration.

> Next with a corslet they defend the heart,
> Not made of steele, but of an old straw-hat,
> With which before they did award that part,
> Against the forces of the greedy *Cat*:
>
> > A piece of leather on their backe they don,
> > Which serues in stead of an habergion.
> > The bottome of a candlestick doth stand,
> > For target or a buckler in their hand:
>
> Small brazen pinnes they brandish like a speare,
> And toss their needles like strong pikes about;
> A walnut shell for helmet they doe beare,
> After that they had eate the kernell out.
>
> > And thus they march to fight that bloudy fray,
> > Vaunting in armour and their proud array
> > For weapons vnto force fresh courage bring.
> > A *Mouse* in armer doth thinke himselfe a King.[21]

---

[21] Sig. Eiii *r.* (Ed. 1603).

Sir Thomas Wrothe (not unknown to Americans from his connection with the colonization of this country) printed as a good many gentlemen did some of his literary exercitations, including the second book of the *Aeneid,* (1620) under the title *The Destruction of Troy,* bound with *A Centurie of Epigrams,* and *A Motto upon the Creede.* The work, being dedicated to Viscount Lisle, must antedate 1618, when Lisle became Earl of Leicester.

Wrothe prints at the beginning:

A request to the reader . . . Give not vp your casting verdict rashly, though you find mee sometimes wandering (which I purposely do) out of the visible bounds; but deliberately take notice that I stray not from the scope and intent of the author, iustified by the best commentaries: so I leaue you to reade, to vnderstand, and to encrease.

Th. W.

As might be inferred, the version is an inexact paraphrase largely expanded. The version is in the obsolescent fourteener, almost a guarantee of dilution and clumsy homeliness. Wrothe makes some attempt to escape the monotony of the form by enjambement, but the verse resists this treatment at his hands. A brief specimen of this late example of the decaying form may be of interest.

This way I tooke (well knowne to me), unto the highest place
Of all the Pallace; from whose top the Troians flung apace,
Both tymber, stones, and other loades; the turret soard'd so hie,
That from the same a man might all the Citie well descrie,
The ships, and tents pitcht by the Greekes; who then augment so fast,
That I aduis'd to ripp the floore, and boards at random cast [*ea lapsa*
    in W.'s text.]
The fall whereof rais'd fearefull shriekes, and murdred many men,
Yet still a new supplie succeades; nothing omitted then,
Nor stones, nor any kind of force, that might cause death, and blood:
At th' entrance of the Pallace gates the ruddy Pyrrhus stood;
Most proudly vaunting of himselfe, and glittering all in brasse
His wonted warr-like muniments: much like the snake he was,
Who lurkes in crannies of the earth whilst winters rage doth last,
But when the warmth of summer comes, and his old garment cast,
And new put on, brings forth himselfe, of late made fresh and young,
And seekes the poysonous hearbes againe, licking his triple tongue,
And now fierce Pyrrhus did approach, and Periphas ensu'th,
Automedon the Charioteer, and all the Scyrian youth

Follow'd him close into the house, whilst we vpon them drop
Death and destruction; they again tosse fire to vs o' the top:
But when the barricado'd dores did giue them all repulse,
Their leader with an Engine comes, and therewith did impulse
The brazen dores to yeeld him way, who no resistance brookes,
But with the forwardst was the first to lift them off the hookes.
When this was don, his irefull mind not pleased therewithall,
The postes and beames he hewed downe, and so lookes through the
     wall,
As through a window, for he made his sight so wide a way,
That he and his confederates without did plaine display
The roomes, and all that was within, and how we did prepare,
To frustrate their attempt; this while, within the pallace women were,
Weeping and wailing, with whose cries the spacious pallace rings,
And in the ayre to their laments a dolefull eccho sings;[22]

A paraphrase of Juvenal's tenth satire was licensed in 1617, with the title, *The World's a liar and will deceiue you,* and published with the title *That which seems best is worst, with the tragicall narration of Virginia's death inserted.* The author, "W. B.," frankly avows his purpose of dealing freely with the poem. His motto is: *Nec verbum verbo curabit reddere fidus interpres,* to which he subjoins,

> The pith is Iuuenals, but not the rime
> All that is good is his, the rest is mine.

(If Juvenal had been writing rime, he would not have written this one.) The whole story of Virginia is worked in as an integral part of the poem, the references to Hippolytus and Bellerophon are greatly enlarged; the whole poem, indeed, has received many additions, especially toward the end. The author has some rude vigor, diminished by his errors in translation, which not merely depart from the original but blunt its point. The work is crude alike in its assault on sin and in its pathos, and disfigures Juvenal's dignified conclusion with an essentially vulgar diatribe against lust, especially that lust "which honestie itself doth call." The work is in a rough enjambed heroic couplet. It has been attributed to William Barksted, but can by no possibility be his. W. B. could never have written:

> As glow wormes adde a tincture to the night
> Glimmering in pallid fire vpon some greene;

---

[22] Ll. 445 ff.

or :

> Eyes like two stars falne from their proper spheares
> As if they scorn'd the beaten pathes of heauen.

Barksted could not have written the diatribe on lust; and indeed, as Dr. Grosart suggests, was too illiterate to undertake a satire of Juvenal.

These minor translations (except of course Marlowe's) are all the divertisements of men whose minds were engaged elsewhere—done without a sense of the obligations of scholarship or the severe labor required to obtain effective expression. This, at least, is not true of Ben Jonson's professed translations of Latin verse (*Ars Poetica,* a few odes of Horace, a fragment attributed to Petronius, and Martial's epigram to Julius Martialis on *A Happy Life*). These ill-starred versions, though not printed until 1640, were done and made known to Jonson's circle of literary friends before 1619, as is shown by his references to them in his conversations with Drummond. They are in curious contrast with the felicitous adaptations scattered through his works. Swinburne's comment,—"A worse translator than Ben Jonson never committed a double outrage on two languages at once,"[23]—though it can only have been written in ignorance of Drant,—has its justification in the perverseness with which Jonson, a scholar and a poet, having once adopted a wrong principle of translation applied it obstinately, in spite of the failures which it brought about, and at which he would have scoffed in another man. His *Ars Poetica* is singled out by Dryden as the horrible example to illustrate the unsoundness of literalism. The others are all *tours de force,* being translated in defiance of the laws of poetry, of the Latin language, of the English language, and of Ben Jonson, line for line into rhymed verse with the closest possible literality. The *Beatus ille,* apparently his favorite, was indeed, the least unsuccesful.[24] Barten (Bartram) Holyday's versions of Persius, (1616 &c), Horace (1652, 1653) and Juvenal (posthumously printed, 1673) if not adequate in style are at least conscientious in their effort to understand the original by serious study with the assistance of the best learning of the age. In the Persius Holyday cites twelve commentaries as having been consulted by him. In their notes

[23]Swinburne, Algernon C., *A Study of Ben Jonson,* (1889) p. 111.
[24]Jonson, B., *Works,* ed. Herford and Simpson, vol. ii (1925), p. 407.

there is, of course, much repetition; but of them all Bond
(1614) has the most influence. Bond's occasional suggestions
of English equivalents for the original are commonly adopted,
and most of his individual suggestions are followed; even the
turns of phrase in his notes are often to be found in the version.

In a translation of Persius's so-called Satires probably the
most that can be done is to produce a readable expression of
the ideas, with such occasional plays on words or ingenious
equivalents of phrase as luck may bring the translator. Barten Holyday makes no effort to reproduce the plays on words;
and in many cases seems to have missed the point, the ingenious
idea underlying the paronomasia. He has embodied the explanation in his translation, thus expanding the text, and inevitably weakening it, and the familiarity of his diction is less
appropriate to the original, strained and perverse as it is, than
a more dignified level of expresion. The version is in the
run-on couplet almost conventional by this time, and moves
fluently though ungracefully. The Juvenal of Holyday, though
not printed till 1673, must be a product of this same period,
and is based on the same careful preliminary study, including
the examination of the manuscript of Juvenal the possession
of which gratified Ben Jonson so highly.

Chapman's translations may well conclude this survey of the
verse.

The quality of Chapman's character which is most fundamental in his poetry and in all that we know of his life is his
ardor, his capacity for warm and sincere emotion. In all his
poems, in spite of his obscure and perversely tormented style,
this ardor here and there bursts into a flame, and continues
throughout his life, supporting him and giving him eager delight through the long labor of his Homeric translations. This
emotional force, it is true, often leads him astray. He is too
often testy, too often arrogant and self-assertive. He has a
power of scorn, as well as of admiration and reverence. But
in the main, his mind is turned toward noble and admirable
things. He takes that "delight in the goings-on" of nature and
of men which Wordsworth declares is the poet's fundamental
endowment. Hence he approaches Homer with an eager reverence and devotion, and with an essential sympathy that went
far to qualify him as a translator.

He accepts literally the Greek view of Homer as "of all books extant in all kinds, . . . the first and best," as the "president of all learning, virtue, valour, honour, and society," as the "great inflamer of all powers that move in human souls." "Out of him, according to our most grave and judicial Plutarch, are all Arts deduced, confirmed, or illustrated." He was a philosopher and a teacher, "full of direction and government to all estates; stern anger and the affrights of war, bearing the main face of his subject, soldiers shall never spend their idle hours more profitably, than with his studious and industrious perusal; in whose honours his deserts are infinite. Counsellors have never better oracles than his lines; fathers have no morals so profitable for their children as his counsels; nor shall they ever give more honoured injunction than to learn Homer without book, that being continually conversant in him, his height may descend to their capacities, and his substance prove their worthiest riches. Husbands, wives, lovers, friends, and allies, having in him mirrors for all their duties . . . ."[25] Earnest, energetic, high-minded, reverent, with a devotion to Homer that might fairly be called superstitious, if Chapman could give expression to these qualities in his translation, he could not fail of producing a noble and vital work. And as the world knows, he did.

Chapman's method of translation is the same as North's, except that Chapman labored longer and harder than North to get at his author's meaning. He was not simply the follower of another man's mind. He read the Latin translations of Valla and Eobanus Hessus, he read the commentaries especially of Spondanus, and he painstakingly read the Greek. His few notes on his interpretations shew that he thought long and earnestly over the meaning of Homer, and though his divergences from the earlier commentators are nearly all crotchety and over-ingenious he was at least genuinely independent; and when he accepts an interpretation, he accepts it because he is convinced, not because he bows to authority. He labored and reflected until he had a clear conception of the general design of his original, of the characters and the moral ideas of the work, and of the meaning of individual passages.

---

[25]*Achilles Shield* (1598) "To the Understander"; Shepherd's edition of Chapman, III, 14.

Having brooded upon the thought of a passage until he had become possessed by it, he took it not bit by bit but in large masses, and expressed the idea freely and as energetically as possible, in his own style, without anxious or critical reference to the original. He believed in inspiration, and in his own inspiration, and rushed at his work, making not a mosaic of carefully fitted small fragments, but a connected composition, done at a heat. Such a method of translation, if the result of faithful preparation, should become steadily easier, and so it was with Chapman. The first part of the *Iliad* was the most difficult for him; the first two books were twice completely written: when the first twelve books were issued, and when the complete version appeared. There were on the whole but few corrections in the other books from the "twelve books" to the "twenty-four books"; and Chapman tells us that the last twelve books were the work of only fifteen weeks. Perhaps they should have taken more; but it seems unlikely that Chapman would have effected much by detailed and petty correction. The faults of his version were inherent in his conception of poetic style, and no revision would have affected them. As regards the literal sense of Homer, Chapman nearly always understood it, and cannot be charged with many errors in his actual rendering. It is the point of view and the style of Chapman that are un-Homeric.

Chapman thought of poetry not merely or primarily as a source of delight but as the best and deepest of teachers, either by its typical presentation of the heights and depths of human nature, or by having a divine origin. And he believed that true poetry can be created and even understood only by inspiration, as the allegorical communicating of moral truth. As he himself says in the Epistle Dedicatory of the *Odyssey*.[26]

.... Nor is this all-comprising Poesy fantastic or mere fictive; but the most material and doctrinal illations of truth, both for all manly information of manners in the young, all prescription of justice, and even Christian piety, in the most grave and high governed. To illustrate both which, in both kinds, with all height of expression, the Poet creates both a body and a soul in them. Wherein, if the body (being the letter or history) seems fictive, and beyond possibility to bring into act, the sense then and allegory, which is the soul, is to be sought, which intends a more eminent expressure of Virtue

[26]Ed. Shepherd, II, 237.

for her loveliness, and of Vice for her ugliness, in their several effects; going beyond the life than any art within life can possibly delineate. Why then is fiction to this end so hateful to our true ignorants? Or why should a poor chronicler of a Lord Mayor's naked truth (that peradventure will last his year) include more worth with our modern wizards than Homer for his naked Ulysses clad in eternal fiction? But this proser Dionysius, and the rest of these grave and reputatively learned—that dare undertake for their gravities the headstrong censure of all things, and challenge the understanding of these toys in their childhoods; when even these childish vanities retain deep and most necessary learning enough in them to make them children in their ages, and teach them while they live—are not in these absolute divine infusions allowed either voice or relish: for, Qui Poeticas ad fores accedit, etc. (says the divine philosopher) he that knocks at the gates of the Muses, sine Musarum furore, is neither to be admitted entry, nor a touch at their thresholds; his opinion of entry ridiculous, and his presumption impious. Nor must Poets themselves (might I a little insist on these contempts, not tempting too far your Lordship's Ulyssean patience) presume to these doors without the truly genuine and peculiar induction. There being in Poesy a twofold rapture,—or alienation of soul, as the abovesaid teacher terms it,—one insania, a disease of the mind, and a mere madness, by which the infected is thrust beneath all the degrees of humanity: et ex homine, brutum quodammodo redditur:—(for which poor Poesy, in this diseased and impostorous age, is so barbarously vilified;)—the other is, divinus furor, by which the sound and divinely healthful supra hominis naturam erigitur, et in Deum transit. One a perfection directly infused from God; the other an infection obliquely and degenerately proceeding from man. Of the divine fury, my Lord, your Homer hath ever been both first and last instance; being pronounced absolutely, τὸν σοφώτατον, καὶ τὸν θειότατον ποιητήν, "THE MOST WISE AND MOST DIVINE POET."

Poetry of any value, then, must be difficult,—

that Poesy should be as pervial as oratory, and plainness her special ornament, were the plain way to barbarism, and to make the ass run proud of his ears, to take away strength from lions, and give camels horns.

That Energia, or clearness of representation, required in absolute poems, is not the perspicuous delivery of a low invention; but high and hearty invention expressed in significant and unaffected phrase . . . Obscurity in affection of words and indigested conceits, is pedantical and childish; but where it shroudeth itself in the heart of his subject, uttered with fitness of figure and expressive epithets, with that darkness will I still labour to be shadowed. Rich minerals

are digged out of the bowels of the earth, not found in the super-
ficies and dust of it . . .[27]

These words were indeed penned in an introduction to one
of Chapman's earliest and most affectedly ingenious poems,
but the doctrine which they inculcate was always religiously
accepted by him. Indeed, he takes a pleasure in his ingenuity
and uncommonness of style.

> . . . the truth is, my desire and strange disposition in all things I
> write, is to set down uncommon, and most profitable coherents for
> the time: yet further removed from cold affectation than from the
> most popular and cold disgestion. And I ever imagine that as
> Italian and French Poems to our studious linguists win much of
> their discountried affection, as well because the understanding of
> foreign tongues is sweet to their apprehension, as that the manner
> and matter is pleasing; so my far-fetched, and as it were beyond-
> sea manner of writing, if they would take as much pains for their
> poor countrymen as for a proud stranger when they once understand
> it, should be much more gracious for their choice conceits than a
> discourse that falls naked before them and hath nothing but what
> mixeth itself with ordinary table-talk. For my variety of new words,
> I have none ink-pot I am sure you know, but such as I give passport
> with such authority, so significant and not ill-sounding, that if my
> country language were an usurer, or a man of this age speaking
> it, he would thank me for enriching him. Why, alas, will my young
> master the reader affect nothing common, and yet like nothing extra-
> ordinary? Swaggering is a new word amongst them, and round-
> headed custom gives it privilege with much imitation, being created
> as it were by a natural Prosopopeia without etymology or derivation;
> and why may not an elegancy authentically derived, and as I may say
> of the upper house, be entertained as well in their lower consultation
> with authority of Art, as their own forgeries licked up by nature?
> All tongues have enriched themselves from their original (only the
> Hebrew and Greek tongues which are not spoken amongst us) with
> good neighbourly borrowing, and as with infusion of fresh air, and
> nourishment of new blood in their still growing bodies, and why may
> not ours? Chaucer, by whom we will needs authorize our true
> English, had more new words for his time than any man needs to
> devise now. And therefore for current wits to cry from standing
> brains, like a brood of frogs from a ditch, to have the ceaseless
> flowing river of our tongue turned into their frog-pool, is a song
> far from their arrogation of sweetness, and a sin that would soon
> bring the plague of barbarism amongst us . . .[28]

Such ideals of style are in themselves unimpeachable, but
as they were applied by Chapman they encouraged his propen-

---

[27]Epistle dedicatory to *Ovid's Banquet of Sense* (1595). Shepherd II, 21.
[28]*Achilles Shield* (1598) "To the Understander." Shepherd III, 14.

sity to write in a style difficult not because of the inherent profundity of his ideas, but because of an excess of involution in syntax and of ingenuity in diction. Matthew Arnold has put with clear finality Chapman's un-Homeric quality in saying that Homer is simple in thought, plain and direct in expression, while Chapman is complex in thought, ingenious and elaborate in expression.

But more profound and more subtle than Chapman's alterations of Homer's style is his alteration of Homer's spirit, from its objective delight in the energetic manifestation of human activity, its *gusto*, to a tone of moral judgment, expressed in words of approval or reprobation. To this radical departure from his original Chapman was directed by the fundamentally false principle accepted from the Greek tradition, which made of Homer a sacred book, the source and guide of all human arts, reasoning that because he was a great poet and in some sort a great teacher he must therefore be filled with a moral spirit and communicate definite and useful lessons about conduct. First of all, Chapman changes the sentiment of the original by the addition of epithets, involving admiration, sympathy, or disapproval. Thus Priam in Homer is *aged,* or *the aged man;* in Chapman he is the *kind old king,* (xxii, 36). In Homer he beats his *head;* in Chapman his *reverend* head (xxii, 32). In Homer, Hector is bid not to *await this man;* in Chapman to fly this man, this *homicide* (xxii, 36). Chapman, without warrant in any words of his original, makes Achilles *constant* in his mourning for his dead friend, Patroclus (xxiv, 2); Paris becomes *proud* Paris, his *licentious son* (xxiv, 28); Nestor addresses Achilles not as my *son* but as my *honourable* son (xxiii, 542); childish, *unworthy,* dares are not enough without blows to end the conflict between Aeneas and Achilles (xx, 196); Achilles is *the loving Cruel* (xxiii, 174). These epithets are nearly or quite conventional; and may well have been employed with little thought, or almost unconsciously; but they are opposed to the whole spirit of Homer and deeply color the version with an alien hue. But in addition to these apparently casual words Chapman adds phrases or whole passages which must have been consciously intended to bring out the moral judgments that Chapman believed to be latent in Homer. Thus Achilles gives to Nestor a prize without a con-

test, saying not only, *"harsh age fetters you,"* but "Harsh age
. . . fetters you, *and honour sets you free"* (xxiii, 540). The
Myrmidons will eat, not merely *"when we have taken our fill of
bitter lamentation,"* but, "When with . . . woe our hearts have
felt delight *to do a virtuous soul right* (xxiii, 8)." Nestor tells
his son Antilochus that Jove and Neptune love him; Chapman
makes him say, *"thy grave virtues live,* Beloved of Jove and
Neptune (xxiii, 280)." Aeneas could taunt Achilles if he
would;—"we both know the race we are sprung of"; Chapman
adds, *"too gentle to bear fruits so rude* (xx, 187)." Hector
proposes to Achilles reciprocal vows before the gods that the
victor in the impending conflict shall do no outrage to the
body of the vanquished. He in abstract moral terms prays,
"do not see a *cruelty so foul* inflicted on me (xxii, 292-3)"
where Homer uses specific physical terms, "leave me not for
the dogs of the Achaeans to devour by the ships"; in Chapman
he begs, "to *sacred* fire turn thy *profane decrees* (xxii, 295),"
where Homer has him beg, "give me my due of fire after my
death." The additions of Chapman give to the gods moral
grounds for upholding vows:

> . . . they being worthiest witnesses
> Of all vows, *since they keep vows best,* before their Deities
> Let vows *of fit respect* pass both. (xxii, 217-219).

The refusal of Achilles is not alone stated, but formally
condemned:

> *These fair and temp'rate terms*
> *Far fled Achilles;* his brows bent . . .[xxii, 222-3) ;

and Hector responds with a reference to the common judgment
of civilized men in terms which Plutarch would have understood, but which would have been meaningless to Homer:

> I, knowing thee well, foresaw
> Thy now tried tyranny, *nor hop'd . or any other law,*
> *Of nature or of nations;* and that fear forc'd much more
> Than death my flight, which never touch'd at Hector's foot (xxii,
> 307-310). (Homer had said: "With full knowledge of thee do I
> look upon thee; I was not destin'd to persuade thee.")

Chapman's un-Homeric qualities, then, in both thought and
style, are not the result of haste, thoughtlessness, or negligence;
they are the consequences of a deliberate perversity, a theory of

poetry consciously accepted and carefully and consistently followed. Of such a translation done in such a spirit there are two diverse points of view,—Matthew Arnold's judgment of it on the basis of its fidelity—

> No one can tell [the translator] how Homer affected the Greeks; but there are those who can tell him how Homer affects *them*. These are scholars; who possess, at the same time with knowledge of Greek, adequate poetical taste and feeling. No translation will seem to them of much worth compared with the original; but they alone can say whether the translation produces more or less the same effect upon them as the original . . . Let [the translator] ask how his work affects those who both know Greek and can appreciate poetry . . . . I consider that when Bentley said of Pope's translation, "It was a pretty poem, but must not be called Homer," the work, in spite of all its power and attractiveness, was judged.[29]

The other is Swinburne's:

> . . . . considering the poems as in the main original works, the superstructure of a romantic poet on the submerged foundations of Greek verse, no praise can be too warm or high for the power, the freshness, the indefatigable strength and inextinguishable fire which animate this exalted work, and secure for all time that shall take cognizance of English poetry an honoured place in its highest annals for the memory of Chapman.[30]

It is the latter view which must ultimately be accepted. Let us be grateful for a fine and noble poem on any terms, and with any faults. Those translations which have meant the most in our literature have not been those most conspicuous for fidelity, but those which compensated for the loss inevitable in transplanting a great work from one language to the alien soil of another by the contribution of individual qualities of their own. It probably would be unfair to cite Fitzgerald's Omar Khayyam, for its compensating qualities are so much its own that it practically ceases to be a translation, but Frere's Aristophanes, even Jowett's Plato are not only free translations, but their literary qualities are independent—personal, added to or supplementing the original. The same is true of the finer Elizabethan translations—North's Plutarch, Adlington's *Thea-*

---

[29]Arnold, M. *On the Study of Celtic Literature and on Translations of Homer*, (1909) p. 143-4.

[30]Swinburne, Algernon, C. in the 9th edition of the *Encyclopedia Britannica*.

genes and Chariclea, Holland's Suetonius, Shelton's *Don Quixote.* Even the translators of the sacred words of Scripture gave to their version a manner different from that of the original; the New Testament in English has certainly a literary quality very different from the simple colloquialism of the original Greek, and obedient as the Old Testament is to the Hebrew, it is compelled at times to give a smoother quality to the violent energy of that powerful but rugged language. Chapman's Homer has a style,—a manner that was a real expression of Chapman's nature,—and not merely a conventional rhetoric, such as Pope's. Pope's simpler and easier version was naturally more popular; but a reader willing to give to Chapman the necessary attention will draw enough from his version to reward him for his trouble.

The fourteener in Chapman's hands is not a ballad meter. He has abandoned the cesural regularity of the earlier translators, and writes in swinging periods of boldly run-on lines. His verse strides forward with great steps, not graceful, but large and firm.

The *Odyssey* of Chapman is in many points like the *Iliad.* It has the same warmth in the expression of emotion; such passages as the hospitality shown to Odysseus by Eumaeus, the death of Argus, the cautious reserve of Penelope when her husband is made known to her, all being full of Chapman's fine and noble sense of the greatness of human feelings. The translation, also, manifests the same ingenuity of paraphrase, and only too often substitutes abstract nouns for Homer's direct personal verbs. The sentences, however, are not so parenthetical or the syntax so inverted as in the *Iliad*, and hence the reading of the *Odyssey* is easier. But Coleridge's preference of Chapman's *Odyssey* to his *Iliad* is plainly due to his enjoying the *Odyssey* itself the more—as must people do, until they come to know the *Iliad* very well. In spite of its tedious monotony of too similar slayings and the interruptions of the main story by episodes, the *Iliad* is nobler and more full of spirit than the *Odyssey,* and the noblest and most spirited of Chapman's work is to be found in it.

The *Odyssey,* like all of Chapman's translations except the *Iliad* itself, is in the enjambed heroic couplet which had by this time established itself as the accepted form for the trans-

lation of continuous verse. In Chapman's hands the couplet
is varied, fluent, and vigorous, but not so stirring or powerful
as the fourteeners of the *Iliad*. Chapman carried on his work
to include all the poems associated in antiquity with the name
of Homer: the *Hymns,* the *Epigrams,* and the *Batrachomyomachia,* and finished his labors in the field of Ionic poetry with
the *Works and Days* of Hesiod. They are pieces of honest
work, possessing and requiring little distinction of manner or
poetic energy. In the notes on the Hesiod, Chapman constantly
cites Melanchthon; but I have not been able to find in Melanchthon's commentary a great deal of what Chapman gives him
credit for. Unfortunately the other editions of Hesiod from
the late sixteenth and early seventeenth century have not been
accesible to me, so that I have not found the source of Chapman's commentary.

Last of all we have to speak of translations meant to aid
pupils in their study of Latin. Richard Bernard, adopting
Maurice Kyffin's version of Terence's *Andria,* completed the
rest of the plays, and issued the Terence as a book suitable for
young students. He dedicates his work,—

> To the vvorshipful yong gentleman and of vertuous education M.
> *Christopher Wray,* sonne and heyre to the Right worshipfull Sir
> William Wray knight, and to the rest of the toward yong Gentle-
> men his brethren, nephewes of the vertuous and true religious Ladies,
> the Ladie *Bowes* and the Ladie *Sainctpoll* his very bountifull Patron-
> nesses, R. B. wisheth encrease of knowledge, vertue, and honour,
> with happie daies. . . .

The tone of the dedication is that of an elderly tutor addressing
his pupils :—

> . . . Your tender yeares . . . I offer you here, that which *Fortune*
> hath vouchsafed to fauour me withall, a Latin authour taught to
> speake English; a comicall Poet, pithie, pleasant, and very profitable:
> as merry as Eutrapeles, as graue as *Cato,* as ethicall as *Plato.* He
> can play craftily the cousener, and cunningly the clowne: he will
> tell you of the nature of the fraudulent flatterer, the grimme and
> greedie old Sire, the roysting ruffian, the minsing mynion, the beastly
> baud; that in telling the truth by these figments, men might become
> wise to auoid such vices, and learne to practise vertue: which was
> *Terence* purpose in setting of these comedies forth in latin; mine in
> translating them into english: & this end I desire you to propound

to yourselues in reading them, so shall you vse them, & not as
most doe such authors, abuse them . . . .

Farewell. *Epworth* in Lincolneshiere this 30. of Maie

Yours in the Lord

Rich. Bernard.

In a Latin letter, *"ad lectorem,"* he says in effect, "Some of the
reasons why I have translated Terence you may find in the preceding letter; some if you read the work. For in my view it is
of much consequence that tender and youthful minds, which
should be led, not driven, to learning, should at first read such
authors as may at once form the style and delight the soul.
Terence both charms and instructs by the richness and beauty
of his expression, with which it is easy to enrich one's style, and
by the truth and variety of his representation of humanity,
such that he becomes in jesting a teacher of morals. Hence
no author is better suited to youth. Some will scorn me for
translating him into English; yet he translated his own work
from Greek."

Each division of the play, *i.e.,* prologue, or scene, contains:
(1) The Latin text with marginal notes on the rhetorical points,
(*argumentum a maiori; praeteritio*), or the character exhibited
(*prudens Simonis consilium; Sedulitas paterna erga filios*),
or grammatical difficulty, or a moral sentence (*nemo repente
fit turpissimus*); (2) *Expositiones morales*: the fundamental
moral ideas of the passages; (3) The English translation;
(4) *Formulae loquendi,* Latin and English; (5) *Sententiae,*
Latin.

The *Formulae loquendi* are drawn mainly from Udall's
Flores: Nos opinantes ducimur falso gaudio. He makes us
beleeue the moone is made of a greene cheese. He brings vs
silly ones, into a fooles paradise—*Circuitione vsus est.* He
went about the bush with him—*Quid agam incertum est.* I
am in a mammoring what I should doe. *Pereo funditus* . .
I shall neuer be my owne man. *Paulo momento huc illuc im-
pellitur.* He is as wavering as a wether-cocke. He is heere
and there all in a moment. Theires as much holde to his woord
as to take a wet eele by the taile.

The *sententiae,—Meritorum simus memores; amatores,
stulti, temerarii, pervicaces, & tandem miseri sunt,*—are not al-

ways from Terence, but are often commonplaces of reflection on the preceding scene.

The *Andria,* as has been said, is from Kyffin, with a few unimportant changes. The *Hecyra, Adelphi,* and *Phormio* are stiff and awkward in expression, and have the shadow of the Latin idiom hanging over them. The *Eunuchus* and *Heautontimoroumenos* are more spirited; but the book as a whole in spite of its abundance of English colloquial expressions is nothing more than a creditable school-book.

Corderius's plan of helping pupils by giving them in print the detailed construing and parsing of elementary texts had already been introduced into English by a version of his construing of Cicero's *Letters* (1575) and of Cato's *Distichs* (1577, 1584). A certain Simon Sturtevant applied the system in his work entitled, "The Etymologist of Aesop's Fables, etc." (1602) to the construing of Aesop and Phaedrus word by word, thus going further than Corderius. He defends his system against the obvious objections that *viva voce* assistance is more effectual, that the system will make the pupil lazy, and that the book will be used as a trot in class; and maintains that the use of his book will correct faulty pronunciation, inaccurate interpretation, and misconstruing, and will assist the pupils' memory.

Finally, John Brinsley the elder put forth a great body of laborious translations for the use of schools. His purpose was to make it easy to apply generally the method of studying the classics urged by Ascham in the *Schoolmaster.* This method, suggested to Ascham by a passage in the first book of Cicero's *De Oratore,* was to translate a passage from a foreign author into English, and then to translate the English version back into the original, keeping up the practice until the student became able to write fluently in the foreign language. (It was by similar practice in first taking to pieces papers from the *Spectator* and then recreating them that Franklin formed his English style.) As Brinsley says, the double translation though well suited to private instruction, "is very hard to be performed in the common schooles, especially for lacke of time to trie and compare euery schollar's translation." His plan was to provide pupils with a translation of their Latin arranged after a standard "grammatical or natural" order. With

each passage studied the pupils went through five steps: (1)
they recast the Latin in the natural order; (2) they construed
the passage word by word; (3) they parsed it similarly; (4)
they turned the English back into Latin word by word; (5)
they compared their version with the original, rearranging
their material, and thus gradually learning the principles of
the Latin order. The practical use of the book was to make it
possible for a pupil-teacher to keep a check on the pupil's work,
and for the pupil to learn his lessons without continual recourse to the master. The translation is not interlinear, but
separate from the text, to avoid idleness and deceit, and the
recitations test the pupils and keep them to their work. The
ultimate purpose is to give the pupils the ability to write and
speak Latin, getting moral good by the way from the text
studied.

The translations are printed usually in three columns. In
the inner column the substance of the Latin is set forth and explained briefly. The middle column contains the translation;
the outer column alternative translations, either more or less
literal than that in the second column.

As Brinsley explains his scheme in his translation of part
of the first book of the *Metamorphoses*:

> The inmost columnes containe the sum of the history, which is to
> be first read and vnderstood.
>
> The second containe the Grammaticall translation made plaine and
> easie according to the propriety and purity of our own tongue so
> far as Grammar will well beare.
>
> The third haue variety first of grammaticall constructions where
> the English is ouer harsh to be placed in the translation, noted with
> an *Asteriske,* or little starre thus (*) ; and secondly variety of other
> phrases better to expresse the meaning, directed by an ( ).
>
> The fourth [the Ovid alone has a fourth column] sheweth the
> resoluing of sundry difficulties or allusions and the like, for better
> vnderstanding of the author, with some more obscure notations,
> notes & other necessary points of learning.[31]

Obviously the translation must be absolutely subservient to
the Latin; it must be as near the Latin as the English idiom
will permit. No freedom, power, or grace is possible in such

[31]Sig. Aii *v.*

wooden work. An example from Cicero's *De Officiis* (1616)
p. 157, illustrates the method clearly.

Inner	*Middle*	*Outer*
	Q Howbeit this case indeed is not onely of a ciuill consideration, For it concerneth also the warlike; because it was done by force and by *Q* strong hand: yet the very same was	*Q* Although this thing in truth is not onely of the domesticall reason, [or a ciuill matter] for it toucheth also the warlike [or belongeth to martiall feats] &c.
This point hee further confirmeth by a worthie and general approued speech of his owne, howsoeuer soon enuious and lewde persons did carpe at him for it: to wit, this;	done by *q* the counsell of the citie, without an army. That also in *Q* a worthy [speach] vvherein I heare *q* that I am wont to be *q* taxed of enuious and lewde [persons].	*Q* hand *Q* citie counsell *Q* the best *Q* me to be wont *q* inuaded, set vpon or touched.
Let armes giue place to the gowne; the laurel to the oratours tongue.	*Let *q* armes giue place to the *q* gowne; Let the *q* laurell yeeld to the [Oratours] tongue.	*Let wars giue place to peace, let the laurell branch [or garland] be graunted to the oratour. *q* weapons or wars, because weapons are a signe of war. *q* gowne put for peace whereof it is a signe, or for ciuill magistracy. *q* the laurell branch a signe of eloquence or a reward thereof.

Directions for the use of the books in schools are given with
each translation, and more fully in Chapter VIII of *Ludus
Literarius*. The instructions given with Cicero's *De Officiis*
(1616) are briefest of all, and as clear as any.

An Admonition to the louing Reader.

Vnderstand, first, the matter contained in each Chapter, by reading
ouer and obseruing wel the inmost columne. Then, try so farre as
need is, for the true construing and resoluing therof out of the
Authour it selfe, both for Grammar and phrase; and also to read
it into a good english stile, by the helpe of the second columne and

the margents. And lastly (which is the principall) practice, out of the same (viz. the second columne and margents alone) to read daily some part of it, out of the translation into the Latine of the Author, studying it out of the English alone; trying by it, and a little help of the latine booke, where, need requireth (as I haue aduised chiefly for *Corderius*) how neer you can come to expresse *Tully* liuelily for Latine, phrase, composition, and whatsoeuer elegancy besides. After each sentence, reading the author, to see how neer you came, marking where you failed, with the reason of it. So in a Schoole, cause euery one in a Forme, or so many as you would haue to practice this together, thus first to construe *extempore* daily euery one a peece out of the Latine bookes alone, without the English; onely one of them by the English to aske and direct, where any one failes. Afterwardes, or euery other day, let euery one read his peece out of the English alone, none hauing any Latin book, but onely some one to be in place of the Master, to obserue, and where they faile to direct; first by asking of him who readeth, and then of others, after helping; so posing for sense, phrase, latinisme, both out of the Latin and English, as it is directed in the *Grammar-Schoole*. And then, I hope, you will in time seale with me vpon experience, whatsoeuer I haue written, concerning the benefit of such Grammaticall translations in this behalfe.

Brinsley in *Ludus Literarius* gives the following "list of school authours translated or in hand."

Pueriles confabulatiunculae [Ptd. 1617]
Sententiae pueriles [Ptd. 1612]
Cato [Ptd. 1612]
Corderius dialogues [Ptd. 1636]
Esops fables (Lic. 1617. Ptd. 1624]
Tullies Epistles gathered by *Sturmius*
Tullies office, with the books adioind to them *De Amicitia, Senectute, Paradoxes* [Ptd. 1616 &c.]
Ouid de Tristibus
Ouid's Metamorphoses [i.e. Bk. i, ll.1-567, Ptd. 1618, 1656]
Virgil Eclogues with de Apibus [Ptd. 1620, 1633, &c.]

In addition to these translations, Brinsley printed a version of Publilius Syrus and of Isocrates *Ad Demonicum* in 1622.

Brinsley had a firm conviction of the importance of his work for the whole British realm, and especially for the poor schools in the backward parts of it. His dedication of *Ludus Literarius* to the two princes, Henry, Prince of Wales, and Charles, then Duke of York, expresses his manly confidence in the value of his method, and his devotion to the idea to which he gave his whole activity.

. . . And what is it, which might still more aduance you in the eyes and hearts of all the people of your most noble Fathers Dominion; then if now from your first yeares, you might beginne to be the blessed instrument, of the Almighty, of an euerlasting benefite to the present and all succeeding generations? whereby you might knit all hearts more surely vnto the holy God, and his supreame deputy here amongst vs; as also to your selues his Regall issue, and vnto yours for euer. Accept therefore, to this purpose (I beseech you) this weake labour thus begun, of searching out, and inquiring of all the speediest, surest and most easie entrance and way to all good learning in our Grammar schooles. To the end that those rare helpes of knowledge, which the Lord hath graunted to this age (some of the principall wherof haue been scarce knowen, or very little practiced, so farre as I can find; and most of the rest haue bin only knowen amongst some few) might by your Princely fauours, be made common vnto all, for the publique good of the present age, and of all times to come. The Lord hath giuen vnto your Highnesse and Excellency, to be born, and to liue in the time of most glorious light, and knowledge; in which, if the experiments of sundry of the learnedest, & most happily experienced Schoolemasters and others, were gathered into one short sum, all good learning (which is the chiefest glory of a nation) would daily flourish more & more, and be conueyed to all places & times; that not only this age present, but also al posterity should haue iust cause euermore to magnifie the God of glory for you: for how must this needes oblige all sorts, if this heauenly gift of learning, might thorough you be attained with much more ease, delight, & certainty; and also in shorter time, with lesse charges to Parents, without that extreame sharpnes vsed ordinarily in schools amongst the poore children? How shall it increase your lasting comfort & honour, if for your Highnesses fauours, the work thus entred into, shall soone come to a happy end! For as some very learned and of much experience, haue begun already to help herein, so others of the chiefest gifts and imploiments in this kind, shall not disdaine to lay to their hands to bring it in time to some perfection. Why should wee the liege subiects of *Iesus Christ,* and of this renowned kingdome, be ouergone herein, by the seruants of Antichrist? many of whom bend all their wittes and ioine their studies, for the greatest aduantage of their learning euen in the Grammar schooles, onely to the aduancement of Babylon, with the ouerthrow of this glorious nation, and of all parts of the Church of Christ; to bring vs under that yoake againe, or else to vtter confusion. Or why should we omit any time or opportunity, which the Lord offereth hereunto? The hope therfore of your poore seruant is, that your Highness and Excellency will not impute anie presumption to this indeuor, (though thus vndertaken by me the vnablest of many thousands) but that you will accept it, according to the desire that hath bin in me, to do good thereby to this Church and Nation. . . . . .

Joseph Hall, to whom Brinsley dedicated his version of
Cato's *Distichs,* speaks in his *Comendatorie Preface* with an en-
thusiasm which must have gratified Brinsley (his brother-in-
law) of Brinsley's achievements in improving the teaching of
Latin; and of the need of competing with the schools of the
Jesuits, if Protestant Christianity was to be preserved:

> . . . Our Grandfathers were so long vnder the ferule, till their
> beards were growen as long as their pens: this age hath descried a
> nearer way: yet not without much difficulty, both to the schollars,
> and teacher. Now, time, experience, and painfulnesse (which are
> the meanes to bring all things to their height) haue taught this author
> yet further, how to spare bothe time and paines this way vnto others:
> and (that which is most to bee approoued) without any change of 'the
> receiued grounds . . . The Jesuites haue won much of their reputation,
> and stollen many hearts with their diligence in this kinde. How
> happie shall it be for the Church and vs, if we excite our selues at
> least to imitate this forwardness? We may out-strip them, if we
> want not to our selues: Behold here, not feete but wings, offered
> to vs . . . .

The same spirit dictated Brinsley's editions of the first text
books for children. As he says in his preface to the *Pueriles
Confabulatiunculae:*

> Good reader, whereas I haue been and am daily much called vpon
> for performance of my promise in publishing the translations men-
> tioned in my Grammar-schoole, & this specially amongst others, as
> being through long custom accounted by many very fit for the en-
> trance of young scholars, to learne to speake and talke in Latin, I
> haue thought it equall to condescend vnto their requests. . . . .
> Also for so much as there are sundry speeches vnmeete to season
> the childrens mindes, whereof some are Popish, others profane and
> filthie, those I haue for the most part omitted, or else translated
> them in the best and most modest sense. Vpon this ground and
> occasion I haue omitted some few Dialogues in the end of all, which
> are of this nature in many things, *viz.* vnsauorie, Popish, or both;
> & referre both the teacher and learner to *Corderius Dialogues,* which
> is of another straine, and farre more meet . . . .

His labors, as he says, were to assist and improve the poorer
country schools:

> To the louing Reader. Curteous Reader, who tenderest the poore
> Country schooles, for which this labour hath beene vndertaken, or
> didst euer feele or know the wants in many of them, accept my
> vvilling minde for their good . . . . Remember for whome I write,

euen the meanest Teachers and Learners: with whom though I
sometimes vse repetitions, I cannot bee ouer-plaine; sith they commonly get so little of that [in] Treatises, be they neuer so learned.

In the dedication of the Ovid;—"To the right honourable,
Edward, Lord Denny, Baron of Waltham";—he deals more
fully with this object:

> . . . The rather also haue I done this for that full assurance which
> God hath giuen mee, of a rich blessing to accompany the right vse
> of these translations for the generall good of schooles. And first,
> for all the ruder places of the Land, wherein there is not any thing
> vsually to be found, which may afford the least content or comfort
> to parents, children or any other. Chiefly for the poore ignorant
> countries of *Ireland* and *Wales;* of the good whereof wee ought to
> bee careful as well as of our owne; vnto which I haue principally
> bent my thoughts in all my Grammaticall-translations of our inferiour
> classicall schoole-authors. For that as in all such places, so especially
> in those barbarous countries, the hope of the Church of God is to
> com primarily out of the grammar-schools, by reducing them first
> vnto ciuility thorough the meanes of schooles of good learning
> planted amongst them in euery quarter; wherby their sauage and
> wilde conditions may be changed into more humanity; [marginal note,
> *"Adde, quod ingenuas didicisse artes, Emollit mores nec sinit esse
> feros.* Ouid according to the right iudgement of our Poet, which the
> experience of all ages hath confirmed."]
>
> To which purpose, what can be imagined to bee more effectuall,
> then if together with the Latine tongue they shall attaine withall
> vnto our own Language, and both get and keepe the Latine farre
> more easily and merely in each respect, by the meanes of these trans-
> lations without any inconuenience. Yet haue I not so written them
> for our ruder places alone, but that euen our head Grammar-
> schooles may sundry waies receiue their benefit by them, and
> make their profitable vse of them for their great furtherance for
> Grammar, true sense and meaning of the Authors propriety, purity
> of stile, and variety of phrase, both in our owne and the Latine
> tongue, in many other things; especially, when the Lord shall be
> pleased that they may be brought to that perfection, which we hope &
> pray for, daily labouring and striuing thereunto.

Brinsley's efforts, of course, resulted in failure. Experience
has shown again and again that a good school must have a good
teacher—a sufficiently learned and a well-trained teacher—and
that a good teacher makes a good school, even against difficulties of overcrowding and a bad system; that no book or
device can avail to make the pupil-teacher or the raw and
unlearned teacher do the work. And the system of double

translation, however well suited to individual instruction, cannot escape in classes the burden of tedium for the pupils and of impossible labor for the teacher: sooner or later, to be sure, his system, like all systems of the day, which viewed the main object of training to give pupils the power to "make and speake true Latin in verse and prose, *suo ut aiunt Marte*,"[32] must have become obsolete as the modern age came to understand its needs better. But even for its own time and for its restricted object, it could never have justified his high hopes.

The influence of the work of translators on English prose is beyond measurement. In the very earliest days, when the christianization of the English brought them into the intellectual community of western Europe, the most notable and significant prose works were translations, accompanied by imitations and compilations, and thus English prose continued right up to the time of Hooker and Bacon. In the sixteenth century, when England was flooded with new subjects of thought, new models of style, new words, and new points of view, from Italy, from France, from Germany, and from antiquity either directly or flowing through the channels already cut in other countries, the classics contributed an important part but only a part of the enrichment conveyed to England by this vast Nile-like rise of waters. The leading scholars of England gave themselves not to making the treasures of ancient wisdom open and free to their less-lettered countrymen, but to the Scriptures. And the English version of the Bible was from the first set apart from the normal course of prose. It became available as a model of style for special purposes of ennobling eloquence, or for the enrichment of picturesque narrative, it exerted a multiform influence, but it was not in the central line of the development of English prose. The more pedestrian function of schooling and suppling prose for the general purposes of literature, and of civilized communication on a level below literature, was divided between Greek and Latin, which in effect formed one influence, and French. Both tended to give system to the syntax of self-respecting writers, the French in briefer and less highly organized pe-

----

[32]Harvard College entrance requirements in 1642; *New England's First Fruits*, apud Peirce, Benjamin, A History of Harvard (1833), Appendix, p. 4.

riods, the classics sometimes more cumbrously, or more stiffly, sometimes with a nobler and larger ordonnance.

It is easy to perceive in the better writers of the first half of the sixteenth century, the clear evidence of classic discipline upon their syntax; and this is especially evident in the translators, Sir Thomas Elyot and Gentian Hervet. Contrast the inability of Sir Thomas Malory to maintain a construction through a sentence, his shifts from indirect to direct discourse or from dependent to independent clauses, or the breaking down of his parallelism when he essays an elaborate period with the easily parsed sentences of the *Education of Children*, or the *Gouernour*. It is true that Malory's writing is sweeter and more gracious and warmer, but for the general purposes of writing, and especially for the expression of fine discriminations and complex logical relationships the writers of the translations are opening the way to a more usable standard prose. They are opening the way; but almost a century and a half of discipline and experiment were to follow before final mastery was to be achieved by Dryden. Cheke and Ascham and Wilson carry on the tradition and contribute to it. These earlier humanists are analytically detached in spirit, repressed and unimaginative in style. This quality is in part due to the ideal of the "plain style" which they set before themselves, avoiding strange words, and the ingenious extravagances of the rhetoric of the middle ages. They aimed at self-control, practicality, and the rule of reason, with a somewhat Stoic type of rhetoric. The work of Brende marks a new stadium in the same course, wrestling as he does to give English a more elaborate period, and to give energy to his style; and Grimald's Cicero sets a new standard of energetic precision and of the effort to deal with fairly refined distinctions in a prose that strives for literary finish.

The achievement of all these men in point of the command of the period is only relative; they can manage a sentence of moderate length, but their long sentences lack clean central emphasis and run helplessly hither and thither or are cluttered with modifiers, or else they are rigid and un-English.

In contrast with the sober classicists were the ruck of popular writers, the authors of clamorous polemics, who when they write with any idea of style at all exhibit the sharp staccato sentences, chiming rhythm, ingenuity of sense and sound, in brief all of Euphuism except its unnatural natural history, and the finish of its perverse skill. Evidently neither the cold rationalism of the earlier humanists nor the tasteless excess of the sensationalists was appropriate to the material of the translators of classic prose in the era between 1560 and 1580. Golding and Adlington, Underdowne and North were mainly translating narrative: sober history, amatory tales far from sober, and history that was piquant and picturesque as well as serious in intent. They were much affected by French intermediaries and examples, as well as by the standard of previous English translators. And they created a style (for they have a style presenting enough common characteristics to be regarded under one view) which was not a compromise but a combination. The sentences are larger in their sweep than was quite normal to untutored vernacular English, and yet not dilated to the periods of antiquity; flowing and continuous, not abrupt; fairly orderly and regular in syntax; and restrained within the bounds of taste and judgment. In all this, their style is "humanistic." On the other hand, they manifest a sense of the beauty possible to colloquial rhythm, a sense denied to the earlier translators but possesed by more untutored writers. They spice or enliven their writings by occasional free colloquialisms or even bold slang; they are not afraid of metaphors, even extreme ones, though they are not restlessly searching for them. They know the use of variety, of contrast, and they know that the effect of a high light of style is only gained by its standing forth from a background not broken up by too many spots of brilliance. Lofty eloquence was not aimed at by them in general, not appropriate to their material, perhaps not within their reach; but English prose has certainly never been written in a more flowing, picturesque, energetic, melodious, and unaffected fashion. At the same time, it was not precise in distinctions where precision was needed, or neat and easy in subordination, or capable of readily dilating and contracting from a rolling period to a sharp epigram, or sure and definite in logical connection. In substance and manner the prose of this period reaches its climax in North's Plutarch, which noble and generous as it is, is in thought and dialectic immature.

The original work of this period which has most attracted attention and been the subject of most controversy is of course Lyly's *Euphues*. Lyly was a scholar, and the work is full of borrowings from antiquity, most interestingly from Isocrates. But its style is not Isocratean, and not classical. No doubt Lyly's abundant practice in translation (of which the book contains so many examples) developed his resources in the manipulation of syntax; and the works of earlier laborers in the field of organic English prose helped to teach him; but the peculiar features of his style, his excess of elaborate mechanical ingenuity in syntax, his word-play, and his similes are the development not of classical but of medieval methods and ideas. Developed medieval rhetoric though based on the classics ran the art of manipulating syntax into the ground; and its symbolic treatment of the visible universe is far nearer akin to Lyly's similes than any classical treatment of nature. Lyly, then, as far as he is a Euphuist is against the current of prose slowly moving, feeling its way, and gradually forming its channel across the new land of English thought. It should not be forgotten that Lyly is not always a Euphuist, and that he can write a clear and pleasant idiomatic English prose, not so imaginative or full of feeling as Sidney's *Defense of Poesie,* but as sound, graceful, and easy. If the account of sixteenth-century prose given thus far is even sketchily correct, then English prose did not need the tuition of Euphuism to acquire form. Indeed, the practice of Euphuism might in the individual develop a certain rhetorical skill which a better ideal could put to use, and to the language as a whole it might contribute some enrichment of vocabulary; but in the course of English prose from generation to generation it seems to me an excrescence, or at least an outlier or minor channel. For the writers of prose whose work has endured, and who exercised a continuing influence: Sidney at his best, Raleigh, Hooker, Bacon, are not seriously affected by Euphuism. Writers less memorable for their style are often painfully or annoyingly ingenious, but no more so than the secondary writers of the first half of the century, and not Euphuistically so. If they are less crude, better able to put sentences together, the credit should be given to the manifold labors of many writers—not least of all to the translators—who steadily wrote clearer and better formed sentences. And the prose translators of the early seventeenth century carried little further the art of style than their predecessors of the age of Elizabeth. Holland, Lodge, and Bolton write no better than North or Adlington: perhaps their sentences are a little more secure than Golding's. Holland, indeed, surpasses every predecessor in his care for clearness of logical juncture; but in other respects we praise him for much the same qualities as his predecessors, and with much the same reservations. Lodge has gone back to too cool a manner; he does scant justice to Seneca's special qualities of style. Healey and the others, so far as their influence on prose is concerned, are negligible.

But outside of this group of professed translators of complete works there is one translator of prose more important than any of the rest, though he put into English only extracts and disconnected passages—I refer to Ben Jonson. As has always been well known, Ben Jonson's dramas are stuffed with lines, adaptations, even passages taken bodily from the classics. And in the field of prose his *Discoveries* consist in their most important part of passages especially from Silver Latin, and above all from Seneca. It is just before the break of the century that the impact of Silver Latin on English Literature is definitely felt. Seneca to be sure, had never ceased to exert an important influence on English literature, though mostly in ideas and in a large general way. But the spirit of bitter corrective and even disillusioned criticism, the spirit of Juvenal, Tacitus, and Lucan, and of melancholy effort to meet the evils of the world with courage and resignation, but with little hope, the spirit of Seneca and Epictetus, very vigorously entered English literature with Jonson's comedies and grew rapidly in the congenial soil of the age of James I. In English prose the thought of Silver Latin found expression in the compressed, sententious passages in Jonson's *Discoveries*, full of reflective passages from the two Senecas and Quintilian, in a concise style, too rigid and epigrammatic for continuous writing, but powerful and noble in these separate passages. Their style is akin to that of Bacon's *Essays*, themselves affected by Seneca both directly and through Montaigne, and aiming at the same sententious pregnancy as Seneca and Tacitus. It is notable, in this connection, that much of Cicero as appears in the Essays, illustrations from and allusions to later writers, especially Tacitus and Suetonius, accompany the ideas of Cicero, and even the Ciceronian passages lose their elaborate flowing manner, and are reduced to the pointed style of the later era. Jonson's prose so far as its form and manner are concerned, was perhaps more of a symptom than an influence, a part of a general tendency in a rationalistic age toward the development of antithesis as a means of contributing to energy of thought and not as a mere decoration, and toward a close and firm conciseness sometimes reaching epigrammatic brevity —the type of writing reached at the high points in Halifax and Dryden.

Such then are some of the types of prose which translators from the classics had assisted in developing by the end of our period: the relatively orderly but monotonous and cold style of the humanists such as Elyot and Ascham; the warmly imaginative, flowing and vital style of North, winning and powerful, not delicate, exact, or flexible; and the pregnant, close-wrought, powerful, but rigid style of Jonson's *Discoveries*: Hooker had already in his Ciceronian manner attained occasional splendor; but it was reserved for one generation to give a ready command of opulence, and for another to give flexibility, art, sureness, and variety to the plain style. But among the many workers who contributed to create and develop the capacities of English prose either of the lighter or the graver sort, acknowledgment is surely due the Elizabethan group of translators, who have now become obscure.

As for the influence of translation from the classics on style in verse, it is not to be perceived so easily or traced so definitely. It is manifested chiefly in brief passages of adaptation or imitation and hence does not come within the view of this book. Yet it should not be forgotten that it was in the effort to create a worthy equivalent for Vergil that Surrey raised his manner above the merely graceful charm of his personal poetry, and that Sackville and Spenser show the influence of his earlier efforts. But in general the verse translations are too free and too inadequate for any direct influence upon poetical rhetoric to be traced to them.

As for the forms of verse, heroic blank verse was of course created as a compromise between ancient and modern types, in order that poetry in a classic language might be more nobly written in a modern language without the petty embarrassment or the jingle of rhyme. So it was used by Surrey, Grimald, and Turbervile. But the original had only the influence of suggesting rhymelessness; the verse form once originated had to follow its natural development, neither hampered nor forwarded by special peculiarities of its original. I think the heroic couplet, however, does even in its metrical form show some peculiarities due to its being used as a vehicle for translation. Grimald first essayed using it as an equivalent for the elegiac distich; and after a few years it rather gradually replaced the septenarius as the standard English meter for versions first of the elegy, then of the hexameter. The feat of rendering Latin elegies couplet for distich was a challenge which some writers were bound to accept—the most ambitious, as Marlowe and Jonson—and thus the habit of thinking in couplets as units was encouraged. Once viewed in this way, the couplet was bound to develop the special peculiarities of its inner form; and accordingly the practice of translation must be taken into consideration in studying the slow evolution of the classic heroic couplet.[33]

As for the substance of the translations, their service may be briefly put: they gave the English reader who knew no ancient languages a lot to think about. A lot of *things* to think about; not so much things to think a lot about. The translations were valued as providing a store to be drawn upon: the histories a store of information, a store of valuable and applicable human experience, a store of illustrative anecdote; the poems a store of tales, of imaginative enrichment and allusion; the treatises on conduct a store of direction and of wise maxims. From first to last classics were translated mainly with the idea of direct usefulness in mind, moral or directly

[33]Professor Courthope (*History of English Poetry*, Vol. III, p. 101) says strangely, "[Sandys's] version of the *Metamorphoses* [1621-1626] is, I believe (with the exception of Gavin Douglas's *Aeneid*), the first example of the use of the heroic couplet in the translation of a classic author." Marlowe's *Amores* (1590-1591), Chapman's *Odyssey* (1615), and Overbury's *Remedia Amoris* (1620) were fairly conspicuous, to say nothing of Heywood's *Ars Amatoria* (1598), Digges's *Raptus Proserpinae*, 1617, and Holyday's *Persius* (1616). Jonson's *Ars Poetica* and other translations in couplets, though not printed till 1640, were of course translated and circulated much earlier. It is, of course, not strange that Heywood's bits of Ovid in *Troia Britannica* (1609) and "W. B.'s" paraphrase of Juvenal Sat. 10 (1617) should not attract attention.

practical. Their inspiring force was implicit, less realized than their immediate value. Yet the view of ancient history did something to develop the sense of the nobility and tragic interest in English history, and to elevate the idea of the possibilities of human achievement. The philosophy did not essay to stir fundamental questions, and yet it cannot but have played some part in the secularization of the ideas of conduct. We cannot know whether the small free-thinking groups like that which gathered about Harriott and Raleigh[34] owed much to classic thought, but surely the familiarity of English readers with Cicero, Seneca, and Epictetus must have done something to prepare the way for the deism of the seventeenth century, which is saturated with ideas from antiquity.

But in spite of the abundance and variety of the translations, the names absent from the list of great works of antiquity made accessible to English readers is as notable as the names present on that list. The fact that the Greek drama was untouched by the translators of the great age of the English drama has been often remarked. But it is not the Greek drama alone that is absent. It is not too much to say that almost no classic Greek works at all were translated, and that none entered the stream of English literature. Hall's Homer is negligible as a translation and as an influence. Chapman's Homer is a striking English poem, but it came at the very end of the period, too late to be an inspiring force, to become a part of the stock of ideas and images of English poetry when it was being created, as Golding's Ovid had done. In the lyric age of Elizabeth no classic Greek lyrics were translated; of course they could not be. A witty poem of a lyric cast has only to have its point of wit gracefully expressed, and a translation is made. Such is *Drink to me only with thine eyes;* perhaps *Amor Fugitivus* may be reckoned as approaching a lyric. Both turn on conceits, on graceful cleverness. But the higher lyric is too essentially one living unity for its soul to be extracted and to take on a new body in another language. It was the lyric element of the Greek tragedy, it will be remembered, that was

---

[34]Herrington, H. W., *Christopher Marlowe—Rationalist*, in *Essays in Memory of Barrett Wendell*, Camb. Mass., (1926) p. 121; Kyd, Thomas, *Works* ed. Boas, F. S. (1901), p. lxxi; Ingram, John H. *Christopher Marlow and his Associates* (1904), p. 184 ff.; Boas, F. S., *New Light on Sir Walter Raleigh*, in *Literature*, vii (1900) pp. 96, 113; Stone, J. M., *Atheism under Elizabeth and James I*, in *The Month*, lxxxi (1894), p. 174.

the stumbling-block to Erasmus. Naturally, there could be no
Pindar or Sappho in English. Nor is it surprising that there
was no comedy. The comedy, like the tragedy, presents the
difficulties of the lyric. "That merry Greek, tart Aristophanes," even if he could have passed the Elizabethan censor,
could not have been made intelligible either in his humor or
in his poetry. It would not be true to say that there was no
classic history; but there seems to have been little curiosity
about earlier Greek history. No attempt was made to super-
sede Nichols's crude Thucydides, and "B.R." was not encouraged to complete his Herodotus; Xenophon's moral romance, the *Cyropedia,* had the honor of being twice translated;
but nobody cared to translate the *Hellenica* or the *Anabasis.*
As for Greek oratory, the only representative of it is in a
translation intended as a political pamphlet, sincere and simple,
but without the faintest suggestion of Demosthenes's dynamic
power or of the beauty of his expression, which goes far beyond even the rhetorical finish which his translator could not
achieve. There is, properly speaking, no Greek philosophy—
nothing but moral essays. The English reader was not ready,
—and I suppose never has been ready,—for the tough labor
of thought on fundamentals. It is small wonder that Plato
and Aristotle were not made known to the Elizabethans; but
it may fairly raise some surprise that the *Axiochus* should get
a fair share of attention while the *Apology* and *Crito* were neglected. As for Aristotle, he is indeed represented by Wilkin-
son's *Ethics* but the version gives us the clouded medieval view
of Aristotle, and not the real philosopher. Near the end of the
period covered by our study the *Politics* was translated.
Unlike Chapman's Homer, this version did not appear too late
to be a force in thought as well as an object of interest, for
Aristotle was genuinely vital in the political theorizing of the
seventeenth century. Yet on the whole it is not too much to
say that Attic Greek philosophy is as little represented as Attic
drama. Epic, lyric, drama, history, philosophy,—the only
classic Greek writer who really made an impression on sixteenth century England was the excellent Isocrates. There was
a little Alexandrian literature. Aratus was translated; there
was some Theocritus, a trifle of Moschus. But on the side of
imaginative literature it is the lower and the later things that

aroused most enthusiasm: the amatory novels and the worst and latest of the epigrams. On the side of instructive and informative writing it was the Greek historians of Rome and empire and the Greek moral writers of the Roman period to whom the translators turned and who contributed the most vital forces of Hellenic origin to the literature of the age.

How much Greek did the translators know? Not much, perhaps, but what Mr. W. H. Woodward says at the end of Chapter IV of the *Cambridge History of English Literature* is not true; namely, "During the period under review . . . In Greek, not one of the translators, Savile excepted, but works through a French version like North." Elyot translated Plutarch's essay on the education of children direct from the Greek as early as 1530. Hervet translated Xenophon's *Oeconomicus* from Greek about the same time. Bury's *Ad Demonicum* (1557) is probably direct from the original; so is Barker's *Cyropedia* (1560?). Billingsley translated Euclid direct, and Wilson Demosthenes, both translations appearing in 1570. Chapman (1598-1615) may have depended much on translations and commentaries, but he worked from the Greek. Healey's Theophrastus is puzzling, but he seems at least to have checked the Latin translation with the Greek. As the history of the universities indicates, there seems to have been a falling off after the first study of Greek at Cambridge, only slowly repaired after the Elizabethan settlement.

The omissions in Latin literature are as notable. In spite of the Plautine influence on English comedy, but one drama of Plautus was translated. Terence is a school-book, and but one play of his was translated before the end of Elizabeth's reign. Cicero is not an orator to the Elizabethans; a single oration was printed, a fulsome praise of the despot. Elizabeth herself translated another of the same kind. We have not in Elizabethan English Cicero's Verres, Catiline, or Antony. The Elizabethans had no deliberative oratory, and Roman as well as Greek freedom of deliberative speech might well have been suspect to Elizabeth's government. A selection of Cicero's letters was printed in a manual of epistolary style; but on the whole Cicero appealed to the age as a profound and inspiring moralist.

It is not a cause for surprise that an author at once so

profound and so alien in spirit as Lucretius should not have
been translated.   There is no Roman lyric, as there is no Greek
lyric and for the same reasons: a little Catullus, including
Campion's graceful adaptations; no Tibullus, no Propertius.
Even Drant did not venture on Horace's *Odes;* Jonson failed
with the few which he undertook, and it was reserved for Campion, again, to adapt some with skill and charm.   Imperial Rome, again, is the source and theme of translators: Vergil, Ovid, Caesar, Seneca, Martial; Justin, Florus, Ammianus Marcellinus, somewhat later Persius, Livy,
Pliny, Suetonius.[35]   It may well be a matter of accident that
Juvenal did not get into print.   Lucan did not seem to appeal
to the age; it was not till the very end of James's reign that
he was translated as a whole.   Apuleius is a natural companion
of the Greek amatory romances.   But the author of authors,
perpetually retranslated and always with affectionate zeal,
was Boethius.   And most popular of all books deriving from
antiquity was the collection of maxims known as Baldwin's
Moral Philosophy.

---

[35]Jonson, Ben, *Conversations with Drummond*: "He recommended to my
reading Quintilian (who (he said) would tell me the faults of my Verses
as if he had Lived with me) and Horace, Plinius Secundus Epistles, Tacitus, Júvenall, Martiall, whose Epigrame Vitam quae faciunt Beatiorem etc.
he hath translated."—"that Petronius, Plinius secundus, Tacitus speke best
Latine, that Quintilianes 6.7.8. bookes were not only to be read but al-
togither digested.   Juvenal, Perse, Horace for delight & so was Pindar."
Works, ed. Simpson and Herford, I, 132.

CHRONOLOGICAL LIST OF TRANSLATIONS

Cato, *Disticha;* paraphrased by Benedict Burgh   1477–8
    ante 1479, 1481(?), 1558

Boethius, *De Consolatione;* tr. Chaucer   1479

Ovid, *Metamorphoses;* moralized by Berçoir, tr. Caxton   1480

Cicero, *De Amicitia;* tr. J. Tiptoft Earl of Worcester   1481
    ca. 1530

Cicero, *De Senectute;* tr. W. Worcester?   1481

Terence, *"Vulgaria";*   *ca.* 1483
    ca. 1483, 1483-4, 1486, ...(?), 1529, ...(?)

Cato, *Disticha;* tr. Caxton, from French   1483

Aesop, *Fables;* tr. Caxton, from French   1484
    1500(?), ...(?), ...(?), *ca.* 1550, 1551, 156-(?)
    ....(?), 1570(?), 1590(?) etc.

Frontinus and Vegetius, *De re militari;* in Christine de
    Pisan's *Fayttes of Armes,* tr. Caxton, from French   1489

Vergil, *Eneydos;* French romance, tr. Caxton   1490

Ovid, *"Flores";*   1513

Lucian, *Menippus;* tr. John Rastell ?   *ca.* 1520

Terence, *Andria,* "Terens in englysh"; tr. ? ptr. John
    Rastell   *ca.* 1520

Sallust, *Jugurtha;* tr. Alexander Barclay   *ca.* 1520
    ca. 1520, 1557

Boethius, *De Consolatione;* tr. John Walton (1410)   1525

Plutarch, *De Tranquillitate Animi;* tr. Sir Thomas Wyat,
    from Latin of Budaeus   1528 (?)

Plutarch, *De Tuenda Sanitate;* from Lat. of Erasmus, ptr.
    Wyer   1530 (?)
    (at least two edd.)

Caesar, *De Bello Gallico,* "as much as concernyth thys realm
    of England"; tr. from French of Gaguin by Wil-
    liam Rastell ?   1530

Plutarch, *De Educatione Puerorum;* tr. Elyot, from Greek   *ca.* 1530
    1531(?)

Isocrates, *Ad Nicoclem;* tr. Elyot, from Latin of Guarino   *ca.* 1531
    ....(?)

Xenophon, *Oeconomicus;* tr. Gentian Hervet, from Greek   1532
    1537, 1544, *ca.* 1550, 1557, 1573, 1579

Terence, *"Flowers";* tr. Nicholas Udall   1532 (?)
    1538, 1544, 1556(?), 1560, 1568, 1570? 1572, 1575, 1581

Lucian, *Cynicus;* tr. Elyot, from Latin of More   *ante* 1535

Cicero, *De Senectute;* tr. Whytinton   1535 (?)
    1540

Plutarch, *De Capienda ex Inimicis Utilitate;* tr. ?   1535 (?)
    1550(?)

Cebes, *"Table";* tr. Francis Poyntz   *ca.* 1535
    1537(?), 1560(?)

Varii, *The Garden of Wysedome;* compiled and tr. Richard
    Taverner   1538
    enlarged, 1539(?), *ca.* 1550, 1590

Publilius Syrus, *Apothems;* tr. Richard Taverner   1539
    1540, 1540(?), 1553

Frontinus, *Stratagemata;* tr. R. Morysine   1539

Varii, in Erasmus, *Adagia;* tr. R. Taverner   1539
    1552

Varii, *The Bankette of Sapience;* compiled and tr. Elyot   1539
    1542, 1545, 1557, 1564

Cicero, *Paradoxa, De Officiis;* tr. Whytinton   1540

Galen, *Therapeutics;* Bk. IV, fr. French, tr. Robert Copland
    (in *The Questenary of Cyrurgens*)   1541
    rev. by Geo. Baker 1574, 1579

Varii, *Apophthegmata;* compiled Erasmus, tr. Udall   1542

Plutarch, *De Tuenda Sanitate;* tr. John Hales   1543

Livy, *History;* a small part, tr. Sir Anthony Cope   1544
    1561, 1568, 1590

Cato, *Disticha,* with *Sage Sayings of the Seven* and Pub-
    lilius Syrus, *Mimi;* tr. W. Burrant   1545
    1553, 1560, 1622

Pseudo-Seneca, *The Forme and Rule of Honest Lyvinge;*
    tr. Whytinton   1546

Pseudo-Seneca, *The Myrrour or Glasse of Maners;* tr.
    Whytinton   1547

Seneca, *Ad Gallionem;* tr. Whytinton   1547

Aristotle, *Ethics,* from the medieval Italian version of
    Brunetto Latini; tr. J. Wylkinson   1547

Varii, *Treatise of Moral Philosophy;* compiled and tr.
    William Baldwin   1547
    1550, ...(?), 1555, ...(?), 1564, 1567, 1571, 1575,
    1587, 1591, 1596, 1600, 1610,........(?)

Cicero, *De Amicitia;* tr. John Harington   1550

Hippocrates, *Aphorisms;* tr Humphrey Lloyd fr. Latin   1550 (?)
   1585

Proclus, *De Sphaera;* tr. W. Salysburie, fr. Latin   1550

Thucydides, *Peloponnesian War,* fr. French of Claude de
      Seyssel; tr. Thomas Nichols   1550

Cato, *Disticha;* tr. R. Burrant   1553
   1560

Cicero, *De Officiis;* tr. Nicholas Grimald   1553
   1556, 1558, 1558, 1568, 1575, 1583, 1588, 1590, 1596, 1600,
   1610

Cato, Syrus, Erasmus's *Adagia;* tr. R. Taverner   1553

Quintus Curtius, *Alexander;* tr. John Brende   1553
   1556, 1561, 1568, 1571, 1575, 1583, 1584, 1592, 1596,
   1600 (?), 1602, 1614

Vergil, *Aeneid;* tr. Gawin Douglas   ptd. 1553

Vergil, *Aeneid;* Bk. IV, tr. Surrey   ptd. 1554

Cicero, *Pro Marcello,* in *The Figures of Grammar and
      Rhetoric;* tr. R. Sherry   1555

Herodian, *Roman Emperors;* tr. from Latin of Politian; by
      N. Smith   *ca.* 1556
   1564

Boethius, *De Consolatione;* tr. George Colvile (Coldewel)   1556

Isocrates, *Ad Demonicum;* tr. J. Bury, from Greek   1557

Vergil, *Aeneid* II and IV; tr. Surrey   ptd. 1557

Varii, in Tottel's *Miscellany;*   1557

Vergil, *Aeneid* I-VII; tr. Thomas Phaer   1558

Seneca, *Troas;* tr. Jasper Heywood   1559
   1560(?)

Seneca, *Thyestes;* tr. Jasper Heywood   1560

Xenophon, *Cyropaedia* I-VI; tr. William Barker, from Greek 1560 (?)
   1567

Justin, *Abridgment* (two speeches); tr. T. Norton   1560 (?)

Ovid, *Metamorphoses,* III, 342 etc.; tr. J. Howell ?   1560

Cicero, *Tusculan Disputations;* tr. John Dolman   1561

Seneca, *Hercules Furens;* tr. Jasper Heywood   1561

Cicero, *Ad Quintum;* tr. G. Gilby   1561

Plutarch, Three essays from *Morals;* tr. W. Blundeville,
      from Latin   1561
   1580

Vergil, *Aeneid* I-IX; tr. Thomas Phaer   1562

Seneca, *Oedipus;* tr. Alexander Nevyle   1563

Artemidorus, *Oneirocritica,* from French; tr. Thomas Hill   1563
   1571, 1576, 1606

Eutropius, *"Breviary";* tr. Nicholas Haward   1564

Justin, *Abridgment;* tr. Arthur Golding   1564
    1570, 1578

Horace, *Satires,* Bk. I, 1 and 2; tr. Lewis Evans.   1564

Lucian, *Toxaris;* tr. A. O.   1565

Caesar, *Gallic War;* tr. Arthur Golding   1565
    1578, 1590

Ovid, *Metamorphoses* I-IV; tr. Arthur Golding   1565

Pliny, Summary of *Natural History,* from French; tr. J.
    A[lday?]   1565
    1585, 1587

Ovid, *Metamorphoses,* IV, 287 etc.; tr. T. Peend   1565

Seneca, *Octavia;* tr. Thomas Nuce   1566

Seneca, *Agamemnon* and *Medea;* tr. John Studley   1566

Seneca, *Hippolytus;* licensed   1566

Euripides, *Phenissae (Jocasta)* ; tr. George Gascoigne
    and Francis Kinwelmershe, from Italian   acted 1566
    printed 1572, 1575, 1587, 1587

Apuleius, *The Golden Ass;* tr. William Adlington   1566
    1571, 1582, 1596, 1639

Horace, *Satires;* tr. Thomas Drant   1566
    1567

Livy etc. in Painter, *Palace of Pleasure,* tome i   1566

Ovid, *Metamorphoses;* tr. Arthur Golding   1567
    1575, 1584, 1587, 1593, 1593, 1612

Ovid, *Heroides;* tr. George Turbervile   1567
    1569, 1570(?), 1580(?), 1600

Horace, *Ars Poetica, Satires,* and *Epistles;* tr. Thomas
    Drant   1567

Arrian, *Abridgment* of Epictetus; tr. James Sandford   1567

Xenophon, *Cyropedia;* tr. William Barker   1567

Heliodorus, *Aethiopica;* Book IV, tr. James Sandford, from
    Latin   1567

Plutarch, *Morals,* "Amorous and Tragical Tales"; tr. James
    Sandford, from Latin   1567

Livy etc. in Painter, *Palace of Pleasure,* tome ii   1567

Anthology etc. in Turbervile, *Eclogues,* etc.   1567

Polybius, *History;* Bk. I, tr. T. Watson, from Latin   1568

Cicero, *Paradoxa, Somnium Scipionis;* tr. Thomas Newton   1569
    1577

Heliodorus, *Aethiopica;* tr. Thomas Underdowne, from Latin   1569
    1577, 1587, 1605, 1606, 1622

Ovid, *Ibis;* tr. Underdowne   1569
   1577

Diodorus Siculus, *History,* etc.; tr. Thomas Stocker, from
   French   1569

Euclid, *Elements;* tr. Henry Billingsley, from Greek   1570

Demosthenes, *Olynthiacs* and *Philippics;* tr. Thomas Wilson
   from Greek   1570

Seneca, *Hercules Oetaeus;* tr. John Studley   1571

Plutarch, *De Educatione Puerorum;* tr. E. Grant   1571

Dionysius Periegetes, *Survey of the World;* tr. from Latin,
   Thomas Twyne   1572

Ovid, *Tristia;* tr. Thomas Churchyard   1572
   1577, 1578, 1580

Vegetius, *De re militari;* tr. John Sadler   1572

Vergil, *Aeneid;* tr. Phaer and Twyne   1573
   1584, 1596, 1600, 1607, 1620

Varii, in Painter, *Palace of Pleasure,* enlarged   1574

Galen, *Elements;* tr. John Jones, from Latin   1574

Galen, "*Third book of curing wounds etc.*" in *Oil of Oleum*
   etc.; tr. G. Baker   1574

Vergil, *Eclogues;* tr. A. Fleming   1575
   1589

Cicero, *Epistolae;* from Corderius, tr.?   1575

Aelian, *Register of Histories;* tr. Abraham Fleming   1576

Varii, in Fleming, A., *Panoplie of Epistles*   1576

Varii, in Kendall, Timothy, *Flowers of Epigrammes*   1577

Cicero, *Paradoxa, Somnium Scipionis, De Senectute, De
   Amicitia;* tr. Thomas Newton   1577

Cato, *Disticha;* tr. ? from Corderius   1577
   1584

Appian, *Roman Wars;* tr. W. B., from Latin   1578

Seneca, *De Beneficiis;* tr. Arthur Golding   1578

Plutarch, *Lives;* tr. Sir Thomas North, from French   1579
   1595, 1603, 1610-12, 1631

Eunapius, *Lives of the Philosophers;* tr. Anon.   1579

Galen, *De comp. med. per Genera,* 3d book, and *Therapeutics,* 4th book; tr. G. Baker   1597

Synesius, *Laus Calvitii;* tr. A. Fleming   1597

Isocrates, *Three Orations;* tr. Thomas Forrest, from French   1580

Vergil, *Alexis* (in *Lawyers Logike*); tr. Abraham Fraunce   1580 (?)
   (in *The Countess of Pembroke's Ivy Church*)   1591

Homer, *Iliad* I-X; tr. Arthur Hall, from French   1581

Seneca, *Thebais;* tr. Thomas Newton, in *Tenne Tragedies*
    of Seneca   1581

Vergil, *Aeneid* I-IV; tr. Richard Stanyhurst   1582
    1583

Herodotus, *History,* I, II; tr. B. R.   1584

Cato, *Disticha* ("*Cato Construed*") ; tr. Anon.   1584

Isocrates, *Ad Demonicum;* tr. R. Nuttall   1585

Pomponius Mela, *De Situ Orbis;* tr. Arthur Golding   1585
    1590

Solinus, *Collectanea;* tr. Arthur Golding   1585 (?)
    1587, 1590

Aesop, *Fables;* tr. William Bullokar   1585

Cato, *Disticha;* tr. William Bullokar   1585

Galen, *Methodus Medendi;* tr. Thomas Gale, from Latin   1586

Vergil, *Bucolics, Eclogues* I and II; tr. W. Webbe in *A*
    Discourse of English Poetrie   1586

Longus, *Daphnis and Chloe;* tr. Angel Day, from French   1587

Terence, *Andria;* tr. Maurice Kyffin   1588

Theocritus, *Six Idyls;* tr. Anonymous   1588

Anacreontics, 31; tr. R. Greene in *Alcida*   1588

Vergil, *Bucolics* and *Georgics;* tr. Abraham Fleming   1589

Plutarch, *De Tranquillitate;* tr. John Clapham, fr. French   1589

Ovid, *Certain of Ovid's Elegies;* tr. Christopher Marlowe
    in *Epigrammes and Elegies*   1590 (?)
    1593, 1596

Tacitus, *Histories* and *Agricola;* tr. H. Savile   1591
    (with Grenewey's *Annals* and *Germania*)
    1598, 1604, 1612, 1622, 1640

Heliodorus, *Aethiopica,* a fragment of the beginning in
    hexameter, in *The Countess of Pembroke's Ivy*
    Church; tr. Abraham Fraunce   1591

Vergil, *Bucolica, Ecl.* II; tr. A. Fraunce, *ibid.*   1591

Pseudo-Vergil, *Culex;* tr. Edmund Spenser   1591

Lucian, *Galatea and Polyphemus;* tr. Giles Fletcher in
    Lycia   1593

Moschus, *Idyl* 1, from French; tr. Barnabe Barnes, in
    Parthenophil and Parthenope   1593

Lucan, *Pharsalia;* Bk. I, tr. C. Marlowe   (before 1593)

Plautus, *Menaechmi;* tr. W. Warner   1595

Pseudo-Aristotle, *Problemata;* tr. ?   1595
    1597, 1607

Coluthus, *Raptus Primus Helenae;* tr. I. T[russel?]   1595

Achilles Tatius, *Leucippe and Clitophon;* tr. William Burton, from Latin   1597

Hippocrates, *Oath* and *Prognostics;* tr. Peter Lowe   1597
1612, 1634

Ovid, *All Ovid's Elegies;* tr. Christopher Marlowe   1597
1600

Homer, *Iliad* I-VII; tr. George Chapman, from Greek   1598

Homer, *Iliad,* from Bk. XVIII; tr. George Chapman   1598

Terence, *Plays;* tr. Richard Bernard   1598
1607, 1614, 1629

Aristotle, *Politics,* from French; tr. I. D.   1598

Tacitus, *Annals* and *Germania;* tr. R. Greenewey, with
Savile's *Histories* and *Agricola*   1598

Ovid, *De Arte Amandi;* tr. T. Heywood   1598
1600(?) *ca.* 1636, 1640, 1650, 1662, 1672, 1677, 1708

Livy, *History;* tr. Philemon Holland   1600

Caesar, *Bellum Gallicum,* I-V; tr. C. Edmondes in *Observations upon the five books, etc.*   1600

Ovid, *Remedia Amoris;* tr. F. L.   1600(?)

Lucan, *Pharsalia,* I; tr. Christopher Marlowe,   printed 1600
lic. 1593

Pliny, *Natural History;* tr. Philemon Holland   1601
1634

Josephus, *Works;* tr. Thomas Lodge (lic. 1598)   1602
1609, 1620, 1632, 1640

Ovid, *Metamorphoses,* IV, 287 etc.; tr. ?   1602

Aesop, *Fables;* construed Simon Sturtevant   1602

Plutarch, *Moralia;* tr. Philemon Holland   1603

Homer, *Batrachomyomachia;* tr. W. Fowldes, from Latin   1603
1634

Caesar, *Bellum Gallicum,* VI-VII; tr. C. Edmondes in
Observations upon Caesar's Commentaries, pt. 2,   1604
1604, 1609, 1655, 1677, 1695

Suetonius, *Twelve Caesars;* tr. Philemon Holland   1606

Justin, *Abridgment;* tr. G. W.   1606

Pseudo-Plato, *Axiochus;* from DeMornay   1607

Sallust, *Catiline* and *Jugurtha;* tr. T. Heywood   1608

Ammianus Marcellinus, *Roman History;* tr. P. Holland   1609

Boethius, *De Consolatione;* tr. I. T.[*i.e.* Michael Walpole?]   1609

Ovid, *Heroides,* Helen to Paris, [and Paris to Helen]; tr.
T. Heywood in *Troia Britannica*   1609

Caesar, *Bellum Civile;* tr. C. Edmondes (with *B. G.*)   1609
1655, 1677, 1695

Homer, *Iliad,* 12 bks; tr. George Chapman   1610
Arrian, *Enchiridium* (Epictetus *Manual*) and
Cebes, *"Table"*; tr. John Healey   1610
    1616, 1636
Hippocrates, *Aphorisms*; tr. ?   1610
Homer, *Iliad* complete; tr. George Chapman   1611
Cicero, *Epistolae*; selections "Verbally translated," tr. ?   1611
Cato, *Disticha*; tr. John Brinsley   1612
Ovid, *Metamorphoses,* Myrrha and Cinyras; tr. Henry
    Austin in *The Scourge of Venus*   1613
Homer, *Odyssey* I-XII; tr. George Chapman   1614
Lucan, *Pharsalia*; tr. Arthur Gorges   1614
Seneca, *Works, Moral and Natural*; tr. Thomas Lodge   1614
    1620
Homer, *Odyssey,* complete; tr. George Chapman   1615
    Iliad and *Odyssey* together, 1615(?), 1616(?)
Cicero, *De Officiis*; tr. John Brinsley   1616
Aelianus, *Tactica,* Capp. I-XXIX; tr. John Bingham   1616
    Complete 1629, 1631
Theophrastus, *Characters*; tr. John Healey   1616
Persius, *Satires*; tr. Barten Holyday   1616
    1617, 1635
Musaeus, *Hero and Leander*; tr. George Chapman   1616
Claudian, *Raptus Proserpinae*; tr. L. Digges   1617
Juvenal, *Satire* 10; tr. W. B.   1617
Aesop, *Fables*; tr. John Brinsley   1617
    1624
Julius Florus, *Abridgment of Livy*; tr. Edmond Bolton   1618
    1618, 1636
Hesiod, *Georgics*; tr. George Chapman   1618
Ovid, *Metamorphoses,* I, 1-567; tr. J. Brinsley   1618
    1656
Ovid, *Remedia Amoris*; tr. Sir Thomas Overbury   1620
Vergil, *Aeneid,* part of 2d book; tr. Sir Thomas Wrothe   1620

ALPHABETICAL LIST OF TRANSLATORS

Anonymous, Cato, *Disticha,* 1577, 1584

    Cicero, *Epistolae,* construed from Corderius, 1575.

    Cicero, *Epistolae,* "verbally translated," 1611.

    Hippocrates, *Aphorisms,* 1610.

    Lucian, *Philopseudes,* from Latin of More, 16....?, 1669.

    Ovid, *"Flores,"* 1513.

    Metamorphoses, IV, 287 etc., 1602.

    pseudo-Plato, *Axiochus,* 1592.

    pseudo-Plato, *Axiochus,* fr. French of DeMornay, 1607.

    Plutarch, *De Tuenda Sanitate,* from Latin of Erasmus, 1530.

    Plutarch, *De Capienda ex Inimicis Utilitate,* from Latin of Erasmus, 1535(?)

    Terence, *Andria, ca.* 1520.

    Terence, *"Vulgaria," ca.* 1483.

    Theocritus, *Six Idylls,* 1588.

Adlington, William, Apuleius, *The Golden Ass,* 1566.

A[lday?], John, Pliny, *Natural History,* summary of de Changi, fr. French, 1565.

Austin, Henry, Ovid, *Metamorphoses,* a fragment, 1613.

Baker, George, Galen, *De comp. med. per Genera,* Bk. III, *Therapeutics,* Bk. IV, from French, in *Oil of Oleum Magistrale,* 1574. with *Guydo's Questions,* 1579.

Baldwin, William, Varii in *"Treatise of Moral Philosophy,"* 1548 etc.

Barclay, Alexander, Sallust, *Jugurtha, ca.* 1520.

Barker, William, Xenophon, *Cyropedia* I-VI, from Greek (?), 1560, complete 1567.

Barnes, Barnabe, Moschus, *Idyl* I, fr. French, in *Parthenophil and Parthenope,* 1593.

Bernard, Richard, Terence, *Plays,* 1598 etc.

Billingsley, Henry, Euclid, *Elements,* from Greek, 1570.

Bingham, John, Aelian, *Tactica* I-XXIX, 1616, complete 1629 etc.

Blundeville, William, Plutarch, Three essays from *Morals,* from Latin, 1561.

Bolton, Edmund, Julius Florus, abridgment of Livy, 1618 etc.

Brende, John, Quintus Curtius, *Alexander,* 1553 etc.

Brinsley, John, Aesop, *Fables,* lic. 1617, pub. 1624(?)

    Cato, *Disticha,* 1612.

    Cicero, *De Officiis,* 1616.

    Ovid, *Metamorphoses,* I. 1-567, 1618.

Bullokar, William, Aesop, *Fables*, 1585.
> Cato, *Disticha*, 1585.

Burgh, Benedict, Cato, *Disticha*, 1477-78.

Burrant, William, Cato, *Disticha;* Publilius Syrus, *Mimi; "Song Sayings* etc." 1545.

Burton, William, Achilles Tatius, *Leucippe and Clitophon*, from Latin, 1597.

Bury, J., Isocrates, *Ad Demonicum*, from Greek, 1557.

"B. . . . , W.", Appian, *Roman Wars*, from Latin, 1578.

Caxton, William, Ovid, *Metamorphoses* moralized, from French, 1480.
> Cato, *Disticha*, from French, 1483.
> Aesop, *Fables*, from French, 1484.
> Vegetius and Frontinus, *De Re Militari* in Christine de Pisan's *Book of the Fayttes of Armes*, from French, 1489.
> Vergil, *"Eneydos*," from French, 1490.

Chapman, George, Hesiod, *"Georgics" i.e. Works and Days*, from Greek, 1618.
> Homer, *Iliad*, I-VII, 1598.
> *Achilles Shield*, from *Il.* Bk. XVIII, 1598.
>> *Iliad*, I-XII, 1610.
>> *Iliad*, I-XXIV, from Greek, 1611.
>> *Odyssey*, I-XII, 1613.
>> *Odyssey*, I-XXIV, from Greek, 1615.
> Musaeus, *Hero and Leander*, 1616.

Chaucer, Geoffrey, Boethius, *De Consolatione, ca.* 1479.

Churchyard, Thomas, Ovid, *Tristia*, 1572.

Clapham, John, Plutarch, *De Tranquillitate*, from French of Amyot, 1589.

Colvile, George, Boethius, *De Consolatione*, 1556.

Cope, Sir Anthony, Livy, *History*, a portion, 1544 etc.

Copland, Robert, Galen, *Therapeutics* IV, from French, 1541.

Day, Angel, Longus, *Daphnis and Chloe*, from French of Amyot, 1587.

Digges, Leonard, Claudian, *Raptus Proserpinae*, 1617.

Dolman, John, Cicero, *Tusculan Disputations*, 1561.

Douglas, G., Vergil, *Aeneid*, 1553.

Drant, Thomas, Horace, *Ars Poetica* and *Epistles*, 1567.
> *Satires*, 1566.

"D. . . , I.", Aristotle, *Politics*, from French of LeRoy, 1598.

Edmondes, C., Caesar, *Bellum Civile*, 1609, etc. (with *Bellum Gallicum*) *Bellum Gallicum* I-IV, in *Observations* etc., 1600. Complete in *Observations*, pt. 2, 1604.

Elyot, Thomas, Plutarch, *De Educatione Puerorum*, from Greek, *ca.* 1530.
> Isocrates, *Ad Nicoclem*, from Latin of Guarino, *ca.* 1531.
> Lucian, *Cynicus*, from Latin of More, before 1535.
> Varii, in *The Bankette of Sapience*, largely from Erasmus, *Adagia*, 1539.

Evans, Lewis, Horace, *The First Two Satires,* 1564.

Fleming, Abraham, Cicero, Pliny, etc., *Epistolae* in *"A Panoulie of Epistles,"* 1576.
> Aelian, *Register of Histories,* 1576.
> Synesius, *Laus Calvitii,* 1579.
> Vergil, *Bucolics,* 1575, etc.
>> *Georgics,* 1589.

Fletcher, Giles, Lucian, *Galatea and Polyphemus* in *Lycia,* from Latin (?), 1593.

Forrest, Thomas, Isocrates, *Three Orations,* from French, 1580.

Fowldes, W., Pseudo-Homer, *Batrachomyomachia,* 1603.

Fraunce, Abraham, Vergil, *Bucolics* II (in *Lawiers Logike*) 1580, (in *The Countess of Pembroke's Ivy Church*) 1591.

Gale, Thomas, Galen, *Methodus Medendi,* from Latin, 1586.

Gascoigne, George, with Francis Kinwelmershe, Euripides, *Phenissae* (*Jocasta*) from Italian of Dolce, acted 1566, printed 1572.

Gilby, Goddard, Cicero, *Ad Quintum,* 1561.

Golding, Arthur, Caesar, *Gallic War,* 1565.
> Justin, *Abridgment,* 1564.
> Ovid, *Metamorphoses* I-IV, 1565, complete 1567 etc.
> Pomponius Mela, *De Situ Orbis,* 1585.
> Seneca, *De Beneficiis,* 1578.
> Solinus, *Collectanea,* 1585 etc.

Gorges, Arthur, Lucan, *Pharsalia,* 1614.

Grant, Ed., Plutarch, *De Educatione Puerorum,* in *"A President for Parentes,"* 1571.

Greene, R., *Anacreontics* 31, in *Alcida,* 1588.

Grimald, Nicholas, Cicero, *De Officiis,* 1553 etc.
> Epigrams in Tottel's *Miscellany,* 1557.

Grenewey, R., Tacitus, *Annals* and *Germania,* with Savile's *History* and *Agricola,* 1598.

Hales, John, Plutarch, *De Tuenda Sanitate,* from Latin of Erasmus, 1543.

Hall, Arthur, Homer, *Iliad,* I-X, from French of Salel, 1581.

Harington, John, Cicero, *De Amicitia,* 1550.

Haward, Nicholas, Eutropius, *"Breviary,"* 1564.

Healey, John, Arrian, *Enchiridion,* from Greek(?), 1610.
> Cebes, *"Table,"* from Greek(?), 1610.
> Theophrastus, *Characters,* from Greek(?), 1616.

Hervet, Gentian, Xenophon, *Oeconomicus,* from Greek (?), 1532 etc.

Heywood, T. Ovid, *De Arte Amandi,* 1598, etc.
> *Heroides,* Helen to Paris, and Paris to Helen, 1609.
> Sallust, *Catiline* and *Jugurtha,* 1609.

Heywood, Jasper, Seneca, *Troas,* 1559, etc.
> *Thyestes,* 1560, etc.
> *Hercules Furens,* 1561, etc.

Hill, Thomas, Artemidorus, *Oneirocritica,* from French, 1563, 1571, 1576, 1606.

Holland, Philemon, Ammianus Marcellinus, *Roman History,* 1609.
    Livy, *History,* 1600.
    Pliny, *Natural History,* 1601.
    Plutarch, *Morals,* from French of Amyot, 1603.
    Suetonius, *Twelve Caesars,* 1606.
    Xenophon, *Cyropedia,* from Greek, 1621, rev. 1632.

Holyday, Barten, Persius, *Satires,* 1616.

"H. ...., S.", Hippocrates, *Aphorisms,* from Latin, 1610.

Howell, J. ?, Ovid, *Metamorphoses,* III, 342 etc., 1560.

Jones, John, Galen, *Elements,* from Latin, 1574.

Jonson, Ben, Horace, *Ars Poetica;* Seneca; Anthology; Martial; Juvenal; etc.

Kendall, Timothy, *Anthology,* from Latin; Ausonius; Martial; in *"Flowers of Epigrammes,"* 1577.

Kinwelmershe, Francis, see Gascoigne.

Kyffin, Maurice, Terence, *Andria,* 1588.

Lloyd, Humfre, Hippocrates, *Aphorisms,* in the *"Treasuri of Helth,"* from Latin of "Petrus Hispanus" 1550(?), 1585.

Lodge, Thomas, Seneca, *"Works, Moral and Natural,"* 1614, 1620.
    Josephus, *Works,* from Latin, 1602, etc.

Lowe, Peter, Hippocrates, *Oath* and *Prognostics,* 1597 etc.

"L. ...., F.", Ovid, *Remedia Amoris,* 1600.

Marlowe, Christopher, Ovid, *Amores,* tr. before 1593.
    (*"Certain Elegies,"* 1590(?) etc.)
    (*"All Elegies,"* 1597 (?))
    Lucan, *Pharsalia,* Bk. I. lic. 1593, printed 1600.

Morysine, R., Frontinus, *Stratagemata,* 1539.

Nevyle, Alexander, Seneca, *Oedipus,* 1563, etc.

Newton, Thomas, Cicero, *Paradoxa, Somnium Scipionis,* 1569.
    Paradoxa, Somnium Scipionis, De Senectute, De Amicitia, (in *"Fower Severall Treatises"*) 1577.
    Seneca, *Thebais* (in *Tenne Tragedies of Seneca*), 1581.

Nichols, Thomas, Thucydides, *Peloponnesian War,* from French, 1550.

North, Sir Thomas, Plutarch, *Lives,* from French of Amyot, 1579, etc.

Norton, Thomas, Justin, *Abridgment,* 2 speeches, 1560.

Nuce, Thomas, Seneca, *Octavia,* 1566.

Nuttall, R., Isocrates, *Ad Demonicum,* 1585.

"O. ...., A.", Lucian, *Toxaris,* 1565.

Overbury, Sir Thomas, Ovid, *Remedia Amoris,* 1620.

Painter, William, Livy etc. in *The Palace of Pleasure,* 1566, 1567, 1575.

Paulfreyman, Varii in revision of *"Treatise of Moral Philosophy,"* see Baldwin.

Peend, Thomas, Ovid, *Metamorphoses,* IV, 287 etc., 1565.

Phaer, Thomas, Vergil, *Aeneid* Bks. I-VII, 1558, I-IX, 1562; completed
by Twyne 1573, etc.

Poyntz, Francis, Cebes, *"Table,"* ca. 1535.

Rastell, John?, Lucian, *Menippus,* from Latin of More, ca. 1520.

Rastell, William?, Caesar, *De Bello Gallico* "as much as concernyth thys
realm of England," from French of Gaguin, ca. 1530.

"R. ...., B.," Herodotus, *History,* Bks. I-II, 1584.

Sadler, John, Vegetius, *De re militari,* 1572.

Salysbury, Wyllyan, Proclus, *Proclus, De Sphaera,*

Sandford (Sanford), James, Arrian, *Abridgment* of Epictetus, from
French, 1567.
Heliodorus, *Aethiopica,* from Latin, Bk. IV, 1567.
Plutarch, *Morals, "Amorous and Tragical Tales,"* from
Latin, 1567.

Savile, Sir Henry, Tacitus, *Histories* and *Agricola,* 1591 etc.

Shakespeare, W., *Anth. Gr.;* two epigrams paraphrased in *Sonnets*

Sherry, R. Cicero, *Pro Marcello,* in *The Figures of Grammar and
Rhetoric,* 1555.

Smith, Nicholas, Herodian, *Roman Emperors,* from Latin, ca. 1556, 1564.

Spenser, Edmund, Pseudo-Vergil, *Culex,* 1591.

Stanyhurst, Richard, Vergil, *Aeneid,* I-IV, 1582, 1583.

Stocker, Thomas, Diodorus Siculus, *History,* from French of de Seyssel,
1569.

Studley, John, Seneca, *Agamemnon* and *Medea,* 1566.
(*Hippolytus* lic. 1556, perhaps Studley's.)
Studley's *Hippolytus,* 1579
Hercules Oetaeus, 1571.

Sturtevant, Simon, Aesop, *Fables,* construed 1602.

Surrey, Henry Howard, Earl of, Vergil, *Aeneid,* probably from Italian,
Bk. IV, 1554; Bks. II and IV, 1557.

Taverner, R., Cato, *Disticha;* 1553, etc.
Publilius Syrus, *"Apothems,"* 1539.
Varii, in Erasmus, *Adagia,* 1539.
in *The Garden of Wysedome,* 1538, enlarged, 1539.

Tiptoft, John, Earl of Worcester, Cicero, *De Amicitia,* 1481.

T[russel], I., Coluthus, *Raptus Primus Helenae,* 1595.

Turbervile, George, *Anthology* etc. in *Eclogues,* 1567.
Ovid, *Heroides,* 1567 etc.

Twyne, Thomas, Dionysius Periegetes, *Survey of the World,* from
Latin, 1572.
Vergil, *Aeneid,* see Phaer.

"T. ...., I." [*i.e.,* Michael Walpole?], Boethius, *De Consolatione,* 1609.

Udall, Nicholas, Terence, *"Flowers,"* 1532,(?) etc.
Varii, *Apophthegmata,* from Erasmus, 1542.

Underdowne, Thomas, Heliodorus, *Aethiopica,* from Latin of Warsche-
      witzki, 1569 etc.
      Ovid, *Ibis,* 1569.

"W. ...., B.", Juvenal, *Satire X,* 1617.

"W. ...., G.", Justin, *Abridgment,* 1606.

Walpole, Michael, *see* "I.T."

Walton, John, Boethius, *De Consolatione,* 1525.

Warner, William, Plautus, *Menaechmi,* 1595.

Watson, Thomas, Polybius, *History,* Bk. I, from Latin of Perottus, 1568.

Webbe, W., Vergil, *Bucolics;* Ecl. I, II in *"A Discourse of English
      Poetrie",* 1586.

Whytinton, Cicero, *Paradoxa,* 1540.
      De Officiis, 1533(?).
      De Senectute, 1535(?).
    Seneca, *Ad Gallionem,* 1547.
    Pseudo-Seneca, *"The Forme and Rule of Honest Lyuinge"*
      1546, and *"The Mirroure or Glasse of Maners,"* 1547.

Wilson, Thomas, Demosthenes, *Philippics* and *Olynthiacs,* from Greek,
      1570.

Worcester?, William, Cicero, *De Senectute,* 1481.

Wrothe, Sir Thomas, Vergil, *Aeneid,* part of Bk. II, 1620.

Wyat, Sir Thomas, Imitations of Horace,⎫
      Various epigrams   ⎬ in Tottel's *Miscellany,* 1557.
    Plutarch, *De Tranquillitate Animi,* from Latin, 1528(?)

Wvlkinson, John, Aristotle, *Ethics,* from Italian of Brunetto Latini, 1547.

NOTES ON MISS PALMER'S LIST OF EDITIONS AND TRANSLATIONS

(For convenience I have indicated here such modern reprints as have come to my notice; and have added some authors, such as Boethius, of a later period than those included by Miss Palmer.)

ACHILLES TATIUS

The most delectable and pleasaunt History of *Clitiphon* and Leucippe: Written first in Greeke, by *Achilles Statius* an Alexandrian: and now newly translated *into* English, *By W. B.* Whereunto is also annexed the argument of euery Booke, in the beginning of the same, for the better understanding of the Historie. *London. Printed by Thomas Creede for William Mattes, and are to be sold at his shop in Fleetestreete, at the signe of the hand and Plough. 1597. 4.°*

Mr. Stephen Gaselee reprinted the tale from the copy discovered by Mr. Peddie, in a handsome limited edition, with valuable introductions by Mr. Gaselee and Mr. H. F. B. Brett-Smith (1923). While the book was in the hands of the binder, another copy turned up, with the title-page, as above.

AESOP

Brinsley's translation of the *Fables* was printed with *Pueriles Confabulatiunculae,* 1617.
[with CATO, *Distichs*]
tr. Bullokar; reprinted Max Plessow in Palaestra LII (1906).
tr. Caxton; ed. J. Jacobs in Bibliothèque de Carabas, 1877 etc.

ANTHOLOGIA GRAECA

Turbervile, George, *Epitaphes* etc. (1567 etc.) should be mentioned as the source of many of Kendall's versions. Reprinted J. Payne Collier, 1870. There are one or a few epigrams from the *Anthology* in Wyatt, Grimald, Shakespeare's Sonnets, B. Jonson, R. Greene in *Alcida,* Orlando Gibbons, *First Set of Madrigals,* 1612, Thomas Baker, *Second Set of Madrigals,* 1618, not to mention Moschus's *Amor Fugitivus,* printed in the Anthology, and frequently translated or imitated.

APPIAN, *of Alexandria.*

The three parts of the book (pt. i, pt. ii, and continuation) have each a separate title-page and separate dedication.
For "demonstration, that" read, "demonstration, That".

APULEIUS, LUCIUS

Adlington's translation reprinted 1887, with preface by A. Lang; with preface by C. Whibley, 1893, 1897; with preface by R. J. Hughes, 1903; with preface by W. H. D. Rouse, 1904; with drawings by Gilbert James, 1906; with preface by Thomas Seccombe, 1913; rev. by S. Gaselee in Loeb Library, 1915; with introduction by F. J. Harvey Darton, illustrations and decorations by Philip Hagroen, Navarre Socy., 1924.

ARISTOTLE

Problems, Edin. 1595 etc.; supposititious.

Wilson's Logic (*The rule of Reason, conteinyng the Arte of Logike*, 1551; revised and enlarged 1567; several later editions) ought to be mentioned.

Wilson's *Arte of Rhetorique* (1553) is practically not at all Aristotelian, and depends mainly on Quintilian and Cicero.

AUSONIUS

Epigrams translated in Turbervile, George, *Epitaphes* etc.; v. *Anthologia Graeca*.

BOETHIUS

[Fo. 2a] Boecius de consolatione philosophie Carmina qui quondam studio florente peregi Flebilis heu mestos cogor inire modos a Llas. I wepyng am constrained to begynne vers of soroufull matere. That whylom in flourisshing studye made delitable ditees/ . . .

[Fo. 94 b, 1. 7] *Post obitum Caxton voluit te viuere cura*
Willelmi. Chaucer clare poeta tuj
Nam tua non solum compressit opuscula formis
Has quoq[ue] s[ed] laudes. iussit hic esse tuas/

From E. Gordon Duff's *Fifteenth Century English Books*, Bibliog. Socy. Illustrated Monographs No. XVIII (1917), no. 47, p. 13. Fo. William Caxton, Westm. *ante* 1479.

The Boke of comfort called in Latin Boetius de Consolatione Philosophie. Translated in to englesse tonge by John Waltwnem

Here endeth the boke of comfort called in latyn Boecius de consolatione ph i.e. Enprented in the exempt monastery of Tauestok in Denshyre by me Dan. Thomas Rychard monke of the sayd monastery to the instant desyre of the right worshipful esquyer Mayster Robert Langdon. Anno d. M.DXXV. Deo Gracias. [Escutcheon of Langdon]. Bodl. (Rawl. 4° 530; Rawl. 4° L 71 Art. 16)

Boetius de consolationae philosophiae. The boke of Boecius, called the comforte of philosophye, or wysedome, moche necessary for all men to read and know, wherein suche as be in aduersitie, shall fynde muche consolation and comforte, and suche as be in great worldly prosperitie may knowe the vanite and frailtie therof, and consequently fynde eternall felycytie. And this boke is in manner of a dialoge of communication betwene two persones, the one is Boecius, and the other is Philosophy, whose disputations and argumentes do playnly declare the diuersitie of the lyfe actiue, that consisteth in worldly, temporall, and transitory thynges, and the lyfe contemplatyue, that always dyspyseth the worlde, and all things therin, and beholdeth almyghtye GOD, and all heauenlye thynges. Translated out of latin into the Englyshe tounge by George Coluile, alias Coldewel, to thintent that such as be ignoraunt in the Latin tounge, and can rede Englyshe, maye vndersande the same. And to the mergentes is added the Latin, to the end that suche as delyghte in the Latin tonge may rede the Latin, accordynge to the boke of the translatour, which was a very olde prynte. Anno. M.D.LVI. *Colophon: Imprynted at London in Paules Churcheyarde at the sygne of the holy Ghost, by Ihon Cawoode, Prynter to the Kynge and Quenes Maiesties. Cum priuilegio ad imprimendum solum.*

[From E. B. Bax's edition of Colville's translation (Tudor Library, 1897].

De Consolatione—Five bookes, of Philosophicall Comfort, full of Christian consolation, written a 1000 yeeres since. By *Anitius, Manlius, Torquatus, Seuerinus, Boetivs;* a Christian Consul of *Rome.* Newly Translated out of Latine, (by I. T.) together with Marginall Notes, explaining the obscurest places. Device. *London. Printed by John Windet, for Mathew Lownes.* 1609. 8°

CAESAR, CAIUS JULIUS

[Gallic War, I-V.] *read: "In Edmondes,* Sir C. Obseruations upon the five first bookes" etc.

In 1600 Edmondes printed his *Obseruations upon the five first bookes* etc., containing an abridgment of B. G. I-V, with the commentary. In 1604 he printed: (a) Bks. VI and VII, with an epistle dedicatory to the effect that the work had now been completed (Printer Ponsonby); (b) a book made up of these prolegomena, the sheets of the original Bks. I-V and the sheets of Bks. VI-VII, with commentaries, just published (Printer Lownes). In 1609 he printed: (a) a book made up of new prolegomena; Bk. I rewritten; Bk. II—near the end of Bk. V, as in 1600; the end of Bk.V, a complete new translation; Bks. VI and VII as in 1604; and the newly translated Civil Wars, with commentary; (b) a book made up in part of new sheets, in part of a remainder of the sheets used in the previous 1609 edition. The alterations made have to do especially with the commendatory verses, and the epistle dedicatory to Sir Robert Drury (p. 179). There is a valuable ms. note in the Dr. Williams copy by Mr. Percy Simpson, dated 23 July, 1907.

[Civil War] in Edmondes, C. *Obseruations etc.* 1609.

CATO

tr. Burgh, repr. Förster, Max, *Die Burghsche Cato-Paraphrase,* in *Archiv* 115, 298; 116, 25 (1905-06); ed. Jenkinson, F. J. H., *Facsimiles of rare Fifteenth-Century Books in the University Library,* Cambridge University Press, 1906.

tr. Bullokar (1535) *v.* Aesop.

CICERO, MARCUS TULLIUS

Read: Fovvre seueral treatises . . . Eloquente . . . and *Colophon: Imprinted at London in Fleetstreete by Thomas March.* 1597 *cum priuilegio.*

Paradoxa Stoicorum with Cicero's Dream, 1569, p. 29; for, "Translated by Thomas Norton," read, "Translated by Thomas Newton."

[*Cato Major*] tr. Newton. (Another edition). London 1577.

[*De Officiis*] tr. Grimald. (Another edition). 1558. 8° Library of Congress.

[*Laelius*] tr. Harrington; repr. 1904, 1906.

[*De Officiis*] tr. Grimald. (Another edition). 1588; (Another edition) 1590; (Another edition) 1610.

EUCLID

Elements. Heading dropped out on p. 45, so that at first sight Euclid seems to be omitted.

EUNAPIUS

The Lyves, of Philosophers and Oratours: Written in Greeke, by Eunapius, of the Cittie of Sardeis in Lydia. Brought into light, Translated into Latine and Dedicated to the Queenes most excellent Maiestie, our most gracious Princesse and Soueraigne, Queene Elizabeth. By the great learned man Hadrianus Iunius Hornamus. 1568. and now set foorth in English, at his request: and Dedicated to the right Honourable, the Lord Chauncellour of England. 1579. Wherein may be seene, The deepe knowledge of Philosophie. The wonderfull workes of secrete Artes. The marvelous effects of perfight eloquence. The singular giftes of naturall qualities. The enuie of the ambitious, against the learned. The daingerous dayes that then befell for faythe. The one of Christians, the other of Infidels. *Imprinted at London by Richard Johnes, and are to be sold at his shop ouer against S. Sepulchres Church without Newgate. The XX daye of May.* (1579)

EURIPIDES

[*Phenissae*] repr. in Gascoigne, *The Posies,* ed. Cunliffe. (1907)

1. *Supposes and Jocasta* ed. J. W. Cunliffe (Cambridge with an excellent introduction, the text of Dolce and of the English version on opposite pages, and a useful bibliography).

2. *Jocasta,* acted 1566, first printed in *A Hundreth Sundry Flowers,* 1572; then in *The Posies of George Gascoigne* (two issues of this edition), 1575; in *The Whole Works of George Gascoigne,* and in *The Pleasauntest Works of George Gascoigne,* 1587 (These are two issues of the same work); in *Four Old Plays,* ed. F. J. Child, Camb. Mass. 1848; in Roxburghe Library 1868-9; with *Supposes,* ed. Cunliffe, Boston, 1906; in *Complete Works of George Gascoigne,* ed. J. W. Cunliffe, Cambridge 1907; Cambridge 1910; in Bond, R. W., ed., *Early Plays from the Italian,* Oxon., 1911.

GALEN

"The third book" etc. *read:* Baker, George.

HELIODORUS

tr. Underdowne 1569; ed. C. Whibley 1895.

HERODOTUS

tr. B. R. 1584; Bk. II ed. A. Lang 1888; both books ed. Leonard Whibley (Tudor Translation) 1925.

HESIOD

tr. Chapman, 1618, see Homer.

HIPPOCRATES

"The whole Aphorismes" etc., p. 55; *read:* "a short discourse."

HOMER

"The Whole Works" etc., tr. Chapman, must be later than the separate *Odyssey;* perhaps 1616, Modern editions: in Chapman's *Works,* with his other translations—ed. Hooper, Richard, 1857; ed. Shepherd, R. N., 1875; ed. Morley, H., 1884.

PSEUDO-HOMER
Batrachomyomachia, tr. Chapman, see Homer; tr. Fowldes, ed. Wild, Friedrich, in *Wiener Beiträge,* XLVIII (1918).

HORACE
tr. Drant, large extracts reprinted in Jiriczek, O. L., *Der Elisabethanische Horaz,* in *Jhrb. d. deutschen Sh. G.* XLVII (1911) 42.

LONGUS
Daphnis and Chloe, tr. Day, ed. J. Jacobs, 1890.

LUCAN
Pharsalia, tr. Marlowe, see Ovid.

LUCIAN
Doris and Galatea, in G. Fletcher's *Licia,* 1593.

MARTIAL
X, 47, tr. Surrey; a number of epigrams in Kendall, *Flowers,* and in Harington, *Epigrams,* 1618.

MOSCHUS
Idyl I. in Barnes, Barnabe, *Parthenophil and Parthenope,* 1593; see *Anthologia Graeca.*

MUSAEUS
"The divine poem," etc. *read:* "Printed by Isaac Iaggard."

MUSAEUS
tr. Chapman, 1616, *v.* Homer.

OVID
Amores tr. Marlowe, reprinted in Marlowe's *Works.* ed. C. F. Tucker Brooke (Clarendon Press 1910); page for page reproduction (London 1925).
Metamorphoses, tr. Golding, reprinted W. H. D. Rouse, 1904.
Tristia tr. Churchyard, reprinted Roxburghe Club, 1816.
Heroides tr. Turbervile, 1567, reprinted Boas, 1928.

[*Ars Amatoria*] p. 77. "Loues Schoole," etc. *read "Iansz Fisscher."*

[*Heroides*] in *Troia Britannica*

[*Ovid moralized*] Caxton, 1580 reprinted Roxburghe Club, 1819; EETS, 1924.

PLAUTUS
Menaechmi, tr. W. Warner 1595, reprinted in Steevens, *Six Old Plays* 1779, 1795; W. P. Collier, *Shakespeare's Library,* 1844 ed. Hazlitt, 1875, pt. ii, vol. I; W. H. D. Rouse, *The Shakespeare Classics,* 1912.

PLUTARCH
Lives, tr. North, 1579, reprinted: Tudor translations, 1895-6; Temple Plutarch, 1898; Oxford, 1928; Nonesuch, 1929, selections: 1875, 1878, 1906, 1909, 1911.

[*De tranquillitate animi.*] Tho. wyatis translatyon of Plutarkes boke of the Quyete of mynde. *Imprinted at London in Fletestrete by Richard Pynson/ printer to the Kynges moost noble grace.* [1528?] 8°.

This is the "Quyete of Mynde. n.d." listed by Miss Palmer. It is now in the Huntington Library.

POLYBIUS

The *Hystories,* tr. C. Watson. Contains only book I.

PTOLEMAEUS

"The Compost" contains nothing from Ptolemy, being a pirated form of *The Kalendar of Shepheardes,* and being nearest to Notary's edition, 1518. V. *The Library,* Ser. III, vol. V, p. 49 (1914).

PUBLIUS, SYRUS

Mimi Publiani. With the interpretation of R. Taverner; editions in 1539, 1540, 1540?, 1553, 1560?, 1622?
tr. Burrant (with Cato), 1545.

SALLUST

Catiline and *Jugurtha,* tr. T. Heywood, ed. C. Whibley, 1924.

SENECA

His Tenne Tragedies, ed. Thomas Newton repr. 1927, with introduction by T. S. Eliot.
On Benefits, tr. Lodge—reprinted Temple Classics (London, 1899).
Agamemnon and *Medea,* tr. John Studley, 1581, ed. Miss E. M. Spearing, in Bang's *Materialien,* Louvain, 1903; *Troas, Thyestes, Hercules Furens,* tr. Jasper Heywood, ed. H. de Vocht, in Bang's *Materialien,* Louvain, 1913.

SUETONIUS

tr. Holland 1606, repr. C. Whibley, 1899.

SYNESIUS

A paradoxe Prouing by reason and example that Baldness is much better than bushie haire, etc. Written by that excellent Philosopher, Synesius, Bishop of Thebes, or (as some say) Cyren. A prettie pamphlet, to pervse, and plenished with recreation. Englished by Abraham Fleming. Hereonto is annexed the pleasant tale of Hebretes the Hermite, pronounced before the Queenes Maiestie. Newly recognized both in Latine and Englishe by the said A. F.

The badge of wisdome is baldnesse.

Printed by H. Denham. 1579.

Letters, in Fleming, A., *A Panoplie of Epistles,* 1576.

THEOCRITUS

Sixe Idillia, ed. H. Daniel, Oxf., 1883; in Arber's *English Garner* vol. 8 (1896); in *Some Longer English Poems,* from the *Garner,* ed. A. H. Bullen (1903); with prefatory note by S. Gaselee, 1922.

THEOPHRASTUS

tr. Healey, 1616, ed. W. H. D. Rouse (Temple Classics), 1899.

VEGETIUS RENATUS, FLAVIUS

Should precede *De re militari.*

VERGILIUS

"The fourth boke" etc. cannot be so early as 1548; 1554?

VERGIL

Webbe, W. *Discourse of English Poetrie,* 1586.
repr. in Haslewood's *Ancient Critical Essays,* 1811-1815; in Arber's *English Reprints,* 1870; in Gregory Smith's *Elizabethan Critical Essays,* 1904.
Eneydos, tr. Caxton, repr. EETS extra ser. lvii, 1890.

XENOPHON

[*Memorabilia*]   The four bookes of Zenon translated into English of the sayings and doinges of Socrates.   Ent. Sta. Reg. 22 Jan. 1601.

SELECT LIST OF REFERENCES

Allen, P. T., *The Age of Erasmus*, 1914.

The author is the most learned of English students of Erasmus, and is unbiased and fair.

Amos, Flora R., *Early Theories of Translation*, New York, 1920.

Of small value in this period.

Argelati, F., *Biblioteca degli Volgarizzatori*, (supplement by Villa, A. T.), Milan, 1767.

A bibliography, apparently accurate, and practically complete of Italian translations.

Ascham, R., *The English Works*, ed. Aldis Wright, in Cambridge English Classics, 1904.

Aurner, Nellie S., *Caxton, Mirror of Fifteenth Century Letters*, Boston, 1926.

A study of the literary interests manifested by the works selected for printing by Caxton.

Ayres, Harry Morgan, *Chapman's Homer and Others*, in New York *Nation*, CIV, 439, 1917.

Useful brief account of Chapman's textual changes in successive editions of *The Iliad*.

Barnard, Francis Pierrepont, (transl.) *A Fardel of Epigrams, [from French and Neo-Latin Epigrammatists.]* London, 1922.

A good discussion of the badness of Renaissance epigrams.

Baynes, T. S., *Shakespeare Studies and Essay in English Dictionaries*, "What Shakespeare learnt at school." P. 147, London, 1894.

An intelligent account of the curriculum in a good grammar school of the age of Elizabeth.

Beaven, A B., *The Aldermen of the City of London*, Vol. II, p. 1., 1888.

On Sir Henry Billingsley.

Benndorf, Cornelie, *Die Englische Pädagogik im 16 Jahrhundert wie sie dargestellt wird im Wirken und in den Werken von Elyot, Ascham und Mulcaster*, Wiener Beit. XXII, Wien, 1905.

Brief outline of the life and works of each, with a consideration of their pedagogical theories and their influence on style and language.

Berdan, John M., *Early Tudor Poetry, 1485-1547*.

Combines learning, critical intelligence, sound generalizations, and a pleasant style.

Bernigau, Karl, *Orthographie u. Aussprache in Richard Stanyhurst's englischer übersetzung d. Aeneide (1582),* in *Marburger Studien zur engl. Philologie,* Heft 8, 1904.
Small results.

Bischoff, Erich, *Prolegomena zum sogenannten Dionysius Cato.* 2nd ed., Jena, 1893.
Useful.

Blades, William, *The Life and Typography of William Caxton,* London, 1861-3.
This, the first edition, contains really indispensable matter not reprinted in the later, smaller editions.

Blass, F., *Die attische Beredtsamkeit,* 2d ed., Lpz., 1887.
Especially valuable on Isocrates.

de Blignières, Auguste, *Essai sur Amyot et les Traducteurs Français au XVIe Siècle,* Paris, 1851.
Chief value in its analysis of Amyot's scholarship and methods.

Boas, Fredrick S., *University Drama in the Tudor Age,* 1914.
Little of direct importance on translation, but an indispensable part of the background of the time.

Botfield, B., *Prefaces to the First Editions of the Greek and Roman Classics,* 1861.
Contains a store of information as to the point of view of the author.

Brinsley, John, *Ludus Literarius, Repr.,* London, 1923.

Brinton, Anna Cox, *Maphaeus Vegius and His Thirteenth Book of the Aeneid,* Stanford University Press, 1930.

Brooke, C. F. Tucker, ed., *Shakespeare's Plutarch,* London, 1909.
In *The Shakespeare Library;* good introduction.

Brooke, C. F. Tucker, *Tudor Drama,* N. Y., 1911.
One of the most important and convenient works in the field.

Brunet, Gustave, *La France Littéraire au XVe Siècle,* 1865.
Chiefly useful as to poetical translations.

Bucchioni, U., *Terenzio nel Rinascimento,* Rocca S. Casciano, 1911.

Cambridge History of English Literature, Vol. IV, Cap. 1, 1910.
Translators, by Charles Whibley, p. 1.
A pleasantly written, sound general view.

Carpenter, F. Ives (ed.), *Leonard Cox, The Arte or Crafte of Rhetoryke,* Chicago, 1899.
An accurate text, with a thorough and interesting introduction.

Chamard, Henri, *Les Origines de la Poésie française de la Renaissance,* 1920.
An unpretentious work, but full of useful information.

Chase, W. J., *Catonis Disticha,* in *University of Wisconsin Studies in the Social Sciences and History,* Madison, Wisconsin, 1922.
Introduction on the vogue of Cato.

Christianity and the Pagan World, T L S, December 26, 1929, p. 1089.
"No matter how much in detail Christian ethics may owe to ancient philosophy, Christianity remains unique in the power of its motives."

Clarke, Arthur Melville, *Thomas Heywood's Art of Love, Lost and Found, The Library,* 1922, pp. 210-222.
Identifies the *De Arte Amandi,* Anon, 1600? as Heywood's, and gives full titles of the various editions.

Clark, Donald L., *Rhetoric and Poetry in the Renaissance,* Columbia thesis, New York, 1922.
An intelligent study of the gradual supplanting of medieval critical principles by classical ones.

Collins, J. C., *Greek Influence on English Poetry.*
In spite of Professor Collins's fanciful parallels, his learning, ability, and taste give this book value, but it must be used with caution.

Comparetti, Domenico, *Vergil in the Middle Ages,* tr. Benecke, E. F. M; intr. Ellis, R., London, 1895, Esp. Chapters XI, XII, XIII, pp. 156-194.
Accentuates the differences between Middle Ages and Renaissance, on the side of the reawakening of the laity.

Compayré, G., *Hist. Critique des Doctrines de l'éducation en France,* 1880.

Conley, C. H., *The First English Translators of the Classics,* New Haven, 1927.

Cooper, Clyde B., *Some Elizabethan Opinions of the Poetry and Character of Ovid,* Chicago, 1915.
A compact, learned, and intelligent study, having a much wider range than the title indicates.

Crotch, W. J. B., *The Prologues and Epilogues of William Caxton,* [EETS Or. Ser. 176) Oxford, 1928.
Contains in addition to an accurate text of Caxton's prologues and epilogues important documents supplementing Blades.

Cunliffe, J. W., *Early English Classical Tragedies,* Oxford, 1913.
Good introduction; text, and notes on *Jocasta.*

Cunliffe, J. W., *Influence of Seneca on Elizabethan Tragedy,* 1893.
Diligent and thoroughly documented; I find myself unable to agree with some of the most important critical comments and references; in particular, Kyd seems to me more Senecan, Marlowe less.

Delaruelle, L., *Études sur l'humanisme français. Guillaume Budé.* [*Bibl. de l'École des Hautes Études, sciences, hist. et phil.,* fasc. 162.] 1907.
A scholarly account not only of Budé, but of the character and difficulties of scholarship in the early sixteenth century.

Delbrück, Hans, *Geschichte der Kriegskunst,* Berlin, 1920.
On the use of classic theorists in the Renaissance.

Deschamps, P., *Essai Bibliographique sur M. T. Cicéron,* 1863.
There is no adequate study of the influence of Cicero; this work contributes valuable material to the subject.

Dolet, Estienne, *La Manière de Bien Traduire d'une Langue en Autre,* Paris, 1540.
Frequently reprinted in the sixteenth century; a limited edition printed at Lyons in 1830. A summary and the five rules appear in a number of writers, e.g. in Christie, C. R., *Étienne Dolet* (French tr., 1886, p. 343).

Dryden, John, *Pref. to tr. Ovid's Epistles, Wks., ed. Scott—Saintsbury,* (1885), XII, 7; *Pref. to Second Miscellany, op. cit.,* XII, 281.
Dryden's most complete discussion of the various types of translation.

Dufayard, Henri, *De Claudii Seisselli Vita et Operibus,* Paris, 1892.
One of those trustworthy French *Thèses* which illuminate the obscurer corners of literary history.

Elyot, Sir Thomas, *The Boke named the Gouernor,* ed. H. H. S. Croft, London, 1880.
An accurate text with learned and valuable comment.

Fest, O., *Ueber Surrey's Virgilübersetzung,* etc., Palaestra, 34, 1903.
The earliest of the special studies on Surrey's relation to Italian models.

Feuillerat, A., *John Lyly,* Cambridge, 1910.
An intimate study of the circumstances in Elizabethan England which affected Lyly; of his allegory; of his sources; his place in literature.

Foster, F. M. K., *English Translations from the Greek* [from 1476-1918], New York, 1918.
Based wholly on Palmer for this period.

Gascoigne, G., *Supposes and Jocasta,* ed. John W. Cunliffe, in Belles-lettres Series, Boston, 1906.
Useful introduction, notes, bibl. Text of Italian original.

Gascoigne, G., *Works,* ed. Cunliffe, in *Cambridge English Classics,* Cambridge, 1907-10.
Text only.

Gee, John Arthur, *The Life and Works of Thomas Lupset,* New Haven, 1928.
A diligent and intelligent gathering of the information about a scholar of the generation after More; little directly on our subject.

Glöckner, G., *Das Ideal der Bildung u. Erziehung bei Erasmus v. Rotterdam,* in *Jhrb. des Vereins fur wissenschaftliche Pedagogik,* XXII (1890), 1.

Glover, Terrot Reaveley, *Life and Letters in the Fourth Century,* Cambridge, 1901.
A delightfully written, learned, and judicious account of the intellectual conditions of the main writers of the age.

Gordon, G. S., editor, *English Literature and the Classics,* Oxford, 1912.
A group of lectures by various scholars; of unequal value; *Ovid and Romance,* by S. G. Owen, of most use in this period.

Graf, Arturo, *Roma nella Memoria e nelle Immaginazioni del Medio Evo,* Turin, 1882; pp. 1-43, La gloria e il primato de Roma; 182-184, La potenza di Roma; 153-195; Gli autori latini nel medio evo.

Greg, W. W., *Pastoral Poetry and Pastoral Drama,* 1905.
Work done so that it need not be done again.

Gummere, R. M., *Seneca the Philosopher and His Modern Message,* in the series *Our Debt to Greece and Rome,* Boston, 1922.
A clear view of the permanent value and influence of Seneca.

Harris, William J., *The First Printed Translations into English of the Great Foreign Classics,* London, 1909.
Indiscriminate dictionary catalogue of translations from many foreign languages. No value for our purpose.

Hatch, E., *The influence of Greek Ideas and Usages upon the Christian Church,* Hibbert Lectures, 1888; (London, 1891), p. 109.

Hatcher, Miss O. L., *Aims and Methods of Elizabethan Translators* in *Eng. St.,* XLIV, 1912, 174.
Unfavorable criticism on quality; insistence on importance; not much of value.

Hauvette, Henri, *De Laurentio de Primofato, etc.,* Paris, 1903.
Thèse; solidly and adequately done.

Herrick, Marvin T., *The Early History of Aristotle's Rhetoric in England,* in *Philological Quarterly,* V, 1926, 242.
The study of rhetoric by certain scholars, and the use of Aristotle by some writers. Little direct influence.

Hettler, A., *Roger Ascham, sein Stil in seiner Beziehung zur Antike.* Freib. Diss., 1916.

Hirzel, R. *Plutarch* in Crusius, V., *Das Erbe der Alten,* Heft 4, 1912.
A valuable and intelligent consideration of Plutarch's influence and permanent significance.

Hoffmann, Adolf, *Das Psyche-Märchen des Apuleius in der englischen Literatur,* Strassb. Diss., 1908.

Hortis, Attilio, *Studii sulle opere latine del Boccaccio,* 1879.

Huf, H., *Warner, William; Albion's England, Quellen-Untersuchungen zu den ersten Büchern,* diss., Munich, 1912.

Hughes, Merritt Y., *Virgil and Spenser,* in *University of California Publications in English,* II, 1910-11, 263 (*Virgil's Gnat,* 309).

Hutton, James, *The First Idyl of Moschus,* in *American Journal of Philology,* XLIX, p. 105, 1928.

Imelmann, R., *Zu den Anfängen des Blankverses: Surreys Aeneis in ursprunglicher Gestalt,* in *Shk. Jhrb.,* 41, 1905.
Important in insisting on the value of the mss.

Jiriczek, O. L., *Der elisabethanische Horaz,* in *Shk. Jhrb.* XLVII, (1911), p. 42.
A meticulously exact reprint, even to the long s's, of Drant's prolegomena, with long excerpts and a useful introduction.

Jockers, Ernst, *Die englischen Seneca-Uebersetzer des 16. Jahrhunderts,* Strass. diss. 1909.

Jusserand, J. J., *Histoire Littéraire du Peuple Anglais,* Paris, 1904.
Vol. II, pp. 46-48. Enumerates some of the important versions under Henry VIII and Mary, indicating their purpose—a good passage; vol. II, p. 331. Deals with Elizabethan translations.

Kendall, T., *Flowers of Epigrammes* in *Spenser Socy. Publications,* 1874.

Kerlin, R. T., *Theocritus in English Literature,* 1910.

Lathrop, H. B., *The First English Printers and Their Patrons,* in *The Library,* 4th ser. iii, (1922), 19.
Maintains that Caxton, following the tradition of manuscript-writers, depended more upon the suggestions of his patrons than has been commonly believed.

Lawton, H. W., *Térence en France au XIVe Siècle; Éditions et Traductions,* Paris, 1926.

Lee, Sir Sidney, *The French Renaissance in England,* 1910.
In spite of Sir Sidney Lee's inaccuracy at many points, his intelligence and breadth of general knowledge make his views important; but he cannot be relied on for particular facts.

Lohff, Alfred, *George Chapman,* Diss. Berlin, 1903.
A careful and intelligent study.

Lucas, Frank L., *Seneca and Elizabeth Tragedy,* 1922.
An account of Seneca's life, work, and influence, with a chapter giving an outline of Seneca's influence on Elizabethan tragedy.

Luick, Karl, *Die Bedeutung der Renaissance für die Entwicklung der englischen Dichtung.* (Inaugurationsrede . . . . des Rektors der Wiener Univ. für . . . . 1925-26) Wien. 1925, pp. 47-58.

Lupton, J. H., *A Life of John Colet,* 1909.
Important for information as to the point of view as to classic authors in education; still more important in giving a picture of the pious Renaissance scholar.

Lyly, John, *Complete Works,* ed. Bond, R. W., Oxford, 1902.
Admirable.

Manitius, Maximilianus, *Analekten zur Geschichte des Horaz im Mittelalter, bis 1300,* 1893.

Mallet, Sir Charles Edward, *A History of the University of Oxford,* 1924.
Little of direct relevance; but see especially the various statutes of the Elizabethan period.

Matthiessen, Francis O., *Translation an Elizabethan Art,* Cambridge, 1931.
Critical discussion of the literary qualities of the most important prose translations, especially of Holland and North.

Modersohn, Anna B., *Cicero im englischen Geistesleben des 16 Jahrhunderts,* in *Archiv,* 149 (1923), 33, 129.
An industrious collection of parallels, with little interpretative comment.

Mullinger, J. Bass, *The University of Cambridge,* Camb., 1873-84.
Takes a broad view of its subject, and in some chapters gives a general view of the educational tendencies prevalent at a particular period and of their application at Cambridge.

Nathan, Walter L., *Sir John Cheke und der englische Humanismus,* Berlin, 1928.

Norden, Eduard, *Die antike Kunstprosa vom VI. Jahrhundert v. Chr. bis in die Zeit der Renaissance,* Lpz., 1898.
Corrigible in detail; essential for its general view.

Norden, Eduard, *Die lateinische Literatur im Uebergang zum Mittelalter,* in *Die Kultur der Gegenwart,* Th. 1, Abth. 8, 1905.

Olschka, L., *Das literarische Vermächtniss des Mittelalters,* in *Deutsche Vierteljahrsschrift für Literaturwissenschaft,* Jahrg. VII, (1929), Heft 2, p. 329.
On the continuity of the Middle Ages and the Renaissance.

Omond, T. S., *English Hexameter Verse,* Edin., 1897.

Osler, Sir W., *Thomas Linacre,* (Linacre lecture), 1908.

Palmer, Henrietta R., *List of English Editions and Translations of the Classics Printed before 1641.* (Bibliographical society publications) 1911.
The basic work in the field.

Plomer, H. R., *William Caxton,* 1925.
A eulogy of Caxton, popular in form and vigorously written, but based on an intimate knowledge of the original documents; defending Caxton from aspersions on his originality and independence.

Pollard, A. W., and Redgrave, G. R., *A Short-Title Catalogue of Books Printed in England, Scotland and Ireland, and of English Books Printed Abroad, 1475-1640,* London, 1926.

Postgate, J. P., *Translation and Translations,* London, 1922.
An admirable work by a genuine scholar of fine taste; a vigorous confutation of the "libertine" doctrine of translation.

Puech, E., *Maturin Cordier,* 1895.

Rashdall, Hastings, *The Universities of Europe in the Middle Ages,* Oxford, 1895.
Knowledge of the classics in the Middle Ages; I, 63-66; I, 240; II, 603.

Reed, Arthur W., *The Editor of Sir Thomas More's English Works: William Rastell,* in *The Library,* 1924, p. 25.

Regel, M., *Ueber George Chapman's Homerübersetzung,* Diss. Halle, 1881.
Superseded.

Rick, Leo, *Shakespeare und Ovid* in *Shk. Jb.,* LV (1919), 35.
Both thorough and broad.

Riedner, W., *Spensers Belesenheit* pt. 1, in *Münchener Beitr.,* No. 38, 1908.

Rolfe, John C., *Cicero and His Influence,* Boston, 1923.
Well balanced general view.

Rollins, Hyder E., *New Facts About George Turbervile,* in *Mod. Phil.,* XV, (1918), p. 513.

Ruehl, F., *Die Verbreitung des Justinus im Mittelalter,* 1871.

Schanz, M., *Geschichte der römischen Literatur,* Pt. III, p. 32 f., Munich, 1896.
(Förster, M., on the translations and adaptations of Cato).

Schelling, F. E., *Foreign Influences in Elizabethan Plays,* 1923.

Schirmer, Walter R., *Der englische Frühhumanismus,* Lpz., 1931.
Covers thoroughly the obscure fifteenth-century beginnings of English humanism.

Schoell, F. L., *Les Emprunts de G. Chapman à Marsile Ficin,* in *Rev. de Litt. Comparée,* III, 1923, pp. 17-35.

Schoell, F. L., *George Chapman and the Italian Neo-Latinists of the Quattrocento,* in *Mod. Phil.,* XIII, 1915-16, p. 215.

Schoell, Frank L., *Un humaniste français oublié: Jean de Sponde,* in *Revue du XVIe Siècle,* XII, 1925, p. 361.

Schoell, Frank L., *L'hellénisme français en Angleterre à la fin de la Renaissance* in *Rev. Lit. Comp.,* V, 1925, p. 193.
Everything that Mr. Schoell prints is both trustworthy and original.

Schröer, A., *Uber die Anfänge des Blankverses in England* in *Anglia;* IV, (1881), 1.
Laborious and thorough; to me not convincing, as failing to recognize effective variations which interrupt but do not destroy the pattern of the verse.

Schumacher, Aloys, *Des bischofs Gavin Douglas Uebersetzung der Aeneis Virgil etc.*, Strassb. diss., 1910.

Compares Douglas with Jodocus Badius Ascensius's edition of Vergil and the French version of Octavien de Sainct-Gelais.

Scott, Mary A., *Elizabethan Translations from the Italian*, 1916.

Sets a standard for similar studies.

Seebohm, F., *The Oxford Reformers*, 1887.

Little on our subject; not superseded in its intimate view of the problems and difficulties of Colet, Erasmus and More in reaching clearness in their own minds, and of the danger and difficulties by which they were surrounded.

Sheavyn, Phoebe, *The Literary Profession in the Elizabethan Age*, 1909.

Essential to an understanding of conditions in Elizabethan England; little specifically upon translation.

Smith, Preserved, *Erasmus: a study of His Life, Ideals, and Place in History*, New York, 1923.

Sound, solid, thorough, and intelligent; useful bibliography; based on the sources.

Spens, Janet., *Chapman's Ethical Thought* in *Essays and Studies by Members of the English Association*, XI (1925), p. 145.

"Chapman more than almost any other poet presents the unrest and confusion of ideals characteristic of his age."

Stewart, H. F., *Boethius, an Essay*, 1891.

A modest work of wide learning.

Sudre, Leopold, *Ovidii Nasonis metamorphoseon libros quomodo nostrates medii aevi poetae imitati interpretatique sint.*, Paris, 1893.

Surrey and Wyatt, Works, ed. Nott, G. F., 1815-16.

Not entirely superseded.

Taylor, A. O., *The Classical Heritage of the Middle Ages*, New York, 1901.

A good general view with a useful bibliography.

Tilley, A., *The Literature of the French Renaissance*, Cambridge, 1904, I, 7.

On Corderius.

Tilley, M. P., *Euphues and Ovid's Heroical Epistles*, P M L A, 1930, XIV, 301.

Supplements Feuillerat and Bond, and compares Lyly with Turbervile.

Tilley, Morris P., *Elizabethan Proverb Lore in Lyly's Euphues and in Pettie's Petite Pallace*, Ann Arbor, 1926.

Interesting discussion of the vogue of proverbs in 16th century literature.

Tillyard, S. M. W., *The Poetry of Sir Thomas Wyatt*, 1929.

Toffanin, Giuseppe, *Il Cinquecento,* in *Storia Letteraria d' Italia,* Milan. 1929; *Que Cosa fu l'Umanesimo* in *Biblioteca Storica del Rinascimento,* VII, Florence, 1929.
Humanism essentially Italian, orthodox and conservative.

Trench, R. C., *Plutarch, Five Lectures,* 1874.
Not superseded.

Trench, W. F., *William Baldwin,* in *Mod. Quart. of Lang.,* Vol. 1 (1899), p. 259.
Dating and discussion of works.

Viglione, F., *L'umanesmo in Inghilterra e le sue relazioni con l'Italia,* in *Rassegna Nazionale,* XLVI, 1924.

Vocht, H. de, *De Invloed van Erasmus op de Engelsche Tonneelliteratur etc.,* Academiis, Ghent: Koninklighe Vlaamsche Acad. voor Taal en Letterkunde, 1908.
Breaks important new ground.

Voigt, George, *Die Wiederbelebung des classischen Alterthums oder das erste Jahrhundert des Humanismus,* 3d ed; ed. Max Lehnert, Berl. 1893.
Vol. i, pp. 1-11, Classic civilization in the Middle Ages; vol. ii, pp. 248-261, Humanism in England (does not come down to Selling). Little of *direct* use; valuable for reference and background.

Vickers, K. H., *Humphrey, Duke of Gloucester,* London, 1907.

Warren, T. Herbert, *The Art of Translation* in *Essays of Poets and Poetry* (1909) pp. 85-133.
Comments intelligently on the most important translations, types and principles.

Warton, Thomas, *History of English Poetry,* ed. Hazlitt, W. C., London, 1871.
This great work will always be fundamental; if practicable it should be consulted in its original as well as its amplified form.

Watson, Foster, *The English Grammar Schools to 1660,* Cambridge, 1909.
Drawn from the documents; full consideration both of contents of curriculum and methods of teaching.

Watson, Foster, ed., *Vives and Renascence Education of Women,* 1912.
Chapter on More.

Webbe, W., *A Discourse of English Poetrie,* ed. Arber (English Reprints, No. 26, 1870) p. 59.

Whibley, Charles, *Translators* in *Cambridge History of English Literature,* IV, 1.

Whipple, T. K., *Isocrates and Euphuism,* M L R, 11, 1916.
Very valuable.

Whipple, T. K., *Martial and the English Epigram,* University of California publications in Mod. Phil., Vol. 10, no. 4, 1925.
A thorough and well-finished piece of work.

Willcock, Gladys, D., *A Hitherto Uncollated Version of Surrey's Translation of the fourth Book of the Aeneid,* in M L R XIV (1919), p. 163; XV (1920), p. 113; XVII (1922), p. 131.
Useful and minutely accurate.

Wolff, S. L., *The Greek Romances in Elizabethan Prose Fiction* in *Columbia University Studies in Comparative Literature,* 1912.

Woodward, Willam H., *Studies in Education during the Age of the Renaissance,* Camb., 1929.
On Corderius, p. 154.

Wyat, Sir Thomas, *Poems,* ed. Foxwell, 1914.

Zielinski, Th., *Cicero im Wandel der Jahrhunderte,* 3d ed., Lpz., 1912.
Especially useful in the discussion of the influences of Cicero on English thought in the 17-18th centuries.

INDEX

343